Kjetil Selvik is Assistant Professor at the University of Oslo and researcher at the Fafo Institute of Applied International Studies. He has broad teaching experience in Middle East-related topics and holds a PhD from L'Institut d'Etudes Politiques in Paris.

Stig Stenslie specialises in Middle Eastern and Asian affairs at the Norwegian Defence Staff. He holds a doctoral degree in Political Science from the University of Oslo, where he is also a lecturer.

'At a time when there is vigorous debate about the potential for reform in the politics of the Middle East, sometimes slipping into alarm and disillusion, this book provides a much-needed grounding for thinking seriously through these issues. Its focus on the forces and limitations of change is a refreshing corrective to those volumes that lead readers to think that the Middle East is inhabited solely by fighters, victims and ideologues. Perhaps most impressively it draws heavily upon the politics of the smaller and often misunderstood states to illustrate how their politics exemplify many of the key issues that affect today's – and tomorrow's – Middle East.'

Glen Rangwala, Lecturer and Fellow of Trinity College,
University of Cambridge

Stability AND Change IN THE Modern Middle East

Kjetil Selvik and Stig Stenslie

I.B. TAURIS

LONDON · NEW YORK

Published in 2011 by I.B.Tauris & Co Ltd
6 Salem Road, London W2 4BU
175 Fifth Avenue, New York NY 10010
www.ibtauris.com

Distributed in the United States and Canada
Exclusively by Palgrave Macmillan
175 Fifth Avenue, New York NY 10010

Copyright © 2011 Kjetil Selvik and Stig Stenslie

Translated from Norwegian to English by John Meyrick

The right of Kjetil Selvik and Stig Stenslie to be identified as the authors of this work has been
asserted by them in accordance with the Copyright, Designs and Patents Act 1988.

ISBN: 978 1 84885 585 4 (hb)
      978 1 84885 589 2 (pb)

A full CIP record for this book is available from the British Library
A full CIP record is available from the Library of Congress

Library of Congress Catalog Card Number: available

Printed and bound in Great Britain by TJ International Ltd, Padstow, Cornwall

MIX
Paper from
responsible sources
FSC
www.fsc.org   FSC® C013056

Contents

Maps and Tables

Maps

Tables

Acknowledgements

This book aims at presenting research-based knowledge about the Middle East to a broad audience. It was first published in Norwegian in 2007 and builds on a lecture series that we have been giving at the University of Oslo since 2002. In addition, the book is based on both short and more lengthy research trips during the period of writing to most of the countries in the region. A number of colleagues, students, and friends supported us along the way.

We are grateful first and foremost to Nils A. Butenschøn and Knut S. Vikør for reading and commenting upon the whole manuscript. We also owe special thanks to Thomas Hegghammer, Wilhelm Kavli, Leif Manger, Yadullah Shahibzadeh, Kjetil Sæter, Bjørn Olav Utvik, and Reidar Visser who provided criticism and suggestions. In addition, Kåre Annaniassen, Youssef Belal, Bernt Brendemoen, Tore Linné Eriksen, Thomas Brandt Fibiger, Lars Haugom, Jacob Høigilt, Constantin Karamé, Gilles Kepel, Nils I. Lahlum, Gunvor Mejdell, Mary Moubarak, Thomas McNicol, Nefissa Naguib, Øystein Noreng, Thomas Pierret, Jan-Erik Smilden, Nicholas Stivang, Finn Thiesen, Charles Tripp, Endre Tvinnereim, and Hisham al-Zouki also made important contributions. Thanks to I.B.Tauris for believing in the project, John Meyrick for translating the book from Norwegian to English, as well as the Freedom of Expression Foundation and the University of Oslo for generous financial support. Our greatest debt is to Sabreen and Saira, who had patience with our passion for Middle East politics and remained loving and supportive.

KJETIL SELVIK AND STIG STENSLIE
Oslo/Washington DC

Notes on Transcription

We have aimed to introduce the reader to central words, expressions and proper nouns used in the languages of the region. Which language is used in each particular case is indicated by 'Arab.' for Arabic, 'Turk.' for Turkish, and 'Pers.' for Persian and so on. For words in Arabic we have consistently tried to use the standard Arabic norm. Consequently, we have attempted to stick to the vowel phonemes /a/, /u/ and /i/ in transcription, disregarding variations in phonetic value in the various Arabic dialects. The characteristic Arabic laryngeal consonant *ayn* is indicated by /'/ and the glottal stop, *hamz*, by /'/. For the sake of simplicity we have not used the diacritic signs.

However, in the transcription of Persian words we have used the vowel phonemes /o/ and /e/ and indicated the Persian *ezafe* with the hyphen /-/. Turkish words are given in the modern written form.

For certain proper nouns we have made exceptions from the transcription rules. This is in cases where there already exist well-established written forms in English and where a transcription might confuse the reader. For example, we do not correct the spelling of Nasser, Bourgiba, Bouteflika, Lahoud, and Benjedid, and we do not transcribe the names of well-known countries, empires, and ethnic groups such as Algeria, the Ottoman Empire, and the Kurds. Foreign words such as *'ulama*, *jihad*, *shari'a*, *sharif*, and *mujahid*, on the other hand, are printed in italics.

1 Introduction

Algeria killed 289 'terrorists' in 2009 ... Bahraini Shi'as clash over Ashura rituals ... Egypt's Muslim Brothers group says to continue peaceful struggle to attain its goals ... Iran pro-government protestors outside British embassy in Tehran ... Iraqi agency says al-Ramadi blast kills ten, injures governor ... Most infiltrators via Egypt linked with al-Qa'ida ... Libya's al-Qadhafi stresses support for peace in Sudan ... Hunger-striking Islamist detainees in Morocco face death ... Saudi Arabia launches satellite TV channels 'to spread messages' of Qur'an ... Lebanese official call for 'intensifying' Syria-Lebanon meetings ... Palestinian Authority's security cooperation benefits Israel alone ... Security forces clash with al-Qa'ida group in Yemen ...[1]

Viewed from outside, Middle East politics seem confusing, chaotic, and often violent. Every day the media report abuse, suffering, and killings in Israeli-occupied Palestine and in Iraq. Another topic which daily gains column inches is so-called Islamic terrorists, often synonymous with 'al-Qa'ida', which after the Cold War has obtained the role as the West's public enemy number one. Nor do the media grow tired of the eternal sabre-rattling among enemies such as Iran and Israel. Journalists create a picture of a region characterised by war, religious extremism, terror, unpredictability, and rapid upheavals. But is the Middle East really *so* unstable?

If we look behind the media's headlines, we find, on the contrary, that stability is a prominent feature of politics in the Middle East. To be more precise, stability means *regime stability*, which has characterised the region for forty years. By and large the political systems that existed four decades ago have all survived to this day. The exceptions are Iran, where the Shah's kingdom was replaced by the Islamic republic in 1979, and Iraq, where Saddam Hussein's political system was toppled in 2003. Furthermore, there has been little change at the top of these regimes. At the beginning of the twenty-first century the region's Arab rulers – kings, sultans, emirs, and presidents – had been in power on average for over twenty years! Simplifying this, one can say that the regimes in the Middle East 'froze solid' around 1970.

Starting from this observation the book raises the following three questions: how have the rulers in the Middle East tightened their grip? What consequences do their power strategies have for political and socio-economic development? And what forces threaten those in power today?

Stability and Change in the Modern Middle East is an attempt to combine an introductory textbook, presenting an overview of central themes within the topics of comparative politics in the Middle East, with a discussion of regime stability. The latter has been chosen to give the reader a problem-orientated approach to each individual theme. It takes as its starting point four principal topics: the relations between society and state; the quest for legitimacy; the organisation of state power; and the possibilities of regime change. Each topic will be discussed in greater depth through examples drawn respectively from Yemen, Iran, Morocco, Egypt, Oman, Syria, Iraq, and Saudi Arabia. Hence, the reader will also get a deeper understanding of several states in the region.[2] These examples are meant to illustrate central features of several Middle East states. But it is important to avoid generalising about every country in the region from these examples. The book offers no systematic analysis and comparison of the explanations for regime stability in the region as a whole.

In accordance with the tradition of comparative politics we shall concentrate on internal explanations of regime stability. This does not mean external factors are of no significance. In the literature there is an extensive discussion as to what extent political development (or the lack of it) in the modern Middle East can be explained primarily on the basis of internal[3] or external factors.[4] The Middle East has been, and still is, an arena for major power rivalry: it is beyond doubt that the latter has set its stamp on politics in the region. Instead of dealing with external factors as a separate topic, however, the book will treat such influences as they affect the functioning of the regimes.

A Eurocentric term

'The Middle East' is a Eurocentric term. The region is east only from a western European perspective. For an Indian the Middle East is to the west, and for a Russian the region is to the south. The term itself is of recent origin, and is linked to Captain Alfred Thayer Mahan, an American naval officer and strategist, who used the term in the article 'The Persian Gulf and International Relations' in 1902.[5] In this article he argued that the United Kingdom had to bear the responsibility of securing the sea route to India and keeping Russia at bay. For Mahan 'the Middle East' referred to the area between the Turkish-dominated Ottoman Empire, 'the Near East', the expanding Russian empire in Central Asia and the

British crown colony India, 'the Far East'. Mahan himself used the Middle East as a variable strategic concept. For him the location of the Middle East was primarily important for the British authorities because of its strategic significance along the sea route to India.

During the Second World War the British began to use the term the Middle East for the Asiatic states west of India up to and including Egypt. Egypt was included despite most of the country belonging geographically speaking to North Africa. During the war the British, among other things, established the Middle East Supply Centre in Cairo. Soon 'the Middle East' entered common usage, replacing the earlier 'Near East' as the term used for countries along the eastern Mediterranean. Gradually the usage was adopted in several other European languages denoting the countries of south west Asia from Iran to Egypt. Only in certain academic disciplines such as archaeology and ancient history was the term the Near East retained. The term the Near East was also kept in French (*Proche Orient*), German (*Naher Osten*), and Russian (*Bližnyj Vostok*).

Despite the Middle East being a Eurocentric term, it has also been adopted in the languages of the region itself. In the 1950s both Egypt's President Gamal 'Abd al-Nasser and Iran's Prime Minister Mohammed Mossadegh made use of it. Today 'the Middle East' is found respectively in Arabic (*al-sharq al-awsat*), Turkish (*Orta Doğu*), and Persian (*khavar miane*), frequently used in books, periodicals, newspapers, radio, and television. Saudi Arabia's biggest newspaper, for instance, is named *al-Sharq al-awsat*. Interestingly, the concept is most frequently used in discussions about geopolitical strategies in the region. In television debates Arab commentators often discuss 'the USA's policies in the Middle East' or 'Israel's relations with the Middle East'.

In this book the Middle East is restricted first of all to the Arab countries Morocco, Algeria, Tunisia, Libya, Egypt, Saudi Arabia, Yemen, Oman, the United Arab Emirates (known hereafter as the Emirates), Qatar, Bahrain, Kuwait, Jordan, Iraq, Syria, and Lebanon together with the Palestinian territories, the West Bank and the Gaza Strip. In addition, we include Israel, Iran and Turkey. In English this region is often referred to as *the Middle East and North Africa*, just as Arabic distinguishes between *mashriq* and *maghrib* and French between *Le Moyen Orient* and *L' Afrique du Nord*. But because all these countries, as we shall soon see, have important features in common, we choose to use the common term 'the Middle East' for all of them. For diverse reasons Iran and Turkey could have been excluded. Most Iranians are very aware of their cultural heritage, often stressing how different they are from the Arabs. Many Turks, especially in the cities of Istanbul, Ankara, and Izmir, regard themselves as Europeans. Besides, Turkey uses the Latin alphabet, has long been a NATO member, and is negotiating EU membership. Nonetheless, we include both Iran and Turkey because their history, culture, and political development share many characteristics with those of the Arab countries. Despite the fact that Israel belongs geographically to the region, we shall write little about this country in this book. The reason for this is purely analytical: that state formation and politics in Israel break with the pattern to be found in the rest of the Middle East. As Leonard J. Fein puts it, 'though *in* the region, Israel is not *of* the region'.[6] The historical background for this, as several researchers have pointed out, is that the formation of the state of Israel came about through European settler colonisation.[7] If this had been a book about the regional power game in the Middle East, it would have been natural to devote a more central place to Israel.

Diversity and unity

The Middle East, which stretches from Morocco in the west to Iran in the east, is a vast area. The region has often been characterised as a 'mosaic' consisting of diverse ethnic groups, faiths, languages, occupations, and ways of life. However, there are also important common features shared by a majority of the region's population.

History

The Middle East is located at the point of intersection of three continents. Over the millennia it has been the meeting place for diverse populations, all of whom have set their stamp on the region. Arthur Goldschmidt has asserted that '[i]f history can be defined as humanity's recorded past, then the Middle East has had more history than any other part of the world'.[8] Historically, the region has been united by merchants, scientists, religious communities, and empire building. The Prophet Muhammad's successors – the caliphs – founded, between 632 and 661, an empire, which to a large extent coincides with the book's definition of the Middle East. The Umayyad caliphs succeeded the first caliphs, who ruled from Medina. From 661 to 749 these ruled over the empire from Damascus. In theory the caliph had both a sacred and a secular function, respectively as head of the Muslim community (Arab. *umma*) and as political and administrative leader of the newly founded world empire. But gradually, especially under the Umayyad caliphs, the former function became less important than the latter.

The Abbasid caliphs took over power in 749, ruling the empire from Baghdad in Mesopotamia. Political unity laid the foundations for the spread of Islam, the Arabic language and culture as well as a flourishing commerce. The Caliphate reached its zenith under Harun al-Rashid (786–809), famed from the folk tale collection *A Thousand and One Nights*. The Abbasids lost their worldly power in the tenth century but kept the caliph title until the Mongol ruler

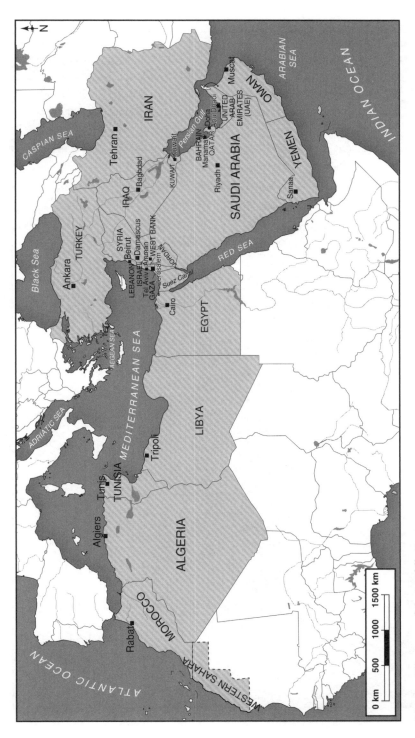

Map 1   The states of the Middle East

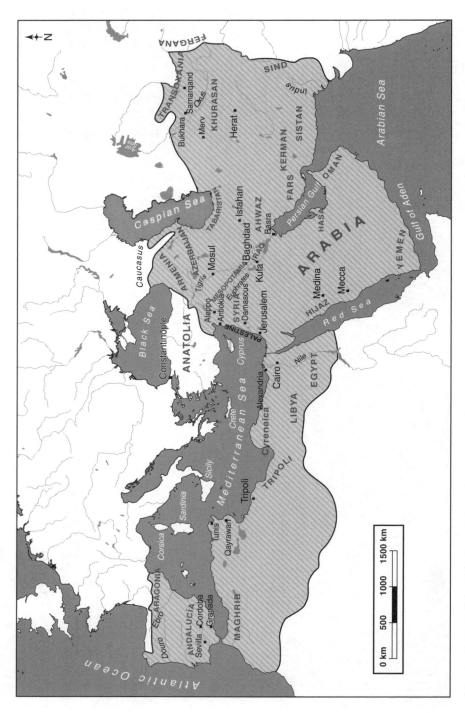

Map 2 Extent of the Caliphate, 750

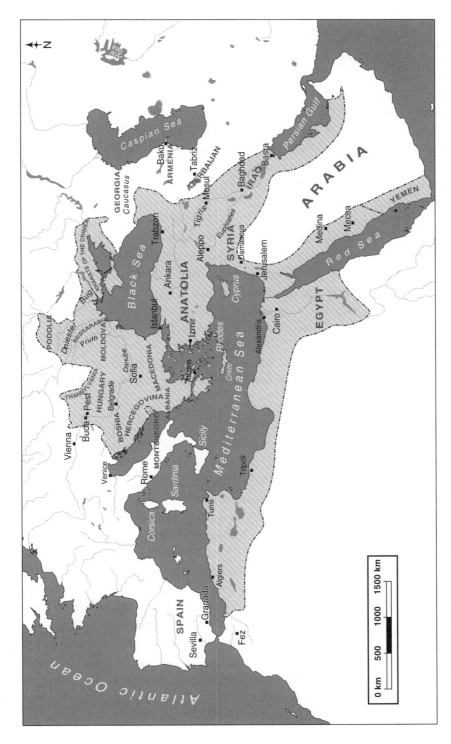

Map 3 Extent of the Ottoman Empire, 1683

Hülegü laid Baghdad in ruins in 1258. The Mongols rolled the last Abbasid caliph, al-Musta'sin, in a carpet and had horses trample him to death. After a period of political fragmentation, the Middle East was again reunited, this time by the Ottoman Turks, who in 1453 ended the Byzantine Empire through the conquest of Constantinople. The city, renamed Istanbul, became the capital of a mighty empire, the Ottoman Empire, which attained its peak under Sultan Süleyman I (1520–66). The Ottoman sultans in later centuries also took the title of caliph to mark that they were the leaders of the Muslim community. The Ottoman Empire came to consist of most of the Middle East until its collapse during the First World War. In 1924 the Caliphate, and with it the Muslim world's symbolic unity, was dissolved.

Napoleon's military expedition to Egypt in 1798 was the start of European dominance and colonisation in the Middle East. At the end of the nineteenth century, as a response to an ever firmer European hold on the region, thoughts arose of political union on the basis of both Islam and the Arabic language. However, the legacy of the European colonial powers was a fragmentation into a number of sovereign states and in consequence, right up to the present, there has existed a tension between, on the one hand, a vision of union and, on the other, the sovereign state. Later we shall see how the state has been challenged from above by supranational ideologies (pan-Arabism, pan-Islamism) and from below by various sub-state groups (language communities, religious groups, clans, tribes, and so on).

Islam

The three big monotheist world religions – Judaism, Christianity, and Islam – all originated in the Middle East. Mecca and Medina in present-day Saudi Arabia are regarded as Islam's two holiest places, followed by Jerusalem, which is also a holy place for Jews and Christians. Over the centuries these religions have subdivided into various directions and factions and as a result the region is a patchwork of religious groups. The most extreme example is Lebanon, where all eighteen Muslim and non-Muslim confessions are recognised by the state and representatives to the country's parliament and government are allotted on a confessional basis. Lebanon is the only country in the region where Christians exert considerable political influence. However, it is the Egyptian Copts who are the largest Christian group. Approximately four million Egyptians are Christian Copts (6 per cent of the total population).[9] Today the Jews live mainly in Israel, even if Jews are still spread throughout the region. But the big majority, almost 90 per cent of the regions inhabitants, are Muslims. More than 80 per cent of these belong to the Sunni faith within Islam.[10] In Iran, Iraq, and Bahrain, however, Shi'a Muslims are in the majority, and in Lebanon the Shi'as make up the biggest single confessional group. In addition the ʿAlawi and Zaydi Shiʿas play a significant role in the history of Syria and Yemen. The Ibadis, who live in Oman, represent a third direction within Islam.

Arabic language

In the Middle East we also find a number of languages belonging to different families. Three major language families are represented: Arabic, Berber, and Hebrew are Afro-Asian; Turkish is Altaic; and Persian and Kurdish are Indo-European languages. Iran is the most multi-ethnic state in the region. Here the core Persian population is ringed by, among others, Azerbaijanis, Kurds, Turcomans, Arabs, and Baluchis. Nevertheless the majority of the inhabitants of the Middle East, around 70 per cent, speaks, reads, and writes Arabic,[11] as Persian is written in the Arabic alphabet. Arabic, which spread as a result of Islam's expansion under the first caliphs in the seventh century, is the holy language for all Muslims. Arabic has a number of different dialects but one standard written form (Arab. *al-ʿarabiyya al-fusha*) that is understood across all the state borders in the region (see Table 1).

Social and economic conditions

Furthermore the economies and the degree of economic integration into world trade vary from country to country. In 2007 Bahrain and Qatar each only had some one million inhabitants, while the population figures for each of the countries Egypt, Iran, and Turkey exceeded 70 million. The Gulf States, Algeria, and Libya have enormous incomes from the sale of oil and gas, while the other countries in the Middle East earn a living through far less profitable sources. Consequently, there are big differences in national incomes. In 2007 the per capita Gross Domestic Product (GDP) was less than US$ 2,500 in Yemen, while

Table 1 Principal religious and language groups in the Middle East

	Muslims	**Non-Muslims**
Arabic speaking	Majority	Copts Maronites Catholics Orthodox Christians
Non-Arabic speaking	Turks Persians Kurds Berbers	Armenians Israeli Jews

the GDP was higher than US$ 40,000 in the Emirates, Kuwait, and Qatar. The states also vary considerably in their ranking on the so-called Human Development Index (HDI). This is a gauge the UN uses to measure the level of development in each country. Factors such as life expectancy and the literacy rate are weighted. For example, in Israel in 2007 about 97.1 per cent of the entire adult population could read and write, while the corresponding figure in Yemen and Morocco was less than 60 per cent. However, the Middle East countries have socio-economic similarities, too. One common feature is an explosive population growth, coupled with rapid urbanisation after 1950. Another common feature is that the economic structure is geared to the export of raw materials, first of all oil and gas, trade, and the service sector (see Table 2).

Table 2   Middle East statistics (2007)

State	Population (in millions)	Expected population 2020 (in millions)	Per capita GDP (in US$)	Life expectancy for newly born	Literacy rate (for over 15s)	HDI ranking
Algeria	33.9	40.6	7,740	72.2	75.4	104
Bahrain	0.8	1.0	29,723	75.6	88.8	39
Egypt	80.1	98.6	5,349	69.9	66.4	123
Emirates	4.4	5.7	54,626	77.3	90.0	35
Iraq	29.5	40.2	–	67.8	74.1	–
Iran	72.4	83.7	10,955	71.2	82.3	88
Israel	6.9	8.3	26,315	80.7	97.1	27
Jordan	5.9	7.5	4,901	72.4	91.1	96
Kuwait	2.9	3.7	47,812	77.5	94.5	31
Lebanon	4.2	4.6	10,109	71.9	89.6	83
Libya	6.2	7.7	14,364	73.8	88.8	55
Morocco	31.2	36.2	4,108	71.0	55.6	130
Oman	2.7	3.5	22,816	75.5	84.4	56
Palestinian Territories	4.0	5.8	–	73.3	93.8	110
Qatar	1.1	1.7	74,882	75.5	93.1	33
Saudi Arabia	24.7	31.6	22,935	72.7	85.0	59
Syria	20.5	26.5	4,511	74.1	83.1	107
Tunisia	10.1	11.4	7,520	73.8	77.7	98
Turkey	73.0	83.9	12,955	71.7	88.7	79
Yemen	22.3	31.6	2,335	62.5	58.9	140
Total	436.8	533.8				

Source: The figures in the table come from UNDP: 'Human Development Report 2009: Overcoming Barriers: Human Mobility and Development', http://hdr.undp.org/en/media/HDR_2009_EN_Complete.pdf.

Regime stability

Apart from the features mentioned above, regime stability is a common characteristic of the Middle Eastern states. According to Webster's Dictionary a *regime* is 'a system of government and administration'.[12] Studies of regimes in the sense of how power is organised within the borders of a state is one of political science's classic topics. Power can be organised in many different ways: a glance at our own times or history reveals great variation and you can scarcely find two alike. The Greek philosophers Plato and Aristotle constructed regime typologies that have been the starting point for categorisation up to modern times. Both divided forms of government into six main types: three legitimate types, 'monarchy', 'aristocracy', and 'moderate democracy', with three distorted types, 'tyranny', 'oligarchy' (rule by the few), and 'extreme democracy' (rule by the mobs). Today it is usual to distinguish between authoritarian and democratic regimes, a clear continuation of the classical typologies.

With the growth of the modern state it has also been usual to distinguish between 'government', 'regime', and 'state'. Robert M. Fishman claims that a regime is a more permanent form of political organisation than a government, but usually less permanent than a state. The state is normally a more permanent structure for dominance and coordination, which includes a repressive system and the means to administer a society and extract resources from it.[13] In most countries in the Middle East it is hard to separate the rulers from the state. This is clear in the example of Saudi Arabia, where the state even bears the name of the ruling Sa'ud family.

David Easton breaks the regime concept into three components: values (aims and principles), norms, and authority structures.[14] The values define the boundaries of what is taken for granted in day-to-day politics without offending the deeply held feelings of important groups in society. The norms specify which procedures are expected and accepted in political decision-making processes. The authority structures refer to the formal and informal patterns of how power is distributed and organised. The values, norms, and authority structures act together to both regulate and legitimise political acts, thus creating a framework for political interaction. In most states this framework is set out in writing in a single document, the country's 'constitution'.

Easton believes that the framework for political interaction changes more slowly than other political relations.[15] Here we approach the question of *regime stability*. By regime stability we mean that a regime maintains its characteristic features – values, norms, and authority structures – over a certain period of time. It is in the period from 1970 to the present that most regimes in the Middle East have had this stability. There are various ways to measure regime stability. One method is to look at the age of its constitution, that is, to find out when the present constitution was ratified or see how many constitutional amendments have been introduced since a given date. In 2009 the constitutions of the Middle East had an average lifespan of 33 years.[16] In several countries, however, a number of amendments have been accepted during this period.

Another method is to focus on regime change, which here refers to a fundamental change in the system of government. An adjustment of the constitution by, for instance, the introduction of a new electoral law is not enough. Regime changes may vary both with regard to direction and speed. Some mark the transition from dictatorship to democracy; others go in the opposite direction; while yet others entail one authoritarian regime being replaced by another. The change may be sudden, the result of a coup, revolution or external intervention, or more gradual. Between 1945 and 1970 the Middle East experienced a turbulent time with a series of regime changes. In several states young officers seized power, deposing monarchs in favour of republics. Examples of this are Egypt in 1952, Iraq in 1958, North Yemen in 1962, and Libya in 1969. But if one looks at the period after 1970, the picture is quite different. There have only been two obvious regime changes in the Middle East in this period, respectively Iran in 1979 and Iraq in 2003. In addition, the union of North and South Yemen in 1990 can be regarded as a regime change. It marked the transition from two authoritarian regimes to one more democratic system of government. Nonetheless, we disregard this as a regime change. The reason for this is that the democratic experiment was very brief. In reality, union meant the north 'took over' the south and that the authoritarian regime of North Yemen's former ruler, 'Ali 'Abdallah Salih, tightened its grasp on power in the whole of the Yemen.

A third method to measure a regime's stability is to examine the turnover among the elite. Most democracies are stable, but because there is a steady turnover among the elite through elections, democracies are not set in stone. In the Middle East, however, rulers tend to stay in power for a long time. A meeting of Arab heads of state at the beginning of the new millennium would include several of the same men who were in power in 1970, among them Syria's President Hafiz al-Asad, Jordan's King Husayn, Libya's President Mu'ammar al-Qadhafi, Morocco's King Hassan II, Oman's Sultan Qabus, and the Palestinian leader Yasir 'Arafat. The year 1999 marked the start of a generation shift at the top of the Arab states. But the new leaders were mainly the sons or brothers of the deceased rulers. These 'dynastic' shifts of rulers have taken place almost without any internal power struggle or popular protest. Lebanon and Turkey have experienced more frequent changes of leadership. This is because they are among the most democratic states in the region. Here the voters decide who shall be head of state, which again has stimulated turnover in the leadership.

No matter what method is used, one finds that Middle East regimes were consolidated around 1970. In spite of this, the old myth lives on that the region's authorities are unpredictable and unstable. Of course, the period has seen military interventions, irregular transfers of power, internal struggles and war. But these disturbances have scarcely affected regime stability. If one takes Lebanon as an example, the bloody civil war between 1975 and 1990 brought only limited changes. Although the constitution was amended in order to revise the division of power between the country's religious so achieve a better balance, in practice, there is a clear continuity as to which parties and personalities dominate the political scene. Nor have international and regional 'earthquakes' such as the collapse of the Soviet Union at the end of the 1980s and the Gulf War of 1990–1 affected the regimes' stability.

Stability and stagnation

Regime stability is not necessarily a good thing in itself. A regime can be stable by oppression and bribery. In the Middle East, regime stability has had its price. This book will show that stability has gone hand in hand with stagnation since 1970 and the signs of stagnation during the last decades are very well documented. It is sufficient to refer to the 'Arab Human Development Report': three reports about development in the Arab countries that were published between 2003 and 2005.[17] These reports attracted much attention, partly because it was exclusively the work of Arab researchers. Moreover, publication was partly financed by the Arab Fund for Economic and Social Development.[18] This gave the reports an extra 'credibility' in the Arab world. The researchers studied a number of topics within Arab societies: economy, health, the environment, education, technological development, gender issues, government, and regional cooperation. The reports concluded that Arab countries are in a midway position, neither underdeveloped nor fully developed. The Arab world is better situated than, for example, sub-Saharan Africa. For one thing the infrastructure (roads, electricity, telephone lines, and so on) is well developed in most countries. Despite this, however, the reports conclude that the Arab world is hampered by three fundamental deficiencies.

First, the Arab countries have a shortage of *freedom*. Authoritarian rulers survive by, among other things, manipulating elections, undermining the distinction between the executive and the judiciary, and censoring the media and controlling civil society. As will be shown later in the book, democracy is weak in the contemporary Middle East. This type of government is least developed in the Arab countries.[19]

Second, there is a shortage of knowledge. Despite Arab countries spending more of their GDP on education than many other developing countries, the level of knowledge is poor. The degree of illiteracy, although declining, is still high. At the turn of the twenty-first century, the 'Arab Human Development Report' estimates that of 65 million adults who were illiterate, almost two-thirds were women; and approximately ten million children had no access to school at all. It is not then surprising that the Arab world is lagging behind both in scientific research and information technology. Investment in research is less than one seventh of the global average. According to the well-recognised *Times Higher Education's* 'World University Rankings 2007', not a single Arab university was included among the world's top 500. The list included, however, four Israeli and four Turkish universities. It is interesting to note that as many as 95 Asian, 12 South American, and four African educational institutions were listed, a fact that underlines the weak position of research and teaching in Arab countries compared with other parts of the world.[20]

Third, there is a deficiency where women's liberation is concerned. Even if illiteracy among women is declining, it is still only half who can read and write. There are few countries in the world where women take less part in politics or where fewer work outside the home than in Arab countries. According to the report, the proportion of women representatives in Arab parliaments remains the lowest in the world. In all these important areas the Arab world lags behind other developing regions such as Latin America, sub-Saharan Africa, and South East Asia.

One particularly serious challenge the Arab countries face is a rapidly growing population. According to the 'Arab Human Development Report', the population of the Arab world is considerably younger than the global average: 50 per cent of the inhabitants of Yemen, for instance, are under the age of fifteen. The reports sketch two different scenarios for demographic development: one where the population in the Arab world is expected to increase from today's 280 million to 410 million by 2020, and a second where the population is estimated to grow to 459 million by the same year. In the decades after 1950 there has been a massive urbanisation. For the authorities it is going to be tough to meet the challenge of the future expectations of such a young and rapidly growing population. This young population, especially in the towns, represents a heavy pressure on labour markets, schools, and health institutions. At around fifteen per cent, unemployment is already the highest in the world and is expected to rise sharply in the coming years. The social problems have already begun to be felt and according to the reports, 51 percent of the young adults interviewed expressed a desire to emigrate.

Culture versus structure

What, therefore, is the best way to approach a theme such as politics in the Middle East? In 1978 Edward W. Said published *Orientalism*,[21] which provided a criticism of what appeared as the dominant Western representation of the people and societies of 'the Orient', the non-Western world. Said's arguments gained a lot of attention and are still being debated. 'Orientalism', he claimed, serves to construct a picture of the non-Western as the West's negative counterpart. According to Said, Western researchers, journalists, writers, and travellers were behind this construction through their dealings with non-Western people and societies. While the Oriental was portrayed as 'irrational', 'religious', 'fatalist', 'emotional', and 'static', the Westerner was, in contrast, described as 'rational', 'enlightened', and 'progressive'. The Orient's backwardness compared to the West was in brief ascribed to the personality features of the Orientals, and Islam as a faith was used to explain political and socio-economic stagnation. Said's main argument was that Orientalism was the basis for Western dominance of non-Western societies – the West was the norm. Colonialism was sanctioned as a normative project, which aimed at 'civilising', but in practice, became the Westernisation of the Orientals. In this way colonialism's true face, dominance and oppression in order to groom the interests of the colonial powers, was disguised.

In spite of the debate that followed in the wake of Said's book, Orientalism's stereotypical interpretations continue to colour our views of people and societies in the non-Western world. This 'neo-Orientalism' also influences our understanding of political systems and processes in the Middle East. The region is frequently looked on as 'mysterious', characterised by intrigues, war, religious extremism, terror, and arbitrary rule. This representation is common within research, journalism, and politics. One of this book's aims, is to try and correct such stereotypical oversimplifications. This is important precisely because neo-Orientalist perspectives contribute towards defining the relations between the West and the Muslim world, centred on the Middle East. In the West Islam is seen as the new major threat since the collapse of the Soviet Union and the fall of communism. Samuel P. Huntington went as far in *The Clash of Civilisations* as to describe this tension as 'a conflict of civilisations'.[22]

Researchers must, in their analyses, be open to the significance of cultural variations, but political systems and processes are not dependent on cultural attitudes and faith alone. The Middle East states are, as we have seen, a natural comparison because they share important common characteristics. But the region's systems and processes are not unique. The region is characterised by poverty, huge income differences, an arms race, urbanisation, a lack of real political participation, and a widespread use of political violence. All these features are also typical of African, Asian, and Latin American states. In brief, these are problems most countries in the third world face today. Instead of limiting ourselves to cultural explanations, this book will analyse structural features of politics in the region.

Content of the book

Part 1 will provide the historical background for the later analysis. Here we will show how the colonial legacy – of the Ottoman Empire, the United Kingdom, and France – laid the foundations of politics in the modern Middle East. Given this difficult starting point, the authorities in the post-colonial states have used various methods to consolidate their power, methods which in their turn have caused new troubles for state- and nation-building. Part 2 of the book (Chapters 3 and 4) carries the title 'Society and State'. Here the focus is on class relations, ethnic conflicts, and the strategies the state authorities have used to control the pluralistic society. The title of Part 3 (Chapters 5 and 6) is 'The Quest for Legitimacy'. In this section we shall explore how the regimes have dealt with the legitimacy crisis that occurred around 1970. The rulers tried to build up a new legitimacy by not only making themselves the spokesmen for both political and economic reform, but at the same time they have Islamised parts of the legislation and judiciary in response to the Islamist challenge. Part 4 (Chapters 7 and 8) is titled 'Institutions and Power'. In the years after independence the state apparatus (police, security services, the armed forces, bureaucracy, and so on) expanded rapidly. Here we show how the regimes have used this state apparatus to preserve their dominant position. In the final section, Part 5 (Chapters 9 and 10), which is titled 'Scenarios of Change', we debate various perspectives for the future from democratisation on the one extreme and state collapse at the other end of the scale. The book concludes with Chapter 11 that summarises and discusses observations made in the light of the three main questions asked in the introduction.

Further reading

Davson, Roderick H.: 'Where Is the Middle East?', in *Foreign Affairs*, 38, July 1960, pp. 665–75.

Keddie, Nikki: 'Is There a Middle East?', in *International Journal of Middle East Studies*, 4 July 1973, pp. 255–71.

Said, Edward W.: *Orientalism*. London: Penguin Books, 2003.

UNDP: 'Arab Human Development Report 2002: Creating Opportunities for Future Generations', New York: United Nations Publications, 2003.

UNDP: 'Arab Human Development Report 2003: Building a Knowledge Society', New York: United Nations Publications, 2004.

UNDP: 'Arab Human Development Report 2004: Towards Freedom in the Arab World', New York: United Nations Publications, 2005.

Zartman, I. William: 'Political Science', in Leonard Binder (ed.): *The Study of the Middle East: Research and Scholarship in the Humanities and the Social Sciences.* New York: John Wiley & Sons, 1976, pp. 265–325.

Part 1
Historical Background

2 Troubled Heritage

The events of 1914–22, while bringing to an end Europe's Middle Eastern Question, gave birth to a Middle Eastern Question in the Middle East itself.[1]

The First World War marked a turning point in the political history of the Middle East. The Ottoman Empire, which had dominated the region for more than four centuries, collapsed and was replaced by a new political order. The modern state system, local versions of nationalism, and modern political institutions took shape in this period. Between the wars all the Arab states – with the exception of Saudi Arabia – were under some form of colonial rule. The degree of colonialisation varied from 130 years of occupation and complete assimilation in Algeria to barely institutionalised treaty relations in the Arab emirates in the Gulf, but for the region as a whole the dominance of the great powers was profound. Even after the states won formal independence, Western interference continued in the Middle East.

The significance of the colonial era for the region's political development is controversial. Some, such as the Israeli historian Avi Shlaim, claim that the Middle East still suffers from a 'Post-Ottoman syndrome' because the old regime was replaced by a set of conflicts – 'Arab–Israeli, Arab–Arab, and Arab–Western'.[2] Others respond that the idea of the destructive consequences of colonialism is a constructed myth that trivialises internal problems and places all the blame on external powers.[3] It is, however, not a complete coincidence that countries such as Algeria, Iraq, Israel/Palestine, and Lebanon have been plagued by war and severe political problems in recent times. As we shall see, these are the countries that, together with Syria, inherited the greatest seeds of conflict from the colonial era.

In this chapter we shall answer the following questions: how has the colonial heritage influenced the Middle Eastern states and politics? We shall study the historical background on three different levels: first, the European colonial powers introduced the modern state system; second, the colonial powers left behind a heritage of the history of ideas and third; the colonial powers exported their political institutions to the region's states.

Pre-modern political organisation

A precious source for insight into pre-modern political organisation in the region is Ibn Khaldun's *al-Muqaddima*, 'The Introduction', from 1377.[4] In this work, which is an introduction to a larger historical work, the author writes about the rise and fall of dynasties in the Maghrib since Islam's first days. Ibn Khaldun was born in Tunis in 1332 and spent much of his life travelling between various courts in Spain and North Africa in a time when the region was characterised by acute political turbulence. He is regarded by many as the world's first 'modern historian' because, in contrast to earlier chroniclers, he went beyond narrating individual events and portraying individual persons by attempting to uncover patterns in history. In *al-Muqaddima* Ibn Khaldun sketches a model of the creation of states in the Maghrib and analyses the forces behind political and social organisation.

The rise and fall of states is presented as a cycle by Ibn Khaldun. A dynasty rises, displacing previous state formations but, in turn, is challenged by the growth of new groups and disappears. The force behind this cycle is called *'asabiyya*, 'group feeling'. Groups possessing a strong *'asabiyya* become powerful and conquer others. The starting point for the formation of states, explains Ibn Khaldun, is the Bedouins' superior group feeling. The Bedouins are uncorrupted by wealth and power, hardened by life in the desert. Once they are mobilised by a cause or a leader, no one can stop them. In this way earlier states are conquered and new dynasties established. However, as soon as the ruling group consolidates its hold on the population, decline commences. The egalitarian spirit of desert life vanishes and the elite enjoys the fruits of its success. Impressive monuments are built, a court is established, and gradually the riches accumulated by the dynasty's founders are squandered. Leisurely town life leads to sloth and decadence, making the state vulnerable to fresh attacks from outside. The elite has lost its original solidarity and is finally deposed by tribal warriors with a strong *'asabiyya*.

An interesting feature of Ibn Khaldun's description of Maghrib's political history is the tension between urban-based kingdoms and the challengers from their margins. Urban society dominated the hinterland but continually had to fight for control of the desert and mountains. Ibn Khaldun uses telling images to describe the control of the dynasties outside the capital. He sees this influence as rays of light that grow weaker the farther they radiate from the centre. Another image is of the rings made when a stone is thrown in the water that become fainter and fainter as they spread outwards. At the farthest reach of the rays or the rings lie the areas that are barely under the dynasty's control. It is here that power will first crumble as the dynasty begins to collapse, and it is here that the foundation is laid for new empires.

The Ottoman Empire

The Ottoman Empire was founded in 1280 and was at its apogee under Sultan Süleyman I (1520–66). The Ottomans conquered Constantinople in 1453 and Egypt in 1517, continuing their expansion under Süleyman until their empire embraced Yemen in the south and Algeria in the west. The only parts of the Middle East that were not annexed in the empire were Iran, Oman, Morocco, and the interior of the Arabian Peninsula (parts of today's Saudi Arabia). The Ottomans also expanded into Europe and conquered Greece, the Balkans, and Hungary. Süleyman went so far as to try to take Vienna in 1539, but the onset of winter obliged him to break off the siege. Mehmet IV made a similar attempt in 1683, but was fought back.

The teaching of *al-Muqaddima* can be applied to the Ottoman Empire. The vast empire Süleyman left behind in 1566 proved hard to defend and administer. In general the Ottoman presence was stronger the closer one came to Anatolia – today's Turkey – and Istanbul, the centre of the empire and stronger along the coast than inland. The central power was particularly weak in mountain and desert regions where outlaws sought refuge and where law and order was maintained by the tribes and different confessional communities. In the empire's shadow there was still room for alternative and competing political organisations. First, the Ottomans suffered their first military defeat against Austria and Russia in the 1690s, leading to constant pressure from European Christians during the eighteenth and nineteenth centuries. Second, Ottoman influence in North Africa diminished in the same period, which created opportunities for military rulers who desired independence from Istanbul. Thus the foundations were laid for Tunisia, Algeria, Egypt, and Libya. For instance, in Egypt the Albanian army commander Muhammad 'Ali took power in 1803 and began to go his own way. Until the country became bound by debt to European creditors in the middle of the nineteenth century, Egypt was for all practical purposes independent. Muhammad 'Ali's forces went so far as to attack the central power in Istanbul by invading Syria and parts of Anatolia. In the end, to stop him, the sultan had to seek military aid from the United Kingdom and France. Third, the Arabian Peninsula was difficult to access and so sparsely populated that the Ottomans could not administer the area. As a result local tribes controlled the outskirts of the Peninsula and gradually developed their own states. Kuwait, Qatar, Bahrain, the Emirates, and Yemen are examples of this. In Yemen the Ottomans met great military resistance and after a while had to cede autonomy to the Zaydis in the mountains. The Zaydis, a Shiʻa Muslim breakaway group, which had settled down in the area in the tenth century, were only under Ottoman rule between 1538 and 1635. In the nineteenth century the Ottoman Empire made fresh advances and finally managed to occupy North Yemen in 1870.

The Arab world

Ilya Harik has systematically investigated the creation of states throughout history in the Arab world and created a typology of what type of authority the states were founded on.[5] He identifies five traditional foundations for authority (see Table 3). The first type is the *imam*-chief states, where the leader has both political and religious authority. He points out two subdivisions. The first comprises states established by a dissident community that has sought refuge in desert and mountain on the periphery of the Sunni empire's centre. Examples of this type of state are the Ibadi *Imamate*, which periodically ruled over Oman between 751 and 1970, and the Zaydi *Imamate*, which controlled northern parts of the Yemen from 897 to 1962. The second type comprises states where the leader claims to be the descendent of the Prophet Muhammad (Arab. *sharif*). Examples of this are the Hashemite state in Hijaz (ended in 1925) and the ʻAlawi royal house in Morocco. As we shall see later in the book, Morocco's King Hassan II (1961–99) took the title 'the commander of the faithful' (Arab. *amir al-muʼminin*) in order to emphasise his religious legitimacy.

The other types of states are *imam* and chief states, or alliance states, where the chief does not himself have religious authority, but gains it through an alliance with a religious authority, an *imam* in Harik's terminology. Harik's example is the kingdom of Saudi Arabia, which is built on an alliance of more than 250 years between the Saʻud family and Wahhabi clerics. Muhammad

Table 3 Traditional authority foundation for states in the Arab world

Traditional authority foundation	States
Imam–chief	Hijaz, Yemen, Morocco, Oman, Cyrenaica (East-Libya)
Imam and chief	Saudi Arabia
Traditional secular system	Qatar, Bahrain, Kuwait, United Arab Emirates
Bureaucratic military oligarchies	Algeria, Tunisia, Tripolitania (North-West Libya), Egypt
Colonially created	Iraq, Syria, Jordan, Palestine, Lebanon

ibn Saʻud and the reformist preacher Muhammad ibn ʻAbd al-Wahhab joined forces in 1744 and laid the foundations of the first Saʻud Emirate's expansion. Beginning at the tiny oasis Diraʻiyyah, the alliance state conquered large land areas in the Arabian Peninsula before Ottoman forces crushed it in 1818. A new attempt at Saudi conquest was defeated in 1891, but when the Ottoman Empire collapsed after the First World War, the project succeeded. The Saʻud family took over much of the Peninsula, founding the kingdom of Saudi Arabia in 1932.

The third type of state in Harik's typology is the traditional secular system where the chief's authority rests on acceptance by traditional local authorities and does not have religious legitimacy for his position. Examples of this type are the small monarchies in the Gulf: the Emirates, Qatar, Bahrain, and Kuwait. The oldest of these chief states is Kuwait, which has been ruled by the Sabah family since 1752. The Ottomans regarded Kuwait as part of their empire, but never took the trouble to subdue local tribes or subject this sparsely populated region to their administration. Thus, in reality, the Sabah family enjoyed autonomy, even if they treaded warily in contact with the Ottomans and used the Ottoman flag. In the latter half of the nineteenth century the chief states in the Gulf accepted separate security agreements with the United Kingdom. Britain, wanting to protect its sea route to India, offered them British protection in return for their promise to end piracy and stay away from other great powers. It was thanks to these agreements that these small and defenceless principalities were able to survive Saudi expansion at the beginning of the twentieth century and enter the oil age first as protectorates and gradually as independent states.

The fourth type is the bureaucratic–military oligarchies, where the leader has authority as a military commander. Harik designates four states created in North Africa in the eighteenth and nineteenth centuries as examples: Algeria, Muhammad ʻAli's Egypt, Tripolitania (in present-day Libya), and Tunisia. These states were led by generals who ruled on behalf of the sultan in Istanbul. Originally, these were all Ottoman officials, most of them recruited from countries outside those they were appointed to administer. In time, however, contact with the central power diminished and the military commanders became interested in increasing local autonomy. Greater independence meant less tax money was transferred to Istanbul, leaving more in the pockets of local leaders. For instance, in Tunisia the Muradi dynasty started to replace Ottoman soldiers by local tribal warriors between 1637 and 1702. Under the Husayni dynasty that came to power in 1706, attempts to win autonomy continued so that in effect the country became independent of Istanbul. The Husayni regime paid no taxes to the central power, nor did it contribute soldiers to the sultan's army. It even declared war and signed peace treaties in its own name.

The fifth type in Harik's model is the colonially created state system. As mentioned in the introduction these are Iraq, Syria, Jordan, Palestine, and Lebanon. These states had their borders drawn on the basis of the colonialists' interests and were therefore, according to Harik, inherently porous and unstable. We shall deal with how these states came into existence in greater detail later in the chapter.

The Europeans arrive

The reason why states such as Egypt and Tunisia could exercise self-government was that the Ottoman Empire was weakened and no longer able to discipline the provinces. This weakening was a combination of internal problems and outer pressure. The Ottomans were under attack from Russian and Austrian forces that had respectively reconquered the northern shores of the Black sea and Hungary. Simultaneously, Greece and the Balkans were in touch with nationalist ideologies and revolt broke out in both Serbia and Greece. The Ottomans retaliated brutally, repressing the rebels, but after the European powers intervened in the conflict, both Serbia and Greece won their independence respectively in 1830 and 1832. Russia declared war on the Ottoman Empire in 1854 and 1877. On the first occasion, the Crimean War, the empire survived thanks to British and French protection, but on the second occasion, the great powers solved the conflicts they had by distributing Ottoman territory between them.

The undermining of the Ottoman Empire

All these wars put increasing pressure on the Ottoman Empire's finances. In order to survive, the empire had to expand and modernise its army, whilst at the same time, weapons and mobilisation expenses were greater than the empire's production apparatus could bear. Its production methods were old-fashioned and ineffective and its tax gathering was flawed with the result that it lagged ever further behind industrialised Europe. Since the Middle Ages Turkey had made agreements, so-called capitulations, conceding protection to foreign merchants and lower customs duties on European goods. To ensure French and British assistance in the war against Muhammad 'Ali the sultan had to sign the Balta Liman Agreement in 1838, which abolished all remaining trade monopolies, leading to the free flow of Western industrial goods into the empire. These free trade agreements made industrialisation of the Ottoman Empire difficult, directing the Middle East into commercial agriculture. Thus an imbalance arose where the region became a raw-material producer for a growing European industry while the cost of manufactured imports outpaced domestic agricultural exports. In this way, as the balance of trade deficit rose, the state treasury was steadily depleted. To meet military expenses and finance other important reforms Turkey resorted to borrowing from European banks. The first loan was granted during the Crimean War in 1854, and during the next twenty years the Ottomans signed fifteen such bank loan agreements. In 1875 the government declared that it could no longer service its many expensive loans. In reality the Ottoman Empire was bankrupt. From the 1850s Muhammad 'Ali's Egypt had been drawn into a similar spiral of debt and was declared bankrupt the following year. This debt crisis led to direct European intervention into Ottoman economic policy and, ultimately, even to occupation. In Istanbul the Europeans were content to introduce international financial control over the Ottoman Empire's budget, but after 1882 Egypt was occupied by British troops. These troops remained in the country until after the First World War and even after the United Kingdom declared that Egypt was a sovereign state in 1922.

Despite economic decline in the nineteenth century, there were forces that counteracted the dissolution of the Ottoman Empire. To start with, sections of the leadership realised that they were faced with a structural crisis and put in place measures to modernise the empire. The first attempt at reform was carried out by Muhammad 'Ali in Egypt. During his rule he introduced conscription for Egyptians, a secular school system, major agricultural reforms, and various measures to rationalise the civil service. He also tried to establish a modern irrigation system and industry. A similar reform wave washed over the centre of the Ottoman Empire between 1839 and 1876. In the empire's history this period is known as the *tanzimat* (Turk. reorganisation) years. The tanzimat reforms involved among other things the modernisation of the army, school system, the law, and the judiciary. A main aim was the centralisation of power by, among other means, reducing the influence of the provincial lords and the Islamic scholars (Arab. *'ulama*). Those who favoured these reforms were Western-inspired bureaucrats.

Second, the life of the Ottoman Empire was prolonged by great power rivalry. The United Kingdom, France, Russia, and, later on, Germany all had interests there, which therefore placed limitations on each other's room for movement. If a state intervened in order to secure its national interests, the others would soon respond. For the United Kingdom its principal interest was in defending the route to India. India was regarded as the Jewel in the Crown and was a main market for British manufactures. To hinder attacks on shipping to and from India, Britain took up positions in the seas around the Arabian Peninsula. Moreover, it was her concerns with India that played a decisive role in Britain's decision to occupy Egypt. Ever since the opening of the Suez Canal in 1869 an increasing share of the transport to India had travelled through that route. For France and Russia it was essential to prevent Great Britain becoming too powerful in the Middle East. They too had interest in Africa and the Levant, and Russia wanted command of the Bosphorus to control traffic into and out of the Black Sea. Towards the end of the century, German presence in Turkey became more visible. Germany assisted the sultan in constructing a railway across Anatolia to Baghdad and contributed towards modernising the Turkish army. However, this alliance with Germany was to prove fateful for the Ottoman Empire, for when Turkey entered the First World War on Germany's side, the last scruples about dismantling the empire disappeared.

From 1830 on the Middle East fell gradually under various forms of European rule and control. The grasp of the great powers in the region was strengthened in three different stages. The first was a free trade phase from the 1830s, where the incipient markets there were opened to European manufactures. This phase also saw two examples of traditional colonialism, since the British annexed Aden in Southern Yemen in 1839 and France occupied Algeria in 1830. On paper Aden was the Middle East's only colony, but the colonisation of Algeria was in reality much more extensive. In 1848 Algeria was formally made a part of France. Under the Third Republic (1870–1940) this declaration of principle was implemented in practice and Algeria came directly under the jurisdiction of the Ministry of the Interior in France. France's secularism led to demands for lay schools in the country in 1882 and Algerians had to be conscripted in the French army. During the First World War, 206,000 Algerian soldiers fought for France and 26,000 of them were killed.[6]

The second phase was the scramble for colonies from 1880s till the First World War. In an era when the European powers were in conflict and rivalry with each other, each tried to secure itself colonies that could provide raw materials for its industry and ensure strategic depth. North Africa was an obvious place to begin because of its proximity and the inability of the Turks to defend their interests there. French forces occupied Tunisia in 1881 and were followed by the British in Egypt the following year. Italy grabbed Libya in 1911–12, and in the same year France and Spain divided Morocco between them. The degree of colonisation varied within North Africa. While the Italians threw the Turks out on annexing Libya in 1912, the European powers retained traditional political institutions in Morocco, Tunisia, and Egypt. The colonial masters controlled politics through their forces and representatives, but never deprived the countries' leaders of their formal right to rule. These states were considered 'protectorates', as if the region's dynasties had sought protection from Europe. In this manner sections of the local power elite survived, such as the 'Alawi dynasty in Morocco, and the breach with pre-colonial practice seemed less brutal. Changes were not as profound as in Algeria, where traditions were turned upside down and the occupying power worked for full assimilation with France.

The third and last phase of Europe's march into the Middle East began during the First World War, when the European powers finally decided to put an end to the Turkish Empire. As early as 1853 Tsar Nicholas referred to it as 'the sick man of Europe'. However, at that time, out of consideration for stability in the region and the danger of war in Europe, the European powers had hesitated to dissolve the Ottoman Empire.

The three agreements of the war

At the outbreak of the First World War the Ottomans took the fatal decision to join the central powers of Germany and Austria–Hungary. Over a million Turkish soldiers were mobilised against the Entente and war fronts were opened in the north and the south. In the north, the Russians pushed the Ottomans onto the defensive until the Bolshevik Revolution brought an end to the war in 1917, and in the south and east the French and British attacked.

McMahon–Husayn correspondence

The United Kingdom and France exploited tensions within the Ottoman Empire to weaken the enemy from the inside. They played on elements such as both a dawning nationalism and internal power rivalry. In 1908 the so-called Young Turks took over the reins of power in Istanbul and strengthened the central government of the empire. This aroused dissatisfaction in the Arab provinces that were at this time beginning to get acquainted with nationalist ideas. Opponents of centralisation accused the Young Turks of 'Turkifying' the empire. They pointed to their increased focus on Ottoman Turkish in schools, the administration, and the courts, and the small proportion of Arabs among the empire's leaders.[7] Great Britain saw the potential in Turk–Arab conflicts and looked around for an Arab ally in the war against the Ottoman Empire. The opportunity offered itself in 1915, when *Sharif* of Hijaz, Husayn Ibn 'Ali, sent a letter to the British High Commissioner in Egypt, Henry McMahon. Husayn belonged to the aristocratic Hashemite family, which claimed to be descended from the Prophet and which was appointed by the sultan to supervise Islam's holiest places, Mecca and Medina. In his letter to McMahon he aired the idea of a strategic alliance with the British, putting forward demands for starting a revolt against the central power in Istanbul. The idea of an Arab revolt was appreciated by the British, who were on the lookout for support from a religious leader to parry the attacks of the sultan in Istanbul. As official leader for the Muslim community the sultan had called for 'a holy war' (Arab. *jihad*) on the outbreak of war in 1914. Having *Sharif* Husayn on its side Britain would take the sting out of the religious rhetoric around the war and reduce the risk of a collective Muslim front. In the course of a correspondence comprising ten letters, Husayn was promised that an independent Arab state would be established in the areas conquered from the Ottoman Empire. However, the exact extent of this state was never formalised in a final agreement, and McMahon, who purposefully expressed himself in vague terms, demanded an exception for Aden, the provinces of Baghdad and Basra in present-day Iraq and the areas west of Damascus, Homs, Hama, and Aleppo (a sort of expanded Lebanon). Husayn insisted that the latter had to be included in the Arab state, but agreed to postpone the issue until after the war.

On 10 June 1916, *Sharif* Husayn's tribal warriors attacked the Turkish garrison in Mecca. With him he had the English officer, Thomas E. Lawrence, whose adventures were immortalised in David Lean's film *Lawrence of Arabia*. Romantic historians have represented the revolt as a general Arab rising after more than 400 years of Turkish despotism. In reality, Husayn's personal ambitions to be king of the Arab world were more decisive, and the tribal warriors he mobilised by no means represented a broad, popular movement. Nonetheless, when these tribal warriors, in cooperation with the British, entered Damascus in 1918, the jubilation was great. Husayn's son, Faysal, rode triumphantly into the city and formed an Arab government.

Sykes–Picot Agreement

Sharif Husayn's dream of a united Arab kingdom was, however, irreconcilable with the interests of the European powers. The United Kingdom's principal interest was the war alliance with France. In addition, London feared it would lose influence in the Middle East if an independent Arab state became too strong or fell into the hands of a rival power. In order to hinder such a scenario during the war, Great Britain negotiated with France a plan to divide the conquered Ottoman territories. This plan took the name Sykes–Picot after the negotiators, the French diplomat François Georges-Picot and the adviser to the British government, Mark Sykes, who signed the agreement in 1916. The agreement was originally secret, but after the 1917 revolution in Russia, the contents became known. France had been promised direct control over Lebanon and the coast into Anatolia and should have Syria (including Mosul province) as its sphere of influence. The British kept direct control over central and southern parts of present-day Iraq, Kuwait and further south along the Gulf, and defined their sphere of interest from Gaza in the south through today's Jordan to Kirkuk in north Iraq. These two spheres coincided to a considerable extent with the areas promised Husayn.

The Balfour Declaration

A question of decisive importance for the future was what should be done with the former area of the Ottoman Empire that went under the name of Palestine. The area was not explicitly mentioned in the McMahon–Husayn correspondence, but for Husayn it was obvious that Palestine should be part of his future Arab kingdom. The Sykes–Picot Agreement would not, however, have it along these lines. Here it was made clear that Palestine should be excluded from Hashemite ambitions and come under part British, part international, rule. The proposal led to quite a reaction when it became known in the Arab world. Great Britain further complicated the issue by making a third promise. In 1917 the then British Foreign Secretary, Arthur Balfour, sent a letter to the Zionist Lord Rothschild in which he promised to work for setting up 'a national home for the Jewish people' in Palestine. The intention was to secure support of the Zionist Movement during the First World War; to prevent a corresponding backing for the enemy Germany; and to create an alternative to Jewish immigration to the United Kingdom in an age in which anti-Semitism in Eastern Europe drove Jews into exile. A British-friendly enclave in Palestine would also give strategic depth for the defence of the Suez Canal. The British deliberately used the vague expression 'a national home' in the declaration and avoided promising the Zionists a state. Nevertheless, the Balfour Declaration became from then on a keystone in the work of the Zionist Movement for recognition of the demand for a state for the Jewish people. Great Britain, too, consistently defended the principle in the peace negotiations after the First World War and the Balfour Declaration was included in the League of Nations' ordinances that regulated the transition to independence of the Arab mandated territories. The Palestinian Arabs could thus not cooperate with the international mandate rule without at the same time accepting the imprecise vision of 'a national home for the Jewish people' within the land's boundaries.

Modern states arise

The question of the fate of the former Ottoman territories was not solved during the peace negotiations in Versailles in January 1919. On the one side stood the British Foreign Office with Thomas E. Lawrence and Faysal, who were against the Sykes–Picot Agreement and for the founding of an independent Arab state. On the other side was France, the oil lobby, and the British India Office, who were for the Sykes–Picot Agreement and against an Arab state. The parties did not reach an agreement at the San Remo Conference in April 1920, and the peace settlement was eventually ratified in the Sèvres Treaty four months later. The main points in the deal were as follows: the Ottoman Empire continued to exist in Anatolia, but lost southern and western part of the Peninsula to France, Italy, and Greece; the Allies recognised an independent Armenian state in east Anatolia and the Caucasus and a semi-autonomous Kurd state in east Anatolia; and the Ottoman Empire's provinces in the Middle East were separated from the empire and partitioned between the United Kingdom and France. The last point was a clear indication of who had won the argument: France, the oil lobby, and the British India

Office had emerged strongest and made sure that the Sykes–Picot Agreement was implemented.

However, the final word on the Ottoman Empire's future had not yet been said. The Allied occupation of Anatolia and the humiliating Sèvres Treaty motivated Turkish nationalists to start an armed revolt. An experienced general from the war, Mustafa Kemal, took over the leadership. He formed a national assembly in the mountain town of Ankara and declared the Istanbul government illegitimate since the city was under foreign occupation. Support for Kemal's movement grew rapidly as Greek forces, which had attacked in 1919, threatened to invade an ever-larger part of Anatolia in cooperation with Russia. The following year Kemal repulsed a Greek invasion and in 1922 he was ready to attack the British to liberate Istanbul. Great Britain summoned a new peace conference to renegotiate the Sèvres Treaty. The final settlement was accepted all over Anatolia, and plans for Kurd and Armenian states were shelved. When the Caliphate was abolished in 1924 the era of the Ottoman Empire was definitively over – a Turkish national state had taken its place. The capital was moved from Istanbul to Ankara as a step in the Turkification of the new state. Turkey was declared a republic in a new constitution, and Kemal became the country's first president. He started a comprehensive reform programme to modernise the country and exercised a unique influence on the shaping of the Turkish national state. In 1934 Parliament gave him the name Atatürk, 'Father of the Turks'.

European mandate rule

No such national hero could save the Arab world from great power manipulation. French troops forced Faysal's state administration out of Damascus and the Sykes–Picot Agreement was implemented. Five new states were founded: Iraq, Syria, Lebanon, Palestine, and Transjordan (present-day Jordan). These states were defined as mandated territories by the League of Nations, which meant that they were placed under European guardianship until they were considered able to rule themselves. The official justification for this arrangement was that the populations of the mandated territories were not sufficiently 'mature' for self-determination. The role of the European powers was to counsel the mandated territories and prepare for the transition to self-government. In reality, France and the United Kingdom regarded the arrangement as a fresh opportunity for international control and for promoting their own interests. A specific plan for transition to self-government was never formulated. The Iraqi mandate was initially put together by the two Ottoman *vilayat*s, or provinces, of Basra and Baghdad before the third northern *vilayat* of Mosul was added in 1926. In Syria European powers' procedure was to the contrary. Instead of building on the provinces that previously had been known as Greater Syria (Arab. *bilad al-sham*), they separated Lebanon, Transjordan, and Palestine, letting the remainder be Syria. The new borders bore an arbitrary character better suited to serve European interests. The crowning example of this was Transjordan, which was drawn on the map in 1921. The reason why this thinly populated area became a mandated territory was twofold: initially, something had to be done to stabilise what was notoriously a turbulent tribal region and prevent warlike attacks against French interests. Second, the two powers were faced with ambitious demands from Husayn's son, 'Abdallah. The problem created by the McMahon–Husayn correspondence during the First World War was still unresolved. The Kingdom of Hijaz was indeed recognised as an independent state since the Sèvres Treaty of 1920, but Husayn's conditions for starting the Arab revolt in 1916 had gone much further than his becoming king of Mecca and Medina. Husayn had three sons with his first wife: the youngest, Faysal, had led the Arab revolt, and the eldest, 'Ali, was the heir to the throne of Hijaz. By far the most ambitious of them though was 'Abdallah, who dreamed of becoming king of Syria. After Faysal had to flee Damascus, 'Abdallah led a group of tribal warriors from Mecca to Ma'n in Jordan, where he settled in order to put pressure on Europe. 'Abdallah's forces constituted no real threat to the British, but nevertheless, Great Britain feared he would make the area even more unstable. By offering 'Abdallah a crown in sparsely populated Transjordan, the European powers killed two birds with one stone. One the one hand, they let an Arab leader take on the job of calming down the Bedouins in the area, and on the other, they helped satisfy 'Abdallah's personal ambitions. In the previous year the British had installed Faysal as King of Iraq.

The United Kingdom thought that by doing so they had helped make up for their breach of promise by arranging for Hashemite rule in three separate kingdoms: Iraq, Transjordan, and Hijaz. The problem was simply that 'Abdallah and Faysal were seen as foreigners in the lands they arrived in. The Hashemites' origins along the Red Sea and the fact that the kings had been installed by the British gave the royal houses a problem of legitimacy. Of the three monarchies only the Jordanian has survived to our times. Hijaz was conquered by 'Abd al-'Aziz ibn Sa'ud (hereafter Ibn Sa'ud) in 1925 and incorporated into Saudi Arabia, and in 1958 a military coup put an end to the monarchy in Iraq.

Divide and rule

Opposition to French and British rule made it hard to maintain law and order in the mandated territories. To make it easier to control the populations there the European powers exploited ethnic differences and governed on the principle of divide and rule. The situation was worst in Lebanon and Syria, where France moved the borders and cultivated religious differences. Lebanon's territory was extended in 1920 and the intention was to increase the influence of the Christians who had until recently enjoyed self-government in the Lebanese mountains since 1861. France had developed ties to this minority during the entire nineteenth century and regarded themselves as protectors of the Christians. By expanding Lebanon in 1920 the French included areas with an overwhelmingly Muslim population. The Muslims were sceptical of being included in a state where Christians dominated politics, and this laid the foundations for ethnic conflict in the country. The two minorities, the 'Alawi and Druze, each acquired their own mini state with their own administration and French governor, and in this way the mandate government mobilised two conflicting forces: on the one hand, and as planned, this division strengthened the inhabitants' sense of belonging to a tribe, a clan, a religious group, and other forms of local identity, and on the other, colonial rule strengthened Arab and Syrian nationalism as a reaction to foreign interference. Consequently, in 1925 a national rising broke out in the Druze Mountains that the French suppressed. This marked the beginning of the Syrians' struggle for independence.

Table 4   Colonial rule in the Middle East

State	Colonial type	Colonial period
Algeria	Part of France	1830–1962
Bahrain	Treaty relations with Britain	1820–1971
Egypt	British protectorate	1882–1922
Emirates	Treaty relations with Britain	1820–1971
Iraq	British mandate territory	1920–1932
Iran	Never colonised	–
Israel/Palestine	British mandate territory	1920–1947
Jordan	British mandate territory	1921–1946
Kuwait	Treaty relations with Britain	1899–1861
Lebanon	French mandate territory	1920–1941
Libya	Part of Italy	1912–1943
Morocco	French/Spanish protectorate	1912–1956
Oman	Informal British influence	–
Qatar	Treaty relations with Britain	1916–1971
Saudi Arabia	Never colonised	–
Syria	French mandate territory	1920–1941
Tunisia	French protectorate	1881–1956
Turkey	Never colonised	–
North Yemen	Never colonised	–
Southern Yemen	British colony in Aden	1839–1967

In Iraq the first revolt against mandate government came in 1920, leading to many fatalities on both the British and Iraqi sides. Great Britain responded with a double strategy to keep control over the country: on the one hand, the heritage from Ottoman times of concentrating power in Sunni hands. This religious group dominated the state administration and court and held top posts in the army. On the other hand, the support of the Shi'a tribes was bought by making them the biggest landowners. In this way, the country's wealthiest people were drawn from the Shi'a Muslim community which at the same time was over-represented among the land's poorest. As their predecessors and successors, the British chose to administer southern Iraq with the support of the tribal leaders. The chiefs were granted judicial authority and great economic power in return for maintaining law and order in the Shi'a countryside.

The transition to independence

In the years between 1918 and 1971 the Middle East states won their independence from the colonial powers. In two of the countries that had formally gained independence earlier, Egypt in 1922 and Iraq in 1932, the British continued to dominate through military intervention and bilateral agreements. The Iraqi-British independence agreement of 1932 gave the British the right to keep its air bases in the country and obliged Iraq to consult the United Kingdom in all foreign affairs. In Egypt the British kept their forces after conceding self-government and in 1936 secured an alliance agreement that gave the United Kingdom the right to occupy the country once more in the event of war.

With the outbreak of the Second World War the great powers' activities in the Middle East increased again. Italy joined the war on the side of Germany and used Libya as a base to attack the British in Egypt. Thus Egypt became a bastion for the Allies during the war, and the victory of El Alamein in October 1942 is considered a turning point in the struggle against Hitler and Mussolini. Great Britain and De Gaulle's French forces invaded Syria and Lebanon in 1941 to oppose the pro-Axis Vichy government that had taken over the government of much of France. In the same year British and Soviet troops invaded Iran in order to stop an increasing German influence in the country, and Iran remained under Allied occupation until 1945. Turkey stayed neutral during most of the war and ceremonially entered on the side of the Allies on 23 February 1945. To hinder an alliance between Turkey and Germany in 1939 France gave Turkey a part of Syria, Alexandretta (Turk. Hatay province), a move contested by Syria as unlawful up to the present time. By the end of the war Italy had lost Libya to Great Britain, and France had lost its foothold in Syria and Lebanon. A British condition for attacking the Vichy government in 1941 had been that Syria and Lebanon should be granted independence after the war. France had tried to renege on this in 1945 and had bombed Damascus, but the French had to give in to international pressure. In 1946 Lebanon and Syria became official members of the UN. In the same year Jordan's 'Abdallah was rewarded for his wartime loyalty and made king in his own country. With three new independent states in the Middle East it was only a matter of time before the remaining countries would follow suit. Opposition to European power was increasing in the region, and politicians in the USA and the Soviet Union put independence on the agenda. The Arab League was founded in Cairo in 1945, numbering seven member countries (Egypt, Iraq, Lebanon, Saudi Arabia, Syria, Transjordan, and North-Yemen). Today it numbers twenty-two members, including Palestine.

The foundation of Israel

The background for the creation of the state of Israel in 1948 is a history apart. It starts with the growth of Jewish nationalism in Europe towards the end of the nineteenth century, and more particularly with Zionism, which linked the dream of a state for the Jewish people to Jerusalem. Emigration to Palestine began among Russian Jews in the 1880s, motivated by the anti-Semitism that made life hard for Jews all over Europe. In 1897 Theodor Herzl founded the World Zionist Organisation with the goal of winning support from the European powers for the creation of a state for the Jewish people. The first breakthrough came with the Balfour Declaration, in which the British Foreign Secretary promised to work for the creation of 'a Jewish national home' in Palestine. However, the road to the founding of Israel was to prove long.

The area the Zionists had begun to emigrate to was part of the mandated Palestine territory that the San Remo Conference had handed over to the United Kingdom to administer. When the mandate was granted in 1920, Jewish immigrants made up scarcely 15 per cent of the population. On the other hand, this minority was focused, well organised, and cooperated with the administration. During the 1920s there was a rapid development of semi-official Zionist institutions such as the trade union Histadrut, the military force Haganah, and the party Mapai. Moreover, the Jews had their own national assembly and government, the Jewish Agency, which provided an efficient representative system. The Arab majority, on the contrary, was disorganised and split. It lacked both institutions and a unifying figure or organisation that could speak for the Arab cause. Two rival families, Nashashibi and Husayni, fought for the right to represent the Palestinians. The British fed the fire under this conflict and awarded the families different positions of power, exploiting the rivalry in order to strengthen their own position. The Zionists benefited greatly from the Palestinians' lack of a purposeful leadership. In an age when Jewish immigration in the area was on the up, the Zionists' financially strong national fund succeeded in buying considerable properties from private Arab landowners.

Gradually, administering Palestine became a headache for Great Britain. The British had committed themselves to setting up 'a national home for the Jewish people' while at the same time promising to respect the rights of the Arab majority. What these promises meant in practice remained unclear to the mandate authority, and it became harder and harder to satisfy both parties at the same time. In 1929 violent confrontations near the Wailing Wall led to the deaths of 133 Jews and 116 Arabs.[8] Throughout the thirties, tension increased and the British mandate administration gradually lost control of the situation. In 1937 the Peel Commission set up by the British, concluded that the Palestine Mandate should be terminated and be replaced by a Jewish and a Palestinian state. The partition plan was rejected by the League of Nations and led to a rising among the Arabs that had to be suppressed by a force of 20,000 British soldiers in 1939.[9] To calm things down the administration formulated a White Paper, in which it was made clear that the United Kingdom did not wish Palestine to become a state for Jews. Limitations were imposed on future immigration and the large-scale purchase of property for Jews prohibited. Zionists vehemently rejected the White Paper and towards the end of the war took up arms against the British. The mandate administration was now under fire from two sides.

In 1947 the British abandoned all attempts to find a solution to the problem. The combination of Zionist sabotage and American pressure to set up a Jewish state led to the British handing over the matter to the UN. The sufferings the Jews had undergone during the Second World War gave the demand that the Jewish nation should have its own state weight and legitimacy. The UN suggested dividing the Palestinian mandate territory into a Jewish and an Arab state with Jerusalem as an international zone. The Zionists accepted the plan but Arab leaders rejected it. On 14 May, 1948, Israel was founded, and the Arab League immediately went to war. The war was a crushing defeat for the Arabs and led to an expansion of Israel's borders. At the truce in 1949 the Zionists had conquered areas in the north, south, and east and over 700,000 Palestinians had become homeless.[10] On top of everything, King 'Abdallah of Jordan, who had not renounced the idea of a greater Arab kingdom under Hashemite leadership, annexed the West Bank in the same year. So no Palestinian state saw the light of day.

The Algerian war of liberation

Of all the transitions to self-determination in the Middle East the toughest was that of Algeria. In 1962 it was the last big country in the region to gain independence. To get this far the population had to endure eight years of bloody war.

Between 1954 and independence probably as many as 300,000 Algerians died out of a total population of over nine million.[11] France invested all its armed forces in the conflict in an attempt to prevent what many saw as a splitting up of the French republic. Algeria was not regarded as a colony, but an integral part of France. Getting on for a million Europeans lived in the country, and over 80 per cent of them had been born there. The French settlers were called 'Black Feet' (Fr. *pieds noirs*): they controlled the best farmland and dominated in the cities and the local administration. They also exerted great influence on the central government in Paris and opposed decisions that threatened their position. When in 1961 Charles de Gaulle was willing to discuss the idea of Algerian self-determination, certain elements of the French army tried to depose him in an unsuccessful coup.

Opposition to colonial rule in Algeria was built on a combination of poor living conditions for the local population and growing nationalism and anti-imperialism. Ninety per cent of Algerians were illiterate, and class differences, both in the towns and in the countryside, systematically followed the division between the 'Black Feet' and Muslims.[12] The opposition movement ranged from local civil servants to clerics and radical activists that wanted a complete break with France or an armed class war. In 1954 the Front de Libération Nationale (FLN) was founded, uniting the country's resistance groups. Starting the 'revolution', it finally emerged as the victor. However, the victory was not military, for the French army was in fact gaining control of the situation when De Gaulle ended the war. In reality, the triumph was political, for France realised that the age of colonialism was over.

The dawn of nationalism

The idea that linguistic and cultural community made 'nations' with a right to their own sovereign states came to the Middle East from Europe. Exactly how and when such thoughts took root in the Ottoman Empire and Iran is hard to say with any certainty. Most historians agree that modern nationalism could not be found in the region before the twentieth century. Nonetheless, one can trace a growing consciousness of linguistic and cultural community there throughout the nineteenth century. One seed of new thinking about identity was sown in 1798, when Napoleon Bonaparte organised an expedition to Egypt and occupied the land for three years. The event had no lasting consequences and has in many ways been seen as a parenthesis in Ottoman history. Napoleon's landing did, however, give the Ottomans the chance to observe French technology and science at close hand, thus symbolising the meeting of the Middle East with the West. As this kind of defeat and occupation grew more frequent when the nineteenth century progressed, this meeting was to provoke a double reaction. To start with it aroused a feeling that something was wrong, since the formerly so strong Muslim world now constantly suffered defeat. In an attempt to make up the loss the sultan introduced the *tanzimat* reforms, while intellectuals called for a fresh interpretation of Islam. Thinkers such as Jamal al-Din al-Afghani and Muhammad 'Abduh tried to promote an Islamic renaissance (Arab. *al-nahda*) in order to heal what they felt was a spiritual crisis in the empire. Second, and partly as a result of the reform of Islam, the feeling of belonging to a community increased. Faced with Western soldiers and traders that had other traditions and spoke foreign languages, the 'us' feeling grew stronger, regardless of whether it was built on religious or linguistic identity.

This increasing consciousness of linguistic and religious communities was long compatible with belonging to the Ottoman Empire. Despite the fact that Arab intellectuals such as Rashid Rida felt that national bonds existed between Arabs and that they used words such as *watan* to express 'fatherland', they were not opponents of the Ottoman Empire. As they saw it, one could have several such fatherlands at the same time, and belonging to 'the Arab nation' was not incompatible with bonds to Istanbul. Arab nationalism in the sense of demands to break away from the empire first arose around the time of the First World War. As the historian Ernest Dawn emphasises, the first supporters of independently governed Arab states were typically ruling class individuals who administered the Ottoman Empire on behalf of the sultan.[13] However, the ruling class had no monopoly on Arab nationalism, and soon came under growing pressure: the modernisation of the Ottoman Empire following the *tanzimat* reforms had created a broader elite, which included officers, journalists, and teachers, and as the century went on this new middle class took over the old aristocracy's role as the main promoter of nationalism.

In addition, the focus on the distinctive character of the Turks grew among the Turkish-speaking members of the empire's elite. Jacob M. Landau has shown how in the last part of the nineteenth century there sprang up a strong interest in Turkish history, language, and literature in academic circles.[14] European Orientalists' charting of the origins of the Turkish people in Central Asia also contributes to this growing interest. At the start of the twentieth century this increased consciousness of Turkish culture acquired a political expression in Pan-Turkism, the desire to incorporate all Turkic-speaking peoples into the Ottoman Empire. The movement was dominated by Turks from Central Asia, refugees from Russia's conquests, and had the character of a reaction to Pan-Slavism.[15] The official Ottoman ideology, based on community in Ottoman culture and Islam, remained, however, dominant until the outbreak of the First World War. Even though the Young Turks who took power in 1908 had this idea of 'a Turkish nation', they hesitated to put it into practice for fear of splitting the empire. Their main project was to strengthen the power of the central authority over the empire. Any exaggerated emphasis on the Turkish would compromise this by provoking ethnic minorities. However, the collapse of the Ottoman Empire after the First World War changed the situation, and when Mustafa Kemal came to define the common factor of the inhabitants of modern Turkey, he seized on Turkish culture. In 1923 former Young Turk and nationalist ideologist Ziya Gökalp wrote *Türkçülüngün esaları*, *The Principles of Turkism*, in which he distinguished 'civilisation' (*medeniyet*) from 'culture' (*hars*).[16] According to Gökalp the key to progress was maintaining Turkish culture while replacing Ottoman Arab-Islamic civilisation with the more modern Western way of living. In accordance with Gökalp's recommendations, Kemal began to work to 'cleanse' Turkish culture and create a new national myth. In 1928 he carried out a language reform in which Arab script was replaced by Roman. A Turkish language council was set up to purify the language of non-Turkish grammatical structures and Arab and Persian vocabulary. Furthermore, Kemal founded a Turkish historical society to reconstruct history. New schoolbooks were written to cultivate patriotism among the population.[17] However, the regime did not carry on with the dream of Pan-Turkish unification. Mustafa Kemal's political project was limited to the inhabitants of Anatolia.

Iranian nationalism arose under different conditions than those of Arab and Turkish nationalism. A first main difference was that Iran as a political unity enjoyed territorial continuity. Unlike the Arabs and Turks the Iranian nation did not have to break away from a larger empire. On the contrary, it was precisely the existing political–geographical unit that provided the foundation for talking about an Iranian nation. Historical memories of Iran go back to the Achaemids (ca. 648–330 BC),[18] and when the Safavids seized power in 1501, an expanded form of the present-day Iranian territory was united. The Safavids made another important contribution to modern Iranian identity by forcibly converting the empire's inhabitants from Sunni to Shi'a Islam. The purpose may have been to create a division between the Safavid dynasty (1501–1722) and the Sunni-dominated Ottoman Empire. Another major difference from Arab and Turkish nationalism was that the demand for political union of Iranian territory (*mamlikat-e Iran*) to a lesser extent corresponded with a single linguistic group. Persian had been the lingua franca in the area's historical empires, but people with Persian as their mother tongue make up less than 50 per cent of Iran's population. Persians share the territory with a number of other linguistic groups such as Arab, Turkish, and Baluchi-speaking. The classic European understanding of nations as linguistic groups was therefore poorly adapted to Iranian reality. Nonetheless, Mostafa Vaziri claims that European linguists and

Orientalists have played an important role in shaping Iranian national identity. Sanskrit researchers and Orientalists at the start of the nineteenth century saw connections between language similarities and ideas of race. Thus arose the 'Arian hypothesis' that asserted that people who spoke Indo-European languages had the same origins; they were all Arians having roots going back to old India. The Orientalists pursued this language-based method in order to distinguish between various peoples in the Middle East. When Iranian nationalism took form at the beginning of the twentieth century, the Arian hypothesis, according to Vaziri, was a significant source of inspiration. Politicians and intellectuals exploited the theory's distinction between Arian and Semitic civilisation to accentuate the Iranian. For instance, the country's history was presented as dividing into two parts: the Antique period of the ancient Persian empires, and an Islamic period where Arab and Turkish dominance brought the nation to subjugation.[19] Under the Pahlavi monarchy (1925–79) the official nationalism continued parts of this presentation, lauding the country's pre-Islamic cultural heritage. Indeed in 1971 Muhammad Reza Shah arranged a gigantic celebration of the Persian monarchy's '2,500 Anniversary', failing to mention that such an empire had not existed between 640 and 1501.

The organisation of state power

The successor states to the Ottoman Empire were organised as republics and monarchies. Whether the new states adopted one or the other of these constitutions was largely a result of whether it was France or the United Kingdom that dominated the state-building process. France set up republics in Syria and Lebanon and exported its state structures to Tunisia and Algeria. Great Britain preferred to base its client states on its own constitution, which led to monarchies in Jordan, Iraq, and Egypt. In addition came the monarchies in the Gulf, Bahrain, Kuwait, Oman, Qatar and the Trucial States (today United Arab Emirates), which were in treaty relations with Britain. The kingdom of Saudi Arabia was a special case. Ibn Sa'ud united his country himself and only indirectly received support from the British. In 1915 the United Kingdom signed an agreement with Ibn Sa'ud to support his conquests on the Arabian Peninsula and prevent him from allying himself with the Ottoman Empire. Under this agreement Great Britain recognised the Sa'ud dynasty's control over the areas Najd, Hasa, Qatif, and Jubayl, and gave him arms and money. In return, Ibn Sa'ud had to keep his distance from the other great powers and respect the borders of the British-supported Emirates, Kuwait, Bahrain, Qatar, and Oman. In 1927, two years after Ibn Sa'ud had defeated *Sharif* Husayn of Mecca, the British recognised the Sa'ud dynasty's right to rule over the biggest part of the Arabian Peninsula. Ibn Sa'ud had himself acclaimed king: the title of king, which was known in Europe, made it easier for him to win acceptance for his rule with the United Kingdom.

Monarchy is often regarded as deeply rooted in the Middle East's tradition and culture. Lisa Anderson and Fred Halliday have, however, pointed out that the way this form of government is understood and practised today is no more anchored in local tradition than republics.[20] Among the eight surviving monarchies there are only two that have reigned continuously prior to the twentieth century. The Arab word for king, *malik*, has, moreover, traditionally negative connotations. During Islam's first centuries *malik* referred to rulers who had mainly secular authority, that is, based on military or political power. On the contrary, a ruler who governed in accordance with God's law, was known as *khalifa* (Caliph, successor of the Prophet) or *imam* (leader, prayer leader). Rulers without religious authority as a rule preferred the title sultan: bearing the meaning 'he who carries the burden of ruling', sultan was a more modest title than *malik*, which from Arabic can be translated as 'he who owns' the state. However, at the start of the twentieth century *malik* experienced a new spring. The title of king obtained its authority and prestige from the fact that it was associated with the institution that at the time reigned over the most powerful empire in the world – the British royal house. The first Muslim ruler who in modern times took this title was *Sharif* Husayn, who declared himself king of Hijaz in 1916.

With the introduction of republics and monarchies came new political institutions to the Middle East as well, such as constitutions, parliaments, elections, and parties. The Ottoman Empire introduced a constitution and parliament as early as 1876, but the despotic Sultan Abdülhamit II (1876–1908) dissolved parliament two years later and ruled without bothering about the constitution. In Iran the constitutional revolution forced the Qajar dynasty that had ruled since 1794 to establish a constitutional assembly in 1906, and in 1907 the country introduced a constitution based on the Belgian model. However, state power was weak and its bureaucracy was rudimentary until Reza Khan deposed the Qajars in 1921 and founded the Pahlavi monarchy in 1925. The new shah carried out a comprehensive development of the military and educational systems, the courts, and state administration in the 1920s and 1930s that was to be the base of the Iranian nation-state. A similar modernisation of the state system took place in Turkey, where Mustafa Kemal took over what remained of the old Ottoman Empire. Compared with the Qajar Empire this state had a more developed bureaucracy and an active standing army, and Mustafa Kemal seized this heritage of the Ottoman Empire. The pillars of the new system were the army and Cumhuriyet Halk Fırkası ('The Republican People's Party'), which Atatürk used to introduce secular reforms and marginalise his opponents.

While the building of the state in Turkey and Iran was driven by domestic national heroes, modern political institutions were introduced in the Arab world by the colonial powers. The United Kingdom and France laid the foundations for the mandate territories' armed and police forces, their courts and state administrations. Since the colonial powers still wished to keep control over these areas for strategic reasons, the prime focus was on security. As Roger Owen points out, more than two-thirds of the colonial powers' expenses related to security measures.[21] More specifically, France and Great Britain gave priority to the establishment and training of police forces. The armed forces came second, since the great powers reserved the right to defend these mandates themselves. But even here the colonial powers took certain important steps. In Syria a military academy was founded in 1920 with French instructors. Local officers trained by the colonial power were appointed to lead the Syrian Legion, which numbered around 6,000 men in the mid-thirties.[22] The opening of the military academy had lasting consequences for Syrian politics. Given that in Ottoman times the Sunni Muslim elite regarded military training as low status and preferred to send their sons to civilian universities in Europe, the Syrian officer corps was dominated by minority groups such as 'Alawi and Druze. When Syria won its independence and the army's importance grew, these groups used the academy as a springboard for social mobility. The 'Alawis in particular managed to position themselves via a series of military coups in the 1950s and 1960s, and have under the leadership of the Asad clan dominated the country's political system.

Another interesting example of the building of the armed forces under European leadership is the Arab Legion (Arab. *al-jaysh al-'arabi*) in Jordan. Founded in 1923 under the command of the British officer Frederick Gerard Peake, it was responsible for internal security in the mandate and patrolling the borders. A regular challenge of this work was dealing with the tribes that created instability in the country as well as making raids into Syria and Saudi Arabia. In order to solve this problem the British sent for Captain John Glubb, a British officer serving in Iraq in 1930. He started his own desert force (Arab. *quwwat al-badiyah*) within the Arab Legion. Glubb recruited tribal warriors to the force, gave them weapons and training in modern battle techniques. At the same time he took care to indoctrinate the tribes to political loyalty. The most important point about Glubb's strategy was, however, to make it in the tribes' own interest that the state should survive. In this way the desert force became a disciplined and effective fighting force, which was loyal to 'Abdallah and the monarchy. Later on Glubb was appointed commander of the whole Arab Legion, which in 1941 consisted of 7,500 officers and men. During the Second World War the legion took part in several military campaigns in the Middle East, and in the war against Israel in 1948 it proved far better trained and effective than the more numerous Egyptian and Iraqi forces. After the war the Legion was reformed as Jordan's regular army.[23]

Even in countries where Britain did not have formal control over the building of the state, British advisers played an important role. The classic example is that of the adventurer Harry St. John Philby, father to the famous spy Kim Philby. Harry St. John assisted Ibn Sa'ud in building the Saudi state administration. Together with a group of advisers from the Arab world, Philby founded the Saudi bureaucracy and was given important tasks by the king. Among other things he led negotiations with the British and American oil companies about concessions to exploit the kingdom's oil reserves. A more state-based British engagement in the region was support for modernisation of Oman under Sultan Qabus. He came to power through a British-supported coup and used Western advisers to build up his state administration. In the sultan's first government, established in 1971, there were both an American and a British colonel. The Omani army is a miniature British army, where the officers are recruited, armed, and trained on a British model. In addition, the Sultan used British soldiers to crush a revolt in the 1960s and 1970s.

Conclusion

The colonial powers left behind a triple heritage in the Middle East. First, the Europeans created the modern state system. When the Ottoman Empire broke down after the First World War, it was Great Britain and France that governed the transition to today's sovereign states. In extreme cases, as in that of Iraq, Lebanon, Palestine, Syria, and Transjordan, the colonial powers manipulated these borders themselves. In North Africa, on the other hand, the Europeans built on the Ottoman administrative division lines. A third variant can be found in the Gulf, where the British entered treaty relations with the local emirs with promises to defend the emirates' integrity. Certain states came into existence through the consolidation of the power of local leaders. This applies first and foremost to Turkey, Saudi Arabia, and Iran, but also, to a certain extent, Yemen. Israel is a special case, because the Zionists who conquered the land were immigrants to the region. Second, the heritage of the colonial powers has left lasting traces on the ideological plane. The colonisation of the Middle East occurred in a period when the West was also a source of inspiration for nationalist ideologies. Awareness of linguistic and cultural communities grew in contact with the Europeans who not only represented 'the other' but also exposed the region to humiliating defeats. Moreover, colonial powers deliberately exploited ethnic divisions in order to weaken their opponents and thereby incited nationalism. Third, the Europeans introduced political institutions that were new to the

Middle East. The British favoured monarchies and the French promoted republics. In both cases states gained political institutions such as parliaments, governments, and parties. In addition, the colonial powers started an expansion of the states' police forces and bureaucracies and since the main goal was to ensure control of the area, emphasis was on the first. Basic sectors such as health and education were allocated fewer resources. As a result, the colonial powers began a negative trend by over focusing on the police and security forces, a tendency that has endured to our own times.

Further reading

Bromely, Simon: *Rethinking Middle East Politics*. Cambridge: Polity Press, 1994.

Cleveland, William L.: *A History of the Modern Middle East*. Boulder, CO: Westview Press, 3rd edition, 2004.

Fromkin, David: *A Peace to End All Peace*. London: Phoenix Press, 2000.

Hourani, Albert: *A History of the Arab Peoples*. London: Faber & Faber, 1991.

Hourani, Albert: *Arabic Thought in the Liberal Age, 1798–1939*. Cambridge, New York, Port Chester, Melbourne, and Sydney: Cambridge University Press, 1983.

Keddie, Nikki R.: *Roots of Revolution: An Interpretive History of Modern Iran*. New Haven and London: Yale University Press, 1981.

Khaldun, Ibn: *The Muqaddimah: An Introduction to History*. Princeton, NJ: Princeton University Press, 1989.

Khalidi, Rashid: *The Origins of Arab Nationalism*. New York: Columbia University Press, 1991.

Mansfield, Peter: *A History of the Middle East*. London, New York, Ringwood, Toronto, and Auckland: Penguin Books, 1992.

Marsot, Afaf Lutfi al-Sayyid: *Egypt in the Reign of Muhammad Ali*. Cambridge: Cambridge University Press, 1984.

Owen, Roger: *The Middle East in the World Economy, 1800–1914*. London and New York: I.B.Tauris, 1993.

Vaziri, Mostafa: *Iran as Imagined Nation: The Construction of National Identity*. New York: Paragon House, 1993.

Yapp, Malcolm E.: *The Making of the Modern Near East, 1792–1923*. London: Longman, 1987.

Zürcher, Erik J.: *Turkey. A Modern History*. London and New York: I.B.Tauris, 2004.

Part 2
Society and State

3 Class

... The exploitation of man by man and the possession by some individuals of more of the general wealth than they need is a manifest departure from natural law and the beginning of distortion and corruption in the life of the human community.[1]

The Middle East states embrace great economic differences, both internally and comparatively. The rich live side by side with the poor, and states possessing modern industry and business structure contrast with stagnant developing countries. According to World Bank statistics, for example, the GDP of Yemen is ten times less than that of neighbouring Saudi Arabia and twenty-three times less than that of the Emirates.[2] Contrasts within the states are just as striking. In *Forbes Magazine*'s 2008 list of the world's wealthiest people, the Egyptian brothers Naguib and Nassef Sawiris were placed respectively number 60 and 68.[3] Yet at the same time, the UN estimates that between 30 and 40 per cent of Egypt's population live under the poverty line.[4] In cities like Cairo, Istanbul, and Beirut fashionable villas are surrounded by dilapidated slums. Class differences are equally striking in Tehran. The city is situated on a slope with a difference in altitude of over 800 metres, where the rich have settled at the top and the poorest at the bottom. Placement on the social ladder can consequently by and far be identified from how far up the slope a person lives.

On several occasions since 1970, poverty and social inequality have given rise to instability and conflict in the Middle East. For instance, in Algeria, an economic crisis in 1988 led to clashes between demonstrators and security forces, in which several thousand people lost their lives. So-called 'bread riots' (Arab. *intifadat al-khubz*) against deteriorating living conditions also took place in Egypt in 1977, Morocco and Tunisia in 1984, Jordan in 1989, Yemen in 2005, Iran in 2007, and again in Egypt in 2008. Such risings have, however, remained isolated incidents, which, for lack of an ideological basis and coordination, have been easily repressed. Economic tensions do not automatically lead to class identification and struggle.

In this chapter we shall examine the following question: how do the Middle East regimes prevent the growth of an organised class-based opposition? To shed light on this issue from another perspective we shall, in the second part of the chapter, devote special attention to the situation in Iran: to what extent is the Islamic Republic characterised by social mobility?

Class in the Middle East

By *class* we mean a social group whose members share a common placement in society's division of labour. In the Marxist tradition the criterion for placement in the division of labour has been expressed as the group's relationship to the means of production. The main difference between the bourgeoisie and the working class has been that the former owned various assets – land, machines, companies, capital, and so on – all necessary for production, whereas the working class only disposed of their own labour. However, a definition that merely takes into consideration ownership of the means of production soon becomes inadequate. Besides economic advantages, the dominance of a class may be built on educational and intellectual background, so-called cultural capital, or networks, social capital.[5] Moreover, one might argue that class differences are created and maintained through social status and political power, rather than through wealth.

The basic idea in class theory is that classes are in conflict with each other and that members of a class therefore share common interests that encourage collective action. In the struggle for the allocation of scarce resources workers will be stronger if they organise themselves and promote their demands in a unified manner. A condition for this is that individuals feel they belong to a class as they must share an identity if they are to stand together and act in unity. Karl Marx introduced the distinction between 'class in itself' and 'class for itself' to clarify this point.[6] By the former he meant an objective class situation that can be observed from without but which is not necessarily clear to individuals. By the latter he meant a subjective class identification that is also felt by the members of the class itself. This distinction can help explain why class differences in the Middle East do not always lead to class-based opposition. As we shall see, even if outsiders can in many cases identify both a working and a bourgeois class, the people concerned do not always think in these terms.

Historical class situation

The descriptions of class structure in the Middle East must allow for the fact that historical and social conditions in this part of the world have been different from those in Europe. Class conflict cannot blindly be written into the standard categories of the bourgeoisie and the working class simply because Marx read developments in his own time as resulting from this struggle. James A. Bill believes that Marxism's definition criterion, control over the means of production, does not go to the core of the class struggle in the Middle East, because what has been decisive here is control over political power.[7] Power created wealth rather than the opposite, and the sources of political power were many. For Bill the upper class in traditional Islamic societies has consisted of a mixture of royalty, tribal chiefs, landowners, officers in the armed forces, and prominent religious leaders who surrounded the ruler and therefore potentially had political influence. Below the upper class, he identifies a middle class mainly made up of civil servants, clerics, and merchants in and around the bazaar. The lower class, Bill claims, has principally consisted of peasants and nomads as well as a traditional working class ranging from servants and labourers to various craftsmen and artisans.

The class structure of the Ottoman and Qajar empires was also less clear-cut than was the case in feudal Europe and the main reason for this is that property rights were weaker in the Middle East. The idea that the feudal lord owned the land was basic to the organisation of feudal society. Property rights were enshrined in the law and contracts and were defended by kings, priests, and laymen. In the Ottoman Empire, however, the sultan regarded all land as belonging to the state. Loyal servants were granted the use of state land, *miri*, but this right was not heritable and could be withdrawn should the sultan so desire. The central authorities, provincial governors, and nomadic tribes moreover lived by squeezing the agricultural surplus from the peasantry. The competition for this surplus led to plundering and other abuses that further weakened property rights.

However, a landowning class did grow up in certain parts of the Ottoman Empire, which came about because the central authorities in Istanbul began renting out disposal rights to land to local tax-gatherers, *muqata'iyun*, but gradually lost the capacity to control how provincial governors administered resources. For instance, during the nineteenth century a strong landowning class grew up in what was later to become south Iraq, because the central authorities were unable to control the Shi'a countryside.[8] A similar development took place in Iran and Egypt, where the central power was weak and the provincial lords were strong. On the other hand, in core areas of the empire the bureaucracy continued to dominate. In 1858 the Ottomans passed a law that formally abolished the subtenant system and introduced direct farm taxation. Where this was actually practiced, as in Anatolia, the law weakened the landowning class. This was also the case in Libya, the future Jordan, and the Arabian

Peninsula, where a combination of poor soils and arid climate did not permit extensive agriculture. On the whole, however, the influence of the landowning class tended to increase. This was a consequence of the region's integration into the new world economy, which turned the Middle East into a producer of raw materials for European industry. The Ottoman Empire became dependent on cultivating and exporting specialised agricultural products, such as cotton, fruit, and tobacco, in order to cover its expenses. The transition to commercial farming also led to larger agricultural units. All of this led to an increase in the power of the landowning class.

In the states that replaced the Ottoman Empire after the First World War this class rapidly became an economic and political elite: due, on the one hand, to the landowners' wealth and experience in leadership from Ottoman times, and, on the other, to the colonial powers' allying themselves with them so as to control the population. Malcolm E. Yapp calls the period from 1923 to the 1950s 'the years of the notables';[9] by which he means that those who had acted as brokers between the central authorities and the population under the Ottomans, the so-called notables, dominated politics in the new states. The colonial powers thus continued a system in which landowners, village heads, tribal chiefs, and clerics guaranteed law and order in return for privileges and political influence. At the same time, the bourgeoisie and working class were weak due to the historical absence of private property rights and industrial development. The middle class was also small, since the educational revolution and large-scale growth of the state apparatus were still in the future. The bulk of the population were peasants or nomads, depending on whether they lived in fertile or infertile areas.

Revolutionary republics and conservative monarchies

As state-building and modernisation processes speeded up under the colonial powers and then the local leaders after independence, state educational institutions and public administration promoted a rapid growth of the middle class. An increasing proportion of the population moved into the towns, becoming what Manfred Halpern described as 'the new middle class', professions such as lawyers engineers, teachers, students, bureaucrats, and officers in the armed forces, and developing into a political power factor.[10]

Meanwhile the old upper class still dominated the apparatus of power, blocking middle class ambitions. In the 1950s and 1960s such class conflicts created an explosive situation in the Arab world and discontent came to expression through military coups. The middle class exploited the hesitation of the upper class to give their sons military training in order to turn the army into a tool for social mobility. So while the children of the elite were sent to prestigious colleges and universities in the USA and Europe, those of lower social standing made careers in the armed forces. Even though they rose in the ranks however, they kept their class feeling and their discontent with the upper class' power monopoly. As a result, the military became a meeting place for critics of the regime and for the planning of revolution – officers in the armed forces seized power in Egypt, Syria, Algeria, Tunisia, Libya, and Yemen. Yapp writes of the period from 1952 to 1970 as 'the years of revolution'. In class terms we can say that the new middle class displaced the upper class from their positions of power.

These revolutionary years created differences in ideology as well as class structure between republics and monarchies in the Middle East. The officers who seized power in the republics (and in the case of Egypt, Iraq, Libya, and Yemen abolished monarchy) mobilised workers and peasantry against the upper class attacking 'feudalism' and 'imperialism'. They criticised France and the United Kingdom for having exploited the Middle East and accused the colonial powers' alliance with the landowning class of stifling development in the region. The West's demand for agricultural products and the landowners' self-interest had, according to the new leaders, turned the Middle East into a producer of raw materials for Europe, while precious little was done to encourage industry in the region. Socially, the officers blamed the landowning class for maintaining an unenlightened feudalism in order to make it easier to control the rural peasantry. From now on the state would promote development, improve the health system, encourage industrialisation, and improve the infrastructure, such as railways, ports, and roads. To reduce dependency on the West and ensure progress, the dominance of the landowners in the countryside had to be broken, so the new regimes expropriated land from the biggest landowners. The way in which these reforms were pushed through was authoritarian: the officers used their new powers to nationalise private property and oppress political opponents. Under conditions that were a mixture of internal instability and external threats, the new regimes attacked the upper classes in the name of the masses and engaged in a state-driven modernisation. In political science such regimes are called populist–authoritarian regimes.[11]

Within the countries with monarchies, conditions were quite different. Whereas the populous, urbanised, and intensive agricultural areas were predisposed for revolution in the 1950s and 1960s, most monarchies were thinly populated and had nomadic tribal societies. These countries lay outside the Arab world's intellectual centres, and because modernisation processes, such as educational expansion and urbanisation, proceeded more slowly, they were less susceptible to contemporary revolutionary ideological ideas. Not least, traditional Islam was stronger than secular Arab nationalism and because revolutionary movements did not get a foothold in these areas, there were no social upheavals in the shape of expropriations and redistribution of the land to lower social classes. The monarchies neither attacked the landowners nor the merchant middle class so that these countries were characterised by a far greater degree of social continuity. After oil riches flooded into the monarchies on the Arabian Peninsula in the 1970s, these states too gained a leading role in economic development. Oil revenues have enabled the regimes to modernise without being overturned by the new middle class, as we shall see in Chapter 7.

The focus on state-led development in the republics as well as in the monarchies has again had consequences for the class structure of the Middle East. Since the state undertook industrialisation and was itself the owner of most of the large companies, the region did not develop a powerful and independent bourgeoisie. Moreover, since these were capital-intensive industries, a smaller working class grew up than might have been the case had the state instead pursued more labour-intensive industries. At the beginning of the 1990s, Nazih N. Ayubi estimated that industrial workers accounted for less than 20 per cent of the labour force in most Arab countries, and the percentage is probably not much bigger today.[12] In addition to these workers there are, however, big marginalised groups that cannot be called workers in the classical sense. Having no legal or regular work, they are what Marxists would call a 'lumpenproletariat'. To this category belong beggars, prostitutes, street sellers, and others who earn a living as best they can. In Algeria in the 1980s this lumpenproletariat got the name *hittiste* (from Arabic *hit*, which means *wall*) because as a rule it stood leaning against a wall. Its role, Algerians said ironically, was to make sure the wall did not fall down. The *hittists* were extremely discontented and became active in the riots that broke out in the late 1980s.

Subjective class identification

However, despite the clear class distinctions in the Middle East, several researchers have pointed out that the degree of subjective class identification in the region is weak. Homa Katouzian, for instance, has claimed that the distinction between *dowlat* ('state' or 'state class') and *mellat* ('society' or 'nation') is more basic in Iranian collective consciousness than the distinction between poor and rich.[13] Katouzian believes the traditional use of the state apparatus to oppress the population has unified the Iranians in a common struggle against despotism. The exploitation of the people is associated with the 'state class', the historian argues, and not with the bourgeoisie or the aristocracy. Therefore the workers do not identify themselves as a lower class versus an upper class but rather as part of *mellat* in opposition to *dowlat*.

Amira al-Azhary Sonbol has a similar analysis of the situation in Egypt.[14] She interprets the country's modern history as a fight between *al-'amma* ('the common people') and *al-khassa* ('the ruling elite'), where the basic difference between the two is that the elite is linked to the state. Sonbol describes *al-khassa* as politicians, the military, and the upper bourgeoisie. The elite distances itself from what it regards as an underdeveloped society, seeing itself as the educator of, and role model for, the people. In contrast are the *'amma*, who are excluded from politics and look on the state with scepticism, obstructing the government's attempts to control, regulate, and tax society. Sonbol shows that the tendency to divide society into *'amma* and *khassa* has been the same since the start of the nineteenth century. This dichotomy is therefore far more rooted in the country than class identification in a Marxist sense. According to Sonbol, what is most important to an Egyptian is whether or not someone is linked to the state, not whether he is rich or poor.

For James A. Bill and Robert Springborg, group identity is more prominent than class identity because social and political conditions favour informal personal alliances and disfavour class organisation.[15] When individuals gather to defend their interests, it is usually hard to organise broadly as a class. Smaller groups based on family relationships, friendship, religious brotherhood, and so on, are better adapted to escape the regime's control mechanisms and promote inner solidarity and trust. Such groups may, however, come together across class barriers. When this is the case – and in addition the family or network of friends is the main supplier of the inhabitants' security and welfare – both class identity and class solidarity are weakened. Friends in 'high places' can help those of lower standing within the group to gain social advancement, instead of opting for class struggle.

In extension of this other researchers argue that the strength of ethnic divisions in the Middle East also weakens class distinctions and subjective class identification. Halim Barakat thinks that awareness of class differences is greater in countries with a more homogenous population such as Egypt and Tunisia than in those such as Lebanon where society is divided confessional lines.[16] Meanwhile Barakat warns against those who exaggerate this argument, forgetting that ethnic divisions can involve hidden class conflict. He refers to Orientalists such as Carlton Coon and C. van Nieuwenhuyze, who in their eagerness to show a mosaic of various societies in the Arab world ended up claiming that the study of class is totally irrelevant for the region. But class divisions may be a contributory factor behind risings, coups, and strikes, even in deeply fragmented societies. And workers may be aware that they belong to an underprivileged group parallel with their ethnic identity. Barakat believes, for example, there are signs of class identity in folk tales, songs, poetry, and literature. He refers to well-known Arab proverbs such as 'Everyone sings for the rich' and 'He who has a shilling is worth a shilling' to illustrate his point.

Generally speaking, subjective class-consciousness may be assumed stronger in the republics than in the monarchies, because the leaders in the populist–authoritarian regimes came to power with an explicit class discourse. As we have seen, the officers claimed to represent the people in their fight against the upper class, promising to wage war on inequality, poverty, and corruption. Formally at least, they all gave their support to socialism. The battle against social inequality has, however, not been followed up. Indeed the revolutionary elite of the 1960s and their successors have themselves become a new political and economic upper class. In this process they have downplayed the class aspect and emphasised the other main component in their populist–authoritarian development project – nationalism. By cultivating the workers' and peasants' Arab, Muslim, and national identities, the rulers hoped to override their class-consciousness and persuade the people to jump to the regime's defence. Nevertheless, renewed class conflict is a real danger in a period when most states adjust to liberal economic policies.

In what follows we shall deal with two key ruling mechanisms that also work against subjective class identification and hinder the growth of an organised class-based opposition.

Corporatism

First, the Middle East regimes use corporatism to prevent the growth of a class-based opposition. By *corporatism* we mean a system of interest representation where social organisations and the state power are interwoven. In democratic states this works by employers' organisations, trade unions, and so on, being able to influence decisions by taking part in official agencies at the same time as the state has a chance of regulating these organisations from above. In authoritarian states, however, influence from the bottom up is minimal. Social actors are forced into a state-defined framework but are not themselves permitted to participate in political decision making. This ruling technique, which Robert Bianchi has called 'corporatisation'[17], allows regimes to maintain a show of freedom for organisations, while, in reality, social actors are put under supervision and, indeed, even partly governed by the institutions of power: workers' movements are infiltrated by intelligence agents; and trade union leaders are co-opted with offers of financial advantage and promotion. In this way the regimes try to turn social organisations into the tools of state mobilisation and avoid strikes and demonstrations.

Classic state corporatism came to the Middle East via the republics in a particular historical phase. It was used to promote state-driven modernisation after independence in a context of external threats and internal social tensions. The first corporative states in the region were Mustafa Kemal's Turkey, Reza Shah's Iran, and Ben Gurion's Israel.[18] In the Arab world, state corporatism came with the revolutionary years and the populist–authoritarian regimes. The monarchies did not establish modern political institutions (trade unions, political parties, and so on) and therefore developed in a different way. Nazih N. Ayubi, though, asserts that a society-based form of corporatism characterises the monarchies of the Arabian Peninsula, because their rulers have undermined the independence of traditional social groups (tribes, linguistic and religious fellowship) by integrating them into their state-building project.[19] Corporatism views society as an organism (Latin *corpus*) in which mutually dependent parts have to be coordinated to function properly. In the republics' state corporatism, the head of state was perceived as the brain and the party was the organism's nerve system.[20] It followed that the ruling party organised countrywide mobilisation with branches in factories, villages, and schools and various social groups were organised in segmented, hierarchical organisations that did not compete with each other but communicated separately with the state leaders. This principle has been described as a 'social pact', in which the state guaranteed the masses' social development and social rights in return for obedience and support for the regime.[21]

Since the state fought for the rights of the masses, the leaders rejected any need for class struggle. Corporatism's pioneer in the region, Mustafa Kemal, expressed his vision for Turkish society as follows: 'It is one of our main principles to consider the people of the Turkish Republic, not as composed of different classes, but as a community divided into various professions according to the requirements of the division of labour for the individual and social life … The aims of our Party … are to secure social order and solidarity instead of class conflict, and to establish harmony of interests'.[22] In Egypt, President Gamal 'Abd al-Nasser had a similar goal of 'melting away class distinctions' though a state-driven socialism.[23] For the leaders in the populist–authoritarian regimes the nation needed solidarity in a vulnerable state-building phase. The main priority had to be preserving the system's unity in order to prevent either the colonial powers or the old upper class from reintroducing their former rule: therefore classes could not be at war with each other. This basic principle meant that, for example, an organisation defending farming interests would typically include everyone from poor landless farm labourers to capitalist farmers and collective farm managers.[24] If any social groups went on strike despite the state-dominated interest-organisation model, the regime would claim that this broke the national consensus and was against the national interest so the state was within its rights to crush the strikers.

One topical instance of how the state subordinates society is corporatism in Libya. Since Mu'ammar al-Qadhafi seized power in 1969, an important part of the ruling ideology has been the myth that 'the people governs Libya'. The leader considers himself the incarnation of a popular revolution that aims to break down all distinctions between the rulers and the ruled. In his manifesto, *al-kitab al-akhdar* (*The Green Book*), Qadhafi invents the word *jamahiriyyah* ('plural' of *jumhuriyya*, republic) to convey his ideal of the 'rule of the masses'. On several occasions he has claimed that there is no state in Libya and that the people are the government of the land. In accordance with this, Qadhafi orders Libyans to take the government into their own hands by participating in popular committees. At first sight, Libyan society can seem very well represented in councils and bodies that officially speak for the people and act as pressure groups on the state. But a careful examination of how the various groups function in practice reveals that their power to influence is hampered by their structural dependency on the state. Lacking any basis in the constitution, since Qadhafi both established them and can abolish them by decree, their structure is ordained from above and their leaders appointed and monitored by the revolutionary committees. Having no independent source of income from membership dues, they are dependent on state funds. Should such groups develop an independent and regime-critical agenda, a withdrawal of state funding would be enough to halt the movement. *The Green Book* makes it clear that the state has the exclusive right to popular mobilisation. All workers have a *duty* to join a trade union, but each occupation shall be represented by one trade union only, and trade unions are forbidden to engage in 'activities' (read, politics) that do not concern their occupation.[25]

Over time, most Middle East republics have abandoned the pure corporative model. One-party states no longer exist in the region, and the regimes apparently recognise the need for pluralism. The main reason for this shift is, as we shall see in Chapter 5, that the populist–authoritarian regimes acquired problems of development and legitimacy. Their leaders have not fulfilled their ambitions for economic development and have therefore found it hard to justify that *unity* is more important than freedom. The result is a formal – if not always real – movement in the direction of political and economic liberalisation. Apart from Libya and the monarchies on the Arabian Peninsula, which do not allow parties at all, this change has led to multi-party systems. In varying degrees, the regimes have rejected the classic corporative model. However, this does not mean that the interweaving of social organisations and state power no longer exists. The states are still corporative in the sense that they refuse to make room for an independent civil society and still regulate the possibilities for political organisation. Although the regimes may formally favour pluralism, in reality, broad popular movements often have no right to organise. Control of trade unions for workers and farmers and of political parties is particularly strict.

Iran's party system may serve as an example. The Islamic republic is one of the most liberal in the Middle East as far as permission to form political parties is concerned. According to the Ministry of the Interior, there are more than 100 registered parties. The state's control of civil society, however, does not lie with acknowledging the establishment of parties but rather in the way parties are allowed to operate. As a rule, a closer look at these parties reveals that they have no regular organisational structure, no permanent working groups, and no clear social base. In most cases there is not even a complete party programme on the basis of which party members can be recruited. The state does not permit the parties to turn into mass movements with an independent income, as a large assembly of people constitutes a security risk for the regime, and because those gathering at mass meetings may decide to demonstrate and demand political change. When thousands of people gather, often no more than a spark is needed to bring the situation out of control. The founding principle of the Iranian state's corporatism is that popular mobilisation shall take place only under the direction of the regime.

In Tunisia, Emma C. Murphy has observed another form of control over society, which she calls 'multi-party-corporatism'. She shows how the heritage of the populist–authoritarian regime has been continued in an apparently liberal context.[26] In a period under President Habib Bourguiba, Tunisia applied a classic corporatism with state socialism and one-party government. Interest groups were organised in country-wide organisations ruled from the top: the workers' union (Union Générale des Travailleurs Tunisiens), the farmers' union (Union Nationale des Agriculteurs Tunisiens), the students' union (Union Générale des Etudiants Tunisiens), and the women's union (Union Nationale des Femmes Tunisiennes). Bourguiba made use of the state's control over the mass-based Dustur Party to gather support for his policies. But in time both the president's popularity and discipline in the party diminished, and the state's resources no longer were adequate to satisfy the interest groups. So, cautiously, from 1981 Bourguiba began to change over to a market economy and allowed certain opposition parties to operate. Under his successor, Zine al-'Abidine ben 'Ali, who seized power in a bloodless coup in 1987, this trend was continued. Economic liberalism speeded up, and Ben 'Ali changed the Dustur Party's name to Rassemblement Constitutionel Démocratique in order to signal that Tunisia was on its way towards democracy. In 1988 multi-partyism was institutionalised through an amendment to the constitution. However, the condition for founding an opposition party was to recognise the state's 'foundation and ideology'.[27] The new electoral law made it quite clear that parties could not be founded on the basis of religion, which prevented the strongest social group in the country – the Islamic movement – from forming its own party. In September 1988 all legal opposition and interest groups signed a 'national pact', al-mithaq al-watani, in which they undertook to work for the unity of the country. In the words of the pact, 'achieving unity (...) is particularly important at the present decisive stage in our country's history, as we strive to usher in democracy and consolidate the legally constituted state'.[28] In retrospect, opposition groups that have gone too far in criticising the regime have been dissolved on the pretext that they had broken the national pact. Movements that challenge the leadership and agenda of the regime have, in practice, no right to organise. Through this type of informal corporatism, regimes hinder independent social groups from organising and challenging the interests of the ruling class.

Clientelism

While as a rule political opportunities are closed to class-based factions, there are openings for individuals. The second main mechanism used by the Middle East regimes to hamper a greater degree of organised class-based opposition is clientelism. By clientelism we mean a form of exercise of power whereby persons in influential positions offer their services to less centrally placed persons in return for political support. This type of patron–client relationship has historical roots in the region. For example, the landowning aristocracy's dominance in the Ottoman Empire and in the mandate period was founded on patron–client mechanisms. Those in authority who dispensed land on behalf of the sultan gave protection, loans, and job opportunities to the peasants. Some also operated a welfare network that offered special services to workers when they were ill, for funerals, and big occasions. In return the landowners obtained labour, soldiers, and various forms of political support. Often the landowners became so powerful that the villagers could not manage without them.

The more powerful element in a patron–client relationship usually has a double function. First, the patron offers protection, and, second, he acts as a broker between the client and the central authorities. The landowning aristocracy in the Ottoman Empire is once again a good illustration. The local authorities were both law and order in the countryside and spoke to the sultan on behalf of the local population. It was only by playing on the same side as the landowner that villagers could gain security and benefits from the state administration. Therefore, most tried to keep in with the local dignitaries. A similar dynamic may be observed today in the Middle East states. The patrons are no longer the landowners but the many officials who control the state apparatus. While villagers in Ottoman times often had one protector, in modern states there are a greater number of patron–client relationships. Clientelism's function is, however, in many ways the same, for the population stills needs protection and a broker to help them in their contacts with the state. An extreme example of this is from Lebanon. The country has a tradition in which the various confessions elect political leaders, so-called *zu'ama;* in return, their clients receive contracts, jobs, health services, and other advantages. In order to mobilise the population the leaders have traditionally had gang leaders at street level, so-called *qabadayat.* The gang leaders' task was to distribute goods from the leader to the inhabitants in their neighbourhood or to punish those clients who were disloyal. Michael Johnson has revealed that gang leaders in Beirut in the 1970s started street brawls or even killed in order to maintain their and the *zu'ama's* authority.[29] Even today, these clientelist structures are essential for securing the leaders' re-election and popularity. As an example, Agnes Favier describes how prominent families dominated the local elections in 1998 by trading in their economic and social capital for political authority. Through their connections with politicians in the central state these modern-day 'notables' attract financial resources to their municipalities and emerge as indispensible service-providers for the population.[30]

A basic problem that strengthens clientelism in the Middle East is the lack of rule of law. Minorities and individuals that have fallen out with the regime may frequently be the targets of discrimination and oppression. Those who have suffered injustice in a conflict with bureaucracy or those in power will seldom find an independent tribunal to which they can appeal their case. The inhabitants have then recourse to one of two alternatives to gain protection. They can organise themselves in interests groups along confessional, tribal or geographical lines, as we shall see in Chapter 4, or they can seek help from those with influence in the regime. As a result, patron–client relationships arise between those in power and the population where the former offer protection in return for political support and loyalty. They can also ensure that their clients are rewarded with services and special advantages: officials can grant school places, grants, and jobs to the sons of clients, and officers in the armed forces can improve conditions for soldiers called up for national service; bank managers can grant cheap loans to faithful supporters and politicians in charge of finance can award subsidies to private firms. The higher up the power hierarchy a patron is the greater the privileges he can secure his clients. At the top of this pyramid sits the leader, king or president, who binds subjects to himself by giving them special privileges. Those who obtain rewards from the head of state can in turn redistribute them, so building up their own client network and in this way can buy support and consolidate their monopoly of power.

Personal dependency in Egyptian politics may serve as an example. Egypt's 1971 constitution gives the president broad powers. He is elected for six years at a time and can be re-elected an unlimited number of times. He appoints and dismisses governments and prime ministers and has the right to dissolve the national assembly. The president is also the leader of the ruling National Democratic Party (NDP). All leading posts in the party are filled by personal appointment of the president and he uses the powers given him by the constitution to fill the state system with reliable supporters and to reward loyal servants. He promotes those who support him and dismisses those who oppose him. Besides members of the government and the leaders of the NDP, Husni Mubarak appoints a number of other key posts in the republic: top judges, senior officers in the armed forces, higher posts in the universities, the media, and the religious institutions are all dependent on his approval. This system has a double advantage for Mubarak: first, state employees realise they cannot pursue successful careers if they challenge Mubarak as any hope of promotion depends on them doing all they can to show their loyalty. Second, the president builds a network and creates a debt of gratitude among those he employs. Heads of prestigious institutions know that that they owe their privileged position to Mubarak. The president is their personal benefactor and they become his clients. Corresponding patron–client relationships may also be seen in the Egyptian electoral system. May Kassem reveals how the regime makes resources available to NPD candidates so that they can buy support:[31] NDP candidates promise money and special advantages to those in their constituency that vote for them and contribute towards expanding the regime's patron–client network. To succeed in politics it pays to join the NDP so as to have something to promise the voters. In this way politicians become isolated individuals that depend on Mubarak's support. Should a candidate challenge the official ideology or develop an independent flock of supporters, he would immediately constitute a threat and the regime would take away his privileges.

A special example of clientelism is what Hazem Beblawi and Giacomo Luciani call *rentier states*.[32] In such states the rulers share out a considerable portion of state income to the population in the hope of securing their loyalty. Beblawi and Luciani present the relationship between the elite and the people as an unwritten pact, in which the governing class takes care of the welfare of the people in return for their acceptance of the former's right to rule. This type of pervasive clientelism is common in states where the ruling powers dispose of natural resources such as oil and gas. The sale of oil generates gigantic revenues that can be channelled into society to purchase political popularity and state income is distributed by financing general goods such as health services, food subsidies, infrastructure, and education. In other words, the rentier state establishes a welfare system from which all the country's citizens' benefit. In addition, the state awards privileges to important groups to ensure support from key players. Thanks to the benefits these groups gain by cooperating with the elite, they buttress the political order and contribute to the regime's stability.

Clientelism facilitates the regime's control of society in two related ways: first, the strategy helps pacify the population, making it dependent on aid and services from the state. The inhabitants lose their independence of those in power and in this way also the chance of making demands on the state. Second, clientelism hinders the development of horizontal alliances in the sense of class solidarity. It becomes harder for social groups to form a common front against the regime, since the people already have individual bonds to those in power. The horizontal loyalty to comparable social groups is in opposition to the vertical bond to the patron. The choice is between class conflict and 'playing on the same side' as the regime. As a rule, the inhabitants go for the latter out of fear of losing security and special privileges.

Case study: Iran – social mobility and political stability

> Father: You must understand that their love was impossible.
> Marji: Why is that?
> Father: Because in this country you must stay within your own social class.[33]

Previously, we have studied one important reason for regime stability in the Middle East by focusing on mechanisms the regimes use to prevent the growth of a class-based opposition. Now we shall turn our attention towards Iran and study another dimension of the class issue, social mobility. By *social mobility* we mean the extent to which an individual can change his/her class position by moving up or down the social hierarchy. The extent to which a society allows members of the working or middle class to climb the social ladder is significant for political stability. If the class structure is so rigid that ambitious individuals from lower classes are barred from opportunities for advancement, this will create popular anger and frustration, which may in turn lead to riots, demonstrations, and revolution. But if a country's class structure is flexible, this acts as a safety valve among those sections of the population that live under difficult conditions. That certain individuals succeed in breaking out of poverty and achieving wealth and power may give hope to others that they too have a chance of improving their fortune within the existing political framework. Social mobility may also contribute towards regime stability by gradually renewing membership of the elite. Vilfredo Pareto observed early on that mechanisms for replacement of the country's political elite are a condition for the chances of survival of a regime.[34] Unless the ruling class is able to include up and coming young hopefuls, not only will the regime invoke the wrath of society but also crumble from inside through aging and decadence. According to Pareto, fossilised elites have a tendency to lose group identity and the will to fight to maintain their position. If the ruling elite is unable to renew itself gradually by co-opting aspiring leaders from lower social ranks, then the probability of its losing power through war or revolution increases.

Is the Iranian elite affected by fossilisation as Pareto warns? The danger is certainly there. As we shall see, a 'state class' has arisen in Iran since the 1979 revolution. Several of the most influential politicians have occupied top posts since the start of the 1980s. The conservatively dominated Guardian Council helps strengthen this power monopoly by hindering opposition politicians from standing for election. If this fossilisation closes all roads to young, ambitious Iranians, then, according to Pareto, it will only be a question of time before the comprehensive socio-economic changes in the country generate counter elites that will challenge the existing order. This is the starting point for the question we shall discuss in this part of the chapter. What possibilities do the working and middle classes in Iran really have to gain a place in the country's elite?

Social mobility under the Pahlavi monarchy

From 1925 to 1979 the Pahlavi shahs Reza (1925–41) and Muhammad Reza (1941–79) ruled Iran and during this period Iranian society underwent a comprehensive modernisation. The shahs built up the state organisation and a powerful army. They improved the transport and communication infrastructure and invested in banks and industry to create a modern economy. Not least the Pahlavis developed a modern school system that greatly increased the literacy of the Iranian population. This modernisation process led to profound changes in the country's social structure. Old social elites were undermined, new ones arose. Among the former were the tribal chiefs, the clerics and, after a while, the landowners too. As part of the Pahlavi monarchy's modernisation strategy, Reza Shah began a large-scale forcible settlement of nomads, killing or imprisoning tribal leaders in order to enforce the state's authority. He took the responsibility for teaching, as well as judicial authority in criminal cases, away from the clerics and this policy was continued by his successor Muhammad Reza. In 1962 he went on to undermine the power base of the landowning class by extensive land reforms. During what the shah called 'The White Revolution' (Pers. *enqelab-e sefid*), the state expropriated properties over a certain size and redistributed them to the peasants who had cultivated the land and, between 1962 and 1971, approaching two million farmers received agricultural land from the state.[35]

While the power of the traditional elites declined, new social groups and elites sprang up as a result of the Pahlavi modernisation. The educational revolution that began under Reza and speeded up under Muhammad Reza was an important cause of this process. As a result, the number of pupils in primary and lower secondary schools rose from 44,819 to 315,355 between 1921 and 1941.[36] Under Muhammad Reza this expansion reached the universities, where the number of students escalated from 5,624 to 60,000 between 1950 and 1970,[37] and by the time of the revolution of 1979, there were 175,675 students in higher education. Consequently, the new middle class increased considerably, members of which were usually more secularised and Western-orientated than the traditional elites. Moreover, many of the most resourceful students had received their education in the West: approximately 32,000 Iranians studied abroad in 1970.[38] Most of the newly educated soon obtained work in a rapidly growing public sector as the number of state employees increased from 203,000 to 1,277,000 between 1956 and 1976.[39] In addition, the shah invested huge sums in the army and from 145,000 soldiers in 1966 the number grew to 390,000 in 1976. Leading positions in the civil service were highly prestigious, and new members of the middle class gained more and more power. In effect, the state education system under the Pahlavi monarchy had become Iran's most important mechanism for social mobility.

The state's key role in the Iranian economy was another important reason for changes in the class structure. Under Muhammad Reza Shah, Iran turned into a typical rentier state whose oil income laid the foundations of the country's economy. Revenues from oil sales made up 45 per cent of the total income in the state national budget in 1963 and had increased to 77 per cent in 1977.[40] Expansion in the civil service, the armed forces, and education were to a large extent financed by rising oil revenues and the same was true for a massive industrial development that started in the early 1960s. Parallel with 'The White Revolution' the shah invested heavily in building up a modern industry. Between 1963 and 1977 the number of factories with more than ten employees rose from 1,902 to around 8,000. Of these, 159 were big factories with more than 500 employees, producing among other things cars and various metals.[41] While the state reserved ownership of the key companies for itself, most of the new industrial plants were in private hands and as a result of this expansion an industrial middle class grew up that greatly benefited from state investments. The state further encouraged private firms with tax exemptions, cheap loans, and other subsidies in order to speed up industrialisation. Enterprising Iranians could thus make a fortune in the industrial market and by the start of the

1970s some of these industrial entrepreneurs had established themselves as the new economic elite: 150 families controlled 67 per cent of the industrial and financial institutions in the country in 1974.[42] Although some of these were traditional landowning or merchant families that had known how to adapt by turning into industrial capitalists at the right moment, a considerable number were in fact newcomers that had climbed the social ladder during the industrial adventure. The legendary Khayami brothers, for example, who had built up the country's biggest car factory, Iran National, as well as a number of other businesses, had started their careers as car mechanics.

The 1979 revolution

The fall of the shah's regime under pressure from a popular movement in January–February 1979 led to most of Iran's elite being replaced. The Pahlavi monarchy's officials, officers, and politicians as well as leading industrial magnates and intellectuals all lost their dominant position. Among the first to be rejected by the revolutionary movement were the old regime's political and military leaders. The most hated symbols of the shah's power establishment were executed; others were imprisoned while the vast majority of the 'state class' was excluded from politics. Next, the revolutionary movement removed the industrial elite that had grown up under the monarchy. In June 1979 the Revolutionary Council, appointed by Ruhollah Khomeini, decreed that the properties of the 51 biggest industrial families should be confiscated.[43]

The explanation given was that the industrial middle class had had close ties with the shah and had enriched themselves by exploiting resources that belonged to all citizens. Aware of how unpopular they were and of the anticapitalist currents in the revolutionary movement, most industrial magnates had fled the country just before the collapse of the Pahlavi regime. The nationalisation of the abandoned companies and factories was therefore relatively undramatic, whereas the attack on the old intellectual class led to far more conflict. The Westernised new middle class lost their posts in the media, universities, schools, cultural institutions, and publishing houses. Suspicion of Westernisation or links with groups that challenged Khomeini was often enough to close a paper, jail a writer or dismiss teachers and researchers. In spring 1980 the new rulers commenced a comprehensive cultural revolution targeting the intellectual elite. Over the next three years, universities and research institutions were shut and cleansed of regime-critical elements.

Social mobility under the Islamic republic

The first decade after the revolution was characterised by a very high degree of social mobility. The replacement of the old elite made it possible for a new generation of politicians, businessmen, and intellectuals to make careers under the Islamic republic. The most extensive renewal was that of civil servants and politicians as not only the Pahlavi state class but also several of the politicians and activists that had taken part in the revolution were deprived of power. Up to 1982 various segments of the revolutionary movement competed over the shaping of the new state. In this process ethnic, liberal, communist, and rival Islamic groups were defined as 'enemies of the revolution' and suppressed. Those who succeeded were supporters of the Khomeini doctrine of 'the guardianship of the Islamic jurist' (Pers. *velayat-e faqih*), young and determined Islamists challenging the generation gap and class barriers to seize positions of power in the Islamic republic. Most of the new elite were recruited from the five following environments: first, from the clerics, particularly the middle ranks, the so-called *hojjat-ol Islam*, of the religious social ladder. Second, they were recruited from the merchant class of the bazaars, especially the coalition of merchant guilds that went under the name Mo'talife. Third, they came from the Organisation of the Mujahedin of the Islamic Revolution (Pers. *sazman-e mujahedin-e enqelab-e eslami*) which was forged as an alliance between revolutionary militia fighting to tighten the hold of the Islamists on the state. Fourth, leaders were recruited from the Students Who Follow the Imam's Line (Pers. *daneshjuha-ye peru-e khatt-e imam*) who took hostages in the US embassy in 1979 and barricaded the building for 444 days. Last, there were those who came from the Revolutionary Guard (Pers. *sepah-e pasdaran*), which was created in 1979 to supplement and monitor the traditional army.

Politics

The most striking characteristic of the new political elite was that its members were young. With the exception of the leading clerics, the great majority of the politicians that took office after the revolution in 1979 were under thirty and this in itself was a little revolution in a country where traditionally age and respect had been a precondition for power and influence. Furthermore, several members of the new political class came from families in quite modest circumstances: for example, the leader of the Revolutionary Guard between 1981 and 1997, Mohsen Reza'i, was the son of a shepherd, and the Minister of the Interior between 1981 and 1985, 'Ali Akbar Nateq Nuri, had been a cleric in very difficult circumstances under the Shah. The war with Iraq (1980–8) contributed towards strengthening previously marginalised groups' access to positions of power. The 1979 revolution had mainly been an urban phenomenon, but mobilisation for the war came to integrate rural groups, too, into the new regime as villagers who had enlisted en masse for the front line gained key posts in the paramilitary Basij Militia and the Revolutionary Guard. When the war was over, the survivors were rewarded for their heroic contribution with state subsidies, educational advantages, and various political posts. In other words, a major portion of the new political elite came from areas which had been little affected by the shah's modernisation strategy. They were underprivileged economically, less 'sophisticated' and far more conservative than the old political elite, and this was seen by the Western-orientated urbane middle class therefore as a defeat for 'modern' Iran. A negative consequence of the Islamic Revolution was that fewer women went out to work. In 1976, 12.9 per cent of women had been employed outside the home while only 8.2 per cent were employed in 1986. Three years later the figure had risen somewhat to 9.2 per cent, but this was no higher than the figure for women's participation in the labour market in 1956.[44]

The economy

The post-revolutionary economy was, nonetheless, another important source of social mobility. Because the most powerful investors from the Pahlavi period had been eliminated, many possibilities opened up for entrepreneurs with ability and some capital of their own. Before the Revolution the market had belonged to the big companies; now small enterprises could take over. Both previous members of the lower-middle class and newcomers seized the opportunity to exploit Iran's growing market. In a period of rapid population growth, scarcity of goods owing to the Iraqi war, absence of competition from imports, and a high rate of inflation, which made it easy to service loans and increase the value of investments, there were plenty of chances to make money. Just as in the sixties and seventies, the state played a key role in the rise of the new economic elite. Not only did the Islamic republic protect industry with high customs duties but the state also channelled oil money into various development projects from which private investors realised substantial profits. Moreover, the authorities established a number of schemes for supporting private companies. Those who benefited from such subsidies could, for instance, borrow money under the market rate of interest and purchase foreign currency at a reduced rate of exchange. The idea was that these subsidies should be reserved for vulnerable economic sectors and stimulate agriculture and industry in particular, but in practice these subsidies were frequently misused. Through embezzlement or personal contacts in the administration, individuals were able to obtain far greater quotas of subsidised loans or dollars than their level of economic activity warranted. As a result, a new upper class arose where the richest were people who had tight links with the politicians. The top division of the new economic elite became merchants in the bazaars who supported the clergy in their struggle against the Pahlavi monarchy and who in return were granted privileges by the regime. The traditional merchant middle class had been looked on with suspicion and partially opposed by the shah, who preferred modern industry. But after the Revolution large-scale industry was the preserve of the state and the old bazaar class took over the economic hegemony. Moreover, the clerics established a client network of friends and relatives that was set to administer enormously wealthy religious foundations and nationalised corporations. Several of those who gained leading positions in this way had working class backgrounds.

Education

A third area for social mobility was the educational system. The new regime continued the efforts of the Pahlavi monarchy to provide education for all. In 1976, 47.5 per cent of the population were literate.[45] By 1996 the figure had risen to 79.5 per cent, and by the beginning of 2006 it was as high as 86.5 per cent.[46] The share of women students in higher education also continued to increase. Whereas 3 per cent of women had been university or college students in 1956, by 1976 the percentage had risen to 14.9 per cent and by 1996 to 26.9 per cent.[47] After the Revolution, many volunteers from the cities went to rural areas to contribute to development there. Under the motto '*jihad* for development' (Pers. *jahad-e sazendegi*) they constructed roads, sewage systems, power grids, and schools. *Jahad-e sazendegi* was institutionalised in its own department, where bureaucracy and politicisation gradually stifled revolutionary zeal. Nonetheless, the significance of *jahad-e sazendegi* for modernising the Iranian countryside is indisputable. The establishment of 'free universities' (Pers. *daneshgah-e azad*) in a large number of small towns was another important contribution to social mobility after the Revolution. Under the Pahlavi monarchy it had been the biggest cities in the country that had universities but now through the new and partly privately funded system, however, all Iranian towns acquired their own universities although the quality of the teaching and the level of the students were usually somewhat lower than at the state universities. Nonetheless, the new offer of university education in the small towns opened up the opportunity for climbing the social ladder to people from outlying districts.

A fossilisation of the Iranian elite?

As we have seen, the high degree of social mobility in the first decade after the revolution was due to a large-scale replacement of Iran's political, economic, and intellectual elite. The opportunities for social advancement after the fall of the Pahlavi regime came as a result of a large number of vacancies to fill. In time, however, the Islamic republic produced its own elite. This made it harder for newcomers to advance up the social hierarchy.

Politics

The Iranian political landscape is characterised by a unique blend of circulation and rigidity. On the one hand, the country's politics is full of surprises and changes as a result of elections and conflicts within the elite. The presidential election victory for the reformist Muhammad Khatami in 1997 led to a big turnover in the political elite and enlivened public debate. Correspondingly, the election of neo-conservative President Mahmud Ahmadinejad turned politics upside down in 2005. Reformists were thrown out of the government and the country changed course. In other words, compared to countries in the region that do not hold elections and/or are characterised by a monolithic elite, Iranian politics are more dynamic. But, on the other hand, the Iranian system is also very rigid. Even if the people elect the president and the national assembly, there are a number of positions of power over which the government, parliament (Pers. *majles*), and the people have no control. This is true for the position of Leader of the revolution (Pers. *rahbar-e enqelab*), which, according to the constitution, is the most powerful in the regime. Since 1989 'Ali Khamene'i has monopolised this office. The same is true of institutions such as the courts, the police, the armed and security forces, and the Guardian Council, where the Leader appoints to positions of authority without any popular check or balance on his power. The task of the Guardian Council is to act as watchdog of the constitution and to ensure that the laws of the land do not conflict with Islam. Moreover, the Guardian Council carefully investigates candidates for the presidency, parliament, and the Assembly of Experts. In order to be approved candidates have to recognise the Islamic constitution and the doctrine of *velayat-e faqih*. The conservative-dominated Guardian Council uses this criterion to exclude its political opponents from the electoral process. For instance, more than 2,500 candidates were rejected for the 2004 elections.[48]

The Guardian Council's censorship of candidates makes Iranian politics the exclusive pursuit of a small community of individuals with 'the right background' from the revolution. Outside the five basic environments from which the political elite is recruited, it is difficult for others to gain entry into the political elite. In other words, the elite consists of those who fought for *velayat-e faqih* in the first decisive years of the history of the republic. Younger politicians can be socialised in as long as they have no history as opponents of the doctrine. The group that supported *velayat-e faqih* in the first years of the revolution have later split into conservative and reform-orientated factions. The conservatives are adherents of 'the absolute authority' (Pers. *velayat-e motlaq*) of the Islamic jurist, whom they consider as raised above popular opinion. On the other hand, the reformists desire a democratic Islamic state in which the authority of the Leader is regulated and bound by the constitution. The most radical reformists have gradually questioned the whole doctrine of *velayat-e faqih*. Because they belong socially to the group that defended it in the early 1980s, they still have, nonetheless, a certain freedom to take part in politics. The reformists get time on radio and television and traditionally have been able to obtain positions of power through election. The same rights are denied those regime critics who stand outside the revolution's hard core. Not only is political office beyond the reach of the outsiders but political opponents are also exposed to oppression.

Nevertheless, what is special about the Iranian political system is that *outward* rigidity is combined with circulation *within* the elite. Although leading positions are reserved for those who historically have closed ranks around *velayat-e faqih*, relations between the system's insiders are characterised by competition and replacement. The reason for this is, as already mentioned, the dynamics of the electoral process. Throughout the republic's history rival political fractions have fought for control of parliament and the government. In the 1980s, leftist radical Islamists were the strongest group. Their agenda was a mixture of the struggle for the Islamic revolution and state-driven economic development. However, in 1989 'Ali Akbar Hashemi Rafsandjani was elected president and introduced a more pragmatic policy: he dismissed leaders of the Islamic left and appointed a government that bore the stamp of market liberal technocrats. Eight years later Khatami won the presidential elections with a programme to strengthen the constitution and civil rights. As did his predecessor, he appointed new ministers and bureaucrats, this time dominated by reform-friendly intellectuals. In 2005 the neo-conservative Ahmadinejad took over the presidency who has made himself the spokesman for a return to the revolution's early ideals of social equality, a strict moral codex, and an uncompromising foreign policy. Ahmadinejad, too, has moved out large numbers of those in the government and the bureaucracy, but whereas Rafsandjani chose technocrats and Khatami intellectuals, Ahmadinejad largely recruited from the Revolutionary Guard. Other important sources of recruitment to the new wave of the elite are the police, the security forces, and the judiciary.

Parliamentary and local elections also play a role in the circulation of the elite. After a conservative-dominated election in 1996 a reform-friendly majority won in 2000, which in turn was replaced by a neo-conservative *majles* in 2004 and 2008. Although the Iranian parliament has less influence than it would have had in a more democratic system, it is nonetheless an important bastion of power. The Parliament also assures geographical representation because it recruits local elites from Iran's 30 'provinces' (Pers. *ostan*). The practice of holding local elections that was started by ex-president Khatami in 1999 has also worked in this direction. Local elections are now held every fourth year in 324 counties (Pers. *shahrestan*), providing broader segments of the population with opportunities for political influence and career. The elections of 1999 and 2003 had an especially renewing effect, because Khatami managed to keep the Guardian Council out of the nomination process, making it easier for candidates to stand for local elections without being directly connected to the 'political class'. Mahmoud Ahmadinejad himself rose to prominence through winning the Tehran city council election in 2003. In 2005, the former Basij militiaman became the first non-clerical politician in twenty-four years to win a presidential election. Ahmadinejad, as the son of a blacksmith, became an 'icon' of social mobility in the Islamic Republic.

Economy

Farhad Nomani and Sohrab Behdad have studied changes in the Iranian class structure on the basis of solid statistical material and they found that in the first decade after the revolution class differences receded: the working class reduced in size while the middle class became bigger and the old upper class fell. According to the authors, the reason for this was that social and political disturbances undermined the existing conditions of production, thus making room for new actors. However, gradually, as the revolution moved out of its more turbulent stage at the end of the war with Iraq in 1988 and with the death of Khomeini the following year, this development began to change. The regime became more occupied with defending private property rights, stabilising the conditions of production, and consolidating the bourgeoisie. The revolutionary ideas aiming to create a class-less society were replaced by a more pragmatic support of the market economy aiming to promote growth. The consequence was that once more class differences became more prominent. The share of wage-earners, lower grade employees, and working class jobs grew while the growth of the independent lower middle class stagnated. Moreover, the economic elite created by the revolution began to consolidate its position. The gain in the levelling out process of the 1979 revolution was not entirely lost, but, according to Nomani and Behdad, the overall tendency was to a renewed proletarisation of the Iranian labour force.[49]

The political preconditions for economic success did also become more evident. Two major developments in the post-Khomeini era created cohorts of 'new rich' that benefited from political connections: first, the 1990s were marked by the emergence of President Hashemi Rafsandjani (1989–97) as the post-war 'strongman' who set Iran on a course of market liberalisation. Under his leadership Iran started to move away from the state-centred development approach of the 1980s to provide greater possibilities for the private sector. As part of its liberalisation policy, the state sold off publicly owned businesses on the cheap. But to profit from such chances you had to have political contacts and those with 'door-openers' inside the system were first in the queue to buy state companies at these prices.

Second, the 2000s saw a growing influence of the Revolutionary Guards. The reason was that Leader Ali Khamene'i felt threatened by the reform movement under President Khatami (1997–2005) and called upon the Revolutionary Guards to defend the Islamic Republic. Armed units were sent in to control student mobilisation and quell popular protests. In return the *sepah-e pasdaran* received economic benefits of which the high ranking members of the Guards and their networks could make personal use.[50]

Besides 'skimming the milk' of the oil rent, politically connected actors are well equipped to handle Iran's bureaucratic business environment. Red tape and unhelpful bureaucrats can in many cases lead to the simplest request being rejected or taking a very long time to answer. In such a situation it is useful to have friends on the inside. Firms with personal contacts find their passage through the rules and regulations smoothed and gain access to more contracts. The total result of all this is that entrepreneurs with the right contacts to the regime have far better chances than others of becoming wealthy and investors with the right political profile and the right personal contacts meet open doors. All the others must compete on the market with a number of handicaps.[51]

Education

Social mobility is still possible in Iran through the education system but for several reasons it has become harder to rise up the social ladder in this way. Weak economic growth since the revolution carries much of the blame as it has led to rising unemployment and has given the state less of a financial margin. In the meantime the population has doubled between 1976 and 2004 – from 33.7 to 67.7 million,[52] and a surge of youngsters stream into educational institutions, where the state is forced to cut its expenses. However, more than two million each year compete for about 150,000 places at the state universities,[53] and for those who do not pass the tough entry exams and who cannot afford tuition fees at the so-called free universities higher education is out of reach. State student grants are not sufficient for students from the working class to be able to study full-time. The state gives them a small grant and often rooms, but many still have to work to feed themselves and their families. Even for those of ability, strength, and courage, there remains the problem of getting a job after they have finished their studies. With an unemployment rate among the young estimated at 20–25 per cent, competition for available positions is very hard. The situation is worst for those with arts degrees (history, philosophy, and social studies) because those with an academic education have to apply for jobs in the state sector and salaries for those lucky enough to get a post are usually low. More practical studies such as engineering and economics give better chances as students of these subjects can more easily cross over to the private sector.

Job opportunities are also greater for men than for women. Although women are well-represented at most Iranian educational institutions, there are still cultural limitations on the type of professions a woman 'should' choose.

Ultimately, there is a strong tendency in many professions for hiring through personal contacts. Both private and public sectors suffer from this type of nepotism, but the phenomenon gains an extra political dimension for state employment. Not only must the applicant go through a test of good behaviour (Pers. *gozinesh*), in which the applicant's convictions and private life are scrutinised, but to win promotion, ties to the political leadership are also mandatory. In this way persons loyal to the regime are awarded.

The 2009 presidential election

In 2009 the Islamic Republic was struck by its biggest ever political crisis. The trigger was the election that resulted in Mahmoud Ahmadinejad's second presidential term, contested by the defeated candidates Mir Husayn Mousavi and Mehdi Karrubi as well as significant parts of the Iranian population. Mir Husayn Mousavi who, according to the government, received the second largest amount of votes accused the Ministry of Interior of massive electoral irregularities[54] and ultimately 'stealing' his victory. A social protest movement which would gain the name 'the green movement' after Mousavi's electoral campaign colour immediately took to the streets and rallied around the slogan 'where is my vote?' Ali Khamene'i and the government responded with threats and violent suppression of the protests. They were not however able to eradicate the green movement.

As argued in this case study, elections have historically contributed to the survival of the Iranian regime by hindering the ossification of the elite, and, not least, by engaging the electorate. Despite the limits of the electoral system, the Iranian population has always turned out in relatively large numbers to vote. By and large nation-wide over 50 per cent have participated in all parliamentary and presidential elections because they believed electors' votes made a difference for the country's policies. At particularly decisive moments such as the election of reformist president Khatami in 1997 and the 2009 presidential election voter turnout has been as high as 80 and 85 per cent respectively. For the regime the participation of the electorate has been an important source of legitimacy. When over half of the population vote of their own free will this means that they implicitly accept the political system. There is also reason to believe that the circulation of the elite strengthens the popular belief that social mobility in the Islamic Republic is possible. However, the contested nature of the 2009 presidential election seems to have created a deep legitimacy crisis. Judging from the post-electoral developments, members of the reformist opposition have lost faith that the road to power through elections is still open, and a broad popular movement refuses to accept the authority of President Ahmadinejad.

Conclusion

An important reason for Middle East regime stability is the rulers' ability to neutralise class-based opposition. Compared to Europe – where politics has been driven by class interests in the formative period – it may seem as though class dynamics have been put out of action. The low degree of class-based mobilisation is not due to the absence of poverty and class differences. On the contrary, a general feature of the social structure of the Middle East is that the ruling class uses control of the state apparatus to enrich itself and its friends and relatives. The reason lies rather in the strategies the state power uses to control society. In this chapter we have seen how corporatism and clientelism contribute to weakening horizontal bonds and prevent class mobilisation. The aim of the authorities is to stop people from organising themselves in independent units and making collective demands. For those who accept the rules of the game, there are opportunities for enrichment and advancement through the client system. The Iranian case study clearly shows this. A combination of political and economic problems makes the system seem rigid for many Iranians, but the Islamic republic does give considerable opportunities for social advancement for those who know how to take benefit from the system.

Further reading

Arjomand, Saïd Amir: *After Khomeini: Iran under his Successors.* New York: Oxford University Press, 2009.

Amin, Galal: *Whatever happened to the Egyptians?* Cairo: American University in Cairo Press, 2000.

Batatu, Hana: *The old social classes and the revolutionary movements of Iraq.* Princeton, NJ: Princeton University Press, 1978.

Gellner, Ernest and John Waterbury (eds.): *Patrons and Clients in Mediterranean Societies.* London: Gerald Duckworth, 1977.

Kassem, May: *In the Guise of Democracy.* London: Ithaca Press, 2000.

Katouzian, Homa: *Iranian History and Politic: The Dialectics of State and Society.* Oxon and New York: RoutledgeCurzon, 2003.

Murphy, Emma C.: *Economic and Political Change in Tunisia.* Basingstoke and London: Macmillan Press, 1999.

Nomani, Farhad and Sohrab Behdad: *Class and Labor in Iran: Did the Revolution Matter?* Syracuse, NY: Syracuse University Press, 2006.

Perthes, Volker (ed.): *Arab Elites: Negotiating the Politics of Change.* Boulder, CO: Lynne Rienner Publishers, 2004.

Richards, Alan and John Waterbury: *A Political Economy of the Middle East.* Boulder, CO: Westview Press, 1998.

Sonbol, Amira al-Azhary: *The New Mamluks: Egyptian Society and Modern Feudalism.* Syracuse, NY: Syracuse University Press, 2000.

Vandewalle, Dirk: *Libya Since Independence: Oil and State Building.* London: I.B.Tauris, 1998.

4 Ethnicity

A dynasty rarely establishes itself firmly in lands with many different tribes and groups.[1]

After 1970 a series of Middle East conflicts has had an ethnic character:[2] the collapse of the confessional system in Lebanon; Sunni Muslim Islamists' revolt against the 'Alawi-dominated state in Syria; the tensions between 'East Bankers' and Palestinians in Jordan; Kurd and Shi'a Muslim revolts in Saddam Husayn's Iraq; clashes between Sunni and Shi'a Muslims in Bahrain; Kurdish separatism in Turkey; the Berbers' struggle for linguistic and cultural rights in Algeria and Morocco, and the Zaydi revolt in Northern Yemen. The list of examples could be even longer.

These conflicts have taken various forms and scope. Their common feature, however, is that substate groups have mobilised for collective political action on the basis of a common identity. What this identity relates to varies from conflict to conflict. In some cases belonging to a religious group is the most important factor, in others tribe, language or homeland. Ethnic conflict has often been seen as a consequence of decolonialisation, which created new states whose colonial borders completely disregarded ethnic boundaries. In such multi-ethnic states it was often difficult for local leaders to unite the population in one nation. But this is far from the whole explanation. Another common view is that ethnic mobilisation is a revitalisation of traditional social organisation in the Middle East. As we shall see, mobilisation is rather an expression of modern mass politics.

In this chapter we shall try to answer the following questions: why did ethnic conflicts seem increasingly to be a source of conflict in the Middle East after 1970? To expand on this theme we shall take a closer look at Yemen. What consequences has 'Ali 'Abdallah Salih's authoritarian rule had for relations between the state and society in Yemen?

Ethnicity

By *ethnicity* we understand identity that is based on narratives about which people have common roots and therefore belong together. Such narratives may build on, among other things, a common language, race, religion, and homeland. The condition for the creation of collective identity is that there is an opposite, 'the other', from which this group can define itself as being different. Within social anthropology there has been a theoretical debate as to what extent this is a given or a construction. Claiming that the feeling of belonging is innate, supporters of the first position consider identity as a stable reality. Those who support the second position look on identity as something constructed by political entrepreneurs who have a particular goal attached to group mobilisation. The anthropologist Fredrik Barth was the first to understand identity in this way.[3] He pointed out that groups in contact have a tendency to emphasise their differences rather than their similarities. According to Barth, the reason for this is that social groups construct borders between themselves and others in order to defend their interests. When people feel solidarity with each other, they find it easier to organise as a group and therefore work more effectively for their political objectives. Ethnicity is in other words suitable for political mobilisation but ethnic identity cannot be created out of nothing. Political entrepreneurs start out from cultural characteristics that people recognise and identify with and give these a new and strengthened meaning.

Middle Eastern societies are, like all other societies, characterised by cultural complexity. One person can feel a sense of belonging on account of sex, language, homeland, nationality, faith, work, among others. In the West there is a tendency to look on the identity of the inhabitants of the Middle East as one-dimensional and based on religion. This is, however, misleading. For instance, a Shi'a Muslim is not just a Shi'a Muslim: this person will also have a number of other identities, which, depending on context, can be even more important than that based on faith. During the Iran–Iraq War in the 1980s most Iraqi Shi'as made cause with the Sunni-dominated Iraqi state despite the fact that the enemy, Iran, was Shi'a. On the other hand, after the Gulf War of 1991 many Shi'as mobilised against the central power in Baghdad. The reason for this revolt was the feeling that in Iraq the Shi'as were an underprivileged group. Political entrepreneurs can make use of this flexibility in identity to further their agenda by influencing whichever identity the inhabitants harbour. So in order to answer the question we asked at the beginning of this chapter, we need to reveal who is responsible for ethnic mobilisation and what is their intention.

Ethnic conflict

Ethnic mobilisation can, at worst, lead to *ethnic conflict* which is less about a blossoming of 'traditional' antagonisms in a society than an ethnicisation created by a conflict of interest. Here we shall examine four important driving forces behind this type of conflict: first, ethnic conflict can be ascribed to tensions between the pluralist society and the state's requirements to regulate the lives of all those who live within its borders. Anthony D. Smith thinks that nationalism flourishes when the state apparatus has been developed and its grip on people's lives has grown tighter.[4] In the post-colonial world the introduction of the sovereign state went hand in hand with the principle of nationalism, which declares that every people has a right to establish a state, and that each state should constitute a nation. A *nation* is an ethnic group that lays claim to – whether successfully or not – sovereign power over a certain territory, and *nationalism* in this context is an ideology that contributes towards legitimising this claim. In order to stabilise the new states post-colonial leaders commenced an active policy of *nation building*, that is, employing measures aimed at unifying the population in a national community. The goal was for the inhabitants to abandon their traditional identities, linked to language, culture, homeland, and so on, in favour of loyalty to the new state. The authorities therefore over-emphasised cultural homogeneity by excluding or forcibly assimilating ethnic minorities. However, the state's efforts at national conformity produced reactions among those minorities that fell outside the norms on which national identity was constructed. Political activists belonging to the minority mobilised their own group in order to win greater autonomy or even to break away from the central power.

Second, ethnic conflict can arise as a strategy in the struggle for scarce resources. The state controls political and economic resources that are of vital importance for the inhabitants' security. In states that have poorly developed formal political channels, such as parties and trade unions or where such channels are controlled and manipulated by the authorities, the inhabitants seek security from 'those nearest'. Individuals do not trust the public sector to make arrangements that will take care of them should they fall ill, become unemployed, and so on, and turn to the family, the clan, tribe or co-religionists as a security net in the absence of a reliable state. When the fight for scarce resources is articulated in this way, one will in a pluralist state find parallel identity-based groups in rivalry with each other. If one section of society feels that it systematically loses in comparison with other groups, this group will finally react to this discrimination by mobilising for political action along ethnic lines. The favoured ethnic groups will in return respond by mobilising to defend their privileges. As we shall see, this dynamic has led to ethnic conflict in several Middle Eastern countries.

Third, external influence can in many cases lead to ethnic conflict. Fragmented societies, found in the region, are highly vulnerable to outside interference. As we mentioned in Chapter 2, the colonial powers made use of divide and rule strategies in order to hold on to power. A typical pattern was of the European colonial powers allying themselves with ethnic minorities, often Christians, such as the Maronites in Lebanon and the Copts in Egypt, or minority Muslim groups, such as the 'Alawi and Druze, at the expense of the majority. For elite families within each minority there were great opportunities for social advancement in allying themselves with the powerful Europeans. In this manner colonial rule created internal friction. Western powers did not however lose interest in the region after decolonisation and to the present day have promoted their strategic and economic interests by 'buying' support with cooperative groups. Regional powers have also proved capable of playing the ethnic card and sought to undermine each other by setting up the others' ethnic minorities against the central authorities.

Fourth, authoritarian government in pluralist societies can lead to ethnic conflict and the danger is particularly great when rulers whose legitimacy is dubious play the 'ethnic card' to safeguard their power. Joel S. Migdal is concerned with the strength of the state *vis-à-vis* society and classifies states as relatively 'strong' or 'weak'.[5] He claims that an important condition for a state to be regarded as strong is that society voluntarily supports its laws and regulations. A state that lacks legitimacy and that has to impose its will by oppression is, in other words, not strong. According to Migdal, rulers who have limited control are obliged to govern through 'the politics of survival'.[6] This can involve recruiting leaders to the apparatus of power on the basis of friendship or blood bonds in order to ensure loyalty. Such recruitment can lead to members of a particular ethnic group monopolising the state apparatus, which in turn will cause reactions in the form of mobilisation among other groups. In that way ethnic conflict can once more break out.

Ethnic conflict in the Middle East

The theoreticians of modernisation, who dominated Western research into the post-colonial world of the 1950s and 1960s, concluded that state-driven modernisation in the Middle East weakened the importance of traditional identities. The idea was that industrialisation, urbanisation, and secularisation broke down such loyalties and exposed the individual to new rights and duties on a foundation of universal ideologies. The theoreticians believed that horizontal identity based on work and class would soon overshadow vertical forms of solidarity. After 1970 it may seem that these theoreticians were mistaken in their suppositions. Ethnicity has gained renewed significance in a number of countries in the region.

Reaction to forced assimilation

Several conflicts in the Middle East after 1970 can – in accordance with Smith's theory – stem from the state's demands for linguistic and cultural conformity. The Kurds and the Berbers failed to benefit when the borders were drawn in the Middle East: neither group was rewarded with its own state. The Kurds, who today number 24–27 million, divided among Syria, Iran, Iraq, and Turkey, have even been referred to as 'the largest nation in the world without its own state'.[7] In both Kurd and Berber mobilisation there has been a desire for recognition as ethnic minorities with a right to their own language, culture, and way of life. In Mustafa Kemal's Turkey, where the largest Kurdish population lives, the authorities tried to build national identity on Turkish language and culture and a Turkification of education, the state administration, and media was implemented in order to homogenise the population. The Kurds, however, with their own linguistic and cultural heritage, fell outside the norms since the Turkish state refused to recognise them as an ethnic minority and sought to assimilate them into the Turkish nation. The problem lay in the fact that the Kurds felt they were treated as second-rate citizens and discriminated against in the allocation of state resources. This led to Kurdish mobilisation for self-government or even total independence from the central authority in Ankara. The group that went furthest in this struggle was the Kurdistan Workers' Party (PKK). In the period 1984–98 the party waged an armed campaign for independence under the leadership of Abdallah Öcalan. Kurdish guerrilla soldiers attacked Turkish security forces in Eastern Turkey, and elsewhere in the country, often from bases in Syria and Iran. Far from all Kurds supported PKK's armed struggle for a separate state, which led to great suffering for the population in Eastern Turkey. The Turkish armed forces responded to the challenge from the PKK with military campaigns, finally managing to defeat the rebels. About 12,000 people were killed, 3,500 villages destroyed, and more than three million people forced to flee the conflict area.[8] In the period after the armed struggle the Turkish authorities have chosen a softer approach to the Kurds, allowing the use of the Kurdish language in schools and certain mass media.

The Berbers have not had independence as a goal but rather sought cultural and linguistic rights within the state. This has been the case in both Morocco and Algeria. However, the worst case has been the situation in Algeria. After the country won its independence from France in 1962, the Algerian state attempted to distance itself from French culture by building a national identity within the framework of Islam and the Arabic language.[9] Articles 2 and 3 of the constitution declare that Arabic is the sole national and official language in Algeria and that Islam is the state religion. This has meant that Arabic is the only language allowed for educational purposes and in the media. This idea of Algerian national culture affected a number of minorities, especially the Berber (*imazighen*), who comprise approximately 30 per cent of the country's population.[10] The Berbers, mainly living in Kabylia and Aurès, opposed the state's attempt at assimilation and in Kabylia, where the biggest and most active Berber group is to be found, the demand for cultural recognition grew stronger and stronger during the seventies. In 1980 a popular rising broke out in Kabylia, resulting in violent clashes with the authorities' security forces. The Berbers continued their struggle against the state's Arabification in both the eighties and nineties, which eventually brought success. In 1996, after a month-long school strike, the state set up an organ for (*amazigh*) Berber culture and amended the wording of the constitution so that it was defined as part of the Algerian national culture. Further riots broke out in Kabylia in 2001. In the wake of this turbulence the authorities decided to accept the Berbers' demand that the constitution should recognise the Berber language (*tamazight*) as a national language in Algeria.

Struggle for scarce resources

Ethnic mobilisation in the Middle East is also a strategy in the battle for political power and access to scarce resources. For instance, in Bahrain the fight for scarce resources has contributed to ethnic conflict. Bahrain's ruling family, Al Khalifa, is Sunni, while, unlike the other monarchies on the Arabian Peninsula, the Shi'a Muslims constitute the majority of the population. Some put the Shi'as as high as 70 percent among a population of 440,000 native Bahrainis; others put the figure at 60 percent.[11] The Sunnis are divided between Arabs with tribal backgrounds and Arabs who emigrated first to Iran and then later moved to Bahrain (*hawwalah*), while the Shi'a are either the aboriginal inhabitants (*baharna*) or belong to a little group of Iranian origin who lack citizenship (*bidun*). The lines of conflict can be traced back to 1782 when a coalition of tribes from the Arabian mainland conquered the island from its Persian masters. The new masters were Sunnis and Bedouins but the native population of Bahrain, on the other hand, were Shi'a and farmers. Al Khalifa took over the arable land, and imposed a quasi-feudal system of exploitation of the *baharna* peasantry. This system ended in the 1920s with British reforms in the bureaucracy and judiciary.

Despite the Shi'a majority in society, Sunnis still dominate Bahrain politically and economically. Sunni Muslims are to be found in most leading positions in the state system. According to the Bahrain Centre for Human Rights, Shi'as occupy merely 18 per cent of the total high-ranking governmental posts and Shi'as do not hold important posts in the defence and internal security forces, although they are allowed to be employed in the enlisted ranks.[12] In addition, Shi'a activists claim, the royal house is pursuing a policy of using citizenship in order to reduce the demographic overweight of the Shi'a. In 1998 the Bahraini government conferred citizenship on between 8,000 and 10, 000 Sunni families from Jordan, Syria, Pakistan, and Yemen. The newcomers are given legal residency, good salaries, and suitable housing.[13] This policy has been hard to swallow for the majority, since some Shi'a families have lived on the island for several generations without being granted citizenship, thus being excluded from the benefits of the welfare state as well as the right to participate in politics.

The Shi'a community did not benefit from the economic boom Bahrain enjoyed in the 1970s and 1980s, when oil production was at its peak. Consequently, the Shi'as also comprise the poorest segment of the population and are those most affected by unemployment. Estimates vary, but it is plausible to assume that between 16 to 30 per cent of Bahraini males is unemployed. Almost all of these are poor Shi'as.[14] The Shi'as claim that they do not have as much access to modern education and good schools as the Sunnis, and that they are subject to systematic discrimination on the job market. Shi'a businessmen claim that the government favours Sunni merchants by awarding them more government contracts and public works projects, while Bahraini unskilled workers cannot compete easily with the skilled foreign workers who are employed in the public and private sectors.[15]

Periodic unrest in Bahrain is often galvanised by high unemployment among young Bahrainis. In 1994–96 the underlying dissatisfaction peaked in the so-called Shi'a *intifada*, which is one of the darkest chapters in the country's history. About forty Shi'a activists were killed, thousands arrested and imprisoned, and several hundred forced into exile.[16]

The first signs that serious political disturbance was on its way were from the early eighties. *Ayatollah* Khomeini's overthrow of the old regime in Iran in 1979 gave ideological nourishment to Shi'a mobilisation in Bahrain, and contributed in this way to ethnification of the country's politics. Since the early eighties, Shi'a organisation has grown in Bahrain. Two institutions, ritual ceremony halls (Arab. *mat'am*) and the charity funds, have played an important role in bringing the community together: the charity funds help poor and unemployed Shi'as financially and the *mat'ams* provide a meeting place. In the past two decades, these institutions have strengthened the sense of Shi'a identity and helped form an increasingly strong bond among members of the community.[17]

When King Hamad bin 'Isa al-Khalifa seized power in 1999 and started a period of political liberalisation, members of the Shi'a community responded by founding a political society. Jama'iyat al-wifaq al-watani al-Islamiyya, usually referred to as al-Wifaq, functions as a moderate Islamist party built on Shi'a demands and identity. It has grown to become the dominating opposition force in the country as testified by the 2006 parliamentary election when al-Wifaq won 62 per cent of the votes and 17 out of 40 seats in the National Assembly.[18]

Another example is the civil war in Lebanon between 1975 and 1990. The National Pact, *al-mithaq al-watani*, of 1943 prescribed that Lebanon's various religious groups should be represented proportionately to their share of the population. The distribution was based on the census of 1932. According to this census the Christian Maronites were the biggest group, followed by the Sunni Muslims. The pact declared that the country's President should be Maronite, the Prime Minister Sunni, the Speaker of the National Assembly Shi'a, and the Head of Defence Druze. In addition to these religious groups there were several other Christian groups represented in the National Assembly. The rules for representation meant that the Christians dominated the assembly, whereas the Muslims had to take a subordinate position.[19] During the 1950s and 1960s the Muslim population grew more than the Christian and growth was particularly fast among the Shi'a, economically the worst off. Today the Muslims make up 50–60 per cent of the population, and of them, the Shi'a are the biggest group with 30–35 per cent.[20] However, these demographic changes did not lead to the remaking of the National Pact. The combination of political under-representation and economic marginalisation of the Shi'a and the Druze was an underlying reason for the civil war. The Druze leader, Kamal Jumblat, made a stand to dismantle Lebanon's confessional system. During the seventies he united a broad coalition of socialist and Arab nationalist groups in *al-haraka al-wataniyya* (The National Movement). A coalition of Christian groups known as the Lebanese Front opposed the National Movement in the first phase of the war. The Shi'a militia, Amal, under the leadership of Musa al-Sadr, originally supported the National Movement, but stayed out of the civil war until 1979. After Israel's invasion of South Lebanon in 1978, which particularly affected the Shi'a, Musa al-Sadr's successors, Husayn Husayni and Nabih Berri, led Amal into the war. As a result of Iran's Islamic revolution in 1979 and Israel's occupation in 1982, another Shi'a movement, Hizbollah (God's Party), was formed with Iranian support. Hizbollah carried on Amal's fight to strengthen the Shi'a position in society and established a welfare network in poor areas such as South Beirut, the Beka' Valley, and South Lebanon. At the same time the movement spread an Islamist ideology and declared war against Israel. After the civil war

Hizbollah was registered as a political party, but upheld its military activities with the object of forcing Israel out of South Lebanon.

The 1989 peace agreement in the Saudi town Ta'if marked the end of the Lebanese civil war and entailed a minor amendment of the arrangement from the National Pact whereby the Christian power monopoly was weakened in favour of the Sunnis. The office of the prime minister was strengthened *vis-á-vis* the president, and the allocation of seats in the parliament between Christians and Muslims was made more equal. The Ta'if agreement, however, did not bring any substantial improvements in the Shi'a Muslims' situation: the country's largest population group still has less influence than the Christians and the Sunni and is still the poorest segment of society. According to Hassan Krayam, the Ta'if Agreement ended the civil war without solving the underlying problems.[21] The agreement declared that the confessional system should gradually be dismantled, but did not specify when or how. The problem is that the Lebanese have not managed to agree on what political system shall replace confessionalism. The Shi'a want proportional representation and claim that the political system is not democratic as long as the majority is prevented from governing. The Christians, on the other hand, argue that Lebanon has a special history as a free place for minorities in the Middle East and must continue some form of confessionalism in order to prevent a dictatorship of the majority. As long as the inhabitants do not agree on an alternative to Lebanon's political system and the marginalisation of the Shi'a continues, the battle for scarce resources will go on being the base for ethnic conflict in the country.

External interference

Another important cause of ethnic conflict in the Middle East generally, and Lebanon in particular, is external interference. In the case of Lebanon, external conditions have contributed towards aggravating internal conflicts in two complimentary ways: first, the influx of refugees after Jordan's clash with Palestinian activists in 1970 unsettled the delicate balance between Lebanese confessional groups, thus contributing to heightened tension. The Palestinians were ardent Arab nationalists, poverty-stricken and allied with the Nationalist Movement in Lebanon. The civil war broke out following skirmishes between Palestinians and the Christian militia Kata'ib.[22] Second, a number of external powers – first and foremost Israel, Syria, and Iran – complicated the civil war by supporting various factions in the conflict. Israel supplied Christian militias with expertise and arms and in 1978 invaded Soth Lebanon in order to defeat the Palestine Liberation Organisation (PLO). The operation was a failure but forced thousands of villagers, mainly Shi'a, to evacuate towards the Beirut area. In 1982 Israel engaged in a new and more extensive attack on Lebanon with massive bombing of PLO-controlled West Beirut. This time the invasion was followed by a three-year occupation of the country, and in South Lebanon Israeli troupes remained stationed until 2000. Syria, too, has a long tradition of intervention in Lebanon to counteract Israeli influence and secure Syrian interests. As early as 1975 Syria intervened in the civil war to hinder an alliance between Israel and Kata'ib. The following year, frightened that Lebanon would disintegrate, Syria joined in on the other side in order to stop an alliance between Kamal Jumblat and the Palestinians.[23] The forces Hafiz al-Asad sent in 1976 signalled the start of a permanent military presence. Iran's intervention in the civil war occurred in the form of support to the Islamist group Hizbollah. Iran regarded Hizbollah as front-line combatants in a larger war against Israel and the West, using the movement to export its Islamic ideology to the Arab world. In 1988, on the eve of the civil war, fights broke out between two Shi'a movements, Amal and Hizbollah. Thanks to Iranian support, Hizbollah emerged victorious as the dominant Shi'a movement at the end of the war.

The Ta'if agreement represented no final solution to the interference of foreign powers in Lebanon. Syrian forces stayed for an indefinite period as a 'security guarantee' against instability. For many Lebanese – especially the Christians – the Syrian presence was looked on as a straight occupation. Only when Syria was accused of standing behind the assassination of former Prime Minister Rafiq al-Hariri in 2005 did Syria withdraw. Moreover, Hizbollah was the only militia not to be disarmed after the civil war. The official reason given was the need to defend Lebanon against Israeli occupation and attack but, in fact, the usefulness of the movement for Iran and Syria in exerting pressure in the regional power struggle was just as important. Israel stayed on in South Lebanon to put pressure on Syria and to control anti-Israeli groups. The total effect of Iranian, Syrian, and Israeli interference was a regular strengthening of Hizbollah, which again challenged the privileged position of the Christians and Sunnis. In 2000, Israel withdrew from South Lebanon, hoping to force Syria to do likewise. However, after an attack on 12 June 2006 in which Hizbollah killed eight and kidnapped two Israeli soldiers, Israel once more attacked the country.

Western powers have also contributed towards ethnic conflict in the Middle East. Over the last few years the USA's invasion of Iraq in particular has had such an effect. Vali Nasr in *The Shi'a Revival* claims that the most important development in today's Middle East is the confessional conflict between the Shi'a and Sunni.[24] In his book he argues that the dynamics were triggered in Iraq in 2003, but that it will not stop there. Nasr asserts that the confessional fight between the Shi'a and Sunni, which will decide the fate of Iraq, has already spread to other parts of the Middle East. According to Nasr, the fall of the Sunni-dominated regime not only brought the Shi'a to power but also aroused a regional Shi'a awakening. This awakening has strengthened Lebanese religious tensions and is changing the regional power balance in Iran's favour. In Sunni Arab countries the fear of such a development sits deep. Not long after Saddam Husayn's fall from power, Jordan's king, 'Abdallah, warned of an emerging 'Shi'a crescent' from Beirut to Tehran. Some militant Sunni, such as Abu Musab al-Zarqawi, former leader of al-Qa'ida in Iraq, went as far as to declare war against the Shi'a.

Nasr's analysis points out a central feature of how affairs have developed: however, the picture is more complex. As Nasr himself admits, Shi'a–Sunni antagonism are hardly new. Long before 2004 Shi'a in such different countries as Lebanon, Bahrain, and Saudi Arabia have organised themselves in order to claim greater political influence and a fairer share of resources. Second, each of these Shi'a communities exists in its unique context and is not to be considered as a unified cross-national movement.[25] In the Kuwaiti and Omani political context, for instance, state-Shi'a relations are not conflictual as in Bahrain and Saudi-Arabia, but on the contrary reflect the fact that Shi'a community leaders have allied themselves with the Sunni rulers.[26] As a consequence, developments in Iraq have a limited significance 'as a model for imitation'. Third, it is important to remember that many Shi'a and Sunni also have other sets of identities that can be far more prominent and that often cross the confessional borders. Both 'groups' can be mobilised as 'Muslims' and 'Arabs' in the fight against Israel and the West. Hizbollah's relative success in the thirty-four day summer war against Israel in 2006 illustrates this. The war also gained the Shi'a movement and its leader, Hassan Nasrallah, great popularity among Sunnis in the Middle East.

Survival politics and ethnic conflict

Ethnic conflicts in the Middle East may also result from authoritarian rule in a pluralist society. In several states in the region, rulers govern through military, security, and party structures that are controlled by their families and relatives. For lack of legitimacy these regimes have had to resort to what Migdal calls 'survival politics' in order to stay in power. Such politics give the impression that today's Syria is in the hands of the "Alawi clan" and that Yemen is run by the 'Sinhan clan'. After 1970 the survival politics of authoritarian rulers have contributed to ethnic mobilisation and conflicts in these countries.

In Syria about 70 per cent of the population are Sunni, the majority of which live in the big towns Damascus, Aleppo, Homs, and Hama. There are also a number of other lesser Muslim groups such as the 'Alawi, the Druze, as well as various

Christian groups. The 'Alawi, who were first recognised as Shi'a by Musa al-Sadr in the 1970s, make up approximately 12 per cent of the population.[27] This minority originates chiefly in the north-western parts of the country around the coastal town of Latakia. The country's Sunni majority, who had a dominant position under the Ottomans, were pushed aside under French rule as the colonial power sought allies among minorities such as the 'Alawi, Druze, and Isma'ili. For these minorities, joining the colonial army gave them the chance to escape the clutches of rich Sunni landowners and to gain social mobility. At independence the 'Alawi were both heavily represented in the army and in the Ba'th Party whose aim of Arab unity and social justice appealed to poor minority groups. During Hafiz al-Asad's rule a handful of 'Alawis took complete control over the repressive system and the Ba'th Party. The elite came largely from the Raslan tribe, in particular from Asad's own Kalbiyya clan as families within this elite clan have close blood bonds through marriage.

The preponderance of 'Alawi in leading positions has created the impression, both among Syrians and Western observers, that the minority has 'hijacked' power. This has motivated other groups to mobilise along ethnic lines. In January 1982 the security forces suppressed violent riots in the towns Homs, Hama, and Aleppo. Resistance in Hama lasted until the end of February, and large parts of this historic town were destroyed. The Muslim Brothers, a Sunni Islamist movement, who had recruited many Sunnis in the own, during the 1970s, organised the uprising. The gap between the Ba'th Party's real policies and its ideology of Arab unity and solidarity across religious divisions was becoming more and more obvious. The Muslim Brothers voiced criticism of the secular 'Alawi-dominated state. In order to take the edge off the criticism, the regime tried to weaken the impression of an 'Alawi state by appointing a number of Sunnis to influential posts. Most of these had been born and had grown up in the countryside – in effect, the men did not belong to the traditional urban Sunni elite and shared the 'Alawis' socio-economic background. Around 1980 Asad also began to build support among the old Sunni aristocracy in Damascus. This elite comprised a large part of Syria's technocrats, intellectuals, and merchants. Several Sunnis were awarded high profile – but low influence – posts in the government. For the Sunni elite this was, nonetheless, an opening, and for Asad it was a relatively successful ploy to muffle Sunni criticism of 'Alawi dominance. Co-opting respected Damascus families kept the Sunnis from organising new uprisings. In addition, Asad made allies of other minorities, for example, the Christians, Kurds, and Cherkessians, all of whom shared the 'Alawis fear of being oppressed in a Sunni-dominated state.

Bashar al-Asad has continued his father's policies when he inherited power in 2000. On the one hand, his closest relatives still control the power apparatus:

his brother Mahir al-Asad commands the Presidential Guard; his mother's cousin 'Adnan Makhluf commands the Republican Guard; his brother in law 'Asif Shawkat is the deputy-chief of staff of the Syrian army and his cousins 'Adnan al-Asad and Muhammad al-Asad command the paramilitary organisation Struggle Companies militia (Arab. *saraya al-sira'*) in Damascus. On the other hand, he has carried on his father's practice of co-opting the urban Sunni elite by opening up the economy and granting Sunni families investment opportunities. Behind the scenes, the regime arranges for confessional representation in parliament, the state administration, and government, while at the same time crushing any explicit sectarian expression in politics. The 'Alawi clan's over-representation in the inner circles of power is not an acceptable theme for public debate but under the surface, however, discontent with minority rule, particularly in Sunni circles, is still palpable. The regime's survival politics have created tensions in Syria that in the worst case can burst into ethnic conflict.

Case study: Yemen – 'Ali 'Abdallah Salih's survival politics

The unluckiest man in the world is he who rides the lion or rules Yemen.[28]

President 'Ali 'Abdallah Salih is one of the legendary rulers in the Middle East – and that despite many analysts prophesying he would remain in power less than six months after he seized power in 1978. Salih ruled the former North Yemen between 1978 and 1990 and has led the united Yemen since 1990. The president is accused of being focused on his own political survival, planning short term, and lacking a vision of how to develop Yemen. The country is one of the most multi-ethnic in the Middle East. The population belongs to various faiths, and tribal and clan affiliations are strong. What consequences has Salih's authoritarian government had for relations between state and society in Yemen?

Strong society, weak state

Southern Arabia, today's Yemen, is one of the oldest civilisations in the Middle East. In what was earlier known as *Arabia Felix*, 'Happy Arabia', there have been a number of states. In Islamic scripts there are many references to a pre-Islamic Yemeni history – in the Qu'ran the breech of the Ma'rib dam is spoken of – and local writers have over the centuries referred to themselves as Yemenis. In oral tradition Yemini consciousness is even more striking.[29] However, the country's history has been characterised by political fragmentation and at any one time, there have always existed several centres of power beside the state. The state has been obliged to fight for the loyalty of its inhabitants in competition with, for example, religious leaders and tribal chiefs, and it did not have the monopoly of the use of force within its borders. It has therefore been usual to regard Yemeni society as strong and the state as weak.[30]

One explanation for this fragmentation is the geography of the land as Yemen is divided by high mountains, deep valleys, and wide deserts. The country is the least urbanised in the Middle East with less than one third of the population living in towns:[31] its biggest city is the capital Sanaa. The majority of the population speak Arabic while the rest are mainly Arabic-speaking Africans who are the descendants of freed slaves. In addition, there are small Indian communities along the south coast and in the port of Aden. As far is religion is concerned, the Zaydi Shi'a, who live mainly in the mountainous north, make up about 50 per cent of the population,[32] the remainder are chiefly Shafi'i Sunni and Isma'ili Shi'a and the small Indian communities are Hindu. Earlier in the country's history, there was a Jewish minority, but today emigration to Israel has much reduced their number. Furthermore, the clans and tribes are very strong in parts of Yemen. In the north the Hashid and Madhhij are the biggest tribal confederations. The tribal people of Yemen claim they descend from Qahtan, one of Noah's sons and that they can trace their ancestry back to pre-Islamic times asserting they are related to the biblical queen of Sheba.

Early history

Yemen has had a series of foreign rulers – Romans, Persians, Ethiopians, Ottomans, and the British. In the sixteenth century North Yemen became part of the Ottoman Empire, but Zaydi *imams*, political leaders with religious authority, managed to expel the Turks in 1636. The Zaydi *imams* soon expanded their sphere of influence to include all of southern Arabia, even Dhofar (in present day Oman) and 'Asir (in today's Saudi Arabia). During the nineteenth and twentieth centuries, however, the *imams* lost their influence because of pressure from an expanding Saudi Arabia and the Ottoman Empire. The Ottomans entered the capital, Sanaa, in 1871. Nevertheless, the Turks' control was very limited, and the Zaydi *imams* led a series of nationalist revolts against the Turkish occupation. In 1911, incapable of defeating the rebels militarily, the Ottomans signed the Da'n agreement. This gave control of the highlands to the Zaydi *imams* and of the Tihamah coast along the Red Sea to the Ottomans.

North Yemen

After driving out the Turks, *Imam* Yahya (1904–48) took over the whole of North Yemen. The country became independent in 1918, and the country's status was guaranteed by the British through an agreement in 1934. The *Imam* and his successors sought to expand their sphere of influence by laying claim to all 'the natural Yemen', but were careful not to directly challenge the British. Their claims were the basis for modern Yemeni nationalism.[33] The *imams* oppressed and excluded the tribal chiefs from political power and *Imam* Yahya's son became known as 'the gruesome' on account of his bloody campaigns to crush the tribes. North Yemen was ruled by the Zaydi *imams* right up to 1962, when a group of army officers seized power and turned the country into a republic. In the wake of this coup a civil war broke out in which Egypt supported the republicans and Saudi Arabia the monarchists. The tribes were very much involved in the war – but on different sides and, as both the republicans and the monarchists mobilised and armed tribes to support their cause, so the civil war became a tribal war. The war ended in 1967, when Egypt withdrew after its defeat in the Six-Day War. However, North Yemen remained under military rule until its union with South Yemen.

South Yemen

South Yemen sprang out of the British occupation of Aden in 1839, which, via agreements with the surrounding emirs and *shaykhs,* became the colony of Aden in 1937. The port's hinterland consisted of several small states under British 'protection'. The British recognised local rulers and gave them money and weapons, in return for which, they agreed not to make pacts with other colonial powers. The Hadramawt Valley, in the east of Yemen, was relatively autonomous and had a stronger local economy based on trade with East Africa, India, and the Dutch East Indies (known as Indonesia after independence in 1949). In 1958 six of South Yemen's local rulers formed, on a British initiative, a federation, which by 1965 came to include all seventeen states in the region. Under pressure from an armed nationalist movement, the British had to withdraw in 1967, and the Democratic People's Republic was formed under the sole Marxist government in the Middle East.

Unification in 1990

Finally, in 1990 the Republic of Yemen was established. The reason for unification was first and foremost that South Yemen was weakened. A civil war had badly affected the country in 1986, and the country had lost its most important ally and trading partner in 1989 when the Soviet Union collapsed. To simplify, we can say that in practice unification meant the North took over the South. 'Ali 'Abdallah Salih was appointed the first president of the unified Republic of Yemen, and 'Ali Salim al-Baydh, the ruler of South Yemen, became vice-president. In 1991 a referendum was held on the new constitution, which was accepted. It was relatively liberal by Arab standards as it allowed political parties and abolished the state monopoly of the press. The following general election of 1993 resulted in the forming of a coalition government, consisting of the People's Congress Party (GPC) and the Socialist Party (YSP), the former governing parties in North and South Yemen respectively, and al-Tajammu' al-yamani li-l-islah (Yemen's Islamic Reform Party), led by the now deceased Grand *Shaykh* 'Abdallah bin Husayn al-Ahmar, chief of the powerful Hashid confederacy. The Islah Party was founded in 1990 by Zaydi *shaykhs*, Muslim Brothers, and conservative intellectuals, who feared that unification would endanger traditions based on Islam and tribal organisation in the North. The Islah Party boycotted the constitutional referendum because it felt that *shari'a* should be the only source of law.

The civil war in 1994

In 1994 'Ali Salim al-Baydh and his colleagues in the YSP declared the founding of an independent republic in Aden. The dissidents were defeated after a mere two months and forced into exile in London. Salih beat the rebels with the aid of an alliance made up of Islamists from the North, including Islah, and opponents of 'Ali Salim al-Baydh from the South. There were several reasons for the civil war: first, after unification a power struggle broke out in Sanaa between former rulers in North and South Yemen respectively as both sides wanted to dominate in the new republic. Second, cultural differences between North and South were huge. The South Yemenis expressed the difference as *nizam* (order, discipline) in the South and *fawda* (chaos, anarchy) in the North.[34] The population in South Yemen was liberal and cosmopolitan in comparison with the North, a legacy from maritime influences as well as more than 150 years of British and then Marxist rule. The South Yemenis were discouraged by what they saw as lawlessness, in the North, where frequent blood feuds raged and there was a deeply rooted culture of carrying arms. The northern 'Hillbillies' held a correspondingly deep distrust of the southerners. Third, the inhabitants of Aden felt economically marginalised. The intention behind unification was that the port should be the economic capital of a united Yemen. Aden, however, was neglected during the power struggle in Sanaa. Besides, just before unification oil was discovered in the border region between North and South with the richest finds being discovered in the South in Hadramawt. The communists in Aden were quick to accuse Sanaa of stealing 'their' oil revenues.

From democracy to authoritarian rule

After the civil war in 1994, Salih has pushed Yemen in an authoritarian direction. The war alliance between GPC and Islah soon crumbled. Islah felt fobbed off with unimportant ministerial posts, despite their members' contribution to the battle against the Aden dissidents. In 1997 GPC won the most seats in the parliamentary elections, and Islah accused the sitting government of electoral cheating – YSP in its turn boycotted the election. The authoritarian tendencies were further strengthened in the presidential election of 1999. Salih manipulated the election so that he won as much as 96 per cent of the votes and at the

2003 general election, GPC won 225 of 301 seats, while Islah and YSP had to be contented with 50 and 7 seats respectively. In July 2005 Salih declared in an address to MPs, tribal chiefs, and other prominent men that he did not intend to stand in the next presidential election. He argued that the time was ripe for 'younger blood' in the presidential palace: some of his supporters shouted: 'No, no, we want you forever!'[35] However, there were few Yemenis who took him seriously as they remembered clearly that Salih had made similar remarks at the previous elections in 2000. This time the GPC organised 'popular campaigns' that were given broad media coverage to get the sitting president to change his mind. The farce ended with Salih choosing to 'sacrifice himself' for his beloved Yemen by undertaking to stand for yet another five-year term. Most Yemenis shrugged this off as pure play to the gallery in order to harvest votes in the coming election and some even accused Salih of referring to his son Ahmad when he spoke of 'younger blood'. Consequently, few were surprised when Salih won in 2006 by an overwhelming margin against his opponent Faysal bin Shamlan, who represented Islah, YSP, and several small parties.

To hold onto power Salih has resorted to what Joel S. Migdal calls 'survival politics'. He has made use of several strategies: first, straight after he came to power in 1978 Salih began to recruit men from his own family and tribe to key positions in the state system. The new political elite were men from Salih's Sanhan tribe, traditionally a marginal branch of the Hashid confederation from villages south of Sanaa. Men from this tribe as well as from the Hamdan tribe from north of the capital, were customarily recruited as soldiers to the *imams'* armies. During the civil war between 1962 and 1967 men from these tribes came to dominate the army and afterwards seized power in the country. Salih has furthermore given key positions in the armed forces and the security and intelligence services to members of his closest family: President Salih is himself Commander-in-Chief of the Armed Forces; his son Ahmad is Commander of the Republican Guards and the Special Forces; his half-brother 'Ali Mouhsin al-Ahmar is Commander of the First Tank Division and the North Western Military Zone; another half-brother Muhammad Salih al-Ahmar is Commander of the Air Force; a nephew Yahya Muhammad 'Abdallah Salih is Commander of the Central Security Forces; and another nephew Tariq Muhammad 'Abdallah Salih is Commander of the Special Guards. Moreover, Salih's relatives fill many other leading posts in the state administration. After unification Salih appointed men from the Sanhan tribe to control the former South Yemen, his son Ahmad was given the job of controlling Abyan, and another relative, Muhammad Isma'il, Hadramawt. Men from Salih's inner circle support the president through thick and thin, because they know that if he loses power, they will also lose their privileges. However, it should be noted that Salih has not based recruitment to leading posts on tribalism as such, but has gone in for building up an inner circle of loyal men from his own tribe. This means that most Hashdis are as marginalised as members of other tribes, such as Bakil and Madhhij.[36]

Second, Salih has made use of co-option to control society, by which we mean granting leaders of social groups a share in the regime's privileges, thereby ensuring the regime's survival. The president has co-opted tribal chiefs, the most important trading families, and the leaders of religious groups (Zaydi, Isma'ili, and so on). In this way they are distanced from their own respective groups. Salih has, for instance, worked to distance the most important tribal chiefs from their tribal kinsmen, a process that in Yemen is referred to as taba'ud.[37] By drawing the shaykhs into businesses in which they have a personal financial interest, the president has been able to reduce their interest in tribal matters and thereby driven a wedge between the chiefs and their tribes. An extreme example of this is Hashid Grand Shaykh al-Ahmar, who was Speaker of Parliament and Islah leader from 1993 till his death in 2007. Despite al-Ahmad's leading positions, the Hashid confederation received few benefits or little more influence. The Grand Shaykh focused on his own and his sons' financial interests at the expense of the welfare of his tribal kinsmen. Today the sons of the deceased al-Ahmar control several hundred businesses in Yemen: organised in the Al-Ahmar Trading & Investment Co. These businesses are the leading companies in all of the sectors of the country's economy in which they are involved, including telecommunication, IT, tourism, retail trade, construction, and petroleum. In addition, the al-Ahmar brothers represent several of the world's biggest multinational corporations operating in Yemen, including Compaq, Emirates Airlines, General Electronic Company, Motorola, Nokia, Oracle, Philips, Siemens, and Sabafon (Yemen's first supplier of GSM-network).[38]

Third, Salih has known how to make use of that well-known strategy divide and rule. Yemen's pluralist society has given him – as it has given earlier rulers in the country's history – the possibility to form alliances with various social groups and to play them off against each other. For instance, Salih allied himself with the communists in the South in order to unify South and North Yemen. Later he formed an alliance with the Islamists and tribal chiefs to crush the uprising in Aden.

Retribalisation

Salih's survival politics has contributed towards creating ethnic conflicts in Yemen. The president's efforts to hang onto power have, according to Sheila Carapico, led to a 'retribalisation'. By this she means that belonging to a tribe or clan has gained renewed importance as a source of political mobilisation in Yemen.[39] Among Yemenis the general impression is that outside the big towns such as Sanaa, Aden, and Ta'izz the 'tribes' dominate.[40] Today the tribes and clans are particularly strong in the north-western Sa'dah province and in the eastern provinces al-Jawf and Ma'rib, where tribesmen claim the right of self-determination over the lands they live in. After 1962 the revolutionary regime in North Yemen gave back some of the power the tribes had lost under the rule of the *imams*. This development has continued under Salih. As well as the state incorporating the tribal chiefs into the political system, the Salih regime has been able to form its own laws combining *shari'a* and norm-based tribal law (Arab. *'urf*). Moreover, the authorities have sought refuge in tribally based explanations of and solutions to political crimes. Several times the state prosecution has refused to investigate killings, kidnappings, and other crimes which they regard as 'tribal tradition'. Several times the state prosecution has refused to investigate killings, kidnappings, and other crimes which they regard as 'tribal tradition'. In accordance with the tribes' customary law, revenge killing is an accepted reaction to murder. This development reflects the Yemeni state's weakness and inability to intervene in society.

At the same time as Salih has tried to incorporate the powerful tribal *shaykhs* into the state system, there has been a revitalisation of marginalised tribes within Yemen. Carapico points to the Bakili tribes in the North as an example of this.[41] In the years after unification these tribes arranged a series of large gatherings that are reminiscent of the clan festivals held in the Scottish Highlands. Tribesmen come from all over to the Bakili gatherings, driving their Toyota pickups, and armed to the teeth with traditional daggers (*jambiya*), AK-47 rifles, and RPGs. In the South there has been a corresponding revitalisation of the clans and tribes. Confederations, such as al-Madhhij, organised themselves after the cooperatives and YSP were dissolved in Aden's hinterland. This is all the more surprising considering that tribal organisation has played a less important role precisely in this part of the country over the last thirty years. The reason for this is that the communists deliberately aimed at undermining tribal structure. Despite egalitarian features of tribal society nomadism was regarded as a primitive production system that should be eliminated in order to realise the communist state. In 1968 a conciliation law was passed to stop tribal feuds, the following year bearing arms was forbidden, and new province borders were drawn ignoring tribal boundaries, and in 1970 tribal organisations were declared illegal. Later indications of which tribe a person belonged to disappeared from personal names.[42] But communist policies never managed to wipe out tribalism and several of the internal power struggles in YSP took place between alliances based on regional or tribal bonds.[43] In the 1990s such tribal bonds gained renewed significance. Furthermore there has been an attempt to build a Madhhij/Bakil alliance to counterbalance the Hashid/Sanhan state.

One might claim that the Salih regime has tried to strengthen the clans and tribes with the aim of ruling through the chiefs. At the same time this revitalisation is a strategy used by marginalised social groups to make themselves heard by central authorities in Sanaa. In the South YSP is still popular, but the party's influence is minimal. Therefore, many South Yemenis look on the revitalisation of the clans and tribes as a way of reinforcing their bargaining position for scarce resources *vis-à-vis* the state.

Revivalist Zaydism

One consequence of Salih's survival politics is the conflict between various religious communities.

In Yemen there has traditionally never been that much opposition between Zaydi, Shaf'i, and Isma'ili Muslims. However, this changed during the 1980s and 1990s. The trend was for traditional religious doctrines to come under pressure from new, imported Sunni doctrines.[44] Salih played on these Islamist currents first to establish an ideological counterweight to South Yemen's Marxist regime, then to mobilise the Islamists against the Aden rebels in 1994. After the civil war, religion has continued to play a central role as a basis for political mobilisation.

An instance of Islam's new politicised role can be seen in the Sa'dah province in north-western Yemen, where, on and off since 2004, a civil war has been taking place. The Zaydi movement's agenda grew from an expression of religious identity and frustration with neglect by the central government, into open criticism of Salih. The president was willing to accommodate Wahhabi inspired Islamists in traditional Zaydis districts. Since the overthrow of the *Imamate* in 1962, Zaydi identity has been undermined as the regime has sought to foster a sense of national identity. President Salih is of Zaydi origin, but does not emphasise his religious background. Wahhabis, led by Saudi-educated *Shaykh* Muqbil al-Wadi'i, gradually expanded their influence in Sa'dah. Many Zaydis are deeply unhappy with this development. Husayn Badr al-Din al-Huthi, a respected Zaydi scholar, became a fierce public critic of the Wahhabis – and thus Saudi Arabia's influence in Yemen – in the mid 1990s. The Zaydi movement gave birth to the Hizb al-haqq party, from which Husayn Badr al-Din al-Huthi developed Muntada al-shabab al-mu'min (The Movement of Young Believers). This messianic movement is the driving force behind today's rebellion.[45]

Husayn Badr al-Din al-Huthi's movement challenged the legitimacy of Salih. This made the movement dangerous for the president, and in the summer of 2004 he seized the initiative to crush the Zaydi movement. The result was a war lasting more than three months up in the mountains south-west of Sa'dah. Husayn Badr al-Din al-Huthi himself was killed, but the fight was carried on by his brothers 'Abd al-Malik, Yahya, and 'Abd al-Karim.

Vested economic and tribal interests, involving trade and smuggling across the Saudi border, have further fuelled the conflict. Tribes from outside Sa'dah, some of them Sunnis, have attempted to seize land in the fertile northern region, thereby provoking the locals. Hashid tribes, who originate from the less fertile Hajja region, now own land in Sa'dah.[46] The Hashid tribal confederation is led by the family of late 'Abdallah al-Ahmar, which has strong links to Saudi Arabia and is an important political ally of Salih.

The rebels receive funding through local Shi'a religious taxes, contributions from the overseas diaspora, especially in Kuwait and the Emirates, as well as cross-border smuggling. Weapons are bought at arms souks in Yemen and the Horn of Africa.[47] The Salih regime has repeatedly claimed that the well-armed rebels receive aid from Iran, allegations that must be seen as a strategy to get political, financial, and military support from the United States, Egypt, and – in particular – Saudi Arabia. In November 2009, the Royal Saudi Air Force bombed rebel positions in Northern Yemen, drawing the kingdom directly into the conflict. This was the first time that the kingdom has taken part in a war directly, and not by proxy, as Saudi Arabia's ruling family fears that the Zaydi rebellion will spill across the border and destabilise the southern provinces.

The war has been characterised by periods of hard fighting interrupted by fragile peace agreements. The Salih regime has offered the rebels amnesty, compensation for the loss of family members, and to set free arrested guerrilla soldiers in return for the rebels laying down their weapons and returning home to the mountains. But all the truces have been broken. By the end of 2009 many villages had been destroyed in the fighting, awn unknown number had been killed, and in all likelihood close to 200,000 had lost their homes.[48] The rebels' support base have been further broadened by the backing of families and communities wanting revenge for the loss of relatives to the regime's attacks. So far, Salih has not been able to permanently crush the Zaydi fighters.

Separatist currents in the south

Besides the mobilisation of the tribes and religious communities, Salih's survival politics have kindled the fire of separatist currents in the South. The support of the movement runs deep, and unites both socialists and traditional tribal leaders. The southern secessionist movement's figurehead is former president 'Ali Salim al-Baydh, while the leader on the ground is former governor of Shabwa province, Hasan Ba'um, a former member of the Yemen Socialist

Party. *Shaykh* Tariq bin Nasir al-Fadhli, the most influential tribal leader in the Abyan province, is the latter's deputy. Al-Fadhli is a veteran *mujahid* from the war in Afghanistan and a former ally of Salih, who led the bloody military campaign to crush the remnants of the old socialist regime in Aden in 1994. The emerging Southern Movement has been hugely boosted by the charismatic al-Fadhli.[49]

In the spring of 2007, seven months after President Salih and his GPC won both the presidential and local elections, a group of ex-soldiers from the southern province Dal'a began to arrange peaceful demonstrations against being forced to leave the army and at their inadequate pensions. These protests became the start of a series of riots in several provinces that made up the former South Yemen. Soldiers, civil servants, unemployed youth, teachers, and lawyers mobilised against what they saw as systematic economic and political discrimination against the southern population. The soldiers accused the authorities in Sanaa of not keeping their promises that they could serve in the army: thousands of soldiers from the south had fled the country after their defeat in the civil war and many had returned because of the amnesty and promises of jobs in the army. Posts in the state administration and the armed forces are the most important sources of employment in Yemen.

Most of the protests were peaceful. However, a group of ex-soldiers under the leadership of General Sa'id Shahtur organised armed resistance against the authorities in Sanaa. Early in 2007 the general declared from his refuge in the Mahfad Mountains in Abayan province that he had started the war to liberate the South from 'Northern occupation'. In June of the same year Shahtur threatened to attack national and international interests in Yemen, including oil companies and tourists.

The regime in Sanaa responded to mass protests in the south with brutal oppression. Peaceful demonstrators were met by tear gas, rubber bullets, and live ammunition. Several were killed or wounded, many were arrested during the spring of 2008, and unrest led to the deaths of at least 19 people between April and June 2009.[50] While many senior figures have been tried co-opted or detained, the regime has failed so far to arrest the top leaders of the Southern Movement. Moreover, a string of tribal leaders, whom the regime had worked hard to cultivate in the wake of the unification in 1990, have declared their support of the Southern Movement.[51] There are fears that the huge frustration with the perceived Northern takeover of power and economic resources in the South, as well as Sanaa's rough handling of the dissidents, will boil over into an eventual civil war.

The authorities' hard-handed suppression has only strengthened discontent among South Yemenis. Their patience is at breaking point. The intensity of the protests that have taken place over the last few months and the fact that it is the grass roots that have mobilised show that dissatisfaction sits deep. For the Salih regime Southern unrest is very alarming, coming at the worst possible time, given that it coincides with the Zaydi rising in the North.

The Salih regime's handling of the Zaydi rising in Sa'dah province as well as the riots in the South with its resort to armed force shows how feeble the Yemeni state is. The regime neither has control over all its territory nor a monopoly of the use of force. For the regime, brutal oppression is the first resort in keeping control. More positive means require resources the state does not possess. That the state is weak does not necessarily mean that society is strong. In the case of Yemen, society, too, is weak. Over decades Salih has by co-option, divide and rule, and oppression effectively weakened all tribal and religious communities and any other social groups he feared might threaten his position as Yemen's absolute ruler.

Conclusion

Ethnic conflict has characterised many Middle Eastern states over the last decades. Common for these conflicts is that there is no question of a blossoming of 'traditional' latent differences within society. Rather these conflicts result from ethnicity being exploited as a rhetoric of mobilisation in the age of mass politics. We have seen how various political entrepreneurs play the 'ethnic card' in order to mobilise the inhabitants in an attempt to realise their agendas. For instance, activists have made use of ethnicity to mobilise resistance to the state power's forced assimilation, and to strengthen their position in the fight for scarce resources. Moreover, external actors have contributed to ethnification by supporting 'their' ethnic allies in order to gain influence in a state. In addition, after 1970 'survival politics' have been an important driving force behind ethnic conflicts. In Yemen 'Ali 'Abdallah Salih's policies have contributed towards sharpening ethnic differences; in Syria authoritarian rulers have similarly served to fragment society. Ethnic tensions may splinter the state from the inside if the strongman or regime that can manipulate and hold these forces in check falls.

Further reading

Barakat, Halim: *The Arab World: Society, Culture, and State*. Berkley, Los Angeles and London: University of California Press, 1993.

Bates, Daniel G. and Amal Rassam: *Peoples and Cultures of the Middle East*. Upper Saddel River, NJ: Prentice Hall, 2nd edition, 2001.

Carapico, Sheila: *Civil Society in Yemen: The Political Economy of Activism in Modern Arabia.* Cambridge, New York, Oakleigh, Madrid, and Cape Town: Cambridge University Press, 1998.

Dresch, Paul: *A History of Modern Yemen.* Cambridge and New York: Cambridge University Press, 2000.

Eickelman, Dale F.: *The Middle East and Central Asia: An Anthropological Approach.* Upper Saddel River, NJ: Prentice Hall, 4th edition, 2002.

Esman, Milton J. and Itamar Rabinovich (eds.): *Ethnicity, Pluralism, and the State in the Middle East.* Ithaca and London: Cornell University Press, 1988.

Hanf, Theodor: *Coexistence in Wartime Lebanon: Decline of a State and Rise of a Nation.* London: I.B.Tauris, 1993.

Hinnebusch, Raymond: 'The Politics of Identity in Middle East International Relations', in Louise Fawcett (ed.): *International Relations of the Middle East.* Oxford and New York: Oxford University Press, 2005, pp.151–71.

Khoury, Philip and Joseph Kostiner (eds.): *Tribes and State Formation in the Middle East.* Berkeley, Los Angeles, and Oxford: University of California Press, 1990.

Lewis, Bernard: *The Multiple Identities of the Middle East.* London: Weidenfeld & Nicolson, 1998.

McDowall, David: *A Modern History of the Kurds.* London: I.B.Tauris, 2000.

Nasr, Vali: *The Shia Revival: How Conflicts within Islam Will Shape the Future.* New York and London: W.W. Norton & Company, 2007.

Weir, Shelahg: *A Tribal Order: Politics and Law in the Mountains of Yemen.* Austin: University of Texas Press, 2007.

Part 3
The Quest for Legitimacy

5 Reformism

The central problem of government in the Arab world today is political legitimacy. The shortage of this indispensable political resource largely accounts for the volatile nature of Arab politics and the autocratic, unstable character of all the present Arab governments.[1]

Michael C. Hudson wrote in 1977 that the biggest problem facing political regimes in the Arab world was the lack of legitimacy meaning that large parts of the population did not regard the leaders and the political systems as legitimate. According to Hudson, the masses recognised neither the political unit (the sovereign state) nor the rulers' right to rule. The consequences of this legitimacy deficit were, first, that the regimes lacked the authority to achieve the goals they had set themselves as the low level of support among citizens led, according to Hudson, to inefficient government. Second, Hudson saw a direct link between the legitimacy deficit and political instability: because the regimes were looked on as illegitimate, he claimed, they were the victims of regular coups and risings. The background for this analysis was the political disturbances that had overturned a series of Arab regimes in the 1950s and 1960s.

Since 1970 two main ideological currents have challenged the Middle East regimes: liberalism and Islamism, both used by opposition groups to criticise the legitimacy deficit and demand a new political order. To meet this challenge the regimes have been obliged to mobilise new ideological resources. In this and the following chapter we shall examine two of the main strategies the rulers have used to redress their weak legitimacy. Two changes in the regimes' ideological profile have been particularly prominent: on the one hand, their agenda is marked by constant economic and political reform and on the other, there are in many cases a clear Islamisation of the political discourse. These changes can be interpreted as a response to the challenges of liberalism and Islamism.

In this chapter we shall address the following question: to what extent have the Middle East regimes succeeded in dealing with the legitimacy issue through reformism? In the second part of the chapter we shall take a closer look at reformism in a Moroccan context: how has Muhammad VI tried to legitimise himself as Morocco's new monarch?

Legitimacy crisis and reform

In comparative politics *legitimacy* expresses a subjective feeling in the people that those who rule have the right to rule and that their laws and decrees should be obeyed. As Max Weber pointed out, that the citizens or subjects feel this way is the best guarantee of an efficient and stable government.[2] When the inhabitants regard their political leaders and regimes as legitimate, they will, in general, voluntarily grant the system their support. Conversely, in states where leaders and political institutions are considered illegitimate, the rulers will have to govern with the help of such mechanisms as bribery, force, and fear. The population will exploit any occasion to cheat the state, and, should the chance arise, to rebel. In other words, legitimacy is a vital resource that leaders should do their best to develop. Nonetheless, the big question is, what does it take for people to regard a political system as legitimate? Hudson gives a general answer by underlining that a regime and a political leadership must be seen as representative of the nation and in harmony with society's values.[3] One may say that leaders and institutions must mirror the community's identity, culture, and convictions.

According to Hudson, in this respect the colonial powers' heritage to the Arab regimes was a poor starting point. The sovereign states that were founded in the Arab world after the First World War were not the product of local nationalist struggles and corresponded badly with the local inhabitants' idea of the nation. The new political units neither matched local identities, such as tribal, regional, or confessional, nor such overarching identities as Arab or Islamic. Nation-building was, therefore, a very difficult task.

Consolidation of the Arab states is not only different from the European model but also from other post-colonial regions in that the states have been challenged both from below (by ethnic groups demanding self-government) and from above (by transnational ideologies such as Arab nationalism's vision of uniting the states in the region and Islamists seeking to restore the Caliphate). According to Hudson, this mismatch between state and nation is one of the main problems of political legitimacy. If neither the population nor the dominant ideologies regard the state system as a natural extension of the nation, neither can the leaders nor the political institutions in the states appear legitimate.

Second, Hudson puts the legitimacy problem in the Arab world in the context of the lack of political development. During the twentieth century, Arab society underwent an extensive modernisation as a result of rising literacy, education, urbanisation, and globalisation. Through these developments the inhabitants have acquired new ideals of social organisation, such as socialism and democracy. At the same time, the region's political systems have not been able to satisfy such expectations. On the contrary, they continue to maintain economic and political inequality.

Third, Hudson links the legitimacy deficit to the regimes' failures in what he calls core issues for Arab opinion. Examples of such core issues are the longing for Arab unity and the desire to be free of Western influence. Foremost among such matters, claims Hudson, is, however, the necessity for defending Palestine. When the state of Israel was founded, people spoke not of a Palestinian but of an Arab problem. It was the Arab League that attacked Israel in 1948 and that founded the PLO in 1964. Only when Yasir 'Arafat and al-Fatah gained control of the organisation in 1969 did the Palestinians take over the resistance struggle. To begin with, the population of the Arab world expected that their leaders would take responsibility for the liberation of Palestine, but after their humiliating defeat in the Six-Day War in 1967, the Arab leaders appeared to have lost all credibility. Israel had conquered the Sinai Peninsula, the Golan Heights, East Jerusalem, the West Bank, and Gaza without the Arab states being able to prevent this.

Considering the legitimacy problem that Hudson described, it is amazing that the Arab world since 1970 has been characterised by regime stability. One would expect that the structural problems mentioned above (which remain unsolved) would lead to political instability. That this did not happen is due to the combination of a number of factors on which this book tries to shed light. In the preceding chapters we have seen how the rulers have exploited divide and rule policies, corporatism and clientelism to hold on to power. Later we shall also show how the institutions of state power contribute to ensuring regime stability. In particular, the system of oppression – the security services, intelligence, and the police – have been important for exterminating political opposition. The difficulty with jailing, torturing or assassinating one's political opponents is, however, that this aggravates the legitimacy problem. The more power the state uses to force its citizens into obedience, the more opposition there is to the regime. To avoid such a vicious circle even the most dictatorial regimes attempt to justify the way they exercise their power to the population. Their opportunity lies in convincing at least some of the inhabitants that they are serving the community's interests.

Traditionally, the Middle East monarchies and republics have attempted to find legitimacy from different sources: while the monarchies emphasised ruling in accordance with tradition and Islam, the republics appealed to the will of the people and secular ideologies. The revolutionary leaders who seized power in the 1950s and 1960s sought legitimacy in ideologies such as socialism, anti-imperialism, and Arab nationalism, which rejected the status quo and looked forward towards an imagined better society. They regarded the heritage from the colonial powers as illegitimate, asserting that the Arab world had been split and weakened. The task that justified their exercise of power was uniting the Arab nation and making the Arab people masters of their own destiny.

The monarchies, for their part, looked with scepticism on this undertaking as implicit in the revolutionary concept was the idea that the Arab royal houses were 'illegitimate children' of British imperialism. Radical presidents made regular verbal attacks against them, claiming that they maintained class differences and a conservative society. Consequently, the monarchs did not cultivate Arab unity. As an alternative they emphasised closer loyalties to the family and tribe, and, at its broadest, to God, as the population had done in earlier epochs. God and family were set before the Arab nation.

The way a regime legitimates itself has much to say for how it will be judged. By selecting a certain legitimising strategy the rulers give a special prestige to certain ideas and symbols, thereby creating an arena in which opponents are able to attack the regime – the greater the fall if the rulers fail to live up to their ideals. For the Middle East, ideologically based legitimacy has been particularly hard to achieve. Promises to abolish corruption and class differences, combat imperialism, and unite the Arab nation have not been kept. As the gap between ideal and reality has widened so have these ideologies deflated. The defeat in the Six-Day War in 1967 was especially harmful for the republics as the promise of a united Arab nation under the existing regimes' leadership lost its appeal and credibility.[4]

Parallel with the weakening of Arab nationalism, problems of a state-led economic development began to increase. Bureaucracy and the growth of industry demanded enormous state resources without bringing the results expected. With the exception of Lebanon, the Arab republics, and also Iran, relied on so-called import-substituting industrialisation (ISI). This development strategy meant that import-dependent countries should begin to produce the goods they had previously imported. To succeed, the state would have to protect domestic industry in the start phase by erecting high customs barriers and subsidies to the manufacturing firms making it easier for domestic industry to get a good start. As a result of the ISI strategy, the Middle East underwent an extensive industrialisation with consumer goods, which up to the sixties had been imported, now increasingly produced locally. The problem was that local industry continued to depend on state subsidies. The theoreticians behind ISI had thought that industry would 'take off' through sales to a growing internal market and become competitive on the world market. But protection against international imports became an excuse for doing nothing to compete in price and quality, since there was no need to do so. With higher production costs and mediocre products, Middle East industries were unable to export their goods. The industrialisation that was intended to promote the region's economic development became instead a drain on the budget.

Around 1970 several of the republics started to re-evaluate their economic strategies. 'Reform' first came on to the agenda in Turkey, Tunisia, and Egypt. During the 1980s and 1990s most of the states in the region followed suit and reform has become a recurring theme in the Middle East. This reform wave must be seen in the light of the legitimacy issue. *Reformism*, in the sense of promises of changes through gradual reform, is, in effect, a survival strategy. The focus on economic, political, and technological reform after 1970 can be seen as an attempt to deal with the legitimacy deficit. Usually, reformism is defined as a belief that gradual change can alter society's basic structures. The concept has its background in the debate on socialism, where it was applied to those socialists who had abandoned the idea of revolution. A parallel to this can be traced to changes in the Middle East republics. Originally, the regimes legitimised themselves through the struggle for revolutionary change but, gradually, replaced their revolutionary discourse with a belief in improvement through reform. Our use of the concept reformism has, however, another aspect. In describing the reform discourse as an '-ism', we wish to underline how the regimes used the reform idea as a replacement for its weakened ideology. Because Arab nationalism and socialism failed to legitimise them, the regimes hope to construct a new ideological legitimacy. What is essential in this context is not whether the specific economic and political measures succeed but to give the impression that the state has a mission. The efforts to bring about reform give the regimes a purpose and emphasise the rulers' energy. However, there is a limit to how long such a strategy can work without economic and political conditions actually improving. As we shall see in what follows, reformism has created fresh challenges for the Middle East regimes.

Economic reform

In 1974 President Anwar al-Sadat proclaimed a change in course towards an 'economic opening', *al-infitfah al-iqtisadi*, in Egypt. The *infitah* initiative was an ideological break with the Arab socialism that had characterised political discourse under Gamal 'Abd al-Nasser. Already after the defeat of 1967, it was clear that plan economics was on its last legs. The war had exhausted the Egyptian state's resources, and its economy lacked investment. The Soviet Union, which since the end of the fifties had subsidised Nasser, was no longer willing to rescue the country from the crisis. First Sadat wanted to make conditions right for an influx of capital from the Arab oil states, which after the 1973 boom flooded over with investment capital. At least as important was the desire for technological and capital transfers from the West. By turning its back on socialism and the Soviet Union, Egypt could change sides in the Cold War in favour of the USA.[5] Moreover, powerful groups in the state apparatus saw opportunities for personal enrichment in closing down state socialism. Those who belonged to the top ranks of the bureaucracy had exploited their power to amass private fortunes which they now wished to invest in a market economy. The opening for foreign investment would also create a market for consultancy services for which members of the state class would have a unique competitive edge because of their access to information and political contacts.[6] International financial institutions such as the World Bank and the International Money Fund (IMF) played a key role in promoting economic liberalisation. They saw the reduction of state expenditure and deregulation of the economy as the solution to Egypt's economic crisis – at this time the World Bank and the IMF were recommending the same medicine for all developing countries. So *infitah* put down roots in most Middle East countries in the seventies and eighties.

The economic goal of the *infitah* reforms was to give fresh life to businesses that either were being choked by bureaucratic injunctions or, cushioned by state subsidies, only making half-hearted efforts. By removing red tape and subsidies, it was hoped to reduce the danger of corruption, to make investment more attractive, and to force firms to increase performance. The ISI safeguards were to be removed and the growth of bureaucracy restrained. More fundamentally, as a rule, economic liberalisation signalled a change in development strategy from ISI to export-driven growth. According to the new strategy, the state should not close the borders in order to build an internal market but rather take up the export of niche products in fields where the country had comparative advantages and therefore could compete without subsidies. Supporters of export-driven growth criticised the ISI strategy for industrialising all sectors simultaneously – under the motto 'Be self-supporting!' – instead of concentrating on certain strategic areas. Countries where conditions were right for agriculture, for example, would be better to specialise in agricultural produce, and industrial development must match access to raw materials, energy, and strategic location. It does not make sense for a desert country such as Saudi Arabia to invest in water-intensive agriculture. The country should instead exploit its access to cheap energy by, for instance, developing sun-cell parks, petrochemical, and smelting plants. Export-driven growth means that highly populated states in the region could exploit the supply of cheap labour by concentrating on labour-intensive industries. In effect, the authoritarian development state had made a big mistake by focusing on capital-intensive industries and down-prioritising agriculture.

The transition to export-driven growth is, however, easier in theory than in practice. To succeed not just comparative advantages but also decisiveness and vigour are required. The political leadership must be ready to take unpopular decisions, and the state apparatus must be able to execute the decisions of the politicians but this has often been missing in the region. With the exceptions of Israel, Turkey, and Tunisia, none of the states in the Middle East have been capable of maintaining, and thereby really carrying out, a transition from ISI to export-driven growth. In most cases the regimes have flinched from the more painful aspects of the reform package and instead only partially liberalised. There are several reasons for this: in states such as Algeria, Egypt, Iraq, and Iran oil and gas revenues, as well as revenues from the Suez Canal and aid from the USA in the case of Egypt, have made it possible to continue ISI much longer than oil-poor Turkey and Tunisia could afford to. In addition, Turkey and Tunisia have had a more market-orientated leadership and a stronger technocrat class than most of the other republics. Furthermore, the will to reform in the Middle East has been caught up by the legitimacy problem. Because most regimes initiated their reform measures from a weakened position as a strategy of survival, they were in a weak position to withdraw privileges. A state enduring a legitimacy crisis will experience difficulties in cutting subsidies, demolishing monopolies, and shutting down unprofitable businesses. As Hudson points out, the legitimacy deficit reduces the rulers' authority.

Parts of the economic liberalisation programme were easier to carry out than others. Typically, the first matters to be liberalised under the *infitah* reforms concerned foreign trade. After decades of high customs duties or even state import monopolies, it suddenly became far easier to import foreign goods into the country. As we have seen, the idea was to pressure domestic companies to perform better. But improvements in industry are a time-consuming process, so exports did not rise at the same pace as imports creating a deficit in the balance of trade. To pay for the increased imports, states that had no oil revenues were obliged to borrow large sums. At the start of the 1980s all the early *intifah* countries, Turkey, Egypt, Tunisia, and Morocco, landed in debt. The crisis forced their regimes to accept the structural adjustment programmes of the World Bank and the IMF. The financial institutions would contribute capital in return for these states cutting their subsidies to agriculture and industry, dismantling the welfare state, and devaluing their currencies. The consequences were worse conditions for the population, especially the urban poor, which in turn prompted 'bread riots'. In Turkey opposition to structural adjustment was a contributory factor behind the military coup in 1980.[7]

As protection against political instability the regimes have slowed the pace of liberalisation and cultivated the clientelist aspect of it. The regimes delay restructuring for as long as possible ensuring that any reduction in the role of the state benefits those who are loyal. This double challenge of reform may be illustrated by experience from privatisation. As a measure in the policy of removing their safeguards, *infitah* recommended privatising state corporations. The idea was to improve productivity through increased competition, but the desired effect has not been achieved for two reasons: first, the regimes have been very cautious and slow to privatise. As Alan Richards and John Waterbury underline, the Middle East reform period, in stark contrast to those of Latin America and Eastern Europe, has not reduced the weight of the public sector in the economy.[8] Quite simply, the regimes have not dared take the chance of large numbers of workers and bureaucrats suddenly finding themselves without a job and privatisation has been used to build a client network and to enrich the rulers' families.[9] The productivity gain to be won by allowing private actors to compete presupposes that they compete under equal conditions. But from the way privatisation has been practiced in the Middle East, certain entrepreneurs have had inside information, bureaucratic shortcuts, and cheap loans, all of which have ensured that they have won the competition without having to improve productivity. The regimes have preferred a loyal private sector to private firms that really perform well. Under *intifah* certain companies grew huge through bonds with the political elite. A crowning example is Arab Contractors in Egypt, which under Ahmad 'Usman Ahmad's management became the Arab world's biggest construction company in the 1970s and 1980s. Ahmad was a personal friend of President Sadat and a former minister and Member of Parliament and, thanks to his political contacts, he gained advantages in purchasing state companies and protection against bureaucratic obstacles.

The hope of *intifah* had been to strengthen support for the regime through economic progress. At the beginning of the eighties, however, economic development in the Middle East stagnated. The region's per capita growth was 0.5 per cent between 1975 and 1998 against 1.3 per cent on a world basis.[10] Only sub-Saharan Africa performed worse in the same period. Partial liberalisation of the authoritarian development state has given the worst of two worlds by keeping the disadvantages of socialism and adding the problems of capitalism. The regimes have increased social differences by dismantling the welfare state without improving productivity. State corporations have been sold without democratic control while large and cumbersome bureaucracies have been kept. Fear of instability has prevented the reforms from working as they should.

Political reform

Far from representing a solution, the failed economic liberalisation of the 1980s became part of the legitimacy problem.[11] Not only did *intifah* raise the cost of living, unleashing bread riots, but the regimes had become bound in debt to Western creditors. It was bad enough for the reputation of those in power to have to starve the public sector, but worse that they do so on the orders of the IMF and the World Bank since the structural adjustment programmes of the 1980s and 1990s could hardly be sold as home-made. Once again, as in the nineteenth century, free trade was undermining the sovereignty of states.

In this context the regimes played a new reform card to strengthen their legitimacy. The next step was to liberalise the political system. The rulers promised to clean up the state and grant freedom to society. Once again the pioneer was Egypt. In 1974 Sadat ended the one-party system and opened up for pluralism. Husni Mubarak continued this positive development by freeing political prisoners, allowing a more critical press, and liberalising political processes. The elections of the 1980s were less marred by obvious manipulation than before, and in the parliamentary elections of 1987 the opposition won 20 per cent of the votes.[12] Other countries showed similar movement. Tunisia first flirted with political liberalisation in 1981 and then opened up considerably after Zine al-'Abidine ben 'Ali took over power in 1987; Algeria and Jordan introduced political reforms in 1989; in 1990 Yemen declared that the unification of north and south would bring democracy to the Arabian Peninsula; Kuwait reintroduced parliamentarism in 1992; and in the same year Morocco, too, liberalised its constitution.

All these reform initiatives had a lowest common denominator, since they all occurred at a point in time when the respective countries were under pressure and had an acute need for popular support. President Sadat was assassinated in Egypt in 1981, a powerful reminder of how unpopular the Egyptian regime had become in certain sectors of society. In Tunisia Ben 'Ali deposed his predecessor Habib Bourguiba in a coup d'état and had to convince the people of the legitimacy of his rule. In Algeria, Jordan, and Morocco structural adjustment unleashed violent protests, and in Yemen and Kuwait the rulers sought national atonement in order to rebuild the country after, respectively, the unification of north and south in 1990 and the Iraqi occupation of 1990. As this book demonstrates, the Middle East regimes have found mechanisms for ruling in spite of legitimacy problems. A regime possessing little legitimacy can survive on a daily basis by a combination of bribery, habit, and fear. But when highly profiled individual events focus people's attention and wrath, a legitimacy deficit can soon be a legitimacy crisis. The danger of a coup or revolution is greatest when symbolic cases incite the people to fight against the state. By the end of the eighties several of the above mentioned regimes were in open confrontation with their inhabitants. The Hashemite royal house in Jordan was badly shaken when a rebellion broke out in tribal areas that traditionally had been an important base for the regime. The rebels in the southern town of Ma'n were not Palestinians, with whom the royal house had long had a strained relationship, but Bedouins whom the monarchy regarded as a bastion of support. Disturbances in Algeria in 1998 were also serious for the Algerian regime, when thousands protested against cuts in state subsidies, and as a result about 500 demonstrators lost their lives.[13] The regime had to resort to reformism to calm the discontent.

In the states that 'eased the pressure', non-governmental organisations (NGOs) and new political parties developed. The classical corporatist period was in decline and 'civil society' seemed to bloom. The NGOs became involved in everything from democracy and civil rights to child labour, the environment, and women's liberation, while the parties challenging the government created debate in parliament. Optimism was in the air after the fall of communism in Eastern Europe. Researchers poured in to examine 'democratisation' in the Middle East.[14] However, the rumours of the death of authoritarianism were exaggerated as, nearly twenty years later, no Arab country has taken the step towards real democracy. Instead the regimes have astonished the world with their ability to modernise their control mechanisms and adjust to new conditions.

The key to the regimes' handling of civil society has been a selective inclusion and exclusion of NGOs and opposition parties. By allowing criticism and independent organisation up to a certain point but ruthlessly repressing those that go too far, the rulers have managed to moderate parts of the opposition and isolate radical regime opponents. Maha M. Abdelrahman, taking Egypt as model, shows how the authorities undermine the NGO's independence with the aid of a mixture of oppression, regulation, co-option, and corporatisation.[15] Through restrictive association laws the regimes, initially, set limits on how civil society organisations can be financed and operate, while the more politicised are gagged. The state further erodes their independence by appointing VIPs as patrons or by founding their own NGOs (GO-NGOs, or government-initiated NGOs). Béatrice Hibou refers to this form of indirect control as 'redeployment of the state' meaning that individuals and groups that share the regimes' interests, ideology, and network move into civil society as 'private' actors. In such cases NGOs present no threat, but instead privatise the control function previously exercised by the state. [16]

As an example, in Egypt, Jordan, Qatar, and Syria the first ladies, Suzanne Mubarak, Queen Rania, *Shaykha* Moza, and Asma al-Asad, profiled themselves by starting and supporting organisations campaigning for everything from youth to women, education, cultural development, micro-finance, and the environment. These activities reap wide international recognition and contribute sorely needed goodwill to elite groups that are otherwise often accused of feathering their own nests.

In encountering opposition groups, the regimes have known how to respond effectively and flexibly. Opposition parties are tolerated to a far greater extent than thirty years ago, but must accept operating under difficult conditions, in that the authorities manipulate the electoral process[17], introduce limits in party law, reduce the challengers' broadcasting time on television, and make political use of election observers and the judicial system. Nonetheless, participation under such conditions is a better alternative for most groups than exclusion. Ellen Lust-Okar has shown how selective inclusion of opposition parties gives opponents of the regime conflicting interests and weakens the will to work together.[18] Through reformism, moderate groups are given the chance to operate openly, criticise political decisions, and recruit voters with alternative programmes. As long as the criticism stays this side of the red line, the challenging group can obtain party or press subsidies. More uncompromising opposition groups, on the other hand, are ostracised, prevented from mobilising their supporters and suffer physical oppression. In this way the rulers create incentives for moderating criticism and seeking influence from the inside. Lust-Okar shows how what she calls such 'divided structures of contestation' muffle political crises. Moderate groups that initially have everything to win by making themselves the spokesmen of popular discontent tend to stop mobilising when they get the support of radical regime opponents.[19]

Technological reform

As well as economic and political reform the rulers have also promoted their ability to bring about change through improvements in technology and infrastructure, or what one might call 'technological reform'. The aim is for the people to associate their leaders with progress and creating national enthusiasm for prestige projects. As those in power all over the world in all ages have understood, the fight for legitimacy partly takes place in the symbolic arena. From the size of the pyramids in ancient Egypt via the height of the church towers of medieval Europe to our era's space programmes, rulers have demonstrated their power and ability. The Middle East regimes, too, distinguished themselves by similar symbolic feats: for example, in 1984, Mu'ammar Qadhafi laid the foundation stone of the world's biggest irrigation canal, the Great Man-made River (Arab. *al-nahr al-sina'i al-'adhim*), from subterranean freshwater springs in south Libya across the country to the Mediterranean coast. According to

Qadhafi, the purpose was to 'make the country as green as its flag' in what he immodestly described as 'the world's greatest wonder'. The irrigation system consists of more than 1,300 wells, most over 500 metres deep, which daily supply agriculture and the cities of Tripoli, Benghazi, and Sirt with 6.5 million m³ fresh water – winning an entry in the *Guinness Book of Records*.[20] In a desert country such as Libya the development and symbolic profit of such a project is obvious. The mega project's contribution to the country's long-term development is, however, a more open question. The subterranean springs are up to 40,000 years old and non-renewable and consequently conservationists and geologists fear that Libya is flushing its most vital resource into the sea at record speed.

On the Arabian Peninsula, the monarchies battle ferociously for who can build the highest skyscraper, the most luxurious hotels, the largest shopping malls, the best high-technology centres, and so on – only the imagination sets the limits – not the finance. Aided by the oil boom since the beginning of the twenty-first century, the monarchies have started their own star premier league for prestige through symbols of modernity, wealth, and progress. The Emirates have engaged in building seven star hotels and attaining skyscraper records. But no sooner had Burj al-Khalifa become the world's highest building with its 828 metres, than Kuwait announced it would build a tower of 1,001 metres (the allusion is of course to 1001 Nights), while Saudi Arabia unveiled plans for a mile high tower (1,609 metres) in Jeddah.[21] Furthermore, in the area around the Ka'ba in Mecca the Saudis are constructing a 130-storey skyscraper complex to house the city's pilgrims.[22] The Emir of Qatar, Hamad al-Thani, made a mark early on in technological reform, when after deposing his father in a coup in 1996, he started the satellite channel *al-Jazeera*. The channel was a media revolution in the Arab world and put the 'Lilliput' country on the map: first in the Middle East, then gradually all over the globe. In 2003 Saudi Arabia challenged *al-Jazeera* by opening the Dubai-based satellite channel *al-Arabiya*. In his attempt to distinguish himself as a world leader the Emir of Abu Dhabi invested on the environmental front: the prestige project, Masdar City, has been presented as the world's first zero-emission city, exclusively based on recycling and solar energy over an area of 6 km². That the rest of Abu Dhabi with its colossal oil production has one of the world's heaviest per capita carbon footprints has not stopped the environmental organisation WWF from celebrating Masdar as one of its flagships.[23]

In Iran the leadership has made mastery of atom technology a symbol of what the nation can do. The regime came under pressure from the Western powers for neglecting to report parts of its nuclear activity to the International Atomic Energy Agency, IAEA, but emerged victorious at home for defending Iran's inalienable right to nuclear technology under the Non-Proliferation Treaty. In the Iranian narrative of the nuclear issue, the crisis is about the West not allowing the country technological development. Not least President Ahmadinejad has made the nuclear question a foundation stone in his populist–nationalist rhetoric. While tensions were at their height with the USA, Ahmadinejad would proclaim, at regular intervals, the so-called 'good nuclear news' (Pers. *khabarha-ye khosh-e haste'i*) that under his leadership Iran had reached new technological heights. In this way he compensated for an irresponsible economic policy and the crackdown on reform activists under his rule, trusting that the nuclear issue would unify the nation. Between February 2006 and January 2007 thirteen other Middle East countries jumped on the bandwagon, announcing new or restarted plans for developing atomic energy.[24]

Technological reform was also pursued in other less spectacular forms, for example, permitting new communication technologies in the strictly controlled republics. The use of internet, mobile phones and satellite television has exploded since the 1990s, changing the lives of millions in the Middle East. The communication revolution represents both a threat and an opportunity for the regimes. On the one hand, the possibility of controlling the flow of information and shaping the consciousness of the citizens is weakened as globalisation brings new voices into the political debate, contributing to a form of pluralism. On the other hand, the development is a trump card the rulers can wave to emphasise that their rule brings progress to the country. Syria's President Bashar al-Asad, for instance, has constructed a modernisation image around his interest in computers and his background as Chairman of the Syrian Computer Society. At the same time the authorities build extensive surveillance and regulatory systems to prevent regime opponents from operating. Access to the internet is particularly strictly regulated with centralised control over servers, censorship of sensitive pages, restrictions on the use of home pages as well as on the opening of internet cafes.[25]

As with economic and political reform, the authorities distinguish between technological reform that strengthens and weakens their position.

Case study: Morocco – from Hassan II to Muhammad VI

> Article 19: 'The King, Commander of the Faithful, Supreme Representative of the nation, Symbol of its unity and guarantor of the permanence and continuity of the State, ensures the observance of Islam and the Constitution.'[26]

In 1999 Muhammad VI took over after his father Hassan II as the King of Morocco. Hassan II had reigned for a very long time, since 1962, and had become the symbol of the regime. He was known as 'the strong man', both at home and abroad. Most of the population had known no other ruler. Father-to-son changes of leadership are critical times in all person-dependent regimes. In Morocco the king has to fill the role of both political and religious head. It was therefore quite a challenge for prince Muhammad VI to fill his father's shoes. During his regency, however, Muhammad VI seems to have become very popular in Morocco. He is spoken of as 'a popular king' and 'a man of action'. Indeed most observers estimate his popularity as greater than his father's. How has Muhammad VI sought legitimacy as Morocco's new monarch?

Tradition and charisma

Max Weber originated a central paradigm in the study of legitimacy. According to Weber, authority may be legitimised in three main ways; through charisma, tradition, and legality (the rule of law). In the first model the exercise of power gains legitimacy by the ruler possessing special personal qualities such as piety, strength or courage. In the second, the ruler justifies his rule by watching over and bearing tradition. Legal authority is founded on the rulers abiding by the law.[27] For Weber, of these three, charisma is historically the 'original' source of legitimacy. Charismatic personalities gain authority in primitive societies because their physical or spiritual strength makes them 'natural leaders'.[28] However, charisma is an ephemeral source of authority: it only ensures support as long as the ruler proves his qualities; it must continuously be defended against challengers and seldom can be passed on from father to son. For authority structures to be maintained over time, charisma must be made a matter of routine. Tradition and the rule of law are here the two principal routes a ruler can follow.

The strategy of the Moroccan royal house builds on a tradition-based institutionalisation of charisma. The corner stone in the monarchy's claim of authority is the image of the king as 'the commander of the faithful' (Arab. *amir al-mu'minin*).[29] Caliph 'Umar, who ruled the Islamic empire between 634 and 644, was the first to use this title of honour, which was later adopted by the succeeding caliphs. In other words the title alludes to Islam's 'golden age', presenting Morocco's 'Alawi dynasty as a continuation of the Caliphate. Since the end of the ninth century a series of dynasties have succeeded each other on the western edge of the Arab world that the Arabs call the *maghrib*, 'where the sun goes down'. The founder of the first sultanate, Idris, was a descendent of 'Ali, the Shi'a Muslims' first *imam* and the fourth caliph in the Sunni tradition, and, moreover, a nephew of the Prophet. He was both the political and religious leader of the Idris dynasty (788–1055), and began thereby a tradition of religious legitimation that has characterised rulers in northwest Africa up to the present day.[30] Under the Almohads (1156–1269) the sultan was acclaimed caliph, and in the fifteenth century, under the Merinids (1258–1471), he took the title *amir al-mu'minin*. Mawlay Sharif, who also claimed he descended from the Prophet through 'Ali, founded the present Moroccan 'Alawi dynasty.

The 'Alawi king's status as *amir al-mu'minin* gives a form of traditional authority that Weber calls 'functional charisma'. By this he means that particular personal qualities are often attributed to a figure of authority through his functions – often in religious contexts. For example, Catholics believe that priests partake of 'holy authority' through ordination – in this case, it is not the priest's personal qualities that give him 'holiness' but the church that is in a holy tradition. Nonetheless, it aids the church's credibility if the priest is, in fact, a moral person. Even if functional charisma is a form of traditional legitimacy and in principle independent of personal charisma, the two mutually influence each other. The function legitimises the person, but his personal qualities also influence the institution. The same applies to the role of *amir al-mu'minin* in Morocco. To enter into a tradition that goes back to the Prophet gives the king an aura of piety. All the same, functional charisma in itself is no guarantee of real authority. If the king is unable to ensure his people's security and welfare, his reputation declines.

In step with political and economic conditions and the rulers' personal suitability the 'Alawi dynasty's authority has varied over time. The rulers have always used their religious prestige to justify the collection of taxes and the raising of armies, but history is full of examples of the sultan being challenged by tribal warriors in alliance with competing religious leaders.[31] As with other pre-modern states, the 'Alawi sultanate's extent varied greatly. Under strong sultans the central power expanded to include new territories and they were able to levy heavier taxes. In periods of decline, in contrast, the dynasty lost authority over the population and came under pressure from rival groups. From early on in the 'Alawi dynasty the relationship between centre and periphery was described as a tension between *bilad al-makhzan*, 'the land of the treasury', and *bilad as-siba'*, 'the land of revolt'. *Bilad al-makhzan* was the dynasty's core area where the sultan had complete military control and powers of taxation. *Bilad as-siba'*, on the other hand, comprised the more peripheral areas where the tribes held back taxes to the central powers and opposed the sultan's authority. To conquer these areas the sultan had to mobilise large forces and force the population into obedience and at regular intervals in Morocco's history there have been such raids on the periphery. The frontier between *bilad al-makhzan* and *bilad al-siba'* could be observed when one ruler died and a new sultan ascended the throne. After negotiations between the sultan and public officials, all those who recognised the new ruler had, according to tradition, to swear allegiance (Arab.

bay'a) in an official ceremony. In this way society signalled that it regarded the ruler as legitimate. In the same way, those who refused to take part in the *bay'a* signalled that they did not recognise the sultan's authority and would expect him to attack them as soon as he had gathered his forces. A consequence of this political game, as John Waterbury has pointed out, was that the sultan was constantly obliged to build alliances with strong groups in society in order to maintain his hegemony.[32] These pacts with elite groups had to be regularly renegotiated: no sultan was capable of establishing his authority over a long time. The apparatus of power (*makhzan*) only existed for as long as it generated profit for those involved and in itself enjoyed no structural legitimacy.[33]

At the start of the twentieth century the 'Alawi dynasty's legitimacy was at its lowest. The sultan was no longer able to carry out basic functions such as keeping law and order and protecting the state from foreign attacks. The state was weakened by internal revolt and by external debt to the Western colonial powers. In 1912 Morocco was divided between a French and a Spanish protectorate. But France and Spain did not abolish the 'Alawi dynasty. Instead the French enthroned a weak sultan, Yusuf (1912–27), as religious and traditional 'alibi' for a government that in reality was under the authority of their local representative. The sultanate was reduced to a cipher and, as a puppet for the occupying powers, the 'commander of the faithful' lacked real legitimacy. But when the sultan as a religious symbol was linked to the nationalist movement under Yusuf's successor, Muhammad V (1927–61), the *makhzan* would regain legitimacy. Muhammad V was less easily controlled than his predecessor, associating himself with the nationalist resistance to the colonial powers. In an attempt to make it easier to govern the protectorate France took away the sultan's political authority and sent him into exile in 1953. But this strategy proved counterproductive, for popular protests increased, and all at once Muhammad V became the Moroccan liberation struggle's symbol and main focus. In other words, thanks to French actions and the liberation movement's support, the religious legitimation potential of the sultan was reactivated. When Morocco won its independence in 1956, Muhammad V emerged as a ruler enjoying broad popular support and a saint-like religious authority.[34]

Hassan II's legitimising measures

Even though the conflict with France had strengthened the position of the 'Alawi dynasty in the national consciousness of the Moroccans, Muhammad V's prestige was not inherited by his successor Hassan II (1961–99). When Hassan II ascended the throne at 32-years-old, he had not the charisma nor the religious aura his father had gained through his conflict with the colonial power. But the unwritten pact between subjects and ruler that had arisen under Muhammad V was institutionalised in the country's first constitution in 1962. Article 19, since unchanged, states as follows: 'The King, Commander of the Faithful, Supreme Representative of the nation, Symbol of its unity and guarantor of the permanence and continuity of the State, ensures the observance of Islam and the Constitution. He is the protector of the rights and liberties of the citizen, social groups, and collectivities.'[35] The constitution was ratified in a referendum by 97 per cent of the votes.[36] But the legitimacy of Hassan II was not secured once and for all and in the same way that Muhammad V had written himself into the hearts of the people during the liberation struggle, Hassan II had to fill his symbolic role with meaning. Observers of Moroccan politics in the 1960s doubted that this was possible.[37] However, analysts underestimated the significance of functional charisma and not least Hassan II's personal abilities.

The nationalist movement in Morocco was strong at this time. Hassan II was under pressure from both the liberation party Istiqlal, and from revolutionary socialism, in Morocco represented by the founder of the socialist party (UNFP), Ben Barka. The anti-imperialist Ben Barka, with support from Gamal 'Abd al-Nasser, wanted to replace the 'feudal' monarchy with a socialist republic. The battle for power between the palace, Istiqlal and UNFP in the 1960s climaxed when Moroccan intelligence agents kidnapped, tortured, and killed Ben Barka in Paris in 1963.[38] After this, for the left, the legitimacy of the royal house had worn pretty thin and in the following years, the *makhzan* had to repeatedly crush student rebellions with the aid of the police and security forces. In two attempted coups d' état, in 1971 and 1972, the king miraculously escaped death. That Hassan II survived these attempted coups helped build the myth that he was protected by God through *baraka* (blessing).

The Green March

Religious legitimacy inherited from forefathers was not enough to ensure Hassan II's seat on the throne, but in 1975, the king finally found a cause that could unite the nation. It was the issue of Western Sahara, a sparsely populated desert region south of Morocco that had been a Spanish province since 1885. UN resolutions of 1972 and 1973 recognised the right of Western Sahara to become an independent state. However, Morocco claimed a 'historic right' to the region based on former times' *bay'a* from desert tribes, asserting that the colonial powers had artificially separated Western Sahara from Morocco. There is broad agreement in Morocco that Western Sahara constitutes a natural part of the country. Hassan II's offensive against the region was, therefore, ideal to ensure support for the monarchy. In 1975 the king gathered 350,000 Moroccans in the south along the border with Western Sahara for a popular march, 'The Green March' (Arab. *al-masira al khadra*), into the territory. This mass gathering stood out as a nationalist triumphal procession – a popular protest against imperialism – that was also loaded with religious symbolism. Hassan II gave the marchers the Qur'an and the red and green flag, the colours of Islam and Morocco, ordering them to face Mecca and worship Allah as soon as they crossed the border.[39] As *amir al-mu'minin* he declared the march a defensive *jihad*, and thereby a duty for all Muslims: the number of volunteers was set at 350,000 to symbolise the number of Moroccans born each year. To mark its faith and its unity the community should sacrifice, as the king put it, 'a year's harvest'.[40] The Green March was like a repeat of the liberation struggle and a masterly piece of political strategy. For not only did Hassan II awaken the Moroccans' national sentiment but at the same time it hastened Spain's retreat. That the Western Saharan independence movement Polisario, with Algerian support, took up the fight against Morocco only contributed to promote even more unity in Moroccan ranks. Even the left recognised Hassan's leadership in this territorial conflict and restarted talks with the regime. By taking a 'national concern' under his own banner, Hassan II took the sting out of the nationalist movement's threat.

A fresh threat to the king's authority, however, was already emerging in the Islamist movement. In 1974 the religious leader 'Abd al-Salam Yasin wrote an open letter to Hassan entitled 'Islam or the Deluge', in which he questioned the monarch's piety.[41] The letter was an attempt to bore a hole through Hassan II's functional charisma and publicly discredit him. According to Article 23 of the Moroccan constitution the person of the king is 'holy' (Arab. *muqaddas*) and 'sacrosanct' (Arab. *la tuntahak hurmatuhu*), a principle Yasin boldly rose above by addressing Hassan II in an informal, direct manner. In the letter Yasin presented himself as the king's religious mentor. After having underlined that he himself is descended from the Prophet, through the founder of the first sultanate, Idris, he corrects Hassan II for his errors and advises him to 'return to Islam'. For a ruler who claims legitimacy for his rule through being the supreme religious authority, this attack was extremely dangerous. Hassan responded by locking Yasin up in a psychiatric ward for three and a half years. But the threat from the Islamic movement was not over. In 1987 Yasin founded the al-'Adl wa-l ihsan movement, 'Justice and Benevolence', to promote his agenda. Two other factors helped to wear down the monarch's popularity in the 1980s. The first was the structural adjustment programme (1983–93), which on the advice of the IMF reduced subsidies, unleashing several 'bread riots'. The second was Hassan II's decision to take part in the Gulf War on the side of the Western coalition. On 3 April 1991, close to a million Moroccans demonstrated against this decision.[42] Towards the end of his reign Hassan II cultivated reformism in order to lessen the pressure and win new support for the regime. He made a truce in Western Sahara and declared the beginning of an inner liberalisation. A constitutional amendment of 1992 increased the authority of parliament and wrote 'human rights' into the constitution. In 1998 for the first time an opposition politician, 'Abd al-Rahman Yusufi, became prime minister.

Muhammad VI's reformism

When Hassan II died on 23 July 1999, the country's elite immediately swore *bay'a* to the new king. Leading clerics reminded people that according to tradition *bay'a* is 'part of God's law, which binds the faithful to their leader and the *imam*'.[43] As Hassan II's successor, Muhammad VI shall have 'inherited his father's secret' (Arab. *waratha sirrahu*).[44] Nevertheless, to succeed as a king it is not enough to inherit his father's charisma. Like Hassan II and Muhammad V before him, the new king must fill the role of *amir al-mu'minin* with meaning. Because of the colonial era his father and grandfather could play on nationalism but at the beginning of the twenty-first century, however, the anti-imperial card was no longer so easy to use: Moroccans today are more concerned with democracy and economic development. Hassan II will not go down in history books as a great moderniser: in 2001 Morocco came a poor 126th place of the 175 countries classified in the UN's Human Development Index. Life expectation was only 68, a mere 30 per cent were registered in lower secondary education, and only 48 per cent of Moroccans over the age of 15 were literate. The difference in development between town and country was enormous. In the countryside on average 72 per cent were illiterate and as many as 82 per cent of women.[45] So Muhammad VI had enough challenges to deal with. He took over the baton from his father and built his platform on 'reform'.

'The king of the poor'

Muhammad VI spent the first months of his reign signalling that he was the king of all his people. He saw the weak and marginalised, and offered reconciliation to Hassan II's enemies. As crown prince Moroccans had become familiar with him as a generous and merciful person and in the 1990s his father had made him head of the Muhammad V Foundation, where he led the fund-raising campaign for children in distress. In Morocco Muhammad VI is spoken of as 'generous towards beggars' and 'respectful towards the weak'. It did not take long before he won the nickname 'the king of the poor'. But it was not just the poor the king brought in from the cold. Muhammad also stretched out his hand to individuals, groups of people, and parts of the country that Hassan II had ignored. In September 1999 he arranged the journey home of Morocco's most profiled exiled opposition figure, Abraham Serfaty, winning much approval for this. Later he also freed Yasin from the house arrest that Hassan II had ordered. In October 1999 Muhammad VI made a symbolic tour of the Rif in northern

Morocco, where, as revenge for a previous uprising, Hassan II had never visited. He also promised to complete the construction of a motorway north that Hassan II had stopped a couple of kilometres south of Tangiers. During his tour of the Rif, Muhammad VI sought direct contact with the inhabitants, moving among them without much in the way of security,[46] and he let himself be filmed in the old town of Fez on his way through narrow, winding alleys. The contrast with Hassan II could not have been greater, since, because of the attempted assassinations, the old king usually stayed within the palace surrounded by an army of guards. The pictures showed that Muhammad VI did not fear his people. The new king also declared he would give greater rights to the Berbers, who constitute about half of the population.[47] In 2001 he opened, with great ceremony, a royal institute for Berber culture, declaring that, as the son of a Berber woman, he could not deny 'his culture and his genes'.[48]

The theme of 'human rights' has been central to Muhammad VI's reformism. In his first speech to the Moroccan people Muhammad VI promised to work for 'the rule of law, human rights and individual and collective liberties'.[49] Shortly after, he asked the Palace's Human Rights Council, Conseil Consultatif des Droits de l'Homme (CCDH), to establish a 'Compensation Committee' responsible for awarding financial compensation to families that had been the victims of abuse committed by the state in the period 1971–90, known in Morocco's history as the 'lead heavy years' (Arab. *zaman al-rusas*/French *les années de plomb*). After the failed coups of the early 1970s, Hassan II had mercilessly suppressed his political opponents, but towards the end of his reign he had wanted reconciliation and to improve his reputation. As part of the liberalisation of the 1990s, he signed the UN convention against torture and founded the CCDH and a separate Human Rights department.[50] Muhammad VI took this reformism to new heights when, in 1999, he dismissed his father's right-hand man and Morocco's Minister of the Interior since 1979, Driss Basri, who for many years was the symbol of breaches of human rights under Hassan II. In 2004 Muhammad VI founded a 'Truth Commission' to chart these human rights breaches during his father's reign. The commission's charter was to 'discover the truth, (...) prevent the recurrence, (...) and make things right for reconciliation'.[51] A former prisoner of conscience, Driss Benzekri, was appointed chairman of the commission and it caused quite a stir that an Arab regime was investigating the human rights situation under its previous leader. The Truth Commission allowed the victims to give testimony of their sufferings in open TV broadcast hearings. This focus on human rights is good news for Morocco, but one should not be blind to the fact that the reform discourse also has its strategic aspect. Muhammad VI cultivates the image of himself as a champion for justice and human rights in order to win inner support and exterior recognition. On the

Truth Commission's home pages one can see pictures of 'moved families of the victims of human rights breaches' thanking the king in his palace.[52] Moreover, Morocco has gained praise internationally for its positive development. As Hassan II understood in the early 1990s, human rights have become a key word in international politics and a source of legitimacy – that none of the abusers from the 'lead heavy years' are actually punished does not seem to spoil the effect. The Truth Commission is the perfect response to the US-led discourse on the need for democracy and human rights in the Middle East.

Muhammad VI's reform of family law (Arab. *mudawwana*) in October 2003 aroused even more international attention. In an area where Hassan II was known for cultivating patriarchal structures, Morocco suddenly introduced one of the most progressive family laws in the Middle East. The new *mudawwana* was a triumph for women's rights as it removed former demands of 'obedience to men' and the need for a male guardian to get married. It also increased the minimum age for marriage from 15 to 18 years. While previously men had the exclusive right to divorce and could do so by simply saying 'I divorce you' three times on the spot, *mudawwana* introduced the right to divorce for women and abolished divorce by word of mouth. The new family law also made it possible for women to gain custody of the children in the case of divorce.[53]

Muhammad VI had long hesitated to introduce family law reform because of resistance from Islamists. However, after the radical Islamist bomb incident in Casablanca on 16 May 2003, the king became more decisive, and the Islamist movement was on the defensive.

The limits of reform

There are, nonetheless, clear limits to the king's reform enthusiasm. Muhammad VI has been particularly lukewarm about transferring power from the palace to elected institutions. In his second speech to the nation in August 1999, the king declared his support for the principle of constitutional monarchy, calling for a new concept of authority in Morocco.[54] He has later described himself as a 'democrat', referring to his reforms as part of a 'democratisation' process.[55] Optimism was great, therefore, when in his first year Muhammad VI dismissed Hassan II's advisers, replacing them with young technocrats. It was envisaged that the autocracy would vanish when democracy-orientated liberals replaced the old guard. However, so far reformism has done more for the king's charisma than for democracy in Morocco – liberalisation has created an image of Muhammad VI as popular, progressive, and vigorous, but not loosened the palace's grasp on politics. Even while praising democracy, Muhammad VI has founded royal committees in strategic areas to monitor the country's government. The king's handpicked men on these committees lay down guidelines that the official government is obliged to follow. It is also Muhammad VI who appoints key members of the government such as the Minister of the Interior, the Foreign Minister, and the Minister for Islamic Affairs. Prime Minister Driss Jettou was not even a representative for the largest coalition in parliament when the king asked him to form a government in 2002.[56]

According to opposition politician and researcher 'Ali Bouabid, Moroccan politics suffers from a division between authority and responsibility. For Boabid democracy is characterised by the decision makers having to answer for their actions, while in Morocco, he continues, 'those who have most power have least responsibility'.[57]

What Bouabid is referring to is the problem of a system dependent on a few people, but that likes to present a democratic façade. Behind this façade of a multiparty system and free elections, politics is still governed by clientelist mechanisms. Only the king and his closest advisers can allocate big funds and take major political decisions. The elected representatives know from experience that they cannot operate independently and therefore try to please the king to get support for their projects. To succeed a politician needs to have the backing of the palace. The paradox, however, is that formally the government bears responsibility for the country's politics: everything is presented as though the elected really governed and could then be held responsible when things go wrong. For example, the Moroccan newspaper *Le Journal* reported in April 2004 that Muhammad VI had scolded his ministers for the lack of results. 'You are a bunch of incompetents', raged the king, 'with one or two exceptions'.[58] The question is, commented the paper, whether the ministers have the authority to act. After the earthquake in al-Hoceïma in February 2004, the members of the government received much criticism because none of them visited the disaster area in the first three days. But the reason, according to *Le Journal*, was that the king had decided to go there and none of the ministers dared to visit the area before Muhammad VI for fear of taking the honour from the king.[59]

In other words, dependency on the monarch's support paralysed the political system. In the short term this way of ensuring the king's legitimacy may seem useful. As the unique, powerful actor the Palace appears 'energetic' and Muhammad VI as 'benevolent'. It is the king that the television cameras focus on when successful or glorious missions are to be carried out. When things go wrong, on the other hand, the government gets the blame. The palace uses the elected as shock absorbers for society's anger, but in the long term such manipulation of 'democracy' is not viable. Muhammad VI and his court technocrats cannot modernise Morocco by themselves. To ensure future social and economic development the country needs a system that works. That means first and foremost clarifying the power relationship between the palace and the government. As long as the decision takers are dependent on the king and the elected have no clear constitutional powers, the Moroccan authorities will continue to be inefficient. The Moroccan constitution, in which the king appoints the government and can dismiss them 'on his own initiative' (Article 24), is a recipe for clientelism. But the public will not remain patient forever with the palace's filibuster tactics. Electoral turnout was at an all time historic low at 37 per cent in 2007 (against 51 per cent in 2002 and 58 per cent in 1997), with a spoilage rate of as much as 19 per cent due to ballot papers being either blank or spoilt, speaks of sinking popular confidence in the system.[60] Opposition politicians, civil society organisations, and intellectuals press for a real democratisation. Up till now, writes Driss Ksikes in the magazine *Tel Quel*, Muhammad VI's reforms has been, as it were, 'a revolt against his father'.[61] The new king strode over the symbolic barriers from the reign of Hassan II but without making fundamental changes and if the king really wanted democracy, concludes Ksikes, he would introduce a new constitution.[62] But so far Muhammad VI's reform portfolio has had no room for this essential change.

Conclusion

After 1970, the Middle East regimes have cultivated reformism to ease the pressure of the legitimacy problem. The aim has been to create an impression of change – that the rulers 'are dealing with problems' – without upsetting fundamental power relations. The Moroccan example illustrates how Muhammad VI tries to represent something new within the status quo. He continues basic principles in the royal house's exercise of power, while at the same time breaking with the past. Other heads of state in the region have made use of similar legitimising strategies. The regimes promise to 'reform themselves', politically, economically, and technologically. After the crisis in the authoritarian development state, the rulers first tried economic liberalisation. The hope of *infitah* was to strengthen support for the regimes by granting special privileges to selected groups and strengthening economic growth. But the power elite soon realised that the reduction of state subsidies increased the danger of instability. So the regimes postponed the heavier parts of the reform package, ending up with a mixture of socialism's inefficiency and capitalism's 'survival of the fittest'. The next step was political liberalisation – popular discontent should be soothed by 'democratisation'. But here too the inhabitants were to be disappointed. Political reforms have been introduced from above, but without altering the fundamental power relations. The rulers have also attempted to diffuse attention through technological reform. By and large, reformism in the Middle East has been a survival strategy. The regimes have bought time – satisfying some – so as to prevent a collapse. All the same, the question is whether this strategy can last. Reformism arouses expectations that real changes will happen. This cannot be put off forever.

Further reading

Abu-Rabi', Ibrahim M.: *Contemporary Arab Thought: Studies in Post-1967 Intellectual History.* London and Sterling: Pluto Press, 2004.

Bourquia, Rahma and Miller, Susan Gilson (eds.): *In the Shadow of the Sultan: Culture, Power, and Politics in Morocco.* Cambridge, MA: Harvard University Press, 1999.

Dawisha, Adeed: *Arab Nationalism in the Twentieth Century: From Triumph to Despair.* Princeton and Oxford: Princeton University Press, 2003.

Heydemann, Steven (ed.): *Networks of Privilege in the Middle East: The Politics of Economic Reform Revisited.* New York and Basingstoke: Palgrave MacMillan, 2004.

Henry, Clement M. and Robert Springborg: *Globalization and the Politics of Development in the Middle East.* Cambridge: Cambridge University Press, 2001.

Hopfinger, Hans (ed.): *Economic Liberalization and Privatization in Socialist Arab Countries.* Gotha: Justus Perthes Verlag, 1996.

King, Stephen J.: *Liberalization against Democracy: The Local Politics of Economic Reform in Tunisia.* Bloomington and Indianapolis: Indiana University Press, 2003.

Navaro-Yashin, Yael: *Faces of the State. Secularism and Public Life in Turkey.* Princeton and Oxford: Princeton University Press, 2002.

Niblock, Tim and Rodney Wilson (eds.): *Economic and Political Liberalisation in the Middle East.* Aldershot: Edward Elgar Publishing, 1999.

Richards, Alan and John Waterbury: *A Political Economy of the Middle East.* Boulder. CO: Westview Press, 2nd edition. 1998.

Tibi, Bassam: *Arab Nationalism: Between Islam and the Nation-State.* Basingstoke, London and New York: Macmillan Press, 1981.

Tozy, Mohamed: *Monarchie et islam politique au Maroc.* Paris: Presses de Sciences Po, 1999.

6 Islamism

Independence, freedom, Islamic republic![1]

When the Shah of Iran had to flee in 1979, and an Islamic republic replaced the West-friendly Pahlavi monarchy, there were few observers who believed their own eyes. The fifty-four-year-old dynasty was regarded as one of the strongest and most stable regimes in the region. Iran's army was well equipped, numbered 400,000 men, and acted as the prop and mainstay of the USA's security interests in the Gulf. At home the Shah was known for encouraging industrialisation, education, and secularisation. According to modernisation theory, such forms of development should undermine the role of religion. However, in practice the results were the contrary, for the 1979 revolution brought Islam to the very centre of politics. Iran's new head of state, Ruhollah Khomeini, was a 77-year-old Shi'a scholar who called for 'the guardianship of the Islamic jurist' (Pers. *velayat-e faqih*). According to this doctrine a scholar learned in *shari'a* law should supervise the government of the country.

The Islamic revolution put Islamism on the map, giving the impression that the political order of the region was about to tumble. The revolution's victory over the Shah inspired Islamist groups throughout the Muslim world, and many dreamed of copying the deed in their mother countries. Since 1970, Islamism has grown into the most important language of opposition in the Middle East and Islamist movements are the best organised social force in most countries in the region. Should the Middle East regimes fall or be democratised, the chances are great that Islamic-orientated groups would come to power. However, so far most regimes have survived the challenge of Islamism. The prophecies of widespread Islamist takeovers in the wake of the 1979 revolution in Iran have not materialised.

In this chapter we shall deal with the following question: why did Islamism gain in strength after 1970 and why have the Islamist movements failed to gain power in any more states in the Middle East? To shed light on the regimes' steadfastness we shall examine the case of Egypt, where the Islamist movement has particularly strong roots. How has President Husni Mubarak dealt with the ideological challenge of the country's Islamists?

What is Islamism?

Islamism is a modern intellectual and political movement that seeks to bring society and politics into agreement with Islam. The underlying idea is that Islam constitutes a 'total system' which should be applied in all spheres of life. In most cases this leads Islamists to call for an 'Islamic state' where *shari'a* is the foundation for the law. In the history of ideas the background for this revivalism dates back to the nineteenth century, when the Ottoman Empire was undermined by imperialist expansion. As mentioned in Chapter 2 this meeting with European superiority led Muslim intellectuals to some soul searching. For reformers such as Jamal al-Din al-Afghani (1839–97) and Muhammad 'Abduh (1849–1905) Muslims had to return to the original, the 'real' Islam in order to revitalise the Middle East.[2] It is this idea that a true Islam is the solution to the region's problems, which inspired twentieth-century Islamist movements. The Muslim Brothers (Arab. *al-ikhwan al-muslimun*) in Egypt is usually looked on as the first Islamist movement. The brotherhood was founded in 1928 by Hasan al-Banna. Originally, it was an Islamic revival and welfare organisation, but early on it began to interpret Islam as a basis for demands for political participation and reform. Through efficient organisation and massive support it was the first political force capable of challenging Egypt's ruling elite without belonging itself to the elite.[3]

It is usual to distinguish between 'moderate' and 'militant' Islamist groups. Beyond the seeming convergence on the ideal of an Islamic state, there is a great deal of disagreement among Islamists about how this state should be organised and what strategies should be adopted to realise it. Moderate Islamists operate within established political channels, working to influence opinion from below at the same time as they strive to Islamise the grass roots in order to gain popular support. Their concept of the Islamic state has room for pluralism and many call explicitly for democracy. Among such currents are the Muslim Brothers in Egypt, Hizb al-'adala wa-l-tanmiya – better known under its French acronym PJD – in Morocco, Jabhat al-'amal al-islami (the Islamic Action Front) in Jordan, and the Islah Party in Yemen.

Militant Islamists reject the moderates' idea of gradual reform in favour of confronting the regime. Their strategy for establishing an Islamic state is characterised by secret organisation and violence. Militant Islamist movements gladly portray *jihad*, in the sense of 'armed battle', as a 'religious duty'. The term jihadism is therefore often used of militant Islamism. Another typical feature of militant Islamist ideology is *takfir,* which means to 'declare (someone) an infidel (*kafir*)'. By stigmatising their opponents as 'infidels' militant Islamist groups seek to legitimise their attacks on them. The model for such *takfir*-orientated groups is often the Egyptian activist Sayyid Qutb (1906–66). In prison under Gamal 'Abd al-Nasser Qutb wrote the militant pamphlet *Milestones* (Arab. *ma'alim fi-l tariq*), where he characterises contemporary Muslim society as 'heathen' (Arab. *jahiliyya*).[4] The expression *jahiliyya* is normally used of society in the Arabian Peninsula before the Prophet's revelation, and in the same way that Muhammad distanced himself from the heathendom of the time, Qutb calls on his contemporaries to reject today's regimes. *Milestones* addresses a vanguard of pious Muslims who must withdraw from *jahiliyya* society and attack the non-Islamic. This recipe for establishing an Islamic state has been adopted by groups such the Groupe Islamique Armé in Algeria and al-Gama'a al-islamiyya in Egypt.

Since the end of the 1990s some militant Islamists have become more global in their orientation. While Islamist movements usually focus on the struggle against the regimes in the Muslim world, new movements have sprung forth primarily concerned with attacking the USA and its allies. This so-called global jihadism sprang directly from militant Islamists from all over the world being gathered in training camps in Afghanistan under the Taliban regime (1996–2001). Battle training, organisation, and the ideological indoctrination in these camps was the starting point for the infamous al-Qa'ida network.[5] Even if the network has been much weakened through 'the war on terror', its ideological heritage lives on, spreading to new groups.

Other Islamists put less emphasis on the political part of their message and concentrate on missionary work (Arab. *da'wa*) and religious practice. The growth of religiously defined political activism since the 1970s has gone hand in glove with a more widely defined religious awakening, which calls people to Islam. Everything from slick TV preachers such as 'Amr Khalid, Tariq M. Suwaydan, and Habib 'Ali, to Sufi-based mass movements such as Nurcu/Fetullah Gülen in Turkey,[6] Jama'at Zayd in Syria,[7] and the world-wide Tablighi Jama'at[8] contribute in this direction. The actors in this awakening have their focus on religious faith and belief and, in some cases, are explicitly apolitical. Nonetheless, they can be accounted part of Islamism because they contribute towards a general Islamisation and have a totalistic conception of public space as 'Islamic'. The so-called Salafi direction (from Arab. *al-salaf,* 'the forefathers') is a scripturalist variant of the awakening-orientated Islamism. Salafi-orientated Islamists regard the Prophet and his closest successors as the perfect role model for Islamic life and conduct, wishing to imitate them in everything. This ambition leads them, among other things, to condemn the Muslim Brothers' use of modern organisation principles such as trade unions and political parties as deviations from a healthy Islamic tradition (Arab. *bid'a*). It also rejects 'Western' ideologies and institutions, such as nationalism, socialism, democracy, parliaments, and presidents, demanding a return to the 'authentic' Islam.

Islamism is in other words a collective term for very different phenomena, and one must therefore be careful when generalising about Islamist groups. The various Islamist movements also represent varying challenges to the Middle East regimes. While the militant groups' use of political violence may appear to be the most immediate threat to regime stability, in many ways moderate Islamism constitutes a bigger structural threat to the rulers. It is in fact moderate Islamism's popularity that would make it hard for the regimes to retain power should they hold free elections.

Why Islamism?

Few questions have created more debate among Middle East experts over the last thirty years than what is the explanation for Islamism's growth. For those who try to find their way in the intricacies of the literature it may seem as though there are as many accounts of Islamism as there are researchers. Certain arguments, however, recur in the analyses, which for simplicity's sake can be sorted into five main categories.[9]

In the nature of Islam

First there is a concept that Islamism is spreading because Islam is a 'political religion'. Adherents of this explanation point out that the founder of Islam, the Prophet Muhammad (570–632), was at one and the same time a secular and a religious leader. While Jesus never possessed political power and Christianity during its first centuries was divided from the state, the Prophet and the succeeding caliphs were society's highest authority in all areas. From a theological viewpoint it is claimed that Islam's basic commandment about *tawhid* (unity, to declare that God is one) prohibits dividing society into a religious and a secular sphere. By pointing to such characteristics of Islam and its history, this argument attempts to explain Islamism by referring to the religion's 'essence'. The belief is that there is a core in Islam that remains the same throughout time and which makes politics and religion one and the same for Muslims. 'Essentialists' such as Bernard Lewis and Emmanuel Sivan draw an unbroken line from the situation at the Prophet's epoch to the struggle to reunite the religious and political spheres in our own time.[10] Explaining current affairs by analogy with events from the seventh century is not without its problems. What Muslims do, say, and think today is influenced by a historical experience, a political reality, and a technological development that did not exist at the time of the Prophet. The essentialistic argument gives little thought to changes that have taken place in the Muslim world over the last two hundred years. But Islamism was precisely produced by developments during the nineteenth and twentieth centuries. It was, for instance, Mustafa Kemal's decision to abolish the Caliphate in 1924 that opened up new thinking about Islam's political organisation and gave nourishment to the demand for the establishment of an Islamic state.

The four remaining categories all take into account that Islamism is a product of modernising processes in the Muslim world: factors such as the Middle East's meeting with Western philosophy, imperialism, capitalism, and globalisation are given more emphasis than seventh-century events. The manner in which the various schools of thought interpret the phenomenon is still very different.

A conservative reaction

The second explanatory model regards Islamism as a conservative reaction. Islamism is understood in this perspective as a rebellion against modernity's way of thinking, against the loss of community, morals, and absolute truth. An example of this approach is found in Bruce Lawrence's classic *Defenders of God*.[11] Those Lawrence calls 'fundamentalists' accept the modern in the shape of material change (such as new technology), but will defend traditional moral values and the absolute truth against modern man's relativism. What is interesting about Lawrence's approach is that Islamism does not appear as a peculiarity of the Muslim world, but puts it in a bigger context of neo-religious movements struggling against the loss of social morals in encountering modernity. However, critics will object that the analysis in presenting Islamism as a conservative reaction exaggerates the reactionary nature of the project. Islamists are not always 'conservative' in the sense of wanting to preserve the status quo; on the contrary, they often attack the existing political order and spokesmen for a passive, traditionalist Islam. Most Islamists agree on the need for *ijtihad* (new interpretation) to adapt Islam to present day society.

A response to development crisis

The third explanation regards Islamism as a reaction to a development crisis and to unfulfilled expectations. Because the regimes in the Muslim world have not given their populations economic and political development, the argument runs, the inhabitants have used Islam to take their fate into their own hands. Supporters of this theory point out that Islamist movements often build welfare networks and help their people with health, education, and security. They also stress how Islamists take on popular demands for a democratic or just society.[12] A pioneer of this type of analysis is the Egyptian Political Scientist Nazih N. Ayubi.[13] His starting point for explaining the growth of Islamism is twofold: first, the Arab world's difficult encounter with the market economy and imperialism, and second, the crisis in the populist–authoritarian development state that has discredited all forms of secular ideology. The transition from economic and political discontent is, however, the crux of the matter in most analyses that consider Islamism as a reaction to disappointed expectations. It is one thing to describe people's frustrations and problems but, in itself, this cannot explain why precisely Islam became the language of opposition. Studies that exclusively explain Islamism against a background of socio-economic conditions fall into the opposite trap to the essentialists. While the latter try to explain everything by religious peculiarities, the former give Islam no explanatory power whatever. In order to understand the dynamics of Islam we must also take religion itself into consideration and recognise Islam's potential as a symbolic language.

Symbolic liberation

The fourth explanatory model focuses precisely on the symbolic aspect of Islamic ideologies and interprets Islamism as cultural liberation and a search for identity. The basic explanatory element for this school is that the Muslim world has gone through the transition to the modern world in a position of inferiority *vis-à-vis* the West. Political and social modernisation has taken place under Western hegemony, both before and after the states became independent. An expression of this hegemony is that political theories and ideals have normally been imported from the West. Westernised elites have thrust alien concepts on a population living in a traditional world picture and who felt the elite's modernisation was an attack on their identity. In contrast the Islamists speak the language of Muslim society: they talk politics using terms and images that appeal to the people. An example of this type of analysis is François Burgat's *L'Islamisme au Maghreb*.[14] The author claims that the core of Islamism is an attempt to regain 'a pre-colonial symbolic universe'. Islam is especially suited to such an attempt since it has a vocabulary which is untainted by the colonial era. 'One cannot express the rejection of the West using its language and terminology', argues Burgat. 'How better to mark the difference (...) than to employ a language that is different from its own, along with a system of codes and symbols that seem foreign to it?'[15] In this perspective Islamism is a parallel to the liberation of US Afro-Americans as it is summed up in the lyrics of a well-known James Brown song: 'Say it loud, I'm black and I'm proud'. However, critics claim that anti-imperialism's self-awareness and Islamism's focus on cultural distinctness have been an excuse for depriving citizens of liberty internally in Muslim society. In this perspective intolerant attitudes render impossible Islamism's supposed liberation potential.[16] To support their claims critics will then refer to political oppression in countries, such as Afghanistan, Iran, and Sudan, which have experienced Islamic rule.

Pietist modernisation

As a final and supplementary explanatory category Bjørn Olav Utvik draws a parallel between Islamism and pietism in the Protestant Christian tradition. According to the Norwegian historian, both are an expression for a modernity-related individualisation and both combine a lifestyle characterised by pains-taking contributions to society and religious reform. Like the eighteenth-century's pietist movement, today's Islamist movements are in opposition to contemporary society and make use of an idealised picture of the past to promote an alternative order. In this perspective the core of Islamism is that the individual feels a moral responsibility for realising God's kingdom as it should truly be: to be a Muslim becomes a *call* to fill one's life with a striving for a moral and just society.[17] Prolonging this argument, Utvik claims that Islamism must be regarded as a modernising force, since it promotes individualisation and, through a broad popular mobilisation, draws new social groups into politics, seeking to adapt Islam to the challenges of the modern state.[18] For instance, many Islamists want the law to be codified in an Islamic state. However, writing down standardised laws based on *shari'a* is a breach of traditional Islamic practice in which the clerics are consulted on each individual case. In many other fields Islamism represents a corresponding new interpretation of religion that points not to the past, but, according to Utvik, rather moves the Muslim world into 'the modern'. Nevertheless, sceptics feel that Utvik is too optimistic in his assertions of Islamism's modernising force. For them the Islamist movements are characterised by reactionary and totalitarian features – linked to their view of women and their organisation culture – which have dragged the Muslim world into a blind alley.

Modern mass politics

No matter whether one shares the view of Islamism as a modernising force for the Middle East or not, it is clear that Islamist movements represent a popularisation of religious authority. While Islamic teachings have traditionally been communicated by the *'ulama*, the Islamist movements are often characterised by non-clerical leaders: the founder of the Muslim Brothers, Hasan al-Banna, was a primary school teacher; Sayyid Qutb was a journalist and bureaucrat, and the al-Qa'ida ideologist Ayman al-Zawahiri is originally a paediatrician. Shi'a Islamist movements in lands such as Lebanon, Iraq, and Iran have traditionally had a larger contingent of clerics, but often young and inexperienced clerics who have also challenged traditional religious authorities. Apart from Ayatollah Khomeini the revolutionary members of the Iranian clergy in 1979 were mostly newly trained students, and the same is true of the Shi'a Islamists in today's Iraq. None of the leaders of al-Majlis al-'ala al-islami al-'iraqi (better known under its English acronym ISCI) bears the title of ayatollah. Muqtada al-Sadr is a mid-ranking cleric, and the Da'wa party has always had a strong lay tradition, placing little emphasis on religious prestige.

Social anthropologists explain the rise of half-educated or unauthorised persons to the leadership of Islamic movements by such phenomena as the education revolution and urbanisation. Whereas people previously lived in a traditional worldview in which they listened to their clerics and obeyed Islam's rules by force of habit, a higher degree of literacy has given Muslims direct access to the scriptures and other religious texts, in addition to which, the encounter with other life styles have enhanced awareness of the self. The result is an individualisation of the relationship to religion that not only explains the growth of self-appointed interpreters of religious injunctions but also the fact that people listen to them.[19] The strengthening of the Islamist movements after 1970 must be viewed in this context.

The last point that needs mentioning in this brief account of the reasons for Islamism's growth is the strength of the Islamist movements' organisation. It is not a matter of chance that Hizballah is the most potent political party in Lebanon, that Hamas has outrivaled PLO in Gaza, or that Sadr supporters and ISCI were the first to set their stamp on Iraqi civil society after Saddam Husayn's fall. Efficient internal organisation has, in many cases, rendered Islamist groups robust when faced with war and oppression. Already in the 1930s the Muslim Brothers were renowned for the strength of their internal organisation. Al-Banna built the brotherhood by careful selection of its members and strict discipline.[20] He obtained his model from the traditional *sufi* brotherhoods with separate local branches coordinated by a strong central leader and gradual promotion through the hierarchy. At the same time the Brothers adopted such modern action activities as appeals, media campaigns, flyers, and mass demonstrations. After more than twenty years' existence, by 1949 the Brotherhood numbered 2,000 local branches, 500,000 members and roughly as many sympathisers.[21]

In her study of the Egyptian Islamist movement's expansion between 1970s and the 1990s, Carrie Rosevsky Wickham has updated the picture of the efficiency of the Muslim Brothers' organisation. Wickham shows how the Islamist movement escaped the corporatism of the Egyptian state by organising in the Islamic sector. Whereas leftist and nationalist oppositions were eradicated by the state's control of parties, trade unions, and various other organisations, the brotherhood used a combination of private mosques, Islamic welfare organisations, and firms to recruit new members and strengthen its hold in society.

By the end of the 1980s the Islamists had established a decentralised mobilisation structure consisting of thousands of mosques, small firms, health clinics, aid organisations, and schools. The structure was hard for the government to control and gave the brotherhood flexibility. Early in the 1990s, with the aid of this decentralised mobilisation network, the Islamist movement gained control over important trade unions such as those of the doctors, the lawyers, and the engineers with more than two million members.[22]

Why have Islamists not gained power?

There is a mismatch between the social and ideological dominance of the Islamist movements in the Middle East, on the one hand, and the small number of states where Islamists have in fact taken over power, on the other. Apart from Iran, Islamist movements have enjoyed greatest success either in weak political units such as Iraq and Palestine or those that are particularly democratic such as Turkey. There is also much debate as to whether the Turkish Adelet ve Kalkinma (AK) Party, which won the 2002 and 2007 parliamentary elections, should be considered an Islamist party. Although its leaders historically emerged from within the Islamist trend the AK Party does not formulate its political ideas on the basis of Islamic identity and explicitly refuses the idea of mixing politics and religion.[23] To explain why Islamist movements have failed to take over power in more countries in the Middle East we shall first study the regimes' survival mechanisms, second, the problems confronting the Islamist movements themselves and, finally, examine how Western governments, out of fear of Islamism, prop up the Middle East's authoritarian regimes.

The battle for authority

In their book *Muslim Politics* Dale F. Eickelman and James Piscatori demonstrate how the Islamist movements make use of the political potential of Islam's symbolic language.[24] The Islamic cultural heritage consists of a number of expressions, images, and myths that may be used to mobilise support, as people associate them with central values. Examples of such symbols are the veil for women (Arab. *hijab*), the Qur'an and the Prophet Muhammad, the Muslim community (Arab. *umma*), holy war (Arab. *jihad*), and the concept of an Islamic state (Arab. *dawla islamiyya*). By linking its demands to the need for the defence of such values, the Islamic movements win moral gravity or what we may call 'symbolic power'. The Islamic movement that overthrew the Shah of Iran in 1979 illustrates well how symbolic power can be applied. The most frequently used symbol during the revolution was the story of Husayn, the third Shi'a *imam*, who in 680 died at the Battle of Karbala (in present day Iraq) against the Ummayad Caliph Yazid. Ever since, the memory of the *imam*'s death has been an important symbol of the suffering of the Shi'a and their identity. The event is the origin of the annual period of mourning *'ashura* in the Muslim month *muharram*, where the faithful beat their chests in memory of Husayn. In the lead up to the 1979 revolution the *'ashura* festival played an important role in mobilising support and demonstrators frequently carried pictures of the *imam*. The revolutionary ideologue 'Ali Shari'ati interpreted the resistance to the Pahlavi dynasty as a repeat of Husayn's fight for justice, and Khomeini compared the Shah with the Umayyad Caliph Yazid. Just as the *imam* had sacrificed his life at Karbala in 680 so must the Iranians be prepared to suffer martyrdom for the sake of the revolution. Shari'ati had formulated the slogan thus: 'Every month is *muharram*, every day is *'ashura* and every piece of earth is Karbala.'[25] Overall, the symbol Husayn functioned as an important mobilising factor in the Iranian revolution. Moreover, it was destructive of the Shah's legitimacy that so potent a symbol should be credited to the opposition to the regime.

Opposition movements are not the only ones to make political capital of Islamic symbols. Learning from episodes such as the 1979 Iran revolution, regimes threw themselves into the struggle for religious authority, the focus of which is what meaning are people are to associate with religious symbols. While regime critics interpret them so as to discredit the rulers, the latter attempt to turn the symbols in their favour. Let us take, for instance, the concept *jihad* used in the Qur'an and mentioned in the sayings traditionally ascribed to the Prophet (Arab. *hadith*). Beyond a broad understanding of *jihad* as a struggle against forces that harm religion there is no agreement among Muslims on how this symbol is to be interpreted.[26] Certain militant Muslims have argued that the *jihad* command must be understood as 'war against the infidel' and that the rulers in the Middle East are to be looked on as infidels. In the book *al-farida al-gha'iba* (*The Forgotten Duty*) from 1981 the founder of the militant Islamist group Tanzim al-jihad, 'Abd al-Salam Faraj, included non-orthodox heads of state as legitimate targets.[27] In the same year that Faraj wrote the book a member of Tanzim al-jihad assassinated the Egyptian president Anwar al-Sadat. Naturally, the Egyptian regime rejects Faraj's interpretation of *jihad*. At the state-controlled university *shaykh* Muhammad 'Abd al-Wahhab al-Tantawi (1928–2010) emphasised that groups such as Tanzim al-jihad were committing heresy and that *jihad* could not be waged against other Muslims. In other words a war is going on between the regime and in this case militant Islamists over the contents of Islamic symbolism. Each side is battling for the symbols to be perceived in such a way as to serve their interests.

A battery of measures is available to heads of state who wish to enhance their religious image: attending public prayer meetings, going on a pilgrimage (*hajj*), referring to the Qur'an in their speeches. Other possibilities are to build beautiful mosques – and name them after themselves – or to use Islam's symbolic language in statues, memorials, and posters. During the Iran–Iraq War (1980–8) Saddam Husayn had the enormous Qadisiyya monument in Baghdad erected in memory of the battle of the same name in 637, when the Arab Caliphate defeated Iran and brought the Persians under Muslim overlordship. The president also had posters printed of himself riding a white horse that he had distributed in Shi'a Muslim areas in southern Iraq. The aim was to appear as a pious ruler and friend of the Shi'as. Shi'a Muslims are used to seeing pictures of the white horse from icons of *imam* Husayn.

It is important to underline that the regimes have different starting points in their efforts to construct religious legitimacy and a main distinction is between republics and monarchies in the region. Most republics are founded on the idea that 'the people' and not God are the basis of the authorities' rule. In addition they have usually gone through phases of socialist thinking causing the leaders to view Islam with scepticism. As we have previously seen, the populist–authoritarian state wanted to undermine the traditional elite, including the religious class, and to modernise Islam. Mustafa Kemal went so far as to forbid the *sufi* brotherhoods, religious dress, Arabic alphabet, and call to prayer in the language of the Qur'an. Popular worship was not compatible with Kemal's concept of progress. Monarchies, on the other hand, do not have the same prehistory of attacks on religious institutions and a state-dictated reform of Islam. Leftwing radical revolutionary ideologists have never governed them. Neither have they ever subjected the clergy to the same degree of corporate control. On the contrary, the royal families of Saudi Arabia and Morocco have tried to present themselves as the guardians of Islam as a measure in a greater campaign for legitimacy that emphasises tradition.

The historical differences between how monarchies and republics have related to religion plays into the way they have tackled Islamism. In the republics the tendency has been to confront the Islamist at the same time as the leaders have used state control of religious institutions to promote a regime-friendly understanding of Islam. Countries such as Tunisia, Egypt, and Syria have prohibited Islamist parties, leaving them very little room for movement. Prominent Islamists are imprisoned, their books banned, and activities such as meetings, demonstrations, and so on, imposed severe restrictions. Violent clashes occurred between police and Islamists; in some cases the rulers have used the army to subdue the movements. Against militant Islamists the regimes used even stronger measures such as torture and abductions. The most extreme example was the oppression during the civil war in Algeria in the 1990s. The occasion was the Islamist party Front Islamique du Salut (FIS) being permitted, in a rare gesture from the government's side, to participate in local and parliamentary elections. FIS won 55 per cent of the votes in the local elections in June 1990 and stood to gain a majority in the national assembly after having secured 188 seats in the first round of the parliamentary elections in December 1991.[28] The traditional ruling party, Front de Libération Nationale, failed to meet the challenge and stood to lose the second round. At this point the army executed a coup to 'save' the situation. President Chadli Benjedid was deposed, the FIS leaders detained, and the second round of elections cancelled. More than 10,000 FIS activists were arrested during the first months of 1992 and the judiciary formally dissolved the party. The oppression led to militant Islamist groups openly attacking the regime. Prior to the armed forces crushing opposition by the end of the 1990s, more than 150,000 Algerians had lost their lives.[29]

Turkey distinguishes itself from the Arab republics in going somewhat further in accepting Islamist parties. In 1996 Necmettin Erbakan became the country's first Islamist prime minister in coalition with Tansu Çillers conservative Doğru Yol party. However, within a year Erbakan was warned to resign by the army in what has been described as a 'post-modern coup'. Four of Erbakan's succeeding political parties have been disbanded.

The monarchies have tackled the challenge of the Islamist movements in a somewhat less confrontational manner. On the one hand this is due to a relatively high threshold for pluralism in lands such as Kuwait, Morocco, and Jordan and, second, that the monarchs are more used to handling Islam's symbolic language than the presidents. The royal houses of Morocco, Jordan, and Saudi Arabia have long included Islam among their legitimising strategies, and even for the more 'secular-based' monarchies such as Kuwait and Oman, it is easier to play on religious symbols without suffering conflict with other ideologies (socialism, republicanism, modernism, and so on). Therefore the monarchies have been able to incorporate Islamists in politics to a greater degree than the Arab republics. Jordan and Morocco in particular have gone far in allowing Islamist parties, and in Kuwait around one-third of the members of parliament are Islamists. The strategy seems to be to co-opt the more moderate elements of the Islamist parties at the same time as harshly oppressing militant Islamists. It is important to stress that Morocco and Saudi Arabia cannot launch a direct attack on all forms of Islamism given that the regimes so clearly have part of their legitimacy based in Islam. The Sa'ud and 'Alawi dynasties' use of religious symbols makes it easier to communicate with the Islamists, but simultaneously obliges the regimes to live up to the religious ideals they assert.

The problems of Islamist movements

Islamism lacked impact not only because of the strategy and manoeuvring of the regimes: it was also inhibited by several internal problems. Naturally, which of

these applied varied from situation to situation, but nonetheless, there are recurring features with Islamist movements. First, the Islamist movements suffer fragmentation and schism, which weakens their impact. In fact, what we designate as
Islamism is as we noted at the beginning of this chapter a hold-all term. Its contents range from politically liberal groups working for public accountability and
democracy to apolitical Salafis that condemn the regimes for allowing society
to drown in 'social disorder' and Western cultural invasion. It houses Western-
orientated intellectuals who consider the regimes illegitimate because they serve
the interests of the upper class, while simultaneously embracing free market ideologists who accuse the regimes for failing to protect private property and for
too much state intervention in the life of the individual. Such tensions combining with personal conflicts have led to schisms within Islamist movements in
most countries. In Iraq the merchant-class oriented ISCI is vying for power with
the Sadr militias that recruit among the urban poor.[30] In Algeria alone, there
are three moderate Islamic parties – Harakat mujtama' al-silm (the Movement
for the Peace of Society), Harakat al-islah al-watani (the Movement for National
Reform), and Harakat al-nahda (the Renaissance Movement), while al-Qa'ida
fi-l maghrib al-islami (al-Qa'ida in the Islamic Maghrib – previously GSPC) and
Humat al-da'wa al-salafiyya (Defenders of the Salafi Mission) fight for control
over the country's militant Islamists.[31] In some cases a strong and charismatic
leader can compensate for this lack of unity. One important reason for the success
in 1979 in Iran was that Ruhollah Khomeini managed to unite the various components of the revolutionary movement. Leaders with corresponding charisma
and the same broad popular appeal as Khomeini are, however, seldom. None of
today's Islamic movements have front figures with similar unifying force.

Second, and partly as a result of internal dissension, many Islamist movements suffer from a lack of a clear political agenda. Criticism of the regimes is
usually specific and well formulated, but lucidity vanishes as soon as it is a question of an alternative political order. Beyond loose slogans like 'the Qu'ran is our
Constitution' and 'Islam is the solution', Islamists are far better at saying what
they are against than what they are for. Most support the establishment of an
Islamic state but have problems expressing what this means in practice. Which
political institutions should such a state possess and what characterises the relation between the rulers and the ruled? What does it mean that the law is based
on *shari'a* and how should the law be codified? Several thinkers have attempted
to answer such questions, but rarely have Islamist movements converted the
answers into a concrete political programme. In this sense, Islamism, with its
modest degree of theorisation, is more a marker of identity and opposition than
a complete political ideology.

Third, Islamism is hindered by a lack of universality. As we have seen, it is based on symbols unique to one religion. Not only does this exclude non-Muslims and the secular, it also easily leads to Islamists landing in cultural conflicts. While an earlier Marxist revolutionary ideology regarded exploitation of the working class as a global problem and appealed to workers in all countries to join in a common cause, the Islamist project is founded on the difference between Muslims and non-Muslims. Admittedly, Marxism, too, was built on a division, that between the bourgeoisie and the proletariat. However, the groups excluded by Islamist ideology are far larger. Even Shi'a Muslims are not granted an equal status in Sunni-dominated states and vice versa. Moreover, this focus on religious differences places the Islamists in danger of 'forgetting' their political project in favour of the cultural project of purifying society of Western or 'non-Islamic' elements. Some Islamists are far more concerned with combating immorality in society – whether it involves the use of alcohol, unmarried boys and girls partying together or women not wearing the veil – than with removing the rulers.

Fourth, and partly as a consequence of the above, these movements lack alliances with other oppositional groups. Whereas overturning regimes from below in the Middle East requires broad popular mobilisation, the Islamists have only managed to a small extent to gather support among the non-Islamist opposition. There are various reasons for this. In some cases this isolation is due to the above-mentioned lack of clarity in the Islamists' programmes for an Islamic state. Many secular Muslims and non-Muslim regime opponents are simply frightened of what will happen if the Islamists come to power. As long as the Islamists fail to reassure them that the Islamic state will guarantee religious freedom and minority rights, these groups will prefer the existing regime to Islamist rule. In other cases, the reason is that the Islamists themselves are not open to cooperating with others. There are honourable exceptions that show that Islamism has the potential for a broader appeal. In Egypt the moderate section of the Muslim Brothers joined with the Coptic intellectuals in 1996 to gain authorisation to start a political party, Hizb al-wasat.[32] In Turkey the reformist Fazilet Party incorporated non-Islamic conservatives in 1999 and invited three female intellectuals to join the party leadership.[33] The extent of this type of alliance building has, however, been limited. Islamist movements by and large are still cut off from other oppositional forces.

Fifth, the radicalisation of violence among militant groups threatens to undermine sympathy for Islamist movements among the population at large.[34] During the 1990s, the scale of violent actions committed by militant Islamist groups increased, and with the growth of jihadism the attacks have become ever more spectacular. The development in Algerian Islamism after the 1992 military coup is a telling example. Whereas FIS originally kept a clear non-violent pro-file, the dissolution of the party led to violent Islamists going on the offensive. Between 1992 and 1998 militant groups such as the Mouvement Islamique Armé, the Armée Islamique du Salut (AIS), and the Groupe Islamique Armé (GIA) were in armed conflict with the regime. The latter adopted particularly violent methods in their battle to Islamise society and destroy the regime which was a result of warriors returning from the war in Afghanistan occupying dominant positions in the group. These men were accustomed to a far higher level of violence from Afghanistan than the local Islamists. During the civil war the GIA distinguished itself by attacking civilians, kidnapping and killing foreigners, placing bombs in public places, and ambushing travellers. All this peaked between 1996 and 1998 when GIA began its extermination campaign against its opponents, periodically massacring several hundreds each night in villages and small towns. With these atrocities popular support for the Islamists crumbled away in the Algerian population. More moderate groups such as the AIS laid down their arms and the army regained control over the territory. In 2001, the former Algerian officer Habib Souaidia claimed that in the 1990s the regime had actively contributed to the brutalisation of the conflict in order to discredit the Islamists.[35] According to Souaidia, the armed forces had both abstained from preventing massacres by militant Islamists and, disguised as religious fanatics, had themselves killed civilians, so as to be able to blame the Islamist movement. The former Algerian Defence Minister, Khaled Nezzar, sued Souaidia for defamation of character in a French court but suffered a humiliating defeat. Later Nezzar tried to clear his name in a book titled *L' armée algérienne face à la désinformation: le procès de Paris.*[36]

Western fear and support

Since the end of the Cold War, Islamism has overtaken the role of Communism as the West's principal bogeyman. Particularly after 9/11, Islamic terrorism and its international media star, Usama bin Ladin, have been depicted as the incarnation of evil. Academics, politicians, and journalists have all contributed to creating this picture. Intellectuals such as Alain Finkielkraut, Slavoj Zizek, and Hans Magnus Enzensberger have presented Islamism as 'our time's totalitarianism' and a 'danger for Western civilisation'.[37] Politicians in the USA and Europe who defend the 'war on terror' like to compare, as did the former US Minister of Defence Donald Rumsfeld, Islamism with fascism.[38] The focus of the media on spectacular Islamist actions contributes only further to identify Islamism with terror. The result is a general fear of Islamism in the West that does not just include militant groups but also any political movement whatsoever which makes use of Islamic symbolic language.

Regimes in the Middle East have known how to exploit this fear to secure external support in the fight against Islamism. Rulers such as Husni Mubarak, Ali 'Abdullah Salih, Mu'ammar al-Qadhafi, and 'Abd al-'Aziz Bouteflika would not have been able to repress Islamist movements so effectively without Western assistance. After 2001, the Bush administration gave these Middle East regimes weapons, trained their special forces and intelligence agents as well as providing other forms of support as part of 'the war on terror'. Western politicians seldom object when these regimes persecute, torture, and kill suspected Islamists.

Case study: Egypt – Husni Mubarak's high wire act

Article 1: 'The Arab Republic of Egypt is a Socialist, Democratic State (...)'

Article 2: 'Islam is the Religion of the State and (...) the Principal Source of Legislation is Islamic Jurisprudence (shari'a) (...)'[39]

On 6 October 1981, during a military parade in Cairo in memory of the 1973 war against Israel, Egypt's president Anwar al-Sadat was assassinated. He had just greeted the troops from his tribune when infiltrators from the militant Islamist group Tanzim al-jihad opened fire from the procession. Sadat's vice-president, Husni Mubarak, sat by his side. He escaped unscathed from the attack and took over the presidential office. From his first day in power it was obvious to Mubarak that the most pressing challenge he faced was dealing with the threat from militant Islamism. At the time of writing Husni Mubarak has been in office for almost 30 years. You have to go back to Pharaoh Ramses II around 3,000 years ago to find an Egyptian ruler who has held power for longer. How has Mubarak tackled the ideological challenge of the Islamist movement?

Ideological tightrope walk

Egypt is an example of what Daniel Brumberg calls 'liberalised autocracies' in the Middle East. According to Brumberg such regimes are characterised by blending authoritarian rule with pluralism.[40] They are liberal in the sense of permitting a degree of openness in civil society, the press, and the electoral system. In addition to Egypt other instances of liberalised autocracies are Morocco, Kuwait, and Jordan. In these states the ceiling for regime criticism is higher than elsewhere and opposition politicians are allowed to stand for election, sit in parliament, and even hold ministerial office. As long as the opposition operates within certain understood 'red lines', the state does not utilise its repressive system. The liberalised autocracies' selective use of repression is in stark contrast to what Brumberg calls 'total autocracies'. Such regimes, with zero tolerance for political competition and debate, are what are usually referred to as dictatorships. Total autocracies allow their opponents no voice. Opposition leaders are hidden away in jails or executed, the press is gagged, and parliament purely decorative. Iraq under Saddam Husayn was the closest to this model in the Middle East. Other total autocracies, according to Brumberg, are Syria, Libya, and Tunisia.

For Brumberg the liberalised have the advantage over the total autocracies in that they can play various political currents against each other and strike a balancing act between competing groups. The rulers attempt to play the role of broker between social and elite groups in conflict. Ideologically, this results in liberalised autocracies rarely having a clear profile. Jordan's King 'Abdallah, jokes Brumberg, performs as a Westernised businessman on Monday, a liberal intellectual on Wednesday, a military officer on Thursday, and a pious *shaykh* on Friday.[41] Liberalised autocracies do not stake the state's legitimacy on one ideological horse: in reality they have no state ideology but rather navigate between social currents and 'set their sails to match the wind'. In this respect they distinguish themselves from total autocracies that seek hegemony for the state's official ideology. Liberalised autocracies are ideologically non-hegemonic and therefore adaptable. Thanks to their ideological flexibility they can not only tolerate Islamist movements but also integrate them into the state apparatus. Partial inclusion, according to Brumberg, is the best way to ensure regime stability, because it obliges the Islamists to refrain from violence and play by the government's rules, whereas, totally rejecting the Islamist increases the danger of conflict and revolution.[42]

However, in the case of Egypt, ideological flexibility has also produced ideological confusion. Since the change of course under Sadat in the 1970s the Egyptian regime has strived to find its identity. The foundation for the regime's official justification is still that the revolution of 1952 liberated Egypt from imperialism. Mubarak's most important legitimation argument is that he stands in the tradition of the Free Officers who ended the British-dominated monarchy and promised progress and modernisation. In the foreword to the constitution 'freedom', 'development', and 'Arab unity' are promoted as core values.[43] Article 1 describes Egypt as a 'socialist, democratic state.[44] Even though the heritage of Gamal 'Abd al-Nasser is formally carried on in this way, the Sadat regime changed its ideological orientation considerably in the 1970s. With the *infitah* policy Sadat embraced market mechanisms and in 1979 he signed a peace treaty with Israel, but the Camp David agreement was looked on as a betrayal by the rest of the Arab world and undermined the goal of Arab unity. Sadat also broke with the secular revolutionary tone in Nasser's Arab socialism by giving the Egyptian state a more religious profile. The 1971 constitution recognised Islamic law as 'a source for legislation' and in 1980 *shari'a* formally became 'the most important source for legislation'.[45] Personally, Sadat was more religious than Nasser and created for himself an image as 'the devout president' (Arab. *al-ra'is al-mu'min*). He also pandered to the Islamist movement by forming a counterweight to radical leftist *infitah* opponents: imprisoned Islamist leaders were set free and the Muslim Brothers' activities tolerated. During the 1970s the Islamist movement strengthened its position in society.[46]

Mubarak took over a mixed ideology from his predecessors: anti-imperialism, socialism, and secularism from Nasser, and market liberalism, Islam and the peace agreement with Israel from Sadat. The relationship between these mutually exclusive categories was not clarified. Sadat never rejected the heritage of Nasser in its entirety but presented a change of direction in the 1970s as a 'corrective reform'. Mubarak himself had no ideological project when he came to power. He lacked his predecessors' visions and, as a professional soldier, he had no political experience before he became vice-president in 1975.[47] The solution therefore was to continue the main elements of Sadat's reformism in combination with 'bridge building' to the Nasser period. For instance, Mubarak declared his support for the Camp David agreement at the same time as he opposed normalisation of social and economic ties with Israel. In the same manner he maintained Sadat's alliance with the USA while resisting American pressure for a military operation against Libya in 1985 and 1986.[48] Mubarak also took the initiative to improve relations with the Arab world. As a consequence of the peace treaty with Israel in 1979, Egypt was excluded from the Arab league. Nonetheless, ten years later Mubarak succeeded in regaining membership and getting the head office moved back to Cairo. Egypt's conversion to market economics was continued, but here too the new president was more cautious than his predecessor and in line with Brumberg's description, Mubarak steered a middle course. To legitimise himself as Egypt's president Mubarak originally went in for political reform. He spoke warmly of the need for a state rule by law to remind the citizens of his constitutional right, as Sadat's vice-president, to take over after him.[49] The restrictions on political rights towards the end of the 1980s show the hollowness of Mubarak's liberalism. The president's only real vision was political stability.

The challenge of the Islamists

A direct line runs from the legitimacy problem to the growth of a strong Islamist movement in Egypt. First, Mubarak's attempt to increase support for the regime through political liberalisation gave the Muslim Brothers room to organise themselves in the 1980s. The movement gained entrance to student and trade unions, using its network of mosques, welfare organisations, firms, and banks to spread its message. The brotherhood even won thirty-six seats in parliament in 1987 before the regime tightened its grip.[50] Second, and more fundamentally, the Muslim Brothers won popularity in areas where the authorities were at odds with society's values. They criticised the peace treaty with Israel, derided the regime's alliance with the USA, condemned the lack of political liberty in Egypt, and raged against corruption in the administration. During the Gulf War in 1991 the Muslim Brothers used the trade unions to protest against Egyptian participation in the attack on Iraq.[51] Moreover, the Islamist movement revealed the appalling inadequacy of the Egyptian state in helping its own citizens. When an earthquake struck the country in 1992, it was volunteers from Islamic welfare organisations that were the first on the spot with tents, blankets, food, and medicines.[52] The brotherhood's social network emerged as far more efficient in dealing with the crisis than the state itself. TV pictures of the rescue operation at the catastrophe site showed banners declaring, 'Islam is the solution'. In this way the Islamists discredited the regime and appeared as the people's 'rightful representatives'.

On the ideological plane the Muslim Brothers directed a powerful attack on secular Arab nationalism. For the Islamists, Nasserism's attempt to modernise Egyptian society had resulted in Westernisation and secularisation. Islamic discourse stigmatised secularism as an alien, imported ideology that served the colonial powers' cause,[53] and the artificial distinction between state and religion had to be eliminated in order to save Islam. Consequently, the use of *shari'a* in legislation and judicial practice was the Islamists' most consistent demand. During the 1980s the Muslim Brothers pressed in particular for the Islamisation of family law. Another central worry for Islamists was 'immorality' and 'threats against Islam' in culture. As the centre of the Arab entertainment industry and the stage for intellectual debate, Cairo in particular was in a constant state of tension with 'Islamic values'. In the 1970s, the preacher 'Abd al-Hamid Kishk led a conservative attack on this development: in his Friday prayers and recorded sermons, Kishk spread a puritanical understanding of Islam.[54] According to Kishk and other preachers, 'moral decadence' was an instrument of Western 'cultural invasion'. Egypt's only chance to resist this danger was to keep the religious commands, guard women's honour, and fill public space with an 'edifying' culture.[55] For example, the Muslim Brothers criticised the 'indecent' way women were represented in the country's TV series. An article in the Islamist magazine *al-I'tisam* described Egyptian mass media as 'a humiliated slave in the sultan's palace who must undergo a long war of liberation to rewin control over his own destiny'.[56] Conservative Islamists also attacked the regime's cultural policy. In parliament in 1994 parliamentarians accused the Minister of Culture, Galal Gharib, of financing 'sinful and immoral' cultural products, because the state had just given financial support to the reproduction of a provocative painting by Gustav Klimt and the production of a play about homosexuality.[57] On several occasions Islamists have demanded a boycott of intellectuals and artists who give a 'wrong' or negative picture of Islam. When Yusuf Shahin's film of the Biblical and Qur'anic story of Joseph, *al-Muhajir*, was launched in 1994, Islamists brought the director to court because the film 'deviated' from the scriptures and 'blackened' religion, on which basis Islamists achieved a state prohibition on the film being shown.[58] Later, however, the court of appeal overturned the judgment.

Mubarak's reply

Faced with the Islamist challenge, Mubarak was armed with no powerful counter-ideology. The 1967 debacle and the controversy around Camp David had discredited Arab nationalism, the *infitah* policy, and the end of the Cold War undermined socialism and the regime's fear of openness made liberalism impossible. The president's lack of vision limited, not least, the chance of developing any special ideological direction. Beyond vague phrases about the significance of Islam, the nation, tradition, and democracy, under Mubarak, Egypt has never possessed a state ideology.[59] Accordingly, the president has been forced on the defensive by the Islamist movement and obliged to adopt their language. In a move that recalls the monarchies' religious legitimation, Mubarak has tried to disarm the Islamist movement with the aid of a 'selective Islamisation'. The core of this strategy is control over the religious establishment, consisting of the '*fatwa* ministry' (Dar al-ifta'), '*waqf* ministry' (Dar al-awqaf), and the long-established Islamic university, al-Azhar, situated in the heart of Cairo. Since its foundation in the tenth century, al-Azhar has been the most important religious place of learning in the Muslim world and from the twelfth century the guardian of sunni orthodoxy. In 1961, as a step in the Free Officers' corporative control of society, Gamal 'Abd al-Nasser made the university a state institution and nationalised religious foundations (*waqf*). The '*ulama* were put on the state pay roll, thereby losing their financial and political independence. Since then the regime has used al-Azhar as an extended arm of the state in order to legitimise its policy. In the 1960s the university 'blessed' Arab socialism and under the *infitah* policy the learned in religious law attacked communism. Under Mubarak, al-Azhar's role has been partly to discredit militant Islamism and partly to convince the rest of the Islamist movement that the state takes care of the interests of Islam. In step with Islamism's growing challenge the religious institutions have gained greater influence. In 1994, for instance, al-Azhar was granted the authority to prevent the production and distribution of material that 'offends religious principles'.[60] The '*ulama*'s veto on un-Islamic cultural production is formally binding for the Ministry of Culture.

The government's strategic use of conservative Islam has contributed towards the Islamisation of public space in Egypt. Society is permeated by a religious discourse that grants little space to alternative understandings of reality. An eloquent example of the pervasive climate is the reception of Haydar Haydar's novel *Walimah li-a'shab al-bahr* (Banquet for Seaweed) when it was published with the aid of a Ministry of Culture grant. The novel was written in 1983 as a 'necrology' over Arab nationalism and the liberation movements in the region in the 1950s and 1960s. The Syrian author gives a gloomy summary of the real consequences of the revolution and in April 2000, the Islamist-orientated newspaper *al-Sha'b* launched a furious attack on the book. Under the headline: 'Who swears to die with me?' the paper accused Haydar Haydar of blasphemy, triggered by the following cannonade in Haydar's novel: 'In the age of the atom, space exploration, and the triumph of reason, they rule us with the laws of the Beduin gods and the teaching of the Qur'an. Shit!'[61] On the basis of this sentence *al-Sha'b* stigmatised Haydar as 'sinful', 'obscene', and 'apostate', and the Minister of Culture as 'the instrument of Satan'.[62] The author of the article demanded the demotion of the Minister, the shutting down of the Ministry, and a *fatwa* against the book from al-Azhar. To dampen the resulting riots the Minister of Culture ordered an investigation into the publication of the novel and the government also asked al-Azhar to give their evaluation of the book. Subsequently, in May 2000, the clerics forbade the publication on account of 'sentences offensive to religion', 'immoral and erotic descriptions', and 'insults to Arab rulers'.[63] The *shaykh* of al-Azhar (1996–2010), Muhammad 'Abd al-Wahhab al-Tantawi, signed the condemnation himself and held the Minister of Culture responsible for what had happened. The campaign continued at full strength throughout the summer with attacks on several authors and books considered guilty of similar abuses.

The regime's survival policy has also resulted in Islamisation of schools and the judiciary. In an analysis of the religious instruction in Egyptian schools Gregory Starrett demonstrates how the regime's religious instruction has contributed towards Islamising society.[64] In schools, children are given, according to Starrett, an ideological understanding of Islam that in the final instance strengthens the Islamist movement's discourse. Egyptian case law too bears witness of an increasing Islamisation, as that the state recognises the *hisba* principle as the basis for legal prosecution: *hisba* gives individuals the right to bring cases before the courts that they think conflict with 'Islamic morals'.[65] The practice has its background in classic Islamic times when the Abbassids gave market inspectors (Arab. *muhtasib*) responsibility to survey the inhabitants' moral behaviour. The inspectors were given wide powers to punish 'immoral behaviour' and their assessments and procedure at times went beyond the regulations in formal Islamic law.[66] Liberal Muslims have long criticised this practice that is explicitly mentioned neither in the Qur'an nor the *hadith*. Conservative clerics, however, defend *hisba*, saying that the Qur'an encourages Muslims to 'command good and forbid evil' (Arab. *al-'amr bi-l-ma'ruf wa-l-nahy 'an al-munkar*).[67] In Egypt, Islamists have frequently made use of *hisba* in their attempts to Islamise state and society: religious jurists have, for example, led legal campaigns to remove 'immoral' advertising billboards.[68] The ban on Yusuf Shahin's film *al-Muhajir* also arose from a *hisba* civil action. Most seriously, however, was the incident of a group of Islamist lawyers who demanded the divorce of Muslim intellectual Nasir Hamid Abu Zayd from his wife against his will because he was an apostate (Arab. *murtadd*) as Islamic law prohibits marriage between a non-Muslim man and a Muslim woman. Abu Zayd considered himself to be a good Muslim but the way he interpreted Islam was blasphemous for sections of the Islamist movement.[69] They therefore brought a *hisba* action against him, demanding his divorce from his wife. To liberal intellectuals' great despair the highest court of appeal gave its verdict in favour of the Islamists. The court emphasised that Abu Zayd's interpretation of the Qur'an and understanding of religion was adequate proof of his heresy (Arab. *kufr*) and declared him to be an apostate. The Egyptian state would not condemn him to death although by Islamic law this is the penalty for abandoning the faith. Abu Zayd was thereby not only divorced from his wife but also obliged to flee his country for fear of his life.

Examples from Egyptian cultural debate, school policy, and legal practice illustrate how the regime accommodates the demands of the Islamist movement in order to strengthen its own legitimacy. The consequence is a conservative shift and a narrowing of the public space that particularly hurts leftist and liberal players. Nonetheless, there are clear limits to the Islamist movement's influence and how far the religious conservatives can go. The opportunity to influence 'heavy' political areas such as security, financial, and foreign policy is first of all far less than in symbolic issues within family legislation, education, and culture. In sensitive political and economic questions it is still Mubarak and his closest associates that decide. Simply allowing members of the Muslim Brothers access to political institutions has been highly controversial. The party law of 1977 prohibits the creation of religiously based political parties and formally the brotherhood is an illegal movement. Even when a group of reformist Islamists decided to cooperate with Coptic Christians and removed all references to religion in the hope of founding the party Hizb al-wasat, they did not get the regime's approval.[70] Despite certain ideological concessions, the state maintains its corporative control and also exploits any violent actions by militant Islamists as a pretext for getting tough on the Islamic movement in general. After an attempted assassination against President Mubarak in Ethiopia in 1995, the regime arrested 81 of the brotherhood's leading members, including former members of parliament, university professors, and businessmen, condemning

54 of them to prison sentences.[71] Similar measures were continued through-out the nineties in an attempt to keep the Muslim Brothers out of politics and blacken them as the men behind violent actions. In other words, the relation-ship between the regime and the Islamist movement is ambiguous. On the one hand, the state gives way to Islamic pressure, permitting them symbolic victo-ries. But as soon as the Islamists step over a certain line, the regime tightens its grip on the reins and represses the Muslim Brothers. The regime knows that the Islamist movement is too solidly rooted in society to be removed and has not been able to produce its own alternative ideology. For its part, the brotherhood has experienced that an armed struggle against the regime is a cul de sac, and that it needs Mubarak's good will to be able to operate. The Brothers emphasise therefore that their aim is not revolution but a gradual Islamisation of Egyptian society.[72]

The brotherhood has also categorically rejected the militant Islamists' asser-tion of the regime's un-Islamic character. By way of thanks for this defence of the regime's claim to legitimacy, the movement has been rewarded with a certain influence in, for instance, parliament. Mubarak's solution to the challenge of the Islamist movement has, however, not attacked the legitimacy problem at its root but overlooked central political demands such as democratisation and opposition to the alliance with Israel and the USA. The legitimacy deficit that contributed towards the growth of Islamism in the seventies is, therefore, as large as ever.

Conclusion

Today Islamism is the most potent ideology in the Middle East as earlier ideological forces such as Arab nationalism and socialism have lost much of their influence. This is due, in part, to those Arab republics that, founded on such ideologies, suffered a legitimacy crisis, and brought such secular ideologies into disrepute. Why precisely Islamism – and not, for instance, liberalism – has taken over the ideological hegemony in the region is a complicated question. Attempts to answer this must first of all recognise that the Muslim world has undergone a radical change since the nineteenth century. In the Middle East's encounter with Western dominance the inhabitants' relationship with Islam and the religious authorities has altered. At the same time Islamic ideologists have emphasised the religion's political aspect, summoning Muslims to fight against 'un-Islamic' regimes. The effect of the Islamic opposition comes partly from well-organised movements being able to evade the state's corporatism because they work within a religious and charitable frame, partly because of the power of Islam's symbolic language, which stands out as authentic in the Muslim world. The Islamist movements, however, have competition from the regimes in their exploitation of these symbols. Lacking other potent ideologies, Middle East rulers have thrown themselves into the battle for the title of 'defenders of Islam'. The Egyptian example illustrates how a previously secular-inspired regime played the Islamic card in order to counterbalance the Islamist movement. Husni Mubarak embraces bits of the Muslim Brothers' rhetoric and agenda so as to keep the opposition out of political decisions that could affect the regime's survival. The question, however, is how long can this strategy work. For Mubarak's selective Islamisation does not remove the structural reasons for the regime's legitimacy deficit, such as the lack of democracy and dependence on the West. Nor does it contribute to weakening the opposition with which the regime is faced. On the contrary, Mubarak's survival policy contributes towards strengthening the Islamist movement's ideological hegemony. Despite a general failure so far to take over power in the Middle East, Islamism is by no means dead.

Further reading

Ayubi, Nazih N.: *Political Islam: Religion and Politics in the Arab World*. London and New York: Routledge, 1991.

Black, Antony: *The History of Islamic Political Thought from the Prophet to the Present*. Edinburgh and Cambridge: Edinburgh University Press, 2001.

Donohue, John J. and John L. Esposito: *Islam in Transition. Muslim Perspectives*. New York and Oxford: Oxford University Press, 2007.

Eickelman, Dale F. and James Piscatori: *Muslim Politics*. Princeton, New Jersey: Princeton University Press, 1996.

François Burgat and William Dowell: *The Islamic Movement in North Africa*. Texas, Austin: The Center for Middle Eastern Studies, 1993.

Ismail, Salwa: *Rethinking Islamist Politics*. London and New York: I.B.Tauris, 2003.

Kepel, Gilles: *Muslim Extremism in Egypt: The Prophet and Pharaoh*. London and Berkeley: University of California Press, 1985.

Lewis, Bernard: *The Political Language of Islam*. Chicago and London: The University of Chicago Press, 1988.

Martin, Vanessa: *Creating an Islamic State: Khomeini and the making of a new Iran*, London and New York: I.B.Tauris, 2000.

Roy, Olivier: *Globalized Islam: The Search for a New Ummah*. London: Hurst & Co, 2004.

Schwedler, Jillian: *Faith in Moderation: Islamist Parties in Jordan and Yemen*. Cambridge, New York, Melbourne, Madrid, Cape Town, Singapore, and São Paulo: Cambridge University Press, 2006.

White, Jenny B.: *Islamist Mobilization in Turkey: A Study in Vernacular Politics*. Seattle and London: University of Washington Press, 2002.

Wickham, Carrie Rosefsky: *Mobilizing Islam: Religion, Activism, and Political Change in Egypt*. New York: Columbia University Press, 2002.

Yavuz, M. Hakan (ed.): *The Emergence of a New Turkey: Democracy and the AK Party*. Salt Lake City, UT: University of Utah Press, 2006.

Part 4
Institutions and Power

7 Monarchies

The most important of our duties as rulers is to raise the standard of living of our people. Fulfilling our duties is a God-given responsibility and all, young and old, have a responsibility to follow up their work.[1]

Most of the world's monarchies that still have real power are to be found in the Arab countries of the Middle East. Monarchs rule more than a third of the countries in the Arab League. The kings of Morocco, Bahrain, Saudi Arabia, the Sultan of Oman, and the emirs of Kuwait, Qatar, and the Emirates, combined, rule over more than 70 million people[2] (see Table 5). The Gulf Co-operation Council (GCC) states – the six monarchies on the Arabian Peninsula – are among the world's largest oil and gas-producers. Given the world's reliance on energy supplies from these regimes, their stability is not just a regional concern but an international one. Consequently, great powers are jockeying for building political alliances and economical partnership with them. Saudi Arabia is the cradle of Islam, and plays a key role in the Muslim world. In addition, the monarchies have a strategically important location: Morocco and Oman at the Straits of Gibraltar and Hormuz. A few decades ago monarchy as a form of government was even stronger in the region. Monarchs reigned in Egypt up to 1952, in Tunisia to 1957, Iraq to 1958, Libya to 1969, and Iran to 1979.

Despite the significance of monarchy in the Middle East, political scientists devoted far less attention to this form of government than to the republics of the region during the 1950s and 1960s. The reason for this was a widespread conception among researchers, particularly in the USA, that monarchy as a form of government was out of date. Two views dominated: first, monarchies – and the societies they reigned over – were regarded as traditional. What precisely 'traditional' meant was seldom specified, but tribalism and Islam were stressed. Second, monarchies were seen as weak regimes that would soon be replaced by republics. The supposition was that monarchies, which had less developed

Table 5   Monarchies in the Middle East (2010)

State	Head of state	Date of birth of the monarch	Year for formal inauguration
Bahrain	King Hamad bin 'Isa al-Khalifa	1949	1999
Emirates	*Shayhk* Khalifa bin Zayid al-Nahayan[a]	1947	2004
Jordan	King 'Abdallah II	1962	1999
Kuwait	*Shaykh* Sabah al-Ahmad al-Sabah	1929	2006
Morocco	King Muhammad VI	1963	1999
Oman	Sultan Qabus bin Sa'id al-Sa'id	1940	1970
Qatar	*Shaykh* Hamad bin Khalifa al-Thani	1950	1995
Saudi Arabia	King 'Abdallah bin 'Abd al-'Aziz al-Sa'ud	1923	2005

[a] *Shaykh* Khalifa is the president of the Emirates and the Emir of Abu Dhabi. Each of the other six emirates that make up the federation – respectively 'Ajman, Dubai, al-Fujaira, Ra's al-Khaimah, al-Shariqa, and Umm al-Quwain – are also ruled by emirs.

institutions, would collapse as a result of socio-economic turbulence. However, the rumours of the monarchies' imminent death were exaggerated.

In this chapter we shall address the following question: how has monarchy as a form of government managed to survive in the Middle East? In the second part of the chapter we shall direct our attention to civil–military relations in Oman. What strategies has the country's ruler, Sultan Qabus, followed to prevent his own officers from obtaining power by a coup?

'The king's dilemma'

The Middle East monarchs, especially those on the Arabian Peninsula, have undergone enormous socio-economic changes as a consequence of the oil boom of the sixties and seventies. Wealth has made it possible to jump from the early Middle Ages to a hyper-modern era in the lifetime of a couple of generations. Today monarchies on the Arabian Peninsula are among the most 'modern' in the world if modernisation means infrastructure development and adaption of new technology. For example, the emirate of Dubai has developed from a small coastal village, where a few hundred inhabitants made a living by fishing and pearl diving, into a city of millions and a Middle East financial centre. Dubai is strategically placed between Saudi Arabia, Iran,

Pakistan, and India, becoming a magnet for rich investors from both these and Western countries as well as one of the world's most cosmopolitan cities. People from all over the world go there to seek their fortune. Dubai has everything from the world's highest skyscraper to the world's biggest shopping centre, an indoor Alpine skiing resort in the desert, and the world's most luxurious hotels. No other society in world history have probably undergone a faster socio-economic transformation.

A number of researchers have claimed that these huge changes will undermine the 'traditional' political order and in that way bring about the fall of the regime. Samuel P. Huntington was one of those who meant that the monarchs were living on borrowed time.[3] In 1968 he wrote about 'the king's dilemma', meaning that a monarch could hardly avoid satisfying his subjects' desire for social and economic progress. In order to realise such an ambition the monarch would have to develop the apparatus of state, which would rapidly face the monarch with a dilemma: he would have to satisfy the demands of the new middle class created by modernisation without alienating his traditional power base, consisting of, among others, large land-owners, tribal chiefs, and wealthy merchants. According to Huntington, sooner or later the new middle class would demand political power, which, if granted, would bring the monarch into conflict with his traditional power base. In the opposite case, if he refused, he would run the risk of losing power through a revolution. In the short term, claimed Huntington, he could co-opt the new middle class, but in the long term the only way to solve the dilemma was either to stop or slow down the modernisation process.

Manfred Halpern, too, was sceptical of the future of the Middle East monarchies.[4] Like Huntington, he suggested that the creation of classes resulting from the socio-economic development threatened the monarchs. Halpern asserted that they could avoid, or at least delay, the threat from the new middle class by omitting to change or reform. In addition, he suggested two alternative ways out: either the monarch could assume the role of 'chief moderniser' in order to control the social forces in his own favour, or he could make others responsible for political decisions within the framework of a new constitution. By exploiting the second option the monarch kept his power as a unifying symbol above party political divisions. But he would no longer have the last word in the decision-making process.

Huntington and Halpern were writing during the troubled times that followed in the wake of the Middle East countries gaining their independence in the 1950s and 1960s. But in spite of the period's disturbances all of eight Middle East monarchies have not only survived but also in many ways function better today than the region's republics. To understand their strength it is necessary to abandon the idea that these regimes are anachronisms. As a matter of fact many of these monarchies – with the exception of Morocco and Oman – are not much older than the region's republics. In the following analysis the focus will be on how these monarchies have exploited their financial and political resources to respond to the challenges that are linked to rapid social change, and consequently, conserved their political power.

Oil incomes

In 2009 BP Statistical Review estimated that 64.7 per cent of the globe's oil deposits were to be found in the Middle East, and that the countries in the region accounted for 37.3 per cent of the total production. The monarchies of the Arabian Peninsula alone accounted for 39.5 per cent of global deposits and 22.6 per cent of production.[5] In 1932 the Bahrain Petroleum Company, a branch of the Standard Oil Company of California, found oil in exploitable quantities under Bahrain's desert sands. The other countries of the peninsula followed in hot pursuit. But it was not until the price hike of the so-called oil boom of 1973–4 that incomes really began to pile up in the monarchs' state treasuries. This new wealth made it possible for progressive monarchs to avoid 'the king's dilemma' by adopting the role of 'chief moderniser'. As a result, oil incomes are a key factor in explaining how the monarchies have survived.

The rentier states in the Gulf

These huge incomes have produced a particular type of regime – the so-called rentier states. According to Giacomo Luciano, these are states that obtain 40 per cent or more of their incomes through external transfers and which in addition adopt an active redistribution policy.[6] The term is borrowed from Adam Smith,[7] who among others was concerned with analysing the income base of states. He used *rent* to distinguish income derived from natural resources from productive work. Rent is also referred to as 'a gift from nature' – the difference between the costs involved in exploiting a natural resource and the income from its sale. It is usual to distinguish between natural rent on the one hand and strategic rent on the other. Examples of strategic rent are investment objects, aid, and income from the hiring out of military bases. Historically speaking, sixteenth century Spain and Portugal, which were saturated in silver from South America, were the first rentier states. Today the Arabian peninsular monarchies stand as rentier states par excellence. The ruling houses primarily make their incomes from sales of oil and gas and from profits from overseas investments, which in turn are made possible by oil money. Only a marginal part of these states' incomes,

Table 6   Oil/gas revenues in the Gulf monarchies (2004)

State	% oil/gas revenues of total revenues	% oil/gas and refined products of total exports
Bahrain	72.4	72.4
Emirates	73.7	42.1
Kuwait	77.2	83.3
Oman	83.7	81.3
Qatar	65.9	78.7
Saudi Arabia	84.2	87.9

Note: The average price in 2004 was slightly less than 40 US dollars per barrel. The figures in the table are taken from International Monetary Fund, http://www.imf.org/external/country/index.htm

in other words, come from taxation. The rulers of the Gulf monarchies also pursue large-scale redistribution policies.

Neither Morocco nor Jordan fit the definition of rentier states. However, Jordan may be regarded as a semi-rentier state since the country receives considerable loans and other financial support – that is strategic rent income – from the Gulf monarchies and its Western allies.

Three political implications

A number of authors have pointed to oil income as the main reason why the monarchies have survived in the Middle East.[8] In the following we will identify three political implications of oil wealth to evaluate how windfall gains have contributed to strengthening the monarchies on the Arabian Peninsula.

Developing the state apparatus

The most striking consequence of the oil revenues is that the monarchies have developed modern state systems. A few decades ago the monarchies' state structure was poorly developed and the most important institution was the royal court (Arab. *diwan*). The monarch ruled by decree (Arab. *marsum* or *'amr*) and consulted the oligarchs in his daily or weekly open meetings (Arab. *majlis*). The ruler had a handful of trusted men, often foreigners, to whom he delegated various tasks. Ibn Sa'ud, who founded modern Saudi Arabia in 1932 and reigned till 1953, relied, for example, on a small circle of princes and a handful of advisors, many of them foreigners, and employees. All financial matters were exclusively in the hands of the king's friend and 'factotum minister', 'Abdallah al-Sulayman. But since petro-dollars began to fill the state treasury, the state apparatus has vastly increased. Through its bureaucracy the rulers have gained an instrument to implement modernisation projects and hand out 'carrots' to their subjects. In addition to the bureaucracy, the royal families have invested in military systems equipped with the most sophisticated Western arms systems, as well as intelligence, security forces, and police, which have given the rulers a huge 'stick' to deter any internal and external challengers.

But while the state apparatus has enlarged, elected political institutions have stayed underdeveloped, democratically elected parliaments scarcely exist, political parties are prohibited, and trade unions enjoy little freedom to operate. In the Gulf monarchies the *majlis* tradition has become institutionalised in the sense that permanent advisory assemblies have been established. Oman's Sultan Qabus has even introduced his own so-called open *majlis*. This is an annual three-week round trip during which the sultan travels from town to town accompanied by his ministers and advisors in order to meet the inhabitants, an event that is massively reported in the local press. But overall, the advisory assemblies have little real power. The representatives are appointed by the rulers in Saudi Arabia and Qatar, and are partly appointed, partly elected in Bahrain, the Emirates, and Oman. Only in Kuwait are the representatives fully elected. Interestingly, the only parliament with substantial power in the Arabian peninsular monarchies, Kuwait's Majlis al-umma, was established before the oil age. Although the balance of power between the emir and parliament favours the former, they have fought a series of battles. Following political rivalries, the previous and current emirs have used their constitutional right to close parliament and called for new elections in 1999, 2006, 2008, and 2009. Previous rulers have also unconstitutionally dissolved parliament (in 1976–1981 and in 1986–1992) ruling by decrees. However, in each case inner and outer pressures have forced them to reopen the National Assembly.

Distributing welfare

The development of the state apparatus has also made it possible for the ruling houses to distribute welfare directly to their subjects. The relationship between rulers and the people in a rentier state is generally described as an unwritten pact in which the people receive socio-economic welfare in return for political loyalty. In the Gulf monarchies, citizenship grants an apparent cradle-to-grave welfare system, which among other things includes free education and health services, state employment, and heavily subsidised basic commodities such as food, water, electricity, and fuel. In Saudi Arabia the right to work after leaving school is even guaranteed by law. Citizens receive all these welfare services without paying taxes.[9] All those who question the rule of the royal families or the role of the royal family risk sanctions such as imprisonment, travel bans or deportation, and this

Table 7 Demographic data for the Gulf monarchies (2002)

State	National population	Immigrant population	Total population	Annual population growth (%)	National labour force	Immigrant labour force	Total labour force
Bahrain	400,000	270,000	670,000	1.6	100,000	200,000	300,000
Emirates	900,000	2,700,000	3,600,000	1.6	200,000	1,700,000	1,900,000
Kuwait	900,000	1,500,000	2,400,000	3.3	200,000	1,100,000	1,300,000
Oman	1,900,000	600,000	2,500,000	3.4	300,000	600,000	900,000
Qatar	200,000	500,000	700,000	2.9	30,000	250,000	280,000
Saudi Arabia	15,500,000	7,300,000	22,800,000	3.3	2,800,000	5,300,000	8,100,000

Source: The figures are from *Middle East Economic Digest*, 9–15 April 2004.

provides strong incentives to keep on the right side of the monarchy. Since the 1960s and 1970s millions of foreign workers have flooded into the Gulf states and, in 2002, there were about 12.5 million foreign workers there, most of them from India, Pakistan, Egypt, Yemen, Bangladesh, Sri Lanka, and the Philippines[10] (see Table 7). By importing a whole working class the rulers have spared their own population from the hardest jobs. Few of these immigrant workers have obtained citizenship or been able to benefit from the welfare state. The many million guest workers are apolitical for fear of deportation and loss of their livelihood.

Nonetheless, the ruler's potential to 'buy' the loyalty of his subjects has its limits. The ruling houses' modernising policy of recent decades has indisputably given an enormous rise in the average person's living standard, which again has led to considerable support to 'chief modernisers', such as Abu Dhabi's *Shaykh* Zayid and Oman's Sultan Qabus. The rulers have been able to purchase the loyalty of their people through the first phase of modernisation, but gradually many inhabitants now have expectations of political influence. There are two factors in particular that contribute to this development: first, there has been a general increase in the level of education in the Gulf. Many thousands of Gulf Arabs have degrees from prestigious universities and colleges in North America and Western Europe. Second, Gulf Arabs are major consumers of modern media such as satellite TV and internet, and via such channels for globalisation new ideas arise as to how society should be run. Intellectuals in the Gulf monarchies energetically discuss, among other matters, the expansion of the advisory assembly's role and the rights of women. The rulers can only meet the new expectations of the people through a real political opening.

For the rulers it is also expensive to maintain the 'pact'. Should oil prices drop significantly several years in a row, something that cannot be ruled out, it would be difficult to meet the future material expectations of a rapidly growing young population. In such a situation the monarchies could lose popular support. The rulers, aware of the danger, have commenced measures to reduce their vulnerability to possible swings on the world market – by diversifying investments and replacing foreign workers by local citizens. In Saudi Arabia a declared aim is to halve the share of immigrant labour by 2013. But in practice the nationalisation of the labour force is more easily said than done. Indeed ambitious development plans have the opposite effect and it is not improbable that, on the contrary, the share of foreign workers will increase in the immediate future.[11]

Undermining potential rivals

Finally, the ruling houses' oil revenue has been used to co-opt potential political rivals, including business families, religious communities, and tribes. All have gradually been transformed to clients of the state.

The co-optation of the business families is illustrated by the following example: the monarchs have been behind an expansive development of the infrastructure, such as roads, water works and pipelines, airports, and harbours. In order to delegate some of the responsibility for economic development the state has granted concessions to local trading and entrepreneur families. These families consequently have an interest in retaining the favour of the ruling families so as to ensure access to lucrative concessions.

Khaldun al-Naqib has pointed out that present-day political systems in the Gulf monarchies have a corporative character,[12] by which he means that local rulers first broke down traditional authority structures and then incorporated them into the state system: tribes that the state relates to via their chiefs; the key merchant and entrepreneur families; and the religious establishments for Sunnis and Shi'as, the Ibadis, Zaydis, and so on. Associating various social groups to the state in this manner has contributed towards strengthening patron–client relations as social promotion depends on finding a prominent patron either from the ruling family or within the tribe or the bourgeois elite.

Taking Saudi Arabia as an example, all the kingdom's elite formations reflect the strategic alliances formed by King Ibn Sa'ud and the later consolidation of his family's regime. The House of Sa'ud is the centre of gravity of this political system, while royals rely on religious leaders, tribal leaders, business leaders, and bureaucratic leaders. Each of these elite groups gradually gained their institutional power bases within the framework of the Saudi state. Steffen Hertog – like Khaldun al-Naqib – argues that this representation gives the House of Sa'ud a corporative character. The leaders of the different non-royal elite groups are not represented in any formal corporative chambers, but rather in governmental institutions at national and local levels, including the police and the military forces. Hertog refers to this process as 'the policy of segmented clientelism'. The segmented consultation arrangements prevent the emergence of class-based identities, and make it even difficult for interest groups to coordinate their claims *vis-à-vis* the state as communication is far more vertical than horizontal. These corporative mechanisms help the regime maintain its rule.[13]

Non-rentier states: Jordan and Morocco

Jordan and Morocco do not have similar access to financial resources to enable them to dominate their local economies, hand out welfare, develop the state apparatus and undermine potential rivals. This has both positive and negative consequences. On the positive side Jordan and Morocco have progressed further in the development of elected institutions, the organisation of political parties and running elections than is the case with the Gulf monarchies. Because the ruling houses cannot to the same extent 'buy' support of selected social groups, they have instead sought to incorporate groups like Islamists, Palestinians, and Berbers into formal political institutions and processes. Jordan's constitution of 1952 established that the country should be a hereditary monarchy with parliamentary rule where the people are 'the source of all power',[14] although between 1967 and 1991 emergency laws restricted the freedoms granted in the constitution. But in 1991, King Husayn annulled the emergency laws and the following year permitted political parties, which had been prohibited since 1963. Adults have had the right to vote in Jordan since 1973 and relatively free and fair parliamentary elections were held in 1989 and 1993, although Islamist parties boycotted the election of 1997 on account of dissatisfaction with the electoral law. The Islamists participated again in 2003 and in 2007. Morocco's constitution declares that the country shall be a constitutional monarchy with an elected parliament.[15] Parliamentary elections have been held since 1963; adults have the right to vote; political parties are allowed. Freedom House called the Moroccan elections of 2002 the freest and fairest held in the country's history and the results led to a parliament with considerable Islamist representation and 10 per cent of the seats held by women.[16]

The negative effect is that the ruling houses of Jordan and Morocco have used force to keep power to a greater extent than has been the case in most of the Gulf monarchies. The dynasties of Jordan and Morocco have been dependent on the police, intelligence, and security forces to survive a series of uprisings and attempted coups. The Hashemite ruling dynasty of Jordan went through a turbulent period in the 1950s and 1960s, being challenged both internally and externally. This began when the country's first regent, King 'Abdallah I (1921–51), was assassinated by a Palestinian nationalist. His successor, Husayn (1953–99), survived several attempted coups after revolutionary regimes took over power in neighbouring Egypt, Syria, and Iraq. The most serious challenge, however, was the confrontation between Jordanian security forces and the PLO that culminated in 'Black September' in 1970. For his part King Hassan II of Morocco has had to deal with a socialist rising led by Mehdi ben Barka and the Union des Forces Populaires in the early 1960s and a military coup led by Muhammad Oufkir in 1972. The king retaliated brutally: the coup-makers and their supporters were arrested, tortured, and killed.

Dynastic monarchies

Michael Herb claims that in recent times Bahrain, the Emirates, Kuwait, Qatar, and Saudi Arabia have maintained their political stability in spite of socioeconomic upheavals and the growth of a new middle class because they have become 'dynastic monarchies'.[17] This type of regime is the result of the offensive development of the state apparatus made possible by oil wealth. According to Herb, dynastic monarchies take shape when the leading princes try to manoeuvre their way to power by making alliances within their own family. To build these alliances the princes offer attractive resources, such as positions within the state apparatus, to their relatives. Herb describes a dynastic monarchy as an institution where the princes in the ruling family hold most of the key positions, for instance, in the armed forces, ministerial posts, and governorships, as well as sharing lower posts in the state apparatus. This is possible because the princes in the ruling family in the Arabian Peninsula are extremely numerous.

Herb believes that dynastic monarchs are very capable of resisting revolution.[18] He claims that the reason for this is that princes of the ruling family hold the most important positions in the state apparatus. For potential opponents of the ruling house it is hard to build a power base within the state system and almost impossible to kill or imprison all the princes in a first strike. No dynastic monarchy has yet been overthrown, whereas, for example, the Iranian shah's regime collapsed as a result of the Islamic revolution of 1978–9. The Iranian constitution prohibited the shah's relatives from holding leading posts in the state system. Iran's last shah, Mohammad Reza Pahlavi, neither trusted anyone nor delegated power and at the time of the revolution he was suffering from cancer, which led to a paralysing of the Iranian state apparatus. Consequently, the Shah's 'one-bullet-regime', using Herb's terminology, was a manageable match for the revolutionaries. Other monarchies in the region that have had corresponding constitutional restrictions – Afghanistan, Egypt, Iraq, and Libya – have also fallen.

In addition, the ruling families have developed mechanisms for regulating internal conflicts that work well. All families are affected from time to time by internal conflict, and the ruling houses of the Gulf are no exception. In Saudi Arabia, Faysal, with the support of a coalition of allied princes, deposed his incompetent half-brother, Sa'ud, as king in 1964. Oman's Sultan Qabus deposed his father in a coup in 1970. Similarly, *Shaykh* Hamad, ruler of Qatar, deposed his father in 1995 (who had in turn seized power from his own father in 1972). And after *Shaykh* Jabir's death in 2006, Kuwait endured a struggle for succession to the throne between the two main branches of the al-Sabah family, Jabir and Salim respectively. Nonetheless, conflict-solving mechanisms have prevented such serious strife from leading to the fall of the ruling dynasty. Herb emphasises the significance of two principles drawn from Arab Muslim tradition that are continued within the families: consultation (Arab. *shura*) and consensus (Arab. *ijma'*). Before important decisions are taken the most influential princes consult and try to reach a consensus. This is especially important when solving the succession issue, historically the most divisive (see Table 8). Moreover, in

Table 8   Succession to the throne

State	Succession rules	Next in line
Bahrain	First born male	Crown Prince Salman
Emirates	Crown Prince of Abu Dhabi accepted by the other emirs	Crown Prince Muhammad
Jordan	First born male but the king can also choose a brother	Crown Prince Husayn
Kuwait	The Emir designates a member of the al-Jabir or the al-Salim family for Parliamentary approval	*Shaykh* Nawaf al-Ahmad al-Sabah
Morocco	First born male	Crown prince Hassan
Oman	Male member of al-Sa'id-family, either chosen by family council or designated beforehand by the deceased sultan	No crown prince designated
Qatar	The emir designates one of his sons	Crown Prince Tamim
Saudi Arabia	Son or grandson of Ibn Sa'ud, the kingdom's founder, either designated by the king or chosen by family council	Crown Prince Sultan

the absence of well-developed constitutional and institutional requirements, a set of norms regulates the conduct of the members of the ruling house. Khalid bin Sultan, a prominent Saudi prince, indicates in his book *Desert Warrior* what norms are strongest in the Saudi ruling house. He emphasises respect for the king, no matter who he is, honouring older family members, solving conflicts within the family framework, putting what is best for the family before individual interests, and sharing out leading positions among the most qualified princes.[19]

The other three monarchies in the Middle East – Oman, Jordan, and Morocco – are not dynastic monarchies. However, Herb points out that the constitutions of these three non-dynastic monarchies permit members of the royal family to hold top positions in the state apparatus. This, he claims, contributes to strengthening the regimes, which in the long run can turn into dynastic monarchies. This is not, however, the case for Oman, and certainly not in Sultan Qabus' reign.[20] For Oman's ruler has delegated little authority or positions to his own al-Sa'id family, which consists of less than 100 male members. Qabus personally holds a series of ministerial posts in his own government. He is Prime Minister, Defence Secretary, Foreign Secretary, Secretary of Finance, and head of the Central Bank. In other words, it is Qabus, and not the al-Saʿid family, that rules Oman. The succession law is specific in Part 1, Article 6 of the 'constitution', *al-nizam al-asasi li-l-dawla*, from 1996. Here it states that the family council shall appoint a successor within three days after the sultan's death. Should the family council not succeed, the head of the Office of the Supreme Commander shall open a letter written by the deceased sultan, kept in two separate places in the sultanate. The letter lists two possible successors in order of priority.[21] Qabus' reluctance to name his heir probably comes from his fear that the latter might challenge his dominating position.

However, there is reason to question whether Herb's analysis makes sufficient allowance for the possible consequences of the minimal constitutional limitations on the monarch's powers and weak formal institutions. Should the informal mechanisms for internal conflict solving fail, this might have dramatic consequences. As the number of royal princes increases so probably will competition for positions of power that give access to the huge oil riches. In Kuwait, for instance, there is a latent tension between the two main branches of the al-Sabah family. After *Shaykh* Jabir's death this friction was exposed. Traditionally, the position of emir has alternated between the Jabir and Salim branches of descendants of Kuwait's ruler Mubarak 1896–1915. But in 2006 the Salim branch crown prince *Shaykh* Saʿd who suffered from chronic illness was deemed incapable of assuming power. The Parliament instead used its constitutional prerogative to name the popular Prime Minister *Shaykh* Sabah al-Ahmad al-Jabir Kuwait's new emir. Like his predecessor Sabah belonged to the Jabir branch, to the dislike of many of the Salims. Tensions rose further when Sabah appointed his brother, *Shaykh* Nawaf, crown prince. Prior to this it was assumed that Sabah would choose his cousin, *Shaykh* Nasir Muhammad al-Ahmad, who belongs to the Salims, so as to subdue the family strife. Another example is Saudi Arabia, where there are indications of a fragmentation of the ruling house. Powerful princes establish their own dynasties within the Saʿud dynasty, and the future successions are likely to seriously challenge the unit of the ruling family. These norms are very much respected by the royals, which helps preserving the unity within the ruling family.

External protection

Neither must the significance of external protection be undervalued as an explanation of why the monarchies have survived. The stability of these regimes has long been of vital economic and strategic importance for the USA and other Western powers There are two main reasons for this: first, the monarchs rule over the world's biggest known oil and gas finds, and, second, these regimes have a strategically important location.

In the 1950s and 1960s during the Arab world's 'Cold War' Egypt's then ruler, Gamal 'Abd al-Nasser, and the Ba'th parties in Syria and Iraq tried to overturn the region's monarchies. To realise their aims these revolutionary regimes sought support from the Soviet Union and the rest of the Eastern bloc. On their side, the USA, the UK, and other states either of, or friendly to, the West supported the monarchies as a counterweight to the Soviet supported republics. The Western powers intervened several times to save the ruling houses that were threatened by radical political forces. One instance of this is Jordan. In the mid-1950s the Jordanian Ba'th socialists and other anti-monarchist forces began to encourage agitation among discontented Palestinian refugees in the country. The opposition also encouraged military conspiracies against King Husayn. When the monarchy fell in neighbouring Iraq in 1958, the king decided to bring in British paratroopers in order to avoid the same fate. From the 1950s Omani Sultan Sa'id received British military and economic aid with the goal of gaining control over the tribes in the interior and of defeating the *imam* in Nizwa. In the early 1970s his successor, Sultan Qabus, obtained support once more from the UK as well as from Jordan and Iran, in order to combat Marxist rebels in the southern Dhofar province.

The collapse of the Soviet Union in 1989 ushered in a new era in relations between the Middle East and the rest of the world. US hegemony was definitely established during the Gulf War of 1990–1, when more than half a million American troops led the coalition to liberate Kuwait. Today the Western powers and the monarchies have common interests, such as, energy supplies, the struggle against Islamism under the banner of 'the war on terror', and hindering the rise of Iran as a regional great power. US hegemony is underlined by the country having at its disposal military bases in most Middle East countries, including the Gulf monarchies except for Saudi Arabia. As a result Iran is surrounded on all sides by American forces. Western corporations, both state-owned and private, have considerable interests in the regions, which concerns not only oil and gas but also other sectors, for example, armaments. According to Stockholm-based SIPRI, the military spending of Israel, Oman, and Saudi Arabia exceeded 8 per cent of GDP in 2007, mainly due to investments in expensive Western weapon systems.[22] All the ruling houses in the Middle East have become important allies of the USA in its 'war on terror'. The monarchs make common cause with the Americans in combating local Islamist groupings – as well as, in some cases, liberal democracy and human rights activists – that are being accused of having the will and ability to launch 'terror attacks'. In connection with the occupation of Iraq, Kuwait and Jordan have also become important logistic supports for the USA.

Only 3.4 per cent of the worldwide oil reserves are located in the huge Asian land mass where half of the globe's population lives. In recent years, China, India, and other Asian countries have become increasingly dependent on imported oil in order to sustain their goals of economic growth. These countries import the bulk of the oil from the Middle East.

Asian reliance on Middle East producers is the outcome of geographical location, delivery speed, and lack of substitutes. This reliance has translated into greater trade and diplomatic ties between Asian states and the Middle East. Asians are also showing far more interest in the internal and regional security of the Middle East. But neither China nor India is anywhere near being able to offer the security benefits that the United States provide to the states in the region. The Asian states are free riders – relying on American military efforts to secure oil production in the troubled Middle East, as well as protecting the sea lines of communication bringing oil from the region to Asia. China and India have so far neither the willingness to challenge the United States nor the ability to step into its role. Therefore, American hegemony in the region will remain unchallenged in the foreseeable future.

Case study: Oman – Sultan Qabus' men

> Oh Allah, protect for us His Majesty the Sultan,
> And the people in our land;
> With honour and peace;
> May he live long and be supported,
> May his leadership be glorious,
> For him we shall lay down our lives;
> Oh Oman – since the time of the Prophet,
> We are a dedicated people amongst the noble Arabs,
> Rejoice – Qaboos has come,
> With the blessings of Heaven;
> Take courage and protect him with your prayers.[23]

Sultan Qabus bin Saʿid al-Saʿid, the ruler of Oman, seized power from his father in a coup in 1970. During his reign he has expanded the armed forces, making them the most professional on the Arabian Peninsula. The Sultan has used this military power to secure both Oman's sovereignty and his own position as authoritarian ruler. Several monarchies in the Middle East fell because officers in the armed forces seized power in the 1950s and 1960s and the Sultan is painfully aware, therefore, of the danger he runs of his own armed forces turning their weapons against him. It is remarkable that since 1970 no military coup has succeeded in overturning either the Sultan of Oman or indeed any other monarch in the Middle East. What strategies has Sultan Qabus adopted to prevent his officers from carrying out a coup?

'The Praetorian problem'

Samuel P. Huntington introduced the term the 'Praetorian problem' for military interventions against civilian rulers,[24] and today the word 'Praetorian' is associated with intrigues, conspiracies, disloyalty, and assassination. The Praetorians were the Roman emperors' lifeguard who protected the emperor's life, but who also had the power to murder him. After the murder of Emperor Marcus Aurelius (161–80), it was precisely this they were famed for. The political history of the Arab Muslim world is also full of military interventions against civilian rulers. One example is the Mamelukes who were slave soldiers, converted to Islam and trained for service for the caliphs of ninth-century Baghdad. The Abbasids fetched their soldiers mainly from non-Turkish tribes that lived north of the Black Sea on the steppes of present-day southwest Russia and the Caucasus. Mamelukes were often sold as slaves by their own poverty-stricken families or kidnapped and sold by slave traders. But gradually the Mamelukes developed into a mighty military cast, and on a series of occasions seized power from the masters they were meant to protect. For example, this warrior cast founded a powerful state in Egypt between 1250 and 1517. Another example is that of the Janissaries, an elite force, consisting of Christian men and prisoners of war, created by the Ottomans in the fourteenth century. Early in the eighteenth century the Janissaries had won such prestige and influence that they could dominate the government, but in 1826 the Janissaries were dissolved after a failed rising against Sultan Mahmud II in Istanbul.

The 'Praetorian problem' is just as acute today. Huntington was particularly concerned with civilian–military relations in the 1950s and 1960s. During these two decades officers grasped power from civilian authorities in a series of post-colonial countries, in Latin America, Africa, Southeast Asia, and the Middle East, where monarchies were overthrown in Libya, Egypt, North Yemen, and Iraq. Huntington was especially concerned with how to reduce the role of the military in politics. His answer was 'professionalisation' – that control over the armed forces was transferred to the civilian authorities.[25] But in the post-colonial world, particularly in the Middle East, professionalisation did not mean that the military were put under civilian control. Instead it meant that they were equipped with more modern weapons, were better trained, and were recruited and promoted for their skills and led by a specialised officer corps. Such a military machine became a challenge to political leaders and therefore the danger of military coups has obliged the rulers to resort to a number of tricks to hinder their own officers from seizing power. In the following, we will focus on the growth of such a professional military machine in Oman and the strategies Sultan Qabus has used to keep his officers in line.

The sultanate is founded

During the eighth century, the isolated land between the al-Hajar mountains and the al-Rub' al-khali desert (the empty corner) became a refuge for the Muslim Ibadis. The Ibadis ensured the local tribes converted to Islam and created a state led by an *imam* initially chosen by the religious leaders and the tribal chiefs. Later this system of elected *imams* gave way to hereditary dynasties. In 1749 Ahmad bin Sa'id, Sohar's governor who was elected *imam* founded the al-Bu Sa'id dynasty that has ruled Oman up to the present day. The al-Bu Sa'id rulers soon abandoned the title of *imam* and moved the capital from the traditional Ibadi seat in Nizwa in the interior to the coastal town of Muscat in order to concentrate on maritime trade, and the sultanate Muscat was established here around 1775. From this town, and others along the Batina coast, Omani seamen trade over the Indian Ocean in, among other commodities, spices and incense (*myrra*). The sultanate became a maritime great power in the nineteenth century, ruling over areas along Africa's east coast (Zanzibar and Mombassa) and the coast of India (Gwadar in present-day Pakistan).

However, conflicts often arose between the sultanate in Muscat, which was liberal and extrovert, and the more conservative and introvert Ibadi *imams* who still had power over the interior. Early in the nineteenth century the al-Bu Sa'id sultanate came under the influence of the United Kingdom. The sultans depended on British protection against external threats, as well as later against the *imamate* that declared itself independent when Salim bin Rashid al-Kharusi was elected *imam* in 1913. In the last half of the nineteenth century the al-Bu Sa'id sultanate, weakened as a result of a succession dispute, gradually lost control over the interior. In 1920 the Sultan of Muscat was obliged to sign the Sib agreement, granting the *imamate* of Oman *de facto* independence.

A professional army develops

Traditionally the sultanate's armed forces consisted of two types: as a standing army, the sultan's mercenary (Arab. *'askari*) manned the forts in the capital and in other towns along the Batina coast as well as the forts of the governors in the interior. By hiring non-Omanis (Hadramis, Baluchis, Persians, East Africans, and so on) the sultan made sure he had a loyal army that would not intervene in politics. Exceptionally, mainly in the interior, the sultan recruited soldiers from the dominant tribe in a given area. On an *ad hoc* basis for greater military campaigns the ruler sought aid from allied tribes. But the tribal warriors were usually motivated by the chance of winning booty rather than by loyalty to the sultan.[26]

The sultanate in addition sought military support from outside powers, including the British.[27] At the end of the nineteenth century the British established bases in Oman, respectively in Salalah in Dhofar and on Masirah Island in the Indian Ocean. The sultanate became isolated, with the UK as security guarantor and the loss of its overseas territories, the sultanate had no need of soldiers other than the mercenaries for protecting the sultan in Muscat. Nevertheless repeated attacks from the *imams* in the interior showed that a stronger standing force was needed. So in 1921 the British founded the Muscat Levy Corps (MLF), the first modern military force on the Arabian Peninsula. This corps had a British commander and Indian soldiers and was the core of Oman's armed forces up to the 1950s.[28]

The 1950s and 1960s

In the 1950s, during the reign of Sultan Sa'id bin Taimur al-Sa'id, the sultanate's armed forces began to expand. There were three main reasons for this: Saudi invasion, tribal rebellions, and oil prospecting. In 1952 the British started the Batinah Force (BF), driving out the Saudi forces that had invaded the al-Buraymi-oasis that same year. Some years later the Petroleum Development Oman (PDO) financed the establishment of the Muscat and Oman Field Force (MOFF).[29] In 1954, thanks to this force, PDO was able to prospect in the interior. However, this provoked a tribal rebellion that continued right up to 1959, the leader of which was the Saudi-supported *imam* Ghalib in Nizwa. The *imam* regarded the prospecting expedition as a breach of the Sib agreement of 1920. Ghalib wanted complete independence for the *Imamate* of Oman from the Sultanate in Muscat. To combat the rebels Sa'id again had to call in British troops.[30] An agreement between the sultan and the British authorities led to MLF, BF, and MOFF being amalgamated into the Sultan's Armed Forces (SAF) and the sultanate was promised British aid to further develop its military apparatus. Subsequently, the foundations were laid for the Sultan of Oman's Air Force (SOAF) and the Sultan of Oman's Navy (SON) and the agreement prolonged the United Kingdom's base rights in the country.[31]

In 1964 a rebellion broke out in Dhofar instigated by the Marxist movement Dhofar's Liberation Front (DLF). Gradually DLF won the backing of the communist regime in South Yemen (which came to power in 1967), the Soviet Union and China, who all worked to overturn the pro-west monarchies on the Arabian Peninsula. Sultan Sa'id was soon pushed into a defensive position *vis-à-vis* DLF's guerrilla soldiers as his troops were poorly trained and equipped.[32] Sa'id's poor handling of the Dhofar conflict ended in his being deposed as sultan.

After 1970

In 1970, with British backing, Qabus seized power from his father. Relations between father and son had long been strained – rumour had it that this was the result of the father in a rage smashing the son's Bee Gee records. The British were dissatisfied with Sa'id's rule: a few years previously a British diplomat stationed in Muscat sent a report home to the Foreign Office in which he declared that Oman was 'at full steam into the sixteenth century'. Omani society was under-developed and isolated. The sultan personally signed all visas for the country. Only one hospital existed and this was run by Western missionaries. Oman had four schools and only one tarmac road (10 kilometres between Muscat and Matrah). Electric lights existed only in the sultan's palace. Joseph A. Kechichian claims that just as Charles de Gaulle had 'a definite vision for France' so had Qabus for a new Oman.[33] His vision was an opening to the world outside, independence, and modernisation. To realise this Qabus took on the role of 'chief moderniser'. He rapidly took control of the government and the key ministries and began ambitious modernisation programmes. However, the sultan showed little interest in delegating power to his own family or to the people.

A condition for executing these programmes was to end the DLF conflict as it was depleting the state finances and undermining the Sultan's legitimacy. Qabus reorganised the defence and sought support from abroad. The British sent troops immediately, including Special Air Service (SAS) and advisors. In 1971 during the bicentenary of the Iranian kingdom in Persepolis, Qabus requested both the Shah of Iran and King Husayn of Jordan for help. Both felt that it served their interests to prevent Oman from becoming a 'people's republic' – and accordingly sent military aid. Thanks to help from abroad and a successful policy to bring the population of Dhofar over to his side, the forces loyal to the sultan began a decisive offensive against DLF's positions in the mountains. In 1975 the last guerrilla fighters were driven from Oman into South Yemen and Qabus declared the war won.

Qabus, who was trained at the Royal Military Academy Sandhurst and previously had served as an officer in the British Army on the Rhine, has during his reign moved the SAF into 'modern times'. In 2001, Oman's armed forces numbered 31,500 men, including both regular infantry units and various supporting units, and is the largest force on the Arabian Peninsula in proportion to its population. Oman's air force numbers 4,200 men while its navy that guards the 2,000 kilometre-long coast and interests in the strategically vital Hormuz Straits, consists of 4,200. In addition there are two tribally based militia, respectively Firqat with 3,500 and the 85-man strong Shikuk Tribal Militia on the Musandam Peninsula. Included in the army are the estimated 6,000 soldiers in the Royal Household troops whose main task is to protect the sultan and his family. The various components in this unit are the Royal Guard of Oman (4,500 men), the British-trained Sultan's Special Forces (altogether 1,000 men), the Royal Yacht Squadron, and the Royal Flight Squadron. The Royal Oman Police counts 6,000 men and women while the Internal Security Services (ISS) are 4,000 men. The security forces formally have as their principal job to reveal corruption and monitor 'religious extremists'.[34]

Since 1984 Qabus has really gone in for 'Omanising' the sultanate's military system. This policy is consistent with Niccolò Machiavelli's recommendations. He claimed that mercenaries are expensive in peace and unreliable in war.[35] For a long time officers and instructors in the SAF were seconded from the British Army or hired in with, in addition, Jordanians and Pakistanis serving as administrative personnel, engineers, and officers. Now, foreign personnel have gradually been replaced by Omanis and Qabus has initiated a series of measures for training SAF's soldiers. Little by little he has succeeded in training both officers and pilots and by 1990 all SAF's command and staff posts were manned by Omanis.[36] Intelligence and security services were 'Omanised' too: in 1987 the Omani Foreign Intelligence Department, led by former MI6 officer Reginald Temple and long dominated by British advisors, was replaced by ISS under Omani leadership.[37]

Qabus' reforms of the armed forces bore fruit. Many believe Oman's soldiers are among the most professional and best motivated on the Arabian Peninsula.[38] As a consequence of the close cooperation with the UK, the sultanate's armed forces have often been described as a 'mini version' of the British Army.[39] After the British withdrew from their bases in 1977, however, the USA took over the role of guarantor of Oman's external security. The British reluctantly accepted the American presence but tried to maintain their commercial and military interests in Oman. In 1990–1 Oman participated in Operation Desert Shield and Operation Desert Storm both by sending troops to Saudi Arabia and by granting the USA access to its air space and port facilities. At the beginning of the operation the Omani troops were the only GCC forces capable of operating effectively with Western forces on account of their identical equipment and procedures. For Qabus the police and the ISS have also been efficient instruments for the suppression of internal dissidents. During the 1990s there were a number of riots in the country. Between 300 and 400 people were arrested by the security forces in 1994, accused of 'Islamist-inspired violence'. In 1997, there were new clashes between the security forces and demonstrators, then an alleged al-Qa'ida cell was exposed in 2002.[40] In 2005 it was announced that 'at least 100 suspected Islamists' had been arrested for plotting to attack a festival marking the start of the Muslim celebration *'id al-adha*. About 30 of these were convicted to prison sentences for planning to overthrow the sultan and reinstall the *imamate* in Nizwa.[41] Nevertheless it seems more likely these protests were against the elite's corruption and the sultan's authoritarian rule.

Three control strategies

After Sultan Qabus seized power in 1970 the armed forces have been an essential support for his regime. But to keep in power the sultan has also been obliged to prevent ambitious men within his own military apparatus from executing coups. In the following we shall analyse three strategies Qabus has used to hinder his armed forces from seizing power.

Personal involvement

The first strategy Qabus chose is to build loyalty among his men by personally involving himself in the military. Like the former kings Husayn of Jordan and Hassan II of Morocco the sultan has shown great interest in his armed forces and very much favours them. He has declared that his own military experiences, as a Sandhurst-trained officer in the British Army and in the Dhofar War, were milestones in his life.[42] Military uniforms are the only Western clothes the sultan is seen in, which makes him appear an active military commander and Omani media regularly show photographs of Qabus with his soldiers while he is inspecting manoeuvres or competitions. Consequently, the Sultan's commitment makes many Omani soldiers feel personal loyalty to him.[43]

As commander-in-chief, Qabus has personally seen to the military's corporate needs. In the armed forces the sultan has created a well-paid, prestigious career path for men who in the main have been recruited from conservative tribe-dominated parts of the country. High social status goes with training at Sultan Qabus' Military College, the Officer's training School, and the Sultan's Armed Forces Command Staff College and the period of service that follows. In this way Oman distinguishes itself from the other Gulf monarchies, where military service carries low status.[44] Qabus has also given the military high priority on the national budget. After the end of the Dhofar War, the sultan could point to the combination of the Iranian Revolution, the Soviet invasion of Afghanistan, the radicalisation of the Marxist regime in South Yemen, and the Iran–Iraq War to justify the expense. According to Anthony H. Cordesman, during the early 1980s Oman was spending between 16 and 22 per cent of its GDP annually on the armed forces. The money has mainly been spent on the purchase of expensive, primarily British, military equipment.[45] However, since the end of the 1980s, military expenditure has been reduced and this must largely been seen against the background of the end of the Iran–Iraq War and sinking oil revenues. Nonetheless, in 2007 Oman was still in the global 'top list', spending 12.3 per cent of its GDP on the military and employing 6.1 per cent of its work force in the armed forces.[46] A consequence of this continuing high military expenditure, however, is that there is less money left over for developing education and the health sector, house building and other infrastructure, and for job creation for Oman's young and rapidly growing population.

Personal appointments

Qabus' second strategy is to recruit loyal men to key officers' positions. The sultan has made bonds of friendship the basis for recruitment to top positions in the armed forces. The sultan's most trusted man over the years has been 'Ali bin Majid al-Ma'mari, who is head of the Office of the Supreme Commander – a newly founded council for the coordination of SAF's activities – and the Palace Office. 'Ali bin Majid al-Ma'mari is one of Qabus' closest friends and enjoys the sultan's personal confidence. He is a very powerful *eminence grise* in Oman since he is responsible for all matters concerning the sultanate's internal security.[47] Furthermore Qabus has recruited officers from those segments of Omani society that he considers most loyal. The sultan's 'Omanising' policy has replaced British officers with Omanis, but the new officer corps is not representative of Oman's population as a whole. Calvin Allen and W. Lynn Rigsbee show that, disproportionately, many officers come from tribes in North Oman, who have a long tradition of cooperating with the al-Bu Sa'id Sultanate in Muscat. Men of the Ma'mari, Kalbani, Balushi, and Zidgali tribes dominate the highest officers' posts. The latter two are Baluchis, who traditionally have made up the main body of Oman's armed forces, while the Ma'maris have traditionally been recruited as mercenaries to the sultan's army.[48]

Allen and Rigsbee find it striking how certain social groups are scarcely represented in the armed forces. First, there are few Dhofaris in leading officers' positions. Second, certain of the biggest northern tribes are under-represented in the officers' corps.[49] This indicates that Qabus has consciously held parts of Omani society outside the armed forces, parts that earlier had fought against al-Bu Sa'id rule, respectively the *imamate* rebels in north Oman and the DLF rebellion in Dhofar. Third, and most striking, there are hardly any members of Qabus' own family in the military. Up to 2004, Shihab bin Tariq al-Sa'id served as commander of RON. Shihab's brother, Asad bin Tariq, was for a brief period head of the sultan's Armour. A peripheral member of the family, Yusuf bin Khalfan bin Zahirb al-Bu Sa'id, served for a while as Defence Secretary. But none of Qabus' three cousins, often named as his most likely successors, the brothers Haitham bin Tariq al-Sa'id, Shihab bin Tariq al-Sa'id, and Asad bin Tariq al-Sa'id, have military office.[50]

Both Shihab and Asad are today personal advisors for Qabus. The fact that the Sultan keeps his closest relatives away from the armed forces may indicate that he wishes to prevent these potential rivals from building their own power bases. Here too Qabus distinguishes himself from his monarch colleagues on the Arabian Peninsula. According to Michael Herb, the peninsula's dynastic monarchs are characterised by their distribution of princes throughout the officers' corps. In this way the rulers ensure they have loyal officers and a 'spy network' in the officers' corps.[51] In Saudi Arabia, for example, the top military positions are reserved for King 'Abdallah (leader of the National Guard) and Crown Prince Sultan (Defence Secretary) and several princes can be found in the armed forces. In Kuwait, where the number of princes is lower, the officer princes keep their eyes peeled for the least sign of disloyalty from non-ruling colleagues and man the guard that protects the emir. In 2004 the royal family of Bahrain controlled all eight of the top posts in the armed forces.[52]

Foreign mercenaries

The last strategy Qabus has used to hinder the army from executing a coup has been to hire foreign mercenaries for the Royal Household Troops, whose job it is to protect the royal household. The command structure of the units of the Royal Household Troops is only slightly 'Omanised'. The Royal Guard of Oman, the Sultan's Special Forces, the Royal Yacht Squadron, and the Royal Flight Squadron are all under the command of British officers.[53] These Special Forces distinguish themselves in this way from Oman's ordinary armed forces that are to a large extent 'Omanised'. In the late 1990s there were about 3,700 foreigners employed in SAF, of which there are 150 British officers and advisors, that is less than 10 per cent of the total force.[54] This is a low figure compared to neighbouring Qatar and the Emirates, where respectively 70 per cent and 30–50 per cent of military personnel are foreign, among these Omani mercenaries. But apparently Qabus still does not dare entrust the job of protecting himself and his family to Omani soldiers. This might have something to do with the attempted assassination of the Sultan's father, Sa'id, by his own soldiers during a military parade in Salalah in 1967. Moreover, other Arab monarchs have suffered assassination attempts by their own armed men. For example, Morocco's King Hassan II barely escaped when a group of army officers attacked his summer palace Skhirat, south of Rabat, in 1971 and yet again the year after when a Moroccan jet pilot tried to shoot down the plane he was on from Paris to Rabat.

Oman's modern armed forces have contributed to ensuring the sultan's security by combating both internal separatism (the *imam* in Nizwa and the DLF in Dhofar) and foreign powers' attempts at infiltration (Saudi Arabia, South Yemen, the Soviet Union, and China). At the same time Qabus has made use of the police and the security forces to safeguard his position as the country's all powerful sultan. So far Sultan Qabus has succeeded with his three strategies to hinder his men from seizing power. He has built a military structure in which the soldiers' personal loyalty to the sultan is emphasised. In addition he has made sure reliable men are handpicked for key officers' positions and foreign mercenaries are hired for the units that guard the ruling household. Potential coup-makers will find it hard to get close enough to kill the sultan, yet alone to seize power in Oman.

Conclusion

After 1970 the monarchic forms of government in the Middle East had managed to withstand both inner and outer pressures. Thanks to their financial and political resources the monarchies have adapted to the challenges of the modern age. Three structural factors have particularly contributed to their survival: first, the rentier states on the Arabian Peninsula – Bahrain, the Emirates, Kuwait, Oman, Qatar, and Saudi Arabia – have the financial strength to dominate the local economies, distribute welfare, develop the state apparatus, and undermine potential rivals. Second, the ruling houses on the Arabian Peninsula, with the exception of Oman, have developed into dynastic monarchies, where they themselves dominate the state system and have mechanisms that work well to regulate internal conflicts. Third, all the monarchies have greatly benefited from powerful foreign allies that have strategic and economic interests in the survival of these regimes. Morocco and Jordan – which are neither rentier states nor dynastic monarchies – seem more vulnerable. But because of capable kings like Hassan II of Morocco and Husayn of Jordan, who both had the will to use force and the ability to balance various social groups against each other as well as having the support of foreign allies, the royal houses in these countries have survived.

Further reading

Allen Jr., Calvin H. and W. Lynn Rigsbee: *Oman under Qaboos: From Coup to Constitution, 1970–1996*. London and New York: Taylor and Francis, 2002.

Crystal, Jill: *Oil and Politics in the Gulf: Rulers and Merchants in Kuwait and Qatar*. Cambridge: Cambridge University Press, 1995.

Gause III, F. Gregory: Oil *Monarchies: Domestic and Security Challenges in the Arab Gulf States*. New York: Council of Foreign Relations, 1994.

Herb, Michael: *All in the Family: Absolutism, Revolution, and Democracy in the Middle Eastern Monarchies*. Albany: State University of New York Press, 1999.

Kostiner, Joseph (ed.): *Middle East Monarchies: The Challenge of Modernity*. Boulder and London: Lynne Rienner Publishers, 2000.

Luciani, Giacomo and Hazem Beblawi: *The Rentier State: Nation, State and Integration in the Arab World*. London: Croom Helm, 1987.

Milton-Edwards, Beverley: *Jordan: a Hashemite Legacy*. London: Routledge, 2nd edition, 2009.

Peterson, J.E.: *Oman's Insurgencies: The Sultanate's Struggle for Supremacy*. London, San Francisco, and Beirut: al-Saqi Books, 2007.

Valeri, Marc: *Oman: Politics and Society in the Qaboos State*. New York: Columbia University Press, 2009.

Vassiliev, Alexei: *The History of Saudi Arabia*. London: al-Saqi Books, 2000.

Waterbury, John: *The Commander of the Faithful: The Moroccan Political Elite – A Study of Segmented Politics*. London: Weidenfeld & Nicolson, 1970.

Zahlan, Rosemary Said: *The Making of the Modern Gulf States*. Reading, England: Ithaca Press, 2nd edition, 1998.

8 Republics

Egypt is a democratic state! I will let the people choose between my two sons [Gamal and Alaʿa].[1]

In 2001 Saʿd al-Din Ibrahim, Egyptian sociologist and democracy activist, was sentenced to seven years in prison. The authorities' case was that his research institute, the Ibn Khaldun Centre, had received funding from foreign actors that wished to undermine the Egyptian state. A more probable explanation, however, is that Ibrahim was being punished for a satirical article in which he pointed out monarchistic traits in Syria, Iraq, and – far worse in the eyes of the authorities – Egypt. He categorised all of these governments as *jumlakiyya*, a concept made up of the Arabic words *jumhuriyya* (republic) and *mamlaka* (kingdom). The occasion was the shift of leadership from father to son in Syria in 2000. Bashar al-Asad's taking over power led to speculations over similar future dynastic changes in leadership in other Arab republics. Husni Mubarak, Egypt's president since 1981 has never appointed a vice-president, despite having passed the age of eighty. He has several times dismissed speculations that he wants his son Gamal as president. But despite these dismissals, the future of Gamal is the talk of Cairo. That the president's son is being groomed to take over is not only openly discussed in the coffee houses but also widely debated in the media.

Authoritarian presidents such as Habib Bourguiba, Husni Mubarak, Saddam Husayn, Hafiz al-Asad, ʿAli ʿAbdallah Salih, and Muʿammar al-Qadhafi have monopolised power in the Arab republics since 1970. The president's confidence, based either on blood or friendship, is the key to influence. Consequently, to get something done it is far more effective to visit someone close to the president than to operate through the formal state apparatus. Those who dare to criticise the president can look forward to a grim meeting with the police, the justice system, and prison. Dangerous voices are silenced by the ruler's torturers.

Table 9   Republics in the Middle East (2010)

State	Highest executive authority	Year of birth	Year (in which formally) inaugurated
Algeria	President 'Abd al-'Aziz Bouteflika	1937	1999
Egypt	President Muhammad Husni Mubarak	1928	1981
Iraq	Prime Minister Nuri al-Maliki[a]	1950	2006
Iran	Leader *ayatollah* Ali Khamene'i	1939	1989
Israel	Prime Minister Benjamin Netanyahu	1949	2009
Lebanon	President Michel Sulayman	1948	2008
Libya	Colonel Mu'ammar al-Qadhafi	1942	1969
Syria	President Bashar al-Asad	1966	2000
Tunisia	President Zine al-Abidine ben 'Ali	1936	1987
Turkey	Prime Minister Reçep Tayyip Erdoğan	1954	2002
Yemen	President 'Ali 'Abdallah Salih	1942	1978/1990[b]

[a] Maliki, from the Shi'a Islamist Da'wa Party, was the first prime minister to be appointed in accordance with the new constitution of October 2005.
[b] Salih was the president of North Yemen 1978–90 and has been the president of the united Yemen since 1990.

In this chapter we shall discuss the following question: how can one explain the strong concentration of power in most Arab presidents' hands after 1970? (See Table 9 for a summary of republics in the Middle East.) To shed light on this theme we shall take a closer look at Syria in the last part of the chapter. How have war and conflict influenced the government of Syria?

'Monarchistic presidency'

Several researchers, like Sa'd al-Din Ibrahim, have drawn parallels between the republics and the monarchies of the Arab world. One of these is Nazih N. Ayubi, who underlines the similarities by introducing the concept 'monarchistic presidency' of the governments of countries such as Egypt, Syria, Yemen, Libya, and (pre-2003) Iraq.[2] The presidents in the Arab countries, with the exception of Iraq and Lebanon, have constitutional or *de facto* lifetime terms of office. An obvious similarity between Arab republics and monarchies is dynastic transfer of power. In Syria in 2000 Bashar al-Asad inherited the presidency from his father, and in Iraq, up to the USA's occupation in the spring of 2003, Saddam Husayn's son, Qusay, was believed to be the man who would take over the presidency once his father died. In Libya many regard Qadhafi's son, Sayf al-Islam, as the regime's 'crown prince'. Ahmad Salih, son of Yemen's president 'Ali 'Abdallah Salih, has a corresponding role.

Fred Halliday mentions four other similarities between Arab republics and monarchies.[3] First, the presidents are as authoritarian as the monarchs: in spite of a democratic varnish, the republics permit no real competition for the most important positions of power and suppress any tendency for disorder or opposition. Second, the presidents recruit – in the same way as the dynastic monarchies that are described in Chapter 7 – relatives and friends to positions of power. The clientelism we have discussed previously has reduced the importance of formal state institutions. Power is linked to how close you are to the president rather than to your formal position in the state hierarchy. Third, accountancy and auditing are as incomplete and as dubious in the republics as they are in the monarchies. The president personally administers parts of the state's revenue that are never accounted for. Even though several Arab republics call themselves 'socialist', in reality, a tiny elite enjoys a giant share of the state cake. Access to this money makes it possible for the elite to buy the loyalty of potential opponents through bribes and corruption. Fourth, the presidents, just as the monarchs, are the centres of considerable personality cults. Pictures of the president hang in public buildings, taxis, shops, and even private homes. Statues and other public monuments emphasise his grandeur and wisdom. The leader's slogans and quotations cover posters, while books of his speeches and writings fill the bookshops and libraries. Streets and towns are named after him. Authors and poets are commanded to produce panegyrics praising the leader. Some of the presidents have been in power so long they have become an integral part of the national identity.

In his book *Neopatriarchy* Hisham Sharabi describes how modernity (historical development) meets patriarchalism (form of traditional society where the family is the basic unit and the father the highest figure of authority) in the Arab world. Sharabi regards Arab society as 'neither modern nor traditional'.[4] In Arab society, claims Sharabi, patriarchalism has not been supplanted as a result of modernisation. Instead this traditional social arrangement has been strengthened and continued in rejuvenated and partly modernised forms. Despite modern institutions and constitutions that reflect modern ideas, the neo-patriarchal state 'is in many ways no more than a modernised version of the traditional patriarchal sultanat'.[5]

It is important to underline that not all Middle East presidents have as much power. In Israel, where the prime minister is the highest executive authority, the president has only a ceremonial role. The president of Turkey, too, has a ceremonial role, but since the 1960s up to the election of Islamic-oriented Abdallah Gül, this post was also a guarantee for the country's military bureaucratic elite in that the president has the right to use a delaying veto against bills he considers to be in conflict with Turkey's secular constitution. The Iranian constitution prescribes a strong presidency but an even stronger Leader (Pers. *rahbar*). In Lebanon and Algeria various factors moderate the president's powers.

Lebanon's constitution prescribes considerable limits on the president's powers. Article 49 clearly states: 'The President's term is for six years. He may not be re-elected until six years after the expiration of his last mandate'.[6] Lebanese presidents that have tried to amend the constitution in order to prolong their term of office have usually been stopped. In 2004 Emile Lahoud – with strong support from Syria – managed to get parliament to change the constitution so he could cling onto power for a further three years. The year after, however, the assassination of Lebanon's former prime minister, Rafiq al-Hariri, and the victory of the anti-Syrian coalition led by Sa'd al-Hariri in the parliamentary elections led to massive pressure from Sunni Muslims and Christians to reduce Syria's influence in the country. Lahoud's resignation in November 2007 threw Lebanon into a political crisis that nearly unleashed a new civil war. The main fault line divided the Western-supported government of Fuad Seniora from the Hizbollah-led opposition. Half a year later, in May 2008, parliament united behind the compromise candidate General Michel Sulayman as the new president.

In Algeria no president, with the exception of General Houari Boumedienne (1968–78), who was a charismatic and strong personality, has managed to build up a strong position. After Boumedienne, particularly in the period 1992–2004, Algeria was dominated by an elite of six or seven generals – popularly known as *les décideurs* or *le pouvoir*. The generals had total power, appointing and dismissing presidents at will and in 1999 with the generals' support 'Abd al-'Aziz Bouteflika was elected president. Gradually, Bouteflika has strengthened his position, *vis-à-vis* the military oligarchs, as a result of succeeding in bringing Algeria, which was isolated as a result of the civil war in the 1990s, back into the international fold. In 2001 Bouteflika tied close bonds with the EU, and later the same year allied himself with the USA in 'the war on terror'. Moreover, he gained vital support from a new generation of officers that were fed up with the bloody civil war of the nineties. The younger officers wished to distance the armed forces from politics, modernise the armed forces, and normalise relations with the West. In addition, Bouteflika has systematically undermined the military oligarchs. From 2004 to 2005 the president, who is also Minister of Defence, dismissed 1,000 older officers in order to strengthen civilian control over the armed forces. Among those thrown out of office were the powerful Chief of Staff, General Muhammad al-Amari, and his protégé, General Fudhil Sharid, who had become opponents of Bouteflika. Both were replaced by officers loyal to the president.[7] Bouteflika was elected president in 1999 and 2004, and has forced through an amendment of the constitution's Article 74 so that he could stand for election for a third five-year term in 2009.[8] On April 10, 2009, it was announced that Bouteflika had won the presidential election, which was boycotted by several opposition parties.

The constitution

Nathan J. Brown has analysed the role of the constitution in the Arab world.[9] One of the purposes of his study is to show how the rulers can use the constitution to strengthen their rule. Brown asserts that the Arab republics have often introduced constitutions with one or two aims in mind: either to signal national independence or to proclaim a revolutionary breach with an earlier form of government. According to Brown, constitutions formulated with such ends are rich in ideological declarations but poor in principles for the division of powers. Without the division of powers there is no rule of law. In agreement with the desire to proclaim national independence or to break with a former form of government the Arab republics' constitutions prescribe a strong executive. Therefore in most Arab republics the president was given considerable power. Mechanisms that limit the authority of the president, protect the rights of individuals, and hold the executive responsible are, on the contrary, poorly developed.[10] The constitutions emphasise democracy and the rule of law as a basic principle. For instance, Article 1 of Syria's constitution states that Syria is a 'democracy', while Article 50 establishes that '[t]he members of the People's Assembly are elected by general, secret, direct, and equal ballot in accordance with the provisions of the election law'.[11] But despite these clauses, the legislature and the judiciary, both in Syria and in most other Arab republics, have a very subordinate position.

According to the constitutions, the president is usually not just the head of state but also the party chairman and head of the armed forces. He himself appoints the vice-president, the prime minister, and the government. In addition, he often appoints judges. In Article 107 of Syria's constitution one can read, in glaring contrast to Articles 1 and 50, '[t]he President of the Republic can dissolve the People's Assembly through a decision giving the reasons'. Further, Article 110 declares that '[t]he President of the Republic may draft project laws and submit them to the Assembly for approval'.[12] Besides such powers of authority the constitutions grant the executive the right to declare a state of emergency and trial by martial court. In the 1960s the military regimes in Egypt, Syria, and Iraq used the conflict with Israel and the threat from 'fifth columns' as an excuse to do just that. In Syria there has been a state of emergency since 1963, and Egypt has had an almost continuous state of emergency since 1967 despite the country signing a peace treaty with Israel as early as 1979. Military law, for example, enables the secret police (Arab. *mukhabarat*) to arrest persons who are suspected of being a security threat and hold them for an unlimited period without trial. Furthermore, the law allows the authorities to censure the press, prohibit political parties, and restrict the right of assembly to prevent demonstrations. After 11 September 2001 the so-called 'war on terror' has been a godsend to authorities in the Arab world with regard to justifying the continuance of the state of emergency. For instance, in February 2003 the Egyptian parliament voted – with reference to the 'war on terror' – to prolong the state of emergency. Kamal al-Shazly, Secretary of State for Parliament and Advisory Organs, even pointed at the USA's anti-terror legislation as a model for Egypt.[13]

The tendency towards the dynastic transfer of power in the republics underlines the weak position of the legislative and judicial branches. In Article 83 of Syria's constitution it said: 'A candidate for the presidency must be an Arab Syrian, enjoying his civil and political rights, and be over 40 years of age.'[14] In 2000, the year Hafiz al-Asad died, Bashar was only 34. However, the same day that Hafiz died, 10 June, parliament unanimously voted to amend the constitution to lower the minimum age to 34 years of age. A few days later parliament, again unanimously, accepted the Ba'th Party's nomination of Bashar as presidential candidate. The farce ended in a highly manipulated referendum in which 97 per cent of Syrians supported Bashar as the country's new president.

According to Yemen's constitution Chapter 2, Article 111, a president cannot sit for longer than two five-year terms.[15] Consequently, the 2006 election was the last time 'Ali 'Abdallah Salih could stand as a candidate. As in Syria the constitution makes it clear that a presidential candidate must be older than 40 years.[16] But the president's son, Ahmad, is in his thirties. There has been speculation as to whether the authorities have adjusted Ahmad's age upwards in public to make him old enough to stand as a candidate in the next presidential elections.

In Egypt today there is no clear procedure for how Husni Mubarak's successor will be appointed. Article 82 of the constitution makes it clear that the vice-president shall take over the executive power when the president 'is unable to carry out his functions'.[17] Both Anwar al-Sadat and Husni Mubarak had been vice-presidents for a number of years before they became presidents. On those occasions when Mubarak was confronted with the fact that he had never appointed a vice-president, he referred to Article 84, which specifies that the speaker of parliament or the chief justice of the Supreme Court if parliament is dissolved shall function as president in the absence of a vice-president. A new president is to be chosen within 60 days. It would hardly come as a surprise if the National Democratic Party nominated the president's son, Gamal, as candidate.

'Hijacked' state systems

At first sight the Middle East republics have an impressive state system. Their formal state institutions give them the appearance of modern bureaucratised states. However, the real power structures are most often of a subtler sort in the republics, as in the monarchies. In Chapter 4 we saw how groups can 'hijack' whole state systems by playing the ethnic community card. Just as in the family-ruled monarchies, the patriarchs rule in republics such as Egypt, Libya, Yemen, and Syria through bonds of blood and friendship. As, among others, Robert Springborg and Michel Seurat have shown in examples from Egypt and Syria, such bonds create a solid group identity,[18] or as Ibn Khaldun would have said *'asabiyya*. The elite functions as a 'quasi tribe' within the state system that has gained control over the repressive system, the party and the bureaucracy. The division between state and regime is thus rubbed out and the state systems become instruments to promote the ruling elite's special interests.

The repressive system

Military officers were behind the establishment of most republican regimes in the Middle East. Steven A. Cook shows in his book *Ruling but not Governing* how the military establishments still dominate these regimes. The repressive systems in the Middle East are obviously the outer parameter of regime protection. Moreover, the officer corps have, in cooperation with their civilian allies, gradually created political systems that take care of their particular interests rather than those of the society as a whole. According to Cook, civilian institutions – parliaments, courts, political parties, and so on – function as a curtain that hides the real power – the repressive system.[19]

All 'monarchistic presidents' came to power through coup d'états or military careers. Ahmad Hassan al-Bakr (1968–79), Hafiz al-Asad (1970–2000), and Anwar al-Sadat (1970–81) all became presidents in the wake of the defeat inflicted by Israel in 1967. Robert Owen shows how the new rulers expanded the military machine: first, more soldiers were called up, they were better equipped with more sophisticated Russian weapons, and given better training with the immediate result that the armed forces performed far better on the battlefield against Israel as early as 1973. Second, various paramilitary organisations were established with principal responsibility for domestic security. In Egypt this was the Central Security Police, and in Syria the Defence Companies under the leadership of the president's brother, Rif'at al-Asad.[20]

The repressive system soon became the most important instrument of power of the 'monarchistic presidents'. As we shall see, the state of emergency sets ordinary legal procedures aside, granting the ruler justification to use the repressive system to crush any sign of internal disturbance and opposition. The presidents have time and time again used the armed forces against their own people. For example, in 1982 Syrian president Hafiz al-Asad brought in the army against Islamic rebels in the town of Hama. The town was left in ruins and between 5,000 and 10,000 were killed, most of them civilians.[21] In 1987–9 Saddam Husayn carried out his so-called Anfal campaign against Kurd rebels in North Iraq, where, according to Human Rights Watch, tens of thousands of Kurds were killed, among them a great many non-combatants, women and children, and hundreds of thousands were forced to flee. As many as 2,000 villages lay in ruins. And during the campaign Iraqi forces are said to have used chemical weapons against the town of Halabjah, killing 4,000.[22] As a result of these experiences of repression a culture of fear has grown: countless tales of terror have circulated recounting what the thugs of the regime will do to those who defy the ruler. There are many stories of those who have 'disappeared', ending up in the torture chambers of notorious prisons such as Abu Salim in Tripoli, Mezze in Damascus, Abu Ghraib in Baghdad, Evin in Tehran, and Mazra't tora in Cairo. According to the Egyptian Organisation for Human Rights, at the end of the 1990s there were as many as 15,000–20,000 political prisoners in Egyptian jails.[23] In Saddam Husayn's Iraq people hesitated to talk of politics even in their own homes – because 'the walls had ears'.[24]

The repressive system has ensured the survival in power of the 'monarchistic presidents'. But at the same time the armed forces have been a dangerous challenge. The former president of Egypt, Anwar al-Sadat, for instance, was assassinated by Islamists who had infiltrated the army in 1981. Before this, as a result of the 1979 Camp David Peace Agreement with Israel, he had reduced Egyptian forces: both the peace deal and the reductions were highly unpopular with many officers and soldiers. As a result, his successor, Husni Mubarak, reversed the cuts. Another example is Rif'at al-Asad's coup attempt in Syria in 1983. Rif'at tried to seize power while Hafiz was abroad to receive treatment for a heart attack and the battle raged for several days in Damascus before troops loyal to the president regained control. Once bitten twice shy, rulers have used a series of tricks to prevent their own officers from arranging coups. These include taking care of the military's corporative needs and top officers private economic interests by maintaining huge allocations to the repressive system, placing relatives and friends in key officers' posts, rotating officers between military districts and between command and staff posts, and awarding officers equal power and overlapping areas of authority.

The presidents have allowed political control over the military to weigh heavier than the war capability of the state. For instance, the practice of non-meritocratic appointments to officers' posts clearly weakened the military capabilities of the Arab republics and in this context Iraq is a good example. Saddam Husayn was scared of a military coup at the same time as he waged an aggressive foreign policy. Consequently, his efforts to prevent a coup undermined Iraq's ability to wage war. This is an important explanation of the country's catastrophic defeat in the final phase of the Iraq–Iran War in the 1980s and faced with Western military power in 1991 and 2003. A report written by Kevin Woods, James Lacey, and Williamson Murray, based on information obtained under interrogation of Iraqi leaders and the examination of confiscated documents, describes how Saddam Husayn on account of his fears of a domestic rising and a military coup made security decisions that undermined Iraq's defence capability.[25] For example, the President recruited key officers because of their presumed loyalty; he appointed his cousin Barzan 'Abd al-Ghafur Sulayman Majid al-Tikriti as the commander of the Special Republican Guard (Arab. *al-haras al-jumhuri*), the best unit in the Iraqi Army. Yet, his cousin had hardly any military background, was notorious for his drinking, and had failed Officers' College. Another example is Saddam Husayn's military dispositions just before the USA-led invasion in 2003. In this critical phase the President moved divisions of the Iraqi Army from areas near Baghdad to distant regions because of his fear that the forces would try a coup if they were in the capital. Moreover, Saddam Husayn decided that everything had to go via the high command – military divisions were neither allowed to communicate directly with each other nor to move troops on their own initiative. As a result of these restrictions, the various division commanders had to send out reconnaissance patrols to find out where neighbouring Iraqi units were. No officer dared tell the president how bad the situation was for fear of his wrath. Saddam Husayn believed that the USA would not march into the capital fearing it would suffer heavy losses but instead limit itself to taking the strategically vital port of Basra and the oil fields in the south. Even when American troops were knocking on Baghdad's gates, there was nobody who dared warn the President.

Besides being an instrument of repression, this system has also been an important part of the rulers' client network. In states with a high unemployment rate the armed forces are a vital source of jobs, and a military training is a possible career for ambitious young men. The living standard of military employees in poor countries such as Syria and Yemen is above the national average, as well as giving social status to those in the armed forces. Last but not least, the rulers have made it possible for the military to invest in the private sector, and often military firms are subsidised by state capital and concessions, are tax and duty exempt and may enjoy other privileges. Today the military are behind many of the biggest industrial and entrepreneurial businesses in countries such as Algeria, Egypt, Iran, Syria, and Turkey.[26]

In Egypt, for example, the armed forces have been granted a key role in the development of the ambitious Southern Valley Project in the south of the country. The aim of the project, which is to be completed in 2017, is to construct canals, massive irrigation schemes, infrastructure for agriculture, and six larger towns along with four free trade zones. The total budget is 300 billion Egyptian pounds (the equivalent of US$ 3 billion). There are plans for agriculture, industry, and tourism. Fresh water will be transported via the Toshke Canal from Lake Nasir all the way to the Farafra Oasis 500 km into the country. The armed forces are responsible, among other things, for planning, constructing the canal, and the removal of earth, sand, gravel, and stone.[27] State projects of this dimension give officers the chance to enrich themselves, not least through the embezzlement of investment funds.

Table 10　The armed forces in the Middle East (2007)

State	Military expenses in percentage of GDP	Personnel (in thousands)	Weapon imports (in US$ m)
Algeria	3.0	147	471
Bahrain	3.4	8	26
Egypt	2.5	469	770
Emirates	–	51	982
Iraq	2.5	577	268
Iran	2.9	523	340
Israel	8.6	177	967
Jordan	6.2	101	179
Kuwait	3.9	16	276
Lebanon	5.1	56	3
Libya	1.0	76	3
Morocco	3.2	196	32
Oman	10.7	43	4
Qatar	–	12	–
Saudi Arabia	9.3	222	68
Syria	4.4	293	–
Tunisia	1.3	36	–
Turkey	2.1	511	858
Yemen	5.0	67	160
Total		3581	5407+

Source: The figures are taken from Stockholm International Peace Research Institute: *SIPRI Yearbook 2009*, and the International Institute for Strategic Studies: *The Military balance 2009*. Personnel figures taken from 2009 survey.

Since 1970 no other development region has been more militarised than the Middle East:[28] in the 1980s Syria's army, which was engaged in Lebanon, grew to 500,000 men;[29] and in the same decade Iraq, which was at war with Iran, had more than one million men in uniform.[30] The International Institute for Strategic Studies estimates that the region's states together had a total standing army of almost 3.6 million men in 2009; Iran, Iraq, and Turkey all had more than 500,000 armed men.[31] Seen as a whole the region spent around 4 per cent of its GDP on the armed forces and Israel, Oman, and Saudi Arabia spent all above 8 per cent of their GDP[32] (see Table 10).

Militarisation has had adverse development effects. The money spent on the armed forces would have benefited society more had it been invested in civil industry, infrastructure, education, and health – this particularly applies to countries that import arms. The purchase of ready-made weapon systems (fighter planes, rocket batteries, radar systems, and so on) which are operated and maintained by foreign experts does not contribute to development.

The governing party

In the age of mass politics political parties have played an important role in the Middle East. In Tunisia and Algeria, Dustur and Front de Libération Nationale respectively led the struggle against French rule in the 1950s and 1960s. In Syria and Iraq officers connected to the Ba'th Party seized power. And in Egypt and Libya populist military regimes organised mass parties to build broad popular support. The parties were formed by nationalist movements fighting for independence in the colonial period. They logically emphasised discipline and efficient organisation. For leaders of the populist–authoritarian regimes multi-party systems were associated with splits and inefficiency. So most republics acquired political systems dominated by one party.

Gradually, as the nationalist movements gained power, the independence parties took the role as governing parties. At the same time the rulers did their best to reduce their real power. The parties were stripped of ideology and reorganised in order to mobilise popular support and political control. Through the parties – in the same way as through the military systems – the rulers established their client networks. The parties dominated all the associations – for workers, students, women, farmers, and businessmen. Membership became the key to privileges such as student grants, loans, and jobs, for example, in Tunisia every state employee had to be a member of the Dustur Party. In this way politically engaged groups such as students and state employees were co-opted and as a consequence the parties grew rapidly. In 1979 the Iraqi Ba'th Party had as many as 1.5 million members. The party recruited on a broad basis across confessional and ethnic dividing lines, resulting in a party member in every state department, military unit, school, university, and neighbourhood.[33]

The extension of the party and its members' loyalty made it an efficient informer network for the president. The Ba'th Party had a similar role in Syria. Hafiz al-Asad used the party as a counterweight to both the left and to the growing Islamist movement at the end of the 1970s. In Syria in 2003 the Ba'th Party had about 1.8 million members – as much as 18 per cent of the Syrian population over 14 years of age.[34]

Meanwhile, the ideology that had been the starting point for the various ruling parties was gradually erased. In some cases the parties simply voiced the presidents' policies. Iraq went furthest in this direction with Saddam Husayn taking the role of chief ideologist of the Ba'th Party. Early in the 1980s he was credited with writing as many as 200 political books, articles, and essays.[35] Moreover, the Ba'th Party's ideology, both in Iraq and Syria, was diluted by the party gradually attracting people who were simply out to profit from the president's client network. Saddam Husayn wanted above all loyal Ba'th Party members and consequently, a recruit had to undergo seven to eight years' instruction to be accepted as a full member. Manipulation from above led, however, to the party losing its vitality and spontaneous support. Close association with the state wore out the legitimacy gained from the liberation struggle and opportunists came to dominate the mass of members.

Today in practice most Arab republics are one-party states because the laws are manipulated to make sure that the ruling party still wins a majority. This is a formidable obstacle to democratic development. In recent years there has been a movement towards giving competing parties more freedom, but laws are still used such as those putting severe restrictions on the establishment of new parties, and electoral manipulation still takes place, all to ensure a solid majority for the government party. Chapter 1, Article 5 in Egypt's constitution of 1971 declares, '[T]he political system of the Arab Republic of Egypt is a multiparty one'.[36] But in spite of this Husni Mubarak's National Democratic Party always obtains more than a two-thirds majority in parliament. The explanation is electoral cheating and that the electoral system is constructed in order to give the party a majority. Previously, Tunisia's constitution stated that all the seats in parliament should go to the party that received the most votes. This had been an efficient trick to secure a monopoly of power for President Ben 'Ali's ruling party, Rassemblement Constitutionel et Démocratique. In 2002 a constitutional amendment was passed that meant that the opposition parties were guaranteed at least 20 per cent of the 182 seats in parliament,[37] but in practice this hardly affected the ruling party's dominance. In Syria, the Tenth Ba'th Party Congress resulted in more parties being permitted, provided they were not based on religion or ethnicity – this was to exclude Islamic and Kurdish parties. However, delegates did not accept the removal of Article 8 from Syria's constitution, where it states: 'The leading party in society and the state is the Socialist Arab Ba'th Party'.[38] The prime minister, the speaker of parliament, and the leading government posts shall still be reserved for higher members of the Ba'th Party.

Bureaucracy

The bureaucracy expanded in the same way as the armed forces did during the 1950s and 1960s. A large administration was at that time regarded as necessary. Inspired by Gamal 'Abd al-Nasser's Egypt – the bureaucracy was to be the enlightened ruler's instrument for realising the dream of development. Although this dream never materialised, the over-dimensioned and top-heavy bureaucracy remained. Mugamma', an enormous building in central Cairo with 1,300 offices spread over 13 floors, was for decades the symbol of Arab bureaucracy. Here Egyptians and travellers were sent back and forth for hours on end to get their papers in order. The main reason why the bureaucracy has not been slimmed down and made more efficient is that this part of the state apparatus has also become part of the ruler's client network. Goods are distributed through the bureaucracy in several ways.

First, a privileged 'class' has sprung up that uses its position within the state administration for personal profit – from top to bottom in most state offices the employees accept bribes. According to Nazih N. Ayubi, the regimes have long quietly accepted this practice, which he characterises as 'tolerated corruption'.[39] This is a conscious choice made by the rulers to ensure a loyal administration as the regime is scared of losing the support of its civil servants if corruption were no longer tolerated. Second, the bureaucracy has become a 'dumping ground' for freshly educated youngsters. In pace with the population explosion ever bigger numbers enter the job market each year. The rulers fear social turbulence and that young people will be attracted to radical political groups if they fail to get a job after school or university.

To keep control over the leadership in the bureaucracy the 'monarchistic presidents' have used the same tactics as they did with the officer corps, such as, moving top people frequently and unpredictably, recruitment to key posts for loyalty – not ability – and overlapping authority to create interdepartmental rivalry. This policy contributes considerably to undermine the professionalism of the civil service. During the last few decades an overdimensioned, expensive, and inefficient bureaucracy has been under attack from both Western creditors and domestic dissidents. However, the *infitah* policy, started by Anwar al-Sadat, did not mean a downsizing of the state administration. That would have been far too risky for the authoritarian Arab regimes.

A case study: Syria – war and stability

> If I were promised safety,
> if I could meet the Sultan
> I would say to him: O my lord the Sultan!
> my cloak has been torn by your ravenous dogs,
> your spies are following me all the time.
> their eyes
> their noses
> their feet are chasing me
> like destiny, like fate
> They interrogate my wife
> and write down all the names of my friends
> O Sultan!
> Because I dare to approach your deaf walls,
> because I tried to reveal my sadness and tribulation,
> I was beaten with my shoes.
> O my lord the Sultan!
> you have lost the war twice
> because half our people
> has no tongue.[40]

As in most places in the world, war and conflict have played a central role in state building in the Middle East. The First World War laid the foundations for today's sovereign states, and the Second World War led to a breakthrough for the Zionist demand for a Jewish state. Since then the Israel/Palestine conflict has unleashed a series of wars. All the Arab states have in one way or another been engaged and affected by the conflict. The consequences have been greatest for Israel's neighbours. Syria is one of the best examples of a state that has taken shape during the conflict with Israel. Two years after Syria's independence in 1946 the country waged its first war. Since then Syria has had to stand up to the Israeli army in 1967, 1973 and (in Lebanon) in 1982. In contrast to Egypt and Jordan so far Syria has not made a peace treaty with Israel. Since 1970 Syria has been ruled by the 'family firm' Hafiz-al-Asad & Son. How have war and conflict affected the way Syria is ruled?

War and state building

Charles Tilly has studied the connection between war and the creation of states in Europe.[41] He argues that the growth of today's states, with centralised control over given territories, has been closely connected to war. State building, according to Tilly, was both a cause and a result of war in Europe, for not only did rulers go to war to increase their power and influence but waging war also created institutions that were to be the germ of modern states. The cost of war forced the rulers to tax their subjects, and to gather taxes the rulers needed administrative structures that were the forerunners of today's bureaucracy. According to Tilly, the need to collect taxes also promoted the need for legitimacy and building alliances. The rulers who enjoyed the support of their subjects and of elite groups could more easily gather the resources required for waging war. As a consequence, taxpayers, and first and foremost the bourgeoisie, gradually won increased influence.[42] The rulers also cultivated the concept of belonging and of loyalty to the 'nation' to make it easier to collect taxes. As a result, waging war in Europe helped produce strong states with well-developed institutions and that were solidly rooted in the population. After the Peace of Westphalia in 1648, which ended the Thirty Years' War, the European state system found its form.

The context for state building in the Middle East has been quite different from that in Europe. In the Arab world the state system was formed by the colonial powers – at a point in time when the nation-state's borders were perceived as inviolable. The Middle East states were not free to invade and conquer each other in the way European princes had formed their state system. Should there be an attack on the sovereign state system, the militarily superior imperial powers were ready to intervene to defend their interests and 'the world order'. The consequence of this has been that the post-colonial states have fought different types of wars to those of the earlier European states.[43] While European states fought with their neighbours either to expand or defend their own territories, many countries in the Third World have concentrated their war waging capacity on internal conflicts. Another essential difference is that post-colonial states often build up their military systems with the help of foreign aid. During the Cold War, for example, many states received financial aid and military support from the USA and the Soviet Union. Alliances with the great powers have permitted rulers to build up their armed forces without taxing their subjects. The rentier states' incomes from the sale of oil or other natural resources have given similar results. The rulers' expansion of the military machine has therefore not had the same nation-building effect. For Europe, claims Tilly, paradoxically the rulers' efforts to expand their capacity to wage war strengthened the citizens' grasp on the state and on politics.[44] The bureaucracies that arose to raise and supply armies developed into civilian power bastions that gradually gained control over the armed forces. In states that build up their armed forces with outside support and financial aid, on the other hand, the military apparatus stays disproportionately strong. The consequence is that mobilisation for war in post-colonial states has a tendency to create military dictatorships.

Another important reason why military rule is more frequent in post-colonial states than in Europe is that the post-colonial states often suffer from development problems. In many cases civilian governments have been incapable of creating security, peace, and prosperity, thus losing their popularity. On the pretext of a development crisis the armed forces have intervened and dismissed weak civilian leaders. Some even go so far as to claim that a vigorous authoritarian regime is a condition for economic development.[45] But military leaders have also cultivated a feeling of crisis in order to justify their own exercise of power. The feeling of a national crisis, in the sense of a collective perception that the nation is threatened by internal and external dangers, is useful for authoritarian rulers: it prepares the way for the cult of 'the strong man' as 'liberator' or 'saviour'. In *The Prince*, written in 1513, Niccolò Machiavelli emphasised two ideal features for a ruler: he had to be either loved or feared.[46] Of these it were best if the ruler were feared as long as he was not hated. In *The Leviathan*, written in 1651, the Philosopher Thomas Hobbes wrote a variation on this theme.[47] Frightened by the chaos of the English Civil War, Hobbes wrote that humankind's basic need for security could be best served under authoritarian rule. For Hobbes the 'state of nature' was characterised by unbridled desires and therefore the war of all against all. The solution to this anarchic situation was for the inhabitants to conclude a social contract whereby each individual cede their right to rebel to a central power, or Leviathan in Hobbes' terminology, so that people could live in peace. An interesting aspect is that the philosopher underlines the significance of *fear* for maintaining the unity of society.[48] In Hobbes' perspective, fear was a positive force because it helped discipline people. But the right kind of fear had to be created, a task the philosopher left to teachers and priests. Their job was to instruct the citizens in the dangers that threatened human civilisation if the right precautions were not taken. Hobbes, too, had a sense for increasing people's contact with the feeling of fear by using theatrical effects. The state could well exaggerate the dangers, directing fears at certain objects rather than others in order to better control the population. The subjects should also fear the central power (*Leviathan*) in order to ensure respect for the social order.

History provides many instances of rulers who, in agreement with the teachings of Hobbes, have made use of fear to dominate the population. The mechanism has been used by both democratic and authoritarian governments. Researchers such as David L. Altheide, Frank Furedi, and Barry Glassner have shown how the authorities in the USA and the UK have consciously exploited the inhabitants' fears of, among other things, terror and crime to gain social control.[49] Several Middle East regimes with the same aim in view have also played on people's fears. One of the clearest examples was Syria's president for many years Hafiz al-Asad, who exploited the feeling of crisis, after the catastrophic defeat inflicted by Israel in 1967, to monopolise power.

Fear of war under Hafiz al-Asad

When Hafiz al-Asad took over the government of Syria in 1970, the country was in many ways in crisis. Externally, Israel had inflicted a crushing defeat in the Six-Day War, occupying the Golan Heights. Internally, Syria was affected by a conflict of the elites and political instability. Tension and unease marked the ruling Ba'th Party, which had come to power in a coup in 1963 and in 1966 a radical faction carried out a coup within the party, steering Syria towards a 'socialist revolution'. Under the leadership of Salah Jalid the radical Ba'thists had nationalised the economy, forbidden opposition parties and press, and strengthened control over society through corporative mass organisations.[50] However, a confrontational foreign policy triggered a pre-emptive attack from Israel in 1967, which caught Syria – and the rest of the Arab world – off guard. At home, the Syrian armed forces were too occupied in introducing the Ba'th Revolution, as well as being weakened by ideological purges, to be able to withstand the attack. The defeat in the Six-Day War undermined Jadid's popularity in Syria and prepared the way for Hafiz al-Asad. Hafiz had taken part in the radicals' *putsch* but stood for a more moderate and pragmatic line than Jadid. He wanted to tone down the Ba'th Party's class struggle in favour of war preparations and national unity. According to Hafiz, Syria's foremost aim should be rearmament with a view to reconquering the Golan Heights. At a party congress in 1968 the Minister of Defence was given authority to reintegrate excluded officers into the army to strengthen its fighting power. He made use of the chance to build a network of loyal supporters in the forces. When Salah Jadid wanted to send the air force against Jordan during King Husayn's 1970 campaign against the Palestinians – 'Black September' – Hafiz refused to obey orders. Instead he carried out a military coup.

Hafiz al-Asad presented his take-over of power in 1970 as a 'corrective movement' (Arab. *haraka tashihiyya*) within the Ba'thist revolution. Instead of fighting against the bourgeoisie and the landowners at home, the regime would hereafter concentrate 'all its resources and manpower on the liberation of the occupied territories'.[51] The fight against Israel required *unity* – under a strong and united central power. During the sixties, competing political factions had controlled different parts of the state apparatus that they used against each other. So Hafiz introduced a united command over the Ba'th Party, the armed forces, and the bureaucracy to prevent internal strife.[52] As Syria's president he gained the authority to appoint and dismiss party leaders, members of the government, and military officers. From this point on discipline was tightened in the Ba'th Party. The party switched from the collective leadership of the sixties to a hierarchical organisation of its top agencies. The two leading internal agencies, the national and the regional commands, which until then had ensured a certain degree of pluralism, now came completely under the president's control. The earlier practice of internal election to leading posts in the party was replaced by personal nominations.[53] Under Hafiz, the Syrian military came under effective political control, too, for the first time since independence. The president, who himself had entered politics via a military career, changed the army from a playground for coup-makers to guardian of the regime's stability.

As we have shown earlier, the strategic placement of clan and family members in coup-sensitive positions has been an important element in this process. But Hafiz also used the danger of war with Israel to 'tame' the armed forces. The need for mobilisation in case of war was useful in two ways. First, it justified a mammoth rise in the military budget that helped keep the officers happy: military expenses rose from 10 per cent of Syria's GDP in the period 1970–74 to 15 per cent for the period 1974–86.[54] Second, the external threat was used to discipline and apoliticise the army. According to Hafiz, the armed forces had to hand over ideological steering to the politicians and become more professional in order to prepare for 'the great battle'.[55]

Tension between Syria and Israel seldom broke out into war under Hafiz al-Asad. The exceptions were the October War in 1973 and the battles in Lebanon between Syria and Israel in 1982. However, the effects of the conflict lay less in the actual battles than in the *expectations* of a military collapse. War preparations showed in various ways, but not least in the growth of the armed forces. In 1967 Syria's forces numbered 50,000 men, while already in 1973 they had increased dramatically to 170,000.[56] Israel's invasion of Lebanon in 1982 heightened the feeling that the country posed a threat to Syria, accelerating further the armed build-up. Under the slogan 'standing firm and damming up' (Arab. *al-sumud wa-l tasaddi*), Hafiz al-Asad introduced a new doctrine of strategic parity with Israel. Syria should not only be capable of defending itself against Israel but also of launching a pre-emptive strike against the enemy. To live up to this doctrine in the period 1983–85 Syria increased its armed forces from 300,000 to 500,000 men.[57] By 1986 the country had built up an arsenal that included 5,000 tanks, 650 fighter planes, 102 missile batteries, and about 400 ballistic missiles.[58] The most important supplier of war material in this period was the Soviet Union. According to Volker Perthes, Hafiz al-Asad also had economic motives for this intensive build-up of arms.[59] The doctrine of strategic parity increased Syria's geopolitical importance, contributing therefore to transfers of revenue from oil-rich Arab states to the country as 'a frontline fighter' against Israel. Thanks to these rentier incomes, the regime could arm its forces without increasing taxes. Consequently, Hafiz al-Asad avoided the opposition linking the tax burden to demands for reform.

The militarisation of Syria made the state of war an everyday matter both in politics and society. After the Ba'th Party took over power in 1963, it proclaimed a state of emergency, which has never been ended. Hafiz al-Asad used the danger of war with Israel as a pretext for governing Syria by decree. This gave the president the power to accept laws without the approval of parliament and to amend the constitution. In other words, the state of emergency completely wiped out the distinction between the legislature and the executive. Similarly, there is precious little room for the division of powers in the regime's treatment of the judiciary. The prime minister and the minister of the interior can give orders for 'preventive detention' of persons suspected of 'threatening public safety and order',[60] and with reference to the state of emergency, the regime reserves the right to try those suspected before military tribunals. Here the accused can be tried – behind closed doors – by officers or Ba'th leaders without formal legal training.[61] On the social level the state of war has led to a comprehensive militarisation of the school system. Until 2003 pupils in lower and upper secondary schools had to wear military uniforms and 'military training' (Arab. *tarbiya 'askariyya*) was on the timetable – indoctrination in 'military values' began in infant school.

Crisis maximation in Syria under Hafiz al-Asad went hand in hand with a strong personality cult. A short time after the corrective movement of 1970, posters of the president appeared in Syria's streets. Hafiz al-Asad had decided to give the Ba'th Party a face, his. Patrick Seale gives Iskandar Ahmad, the minister of information from 1974–83, the 'honour' for having developed the personality cult of the president. Ahmad made the propaganda machine more efficient by coordinating the heads of radio and TV, the country's biggest papers (*al-Ba'th*, *al-Thawra*, and *Tishrin*), and the state news bureau (SANA) in a massive tribute to Asad.[62]

The personality cult, however, did not become intense until after the confrontation with the Islamist movement in Hama in 1982 and the attempted coup that followed by Rif'at al-Asad. In 1984 the first statue of the president was raised in front of the Asad Library in Damascus and the following year came the first chronicles of Asad's leadership and heroic deeds. In the official rhetoric the president was now spoken of as 'our leader for all time' (Arab. *qa'iduna ila-l-abad*).[63] For the opening ceremony of the Mediterranean Games in 1987, which took place in Lattakia, 'capital' of the 'Alawis, the Ba'th Party's youth organisation prepared an impressive staging to celebrate Hafiz al-Asad's vigour and honour. Thousands of young people held up posters to form a picture of the Syrian president. In front of them tanks rolled across the sports arena, while soldiers simulated an attack on an undefined enemy. In another scene Syrian children were staged to play in the arena before a benevolent, smiling Hafiz al-Asad. Suddenly, the backcloth changed to grey and the silhouette of an enemy soldier sank over the stadium. Army officers hurried into the arena to save the children and make them safe, and in the poster theatre the soldier was forced to retreat by the letters of the word peace (Arab. *salam*). The show was meant to remind the spectators of the need to support the 'father' and protector of the nation. In a third poster illustration the Ba'th youth formed the rebus 'we' (Arab. *nahnu*), 'love' (symbolised by a heart) 'Hafiz al-Asad' (the president as a picture).[64]

In the real world though, the ambition of strategic parity with Israel would prove hard to achieve. In the 1990s, a combination of internal and external conditions obliged Hafiz al-Asad to tone down the war rhetoric. Domestically, the main problem was an economic crisis that stemmed from the inefficiently state-run development model, a highly expensive armament programme, and a sharp fall in the price of oil in 1986. The latter gave lower income from both Syria's own oil exports and transfers from the Gulf states. The absolute growth in GDP was negative, −2.9 per cent for the period 1983–7.[65] The crisis badly affected the balance of trade, too, and in 1988 Syria had built up debts to the Soviet Union of US$19 billion.[66] As was the tendency in the other Arab republics, shown in Chapter 5, Syria gradually adopted a policy of cautious economic reform. Externally, Hafiz al-Asad lost his most important supplier of political, military and financial support as the Soviet Union, which had guaranteed Syria's strategic balance with Israel, disintegrated after the fall of the Berlin Wall. The transition from the bipolar world order of the Cold War to a unipolar reality based on the military hegemony of the USA forced Syria to change course. Hafiz al-Asad responded by normalising his relations with Egypt – and thereby implicitly accepting the Camp David Agreement – and by participating on the side of the Western coalition in the war against Iraq in 1991. As a result, he reduced tension in relations with the USA and found a chance to consolidate his hegemony in Lebanon. In 1990 Syrian troops defeated a rising led by General 'Aoun in a final episode in the Lebanese Civil War. With control over Lebanon as a new and vital means of exerting pressure, Hafiz al-Asad also seemed more willing to begin peace negotiations with Israel. When the PLO accepted 'The Oslo Channel' of face-to-face discussions with Israeli officials, this released Syria from the responsibility that Hafiz al-Asad had taken upon himself in the name of Arab nationalism to ensure justice for the Palestinians. So he began negotiations with Israel about the Golan Heights and after Israel admitted in 1993 that the Heights were Syrian territory, for a long time the talks gave room for optimism. But when the Oslo Process stalled and the Israeli Labour Party lost elections in 1996, this spoiled the outlook for a Syrian-Israeli deal. Indeed three months after the death of Hafiz al-Asad on 10 June 2000, the Second Palestinian *intifada* broke out.

Like father like son?

'The coronation' of Hafiz's son, Bashar al-Asad, was simply interpreted as the start of a change of course for Syria. As the younger brother of Hafiz's original heir, Basil, Bashar was not brought up to head the regime and unlike his father and brother he initially had no military training. In fact, Bashar had studied to be an eye specialist in England, and was known to be good with his hands, academic, and keen on technology.[67] It was only when older brother Basil died in a car accident in 1994 that he was sent to military academy. However, between 1994 and 2000 he rose rapidly through the ranks, becoming lieutenant colonel in 1997, colonel in 1999, and Commander in Chief of the Armed Forces the day after his father's death.[68] This promotion was necessary to make Bashar al-Asad credible as the leader of 'a state at war' and to make sure he had the support among the officers. Nonetheless, the optimists saw him as a different kind of leader from his father and believed in a demilitarisation of the state and of Syrian politics. This belief was strengthened when Bashar al-Asad in his first speech criticised 'old ideas' ideas in the regime and called for modernisation.[69] Moreover, when Bashar al-Asad took over, there was generally more scope for civil society and greater freedom of expression. On 27 September 2000, the newspaper *al-Hayat* printed an appeal from 99 artists and intellectuals, demanding the end of the state of emergency. Four months later those behind the appeal made a fresh and more sharply phrased declaration signed by 1,000 people. The declaration, which was leaked to the press before the signatures were in place, challenged the regime to 'learn from the crisis' in which the country found itself and strengthen civil society. The authors argued that freedom and debate far from weakened but, on the contrary, strengthened the 'vigour and unity' of the nation, and they refuted the idea that one political group alone could define Syria's national interests.[70] The declaration was a scarcely concealed criticism of the Ba'th Party's monopoly of power and repression of political opponents under the pretext of war.

The 'political spring' in Damascus – as the wave of liberalisation under Bashar-al-Asad was called – never, however, became a summer. In February 2001, the regime clamped down on civil activity by requiring state authorisation for the right to gather for discussions, as had happened spontaneously the previous year. A state directive published in the Ba'th paper *al-Munadil* 17 February 2001, warned that the civil society activists, consciously or not, were damaging Syria by 'serving the country's enemy'.[71] The opposition replied in a document entitled 'Towards a Social Contract in Syria' that 'occupied Arab land would not be liberated without a democratic political system'.[72] But on 15 April, Bashar al-Asad stated that national unity, the Ba'th Party, the armed forces, and 'the course Hafiz al-Asad had set' were not topics for discussion.[73] In the autumn of 2001 the regime arrested, charged, tried and convicted the leading members of the opposition of 'the Damascus spring'.

Gradually Syria's foreign relations became more tense, as well. The normalisation trend of the 1990s turned into a fresh war of words with Israel, threats from the USA, and rebellion in Lebanon. After the outbreak of the Second Palestinian *intifada*, Bashar al-Asad spoke of the Israelis as Nazis, labeling Israel's repression of the Palestinians as a new 'Holocaust'.[74] This aroused negative reactions in the Israeli and American media that presented Bashar al-Asad as a warmonger. The goodwill Hafiz al-Asad had won by supporting George Bush senior during the Gulf War of 1991 disappeared under George Bush junior. Syria insured itself against USA's wrath in the immediate period after 11 September 2001 by cooperating in the hunt for supposed al-Qa'ida members. Syria was not included in 'the axis of evil' when George W. Bush held his famed speech on the state of the nation in January 2002. With the 'war on terror', however, tolerance diminished for Syrian support of Hizbollah, Hamas, and Palestinian Islamic Jihad, all movements the USA considers terrorist organisations. In March 2003, a USA-led invasion overthrew the Ba'th regime in neighbouring Iraq, while the Bush administration swore to 'democratise' the Middle East. The hawks in the Pentagon accused the Asad regime of supporting the Iraqi war effort, of letting Arab resistance fighters over the border into the neighbouring country, and helping Saddam Husayn to conceal weapons of mass destruction. In December 2003 Congress passed sanctions (SALSA) against Syria, accusing the country of aiding terrorism, destabilising Iraq, developing weapons of mass destruction, and occupying Lebanon.

Lebanon was the last arena in which Bashar al-Asad was put on the defensive. As long as South Lebanon was occupied by Israel in prolongation of the civil war, it was easy for the Asad regime to justify its presence in the country. But when Israel suddenly pulled out in May 2000, demands that Syria should do the same increased. In 2004 the UN Security Council passed Resolution 1559, demanding respect for Lebanon's sovereignty, the withdrawal of Syrian forces, and the disarming of all militia (read Hizbollah). The nail in the coffin for Syria's hegemony over Lebanon came in February 2005, when former prime minister Rafiq Hariri was assassinated in Beirut. The murder of postwar Lebanon's most highly profiled politician and businessman unleashed such strong protests against Syria locally and internationally that Bashar al-Asad had to pull out his troops. The USA and France have since taken the lead for an international demand for an enquiry to find and punish those responsible for the killing of Hariri. A UN commission led by Detlev Mehlis concluded in October 2005 that 'the tracks pointed to Syria'. A leaked unofficial version of the Mehlis Report went as far as to name persons in Bashar al-Asad's closest circle as possibly being behind the assassination. In the light of international developments many observers speculated that the Asad clan's days in power might be drawing to a close. Syria was in a new and threatening geopolitical situation squeezed between its old enemy Israel in the West and the USA in Iraq, and a strongly anti-Syrian government in Lebanon. The USA, France, and the United Kingdom were relentless in their demands that those responsible for killing Hariri must be brought to trial and punished. On top of all this Syria's vice president 'Abd al-Halim Khaddam deserted in 2005, calling for a change of regime from his exile in France. Those in power in Damascus were deeply concerned about the Bush administration's 'regime change list'. The pictures of the statue of Saddam Husayn being pulled down in Baghdad on 9 April 2003 were not shown on Syrian television, instead the media warned that the US war aim was the 'Israelification of the Middle East, the Americanisation of oil, and the destruction of Arab nationalism'.[75]

On the home front however, Bashar al-Asad knew how to exploit the feeling of being besieged in order to win support for the regime. He appealed to the Syrians' national feeling – and fear – and presented himself as the only safe alternative for the nation. When the Mehlis commission put pressure on Syria, the regime responded with a domestic campaign of nationalist propaganda. It staged mass demonstrations and literally covered Syrian cities with national flags. The outlawed Syrian Socialist Nationalist Party, whose goal of Greater Syria had previously been unacceptable for the pan-Arab Ba'th party, was legalised and taken into the National Progressive Front. Bringing with it an estimated 90,000 members, it strengthened the regime's appeal to Syrian nationalist forces.[76] Bashar al-Asad characterised the West's war in Iraq and intervention in Lebanon as a conspiracy against the country. In a speech on 21 January 2006 the president described the USA's policy towards Syria as:

> ... part of an integrated project to undermine the region's identity and reshape it under different names that finally meet Israel's ambitions to dominate the region and its resources. ... But what is targeted are [not only Syria and Lebanon, but all] the Arabs and even the Islamic nation. ... What is happening now [with Syria and Lebanon] is part of a big conspiracy, as [the occupation of] Iraq is part of this conspiracy ...[77]

Based on this reading of the situation, the regime asked the populace to unite in demanding absolute national sovereignty. Referring to the USA's record in the Middle East, the Syrian authorities accused the West of double morality when it demanded justice for Hariri and respect for Lebanon's sovereignty and a democratically elected government. 'No-one demanded justice for the Palestinians, respect for Iraq's sovereignty, and democracy when Hamas won the election' was the quintessential Syrian line of defence. According to Bashar al-Asad, the great powers manipulate law and order as they see fit in order to dominate the Arab world. Therefore Syria would not give in to the Security Council, as the president explained in a speech to the Association of Journalists:

> ... The so-called 'International Society' consists in reality of a group of states, of which some are members of the Security Council and others their allies ... They wage war

> against us with or without Security Council resolutions...No matter what happens, they will wage war against us. ( ) The solution lies in (recognising) that national decisions always have priority over international resolutions, even when they lead to killings and war. We have no choice.[78]

Bashar al-Asad emphasised the significance of internal security even more strongly than external sovereignty. Hardly an occasion was missed to remind the population that the alternative to today's Ba'th regime is chaos, and that therefore Syria must have *stability* as its first priority. Here Bashar al-Asad played, like his father, on a feeling of national crisis. Naturally, the people of Syria were worried about developments in the region. Many were frightened and repelled by the anti-Syrian sentiment that spread in Lebanon after Hariri's murder. Anger especially affected the close on one million Syrian guest workers, who until the withdrawal, worked in Lebanon. Former exile workers returned telling stories about how they were attacked by Lebanese mobs simply because they were Syrians.[79] The reports of ethnic conflict in the neighbouring countries made an impression – just over the border, millions of Iraqis were driven from their homes and thousands slaughtered in the worst imaginable kinds of ethnic violence; in Lebanon political crisis resulted in regular street battles that, along with the Iraqi war scenes, rolled across Syrian television screens. Like its neighbours, Syria has a multi-ethnic social structure and is ruled by a minority elite as was the case in Saddam Husayn's Iraq. Many are upset by the 'Alawi elite's dominating the power apparatus while being pleased that explicitly sectarian political expression are not publicly tolerated. Against this backdrop of fear of a civil war Bashar al-Asad made 'stability' his number one slogan. After being elected for his second term of office in 2007, he explained why:

> What has happened over the past few years – terrorist attacks, attempts at foreign intrusion, and external pressure on Syria – has made stability top priority. Without stability there is no economy. And what is the value of political development if we do not have stability and economy and can cover the basic health and food needs etc of the population? We must get our priorities right![80]

By these priorities the president meant that Syria must concentrate on security, primary needs and economic development and as a consequence, he speeded up the country's economic reforms, building up his image as 'the chief moderniser'.[81] However, these priorities also meant that the Asad regime froze initiatives for political reform and imprisoned political opponents, as at the start of the populist–authoritarian era, the nation should stand united against all external dangers. For 'what is the purpose of the political reforms they (the West) talk about?' asked rhetorically Bashar al-Asad in a speech to the

University of Damascus: 'They want the country to quiver, to lose all its founda-tions so that they can steal power from the inside'.[82] The Iraqi tragedy was used for all it was worth to discredit the idea of 'Western-style' democracy in Syria. Bashar al-Asad distinguished between democracy on a Syrian premise, which was and remained his aim, and the democracy the USA wanted impose on the region from the outside. When the choice is between 'stability' and democracy *à la mode d'Iraq*, the choice is obvious for Syrians. Local democracy and human rights activists in classic manner became linked to the conspiracy of exter-nal powers against the country. The 2003 invasion of Iraq – in the name of democracy – thus proved a catastrophe for democracy activists in the region.

Such rhetorical tricks have proved effective. In a time when the regime has had its back against the wall Bashar al-Asad has managed to survive by playing on national feelings and not least fear of a civil war and the collapse of law and order. The young president, who took over power with promises of reform and a new course for Syria, has in this respect found considerable inspiration from his father's strategies for ruling the country. Deterioration in the state of the region after 2000 must bear much of the responsibility for this. The normalisation tendency of the 1990s was suddenly reversed by unpredictable circumstances that pushed the Asad regime back to the state of emergency of the 1970s and 1980s. The source of fear in the population, however, seemed to have undergone a gradual change: the prime terror scenario in Damascus was no longer war with Israel but the danger of collapse and civil war as in Iraq and Lebanon.

By 2008 the Syrian regime had grown more confident and the fear of US military intervention had waned. In this context, Bashar al-Asad took care-ful steps to set the country on the course of normalisation again. He softened Syria's position on Lebanon, agreeing to establish diplomatic relations and open an embassy in Beirut. He also built ties with the Iraqi government after long depicting it as the offspring of an illegitimate occupation. Last, but not least, he agreed to Turkish-mediated talks with Israel in the aim of resuming peace nego-tiations.[83] The existence of these indirect talks was early on revealed to the Syr-ian public, signalling the regime's preparedness to normalise relations with the historical enemy in case of an acceptable peace agreement. Sceptics doubt that Syria would break its strategic alliances with Iran, Hamas, and Hizballah that have been important «cards» in its security arrangements. The public embrace of the principal of peace negotiations may nevertheless signify that Bashar al-Asad is still trying new ways to secure the survival of the regime.

Conclusion

The populist–authoritarian development path gave the Middle East a tradition of a very strong executive. This was a reaction to the lack of development during the colonial era and the European powers' divide and rule politics. The post-colonial regimes determined that power should be concentrated in the hands of the leader in order to reach the goal of socio-economic progress and national unity and so the principle of the division of powers was set aside. As a result, regimes have sprung up that are very much dominated by one person. The absence of constitutional mechanisms of checks and balances on the executive have made it possible for presidents such as Mu'ammar al-Qadhafi, Husni Mubarak, 'Ali 'Abdallah Salih, Saddam Husayn, and Hafiz al-Asad to monopolise power. By virtue of their domination of the armed forces, the ruling party, and the bureaucracy, the presidents have an efficient system for controlling and repressing their opponents. To legitimise the maintenance of strong presidential powers the regimes have emphasised the need for 'a strong man'. The example of Syria shows how the Asad dynasty plays on war and fear in its struggle to hold on to power. In this connection the costs have been extremely high. Quite contrary to the idea behind authoritarian development, the absence of the division of power has weakened the state. The 'strong man' has put the loyalty of the state system and of society before its development and efficiency.

Further reading

Cook, Steven A.: *Ruling but Not Governing: The Military and Political Development in Egypt, Algeria, and Turkey.* Baltimore and London: Johns Hopkins University Press, 2007.

Hinnebusch, Raymond: *Syria: Revolution from Above.* London and New York: Routledge, 2001.

Karsh, Efraim and Inari Rautsi: *Saddam Hussein: A Political Biography.* New York: Grove Press, 2003.

Kassem, Maye: *Egyptian Politics: The Dynamics of Authoritarian Rule.* Boulder, CO: Lynne Rienner Publishers, 2003.

Kienle, Eberhard: *A Grand Delusion: Democracy and Economic Reform in Egypt.* New York: I.B.Tauris, 2001.

El-Kikia, Mansour O.: *Libya's Qaddafi: The Politics of Contradiction.* Gainesville, FL: University Press of Florida, 1997.

Lesch, David W.: *The New Lion of Damascus: Bashar al-Asad and Modern Syria.* New Haven: Yale University Press, 2005.

Ma'oz, Moshe: *Asad: The Sphinx of Damascus.* Grove/Atlantic, 1990.

Seale, Patrick: *Asad of Syria: The Struggle for the Middle East.* London: I.B.Tauris, 1988.

Tripp, Charles: *A History of Iraq.* Cambridge University Press: Cambridge, 2002.

Vandewalle, Dirk (ed.): *Qadhafi's Libya 1969–1994.* New York: St. Martins Press, 1995.

Wedeen, Lisa: *Ambiguities of Domination: Politics, Rhetoric, and Symbols in Contemporary Syria.* Chicago: University of Chicago Press, 1999.

Zisser, Eyal: *Commanding Syria: Bashar Al-Asad and the First Years in Power.* London: I.B.Tauris, 2006.

Part 5
Scenarios of Change

9 Democratisation

There is a substantial lag between Arab countries and other regions in terms of participatory governance. The wave of democracy that transformed governance in most of Latin America and East Asia in the 1980s and Eastern Europe and much of Central Asia in the late 1980s and early 1990s has barely reached the Arab states.[1]

It has been thoroughly documented that democracy is weak in the Middle East today,[2] and this form of government is least developed in the Arab countries. For a number of years the region's democratic deficit has been the concern of journalists, researchers, and democracy activists. Representatives of these various groups have a tendency to present the Middle East as the last bulwark against the global development towards democracy.[3] Other popular conceptions are that Arab countries are historically and culturally disposed to authoritarian rule, that the Islamists are the principle obstacle to democracy, and that the USA is pressuring the region's authorities to start a development towards more democracy.

All these conceptions are simplistic and problematic. The region is not the last bastion of authoritarian rule. Democracy is just as feeble in Russia, Central Asia, and South-East Asia (China, North Korea, Vietnam, Laos, Burma, Malaysia, and Singapore). There is not much substance either in claims that historically and culturally the Middle East is immune to democracy. The rulers are reluctant to share power but in several countries, experiences of democracy are an important part of the people's collective political memory, and there is today a growing desire for democracy in the Middle East. Over the last few years more and more both secular and Islamist opposition movements have embraced democracy. To what extent Western pressure for democratisation is real is, on the other hand, more dubious. The USA and other Western countries' strategic and economic interests are well taken care of by the sitting regimes, with the exception of Iran and Syria, so one might argue that the Western powers are well served by the status quo.

The development of democratic rule is a long and difficult process. Not least a successful democratisation presupposes the presence of actors with both the will and ability to lead such a process. In the first part of this chapter we shall look at the following question: are there actors with the will and ability to lead the democratisation of the Middle East? In the second part we shall shed light on the following topical issue: what happened to the USA's attempt to democratise Iraq?

Democracy and democratisation

Before we start the discussion, we should clarify what we mean by the concepts 'democracy' and 'democratisation'. Robert A. Dahl, one of our time's most prominent theoreticians of democratisation, mentions five criteria that must be fulfilled before a form of government can be characterised as a democracy. The first is 'effective participation', that is, citizens must have equal opportunities to express their preferences in the decision-making process. The second criterion is 'equal voting weight', that each citizen must have the same right to vote and that her or his preferences must count just as much as the preferences of all the others in the decisive phase of the decision-making process. The third criterion is 'enlightened understanding', meaning that each citizen must have adequate and equal opportunities to discover and validate the choice that best serves the interests of the citizens. The fourth criterion Dahl mentions is 'control over the agenda', that people must have an exclusive possibility to select what is on the agenda and what needs to be decided on in the democratisation process. Dahl's final criterion is 'inclusion', that the people must include all adult members of society (except for transients and the mentally retarded).[4]

Samuel P. Huntington claims in his book *The Third Wave* that the spread of democracy on a world basis has gone in waves over the last 150 years.[5] The first wave swept over a number of countries in Western Europe, the USA, parts of the British dominions, and in some places in South America from the middle of the nineteenth century till around 1920. But in the 1920s and 1930s democratic governments were replaced by authoritarian regimes in Germany and Austria and in several countries in Eastern Europe and South America. The second wave started after the Second World War with the reintroduction of democracy in the countries that lost the war, and in South America. From around 1960, democracy was experimented with in several of the new states in Africa and Asia but by around 1970 one-party and military rule followed. Military juntas seized power in Greece and in several South American and Asian countries.

Huntington thinks he can observe a third wave of democratisation commencing with the fall of the military juntas in Portugal, Spain, and Greece in the 1970s, continuing in the next decade with the reintroduction of democracy in several South American countries and then sweeping over Eastern and Central Europe and parts of South-East Asia and Africa.

Democracy and democratisation in the Middle East

At first glance there are few signs of a third wave sweeping over the Middle East. Real political freedom is still very limited. Severe restrictions are imposed on party and trade union organisation, freedom of expression suffers under wretched conditions, election results are manipulated, and opposition candidates suffer harassment.

Freedom House is a non-governmental organisation that has assessed political and civil rights in the Middle East and other parts of the world since 1970 and subsequent results of their researches have been published in annual reports. The methodology of Freedom House is based on Robert A. Dahl's operationalisation of democracy. In 2006, *The Economist*, too, evaluated the position of democracy in the Middle East on the basis of a similar system. Both *The Economist* and Freedom House base their assessments on a set of indicators of civil and political rights. On the basis of these indicators they arrive at an index of political freedom. *The Economist* divides countries into categories from 1 (= least free) to 10 (= most free), while Freedom House divides countries into the categories 'free', 'partly free', and 'not free'. Even though they are based on different criteria, the results are, on the whole, the same. Israel, Lebanon, the Palestinian self-governing territories, and Turkey (only assessed by Freedom House) have the most democratic governments, while Libya, Saudi Arabia, and Syria emerge as the worst (see Table 11).

But the third wave has also had its repercussions in the Middle East. The popular presentation of the region as the last bastion of authoritarian regimes needs some amendment. Despite the stability of the regimes, the relationship between rulers and the people is far more dynamic than emerges from the results of the enquiries made by Freedom House and *The Economist*, as has been indicated by Jeremy Jones.[6] Jones points out that democratic government is not 'one size that fits everyone'. Without being culturally relativistic, he points out that there are elements in Arab Islamic culture that have democratic features. Freedom House and *The Economist* base their assessments on criteria from Western democratic governments. It means that culturally specific elements of the Middle East are hardly captured by the indicators. As we explained in Chapter 7, Jones, like Michael Herb, shows how there is a culture of consultation between rulers and various population groups in the monarchies of the Arabian Peninsula. During the last few years, the royal houses have gradually moved towards institutionalising various consultative arrangements, and today all of the countries in the Arabian Peninsula have parliaments or advisory assemblies. In Kuwait

Table 11 Formal political representation and political freedom in the Middle East

State	First elected parliament	Political parties allowed	Vote for women	Political freedom	
				The Economist	*Freedom House*
Algeria	1962	Yes	1962	4.30	Not free
Bahrain	1973	No	1973	4.90	Partly free
Egypt	1866	Yes	1956	3.85	Not free
Emirates	2006	No	2006	3.25	Not free
Iraq	1925	Yes	1980	5.80	Not free
Iran	1906	No	1963	3.40	Not free
Israel	1948	Yes	1948	8.80	Free
Yemen	1993	Yes	1967[a]	4.60	Partly free
Jordan	1952	Yes	1974	4.45	Partly free
Kuwait	1963	No	2005	5.95	Partly free
Lebanon	1932	Yes	1952	6.70	Partly free
Libya	1952	No	1964	1.75	Not free
Morocco	1963	Yes	1963	5.05	Partly free
Oman	2003	No	2003	4.45	Not free
Pal. territories	1996	Yes	1996	6.10	Partly free
Qatar	–	No	1999[b]	4.90	Not free
Saudi-Arabia	–	No	–	1.75	Not free
Syria	1932	Yes	1953	2.5	Not free
Tunisia	1956	Yes	1959	3.10	Not free
Turkey	1920	Yes	1934	–	Partly free

[a] South Yemen
[b] Local election

Source: The table is based on 'Special Report – The Dynamics of Democracy in the Middle East', London: The Economist Intelligence Unit, March 2005; 'Freedom in the World 2006', Freedom House, February 2006, pp. 7–12; and Inter Parliamentary Union, http://www.ipu.org/wmn-e/suffrage.htm#Note3.

the parliament is so powerful that it effectively checks the power of the ruling family. There is also growing tolerance for publicly discussing differing political opinions. In Saudi Arabia, for example, it is usual for political activists to join forces to write petitions and send them to the king or prominent leaders.

In Iran there have been elections for more than thirty years, both to the presidency and to parliament. Political debate is loud, voter turnout considerable, and election results often surprising, which indicates that the elections have real political importance. Turkey has become so democratic that the country has been able to commence negotiations for membership of the EU. Over the past few years relatively free and fair elections have been held in Morocco, Jordan, Iraq, Lebanon, and in the Palestinian territories. Islamist candidates have been allowed to stand for election, and in Turkey even win political power. More and more countries in the region hold local elections, even Saudi Arabia, which scores worst on Freedom House's list. Moreover, women have been drawn more into politics. After Kuwait changed its electoral laws in 2005, women have had the right to vote in all Arab countries except Saudi Arabia.

In Chapter 5 we saw that the rulers use political reform as a survival strategy. Rex Brynen *et al.* establish a distinction between 'liberalisation' and 'democratisation', because these concepts, which have such different contents, are often confused. In a political context, 'liberalisation' means that public space is extended by recognising and protecting the right of assembly, freedom of expression, and so on. 'Democratisation', on the other hand, means that people participate to a larger extent in political processes and decision making.[7]

In what follows, we shall discuss to what extent liberalisation might lead to democratisation in the Middle East. Experiences from democratisation processes elsewhere in the world show that democratisation can be initiated from *below*, as a response to demands from society, democratisation can be started from *above*, by individual leaders or elite groups, or democratisation can be imposed from *outside*, by external institutions or states.

Democratisation from below

Democracy initiatives from below presuppose that the people are politically aware. Some believe that democratic awareness does not exist in Middle East countries, supposedly because various features of Arab history and culture have predisposed people to accept authoritarian rule. The feature of Arab culture that is most frequently designated as an obstacle to democracy is Islam. Elie Kedourie has argued that that there is 'a deep confusion of the significance of democracy in the Arabs' public consciousness' and that 'the idea of democracy is alien to Islamic thought'.[8]

In several of the region's countries, however, historical experiences of democracy are an important part of the people's collective memory. For example, the Middle East's first constitution was introduced in Tunisia in 1861 and served as reference for the Dustur (Turk. constitution) Party that fought for independence and democracy against the French protectorate authorities in the 1920s. In Iran the constitutional revolution in 1906 made the country a constitutional monarchy based on Montesquieu's principle of the division of powers. The constitution also guaranteed freedom of expression and set up a secularised and independent judicial system. In Kuwait the memory of the *majlis* movement in 1938 when prominent merchants forced the Sabah family to found a popular assembly is part of 'the national myth' and the country's political culture. On several occasions the ruling family has defied the constitution and dissolved parliament, but each time it has had to reopen the institution because of expectations and pressures from society at large.

Democratic practice, even when initially this was introduced as a strategy for holding on to power, has a tendency to promote a desire among the people for a bigger say in public affairs. In addition, technological development has clearly had an effect on political awareness in the Middle East. One consequence of this is that ever broader segments of the population have the opportunity to acquaintance themselves with democratic government. Through today's rapid spread of information via the internet and TV stations such as *CNN, MBC, al-Jazeera*, and *al-ʿArabiyya*, the region has long since become part of what Marshall McLuhan called 'the global village'.[9]

The internet widens the array of tools available to those who seek to subvert oppressive regimes and advocate democracy. First, it allows access to free information, undermining the regimes' ability to manipulate the inhabitants' world view. Internet gives politically conscious users the opportunity to communicate with each other on issues such as human rights abuses and the problems of governance in authoritarian regimes. This may encourage citizens to act. Governments can effectively wipe out sensitive information from the domestic media, but the internet is not that easy to control. During the protests following the 2009 Iranian presidential election events in the streets were brought to the world in real time through websites, blogs, YouTube, Twitter, and Facebook.[10] Iran's rulers slowed internet speeds and blocked access to the new social media but the protestors found ways around. Second, the internet has drastically lowered the cost of being a regime critic, leading to a younger, wider group of people in the Middle East being involved in illegal political networking over the web. The sheer number of activists claiming democratic reforms and the fact that they leave few electronic traces makes them difficult to trace and encourages a wider range of people to join the opposition.

A number of opinion surveys have shown that there is a growing wish for democracy in the Middle East today. Moataz A. Fattah has studied people's democratic values in Muslim societies.[11] He asked the following question: are ordinary educated Muslims' attitudes an obstacle to democracy? To answer this Fattah carried out a survey among more than 31,000 Muslims in 34 countries (including three where Muslims live as minorities). In total, 55 per cent replied that they were positive to democratic values, while 60 per cent were positive to democratic institutions.[12] But there were variations between countries. Among those asked, the most positive to democracy came from Turkey, Jordan, Lebanon, Morocco, and Egypt, while those least positive came from

Saudi Arabia, Yemen, Tajikistan, and Nigeria. In Saudi Arabia, where one finds 'the least democratic culture', as many as 74 per cent were firmly convinced that democracy is not compatible with Islam.[13] In addition, results differed within the countries according to such variables as sex, age, and education. According to Fattah, the replies suggest that there are two overarching cultures in Muslim societies, which he refers to as 'the dictator culture' and the 'democratic culture'. Among the supporters of the former, Fattah distinguishes two subcultures; that of traditionalist Islamists, who argue that a just ruler is one that rules according to *shari'a* and defends its teachings, and that of autocratic secularists, who speak up for a Hobbesian ruler that secures the state's sovereignty, defending it against outer enemies. Muslims in both categories conclude that the advantages of an authoritarian ruler more than weigh up against democratic government. 'The democratic culture', on the other hand, has been adopted by modernist Islamists and liberal secularists. The former believe that democracy fulfills Islamic teachings on combating dictatorial rule, while the latter regard democracy as a core element in a modern society that should be adopted on a secular basis.

Besides a desire for democracy, democratisation from below requires that society has the possibility to exert pressure on the authorities and this is a moot point for democratisation from below in the Middle East. Previously in the book we have seen how hard it is to organise political opposition as one of the ways authoritarian regimes control society is through a large network of informers. In addition, they barely tolerate opposition parties and the press is either state-owned or censored. Their security forces brutally repress the least hint of demonstration or disturbance.

It is Islamist movements that have demonstrated the best ability to organise opposition in the Middle East. One should not underestimate the potential of Islamist movements as a driving force behind democratisation. Jean Leca argues that democratisation depends on two conditions: one is populism, which is engaging people in politics; the other is constitutionalism, the rule of law.[14] Leca claims that the Islamists play an important role in populism: Islamist movements mobilise the masses for political action by using modern mass media and by educating people in democratic awareness and skills. But the question, according to Leca, is to what extent the Islamists will manage the transition from populism to constitutionalism. Will Islamic movements compromise on religiously argued positions and accept equality before the law? Will they accept the possibility of losing the next election? Or will they abolish democracy and introduce an authoritarian Islamist regime?

Moderate Islamist parties have been permitted to take part in politics in countries such as Morocco, Algeria, the Palestinian self-governing territories, Jordan, Iraq, Kuwait, and Turkey. Experiences from the Middle East show that in cases where the Islamists have been allowed to participate in elections and won, the armed forces – not the Islamists – have seized power through a coup. This happened in Algeria when the Islamists won the first electoral round during the parliamentary elections in 1991 and in Turkey in 1997. When Hamas formed a government in the Palestinian self-governing territories in 2006, Israel and the West did not accept the Palestinian people's choice and responded with economic and political sanctions. In the West there is a tendency to look on the Islamists as the main obstacle to democracy with reference to developments in Iran, Afghanistan, and Sudan. Additionally, there is a striking reluctance and inability to distinguish between moderates – who make up the large majority – and militant Islamists. In the West after 9/11 'Islamism' and 'terrorism' have become closely associated, so Middle East regimes receive few protests from the West when they oppress Islamist movements.

In Turkey, however, the combination of European pressures for democracy and the AK Party's electoral victories in 2002 and 2007 have given some interesting results. The leader of the AK Party, Reçep Tayyip Erdoğan, who is historically an Islamist opposed to the secularist-authoritarian establishment, used the lure of EU membership to impose reforms on the Kemalist elite.

Beyond Islamist mobilisation, 'the Green Movement' that emerged to protest the outcome of the 2009 presidential election in Iran is a highly significant development. Numbers are debated, but according to Tehran's Mayor, Muhammad Baqer Qalibaf, as many as 3 million demonstrators marched in the streets on one occasion.[15] For the first time since the 1979 revolution, the Iranian regime's monopoly on being able to control the streets was broken. The protesters' sustained public defiance seriously shook the regime and by defying the warnings of the leader and the repressive system, Iranians rediscovered the power of mobilising in the streets.

Democratisation from above

Democratisation can also come from the top. This may happen when a democratically minded Leader comes to power or as a result of elite rivalries.

New 'visionary leaders'

Leaders with a democratic vision can promote democracy. At the end of the 1990s new, young leaders came to power in a series of Arab countries. This has triggered a debate about to what extent a change of leadership might lead to political reform.[16] So far the most interesting developments have taken place in the monarchies: in Morocco, Jordan, and Qatar the new rulers have spoken up for a greater degree of the rule of law, respect for human rights, and freedom of expression. In addition, the wives of the new leaders have fronted women's rights: the first ladies of Morocco, Jordan, and Qatar – Salma, Rania, and

Moza – have become the icons of the new, modern, and liberated Arab woman. Queen Rania has also distinguished herself by directing attention to the issue of so-called 'honour killings'. Qatar's *Shaykh* Hamad established the television channel *al-Jazeera* in 1996, a step towards greater freedom of expression. Even members of the Sa'ud royal house, among them Prince al-Walid bin Talal, have emphasised the need for democracy.[17] On the other hand, in the republics, matters are worse. Certain optimism was aroused when Bashar al-Asad took over power in Syria in 2001, but up to now his policies have been far from democratising. In Libya Mu'ammar Qadhafi's son and 'crown prince', Sayf al-Islam, has spoken up for political reform at meetings with Western journalists.[18] The son of Egyptian president Husni Mubarak, Gamal, whom many regard as his father's probable successor, has also built a reputation as the leader of a reform committee in the National Democratic Party.

However, political reforms from above imply a strategic choice, that is to say, the leadership starts liberalisation because they believe it will serve their interests. An authoritarian regime under pressure both from below and from outside may introduce reforms in order to ease the pressure. But as a rule the regime will be careful not to go so far that it undermines its own power and exposes itself to real competition. Despite the new Arab leaders' keenness to liberalise, they only have a limited will to democratise. As we saw in Chapter 5, an important goal of the reform initiatives is to ensure the survival of the regimes. For instance, by emphasising women's rights the rulers appear as reformers both at home and abroad, thus directing attention away from the question of democratisation. Media reforms are used in the same way. It is symptomatic that the Qatar's emir established *al-Jazeera*, a satellite channel that, while shedding critical light on state and politics in the Middle East, is not permitted to criticise Qatar's own regime.

Even if the rulers have a genuine desire for change, it is most unlikely that the rest of the elite will give them the space to democratise. The rulers do not govern alone but as representatives of a privileged 'state class'. This class does not just govern politics but also dominates the economy, therefore, if the ruler decides to give power to the people, all of the privileges of the upper class are at risk. Another obstacle is that conservative elements in society often regard democracy as a threat to their own identity. For example, the late emir of Kuwait, *Shaykh* Jabir, proposed giving women the right to vote in 1999, but the proposal was defeated in the first vote in a parliament dominated by conservative tribal leaders and Islamists. In Saudi Arabia both religious leaders and conservative princes have voiced criticisms of democracy, which they consider does not belong in an Islamic state. And in Libya the reform proposals of former Prime Minister Shukri Ghanim, a close ally of Sayf al-Islam, were voted down by 'the old guard'. Personal interests locked into the state are a considerable obstacle to altering the status quo.

Another consideration rulers have to take into account is that if they give up their power as a result of a democratic election, they will also lose their immunity. In addition, they will lose control over the judiciary. Many of today's Middle East leaders are associated with corruption and repression, for which they risk being brought to account. History provides many examples of former heads of state, being brought to trial before national or international tribunals, as Chile's General August Pinochet and Iraq's ex-president, Saddam Husayn, painfully experienced. The hanging of the latter was even videoed and the tape distributed all over the world. Several of his henchmen also ended their days on the gallows. The rulers and their allies are fearful about these prospects, which give them little reason to encourage a real democratisation.

Elite rivalries

Democratisation from above may also be a consequence of elite rivalries. In creating alliances with groups in society by offering political rights, a faction within the regime may try to strengthen its position *vis-à-vis* rival factions. Tim Niblock emphasises the possibility for democratisation initiated from above as a consequence of elite rivalries in various Arab countries. He believes, for instance, that factions within the Saudi royal house may build alliances with politically discontented groups in Saudi Arabian society in order to strengthen their position relative to family blocks.[19] So far, it has been in Bahrain that elite rivalries have resulted in initiatives from above for democratisation. In 1999 Hamad bin 'Isa al-Khalifa seized power from his father. Many feared a power struggle would break out between the new king and his uncle, *Shaykh* Khalifa, who had been Bahrain's prime minister and *de facto* ruler since independence from the United Kingdom in 1971 and personally, relations between the two had long been bad. Bahrain's Shi'as, who make up about two-thirds of the total population of the country, were opposed to Khalifa because of his brutal repression in the 1990s when many Shi'as were killed or arrested. Khalifa was also unpopular because many Sunnis regarded him as corrupt. Just after taking over power, Hamad challenged his uncle by signalling that he would be more active in decision making. Rivalries found expression in generous spending when the two overbid each other in order to win popular support. During this time Hamad made promises of democracy. One of the first things he did after he inherited power was to appoint new representatives to the country's advisory council, of whom five were women – including a Christian, an Indian, and a Jew. Furthermore, the king held a referendum in 2001, which gave him a great deal of support for his plan to turn Bahrain into a constitutional monarchy with independent courts. Parliamentary elections were held for the first time in 2002. Later, however, Hamad limited parliament's powers and this decision probably reassured Khalifa and other conservative elements of the royal house, worried that their interests were endangered by democratisation. But Hamad also turned large sectors of the population against his rule whom he had given hopes of a rapid democratisation.

Experiences from Bahrain illustrate an important point. Even if they were first meant as a survival strategy, reforms initiated from above can in the long run have unintended consequences. Historical experiences show that once reforms are carried out, expectations from below will soon grow that more will follow. One example is the result of the reforms Mikhail Gorbachev implemented in the Soviet Union at the end of the 1980s. He intended that the Soviet state could only survive by radically changing the Communist model of society. However, the reform process he initiated proved impossible for the Eastern Block regimes to control. The people, glimpsing hope of quick and fundamental changes, poured out into the streets and the regimes fell. Of course, the former Soviet Union is not directly comparable to today's Middle East regimes, but experience shows that reform processes in general are hard to manipulate. The leadership in the Middle East creates expectations of real change through its reformism. If these expectations are not met, this will strengthen people's discontent and the pressure on the regimes will grow even stronger.

Democratisation from outside

Democratisation from outside presupposes pressure from an external actor, state, or institution, which has both the ability and the will to democratise. Huntington claims that such a pressure is the main reason for the 'third wave'. According to him, Western financial institutions (IMF, the World Bank, and WTO) and the USA and other Western great powers have strengthened their grip on the developing countries since the 1980s and reduced these countries' chances of an alternative economic and political organisation.[20] Nonetheless, in the Middle East, Western pressure for democratisation has been weaker than in other parts of the world. The end of the Cold War has not – as in, for instance, Latin America and Eastern Europe – reduced the support of the great powers for authoritarian regimes. This is mainly because of the need for oil and the Islamist 'ghost' that continues to haunt the West's fears of instability in the region.[21] Since President Johnson's administration in the 1960s, US policy towards the Middle East has been characterised by two main considerations: on the one hand, the USA wanted security for Israel; on the other, access to the region's oil resources. The dominant foreign policy doctrine during the Cold War, the so-called realism school, sought to achieve these goals by securing stability in the region. The USA had to prevent wars, coups, and revolutions that might impede the flow of oil, increase the influence of the Soviet Union, and threaten Israel. If considerations of stability damaged democratic movements or led to breaches of human rights, that was a minor matter.

But under President George W. Bush II the realists' preference for stability was challenged by a powerful pressure group, the so-called neo-conservatives, who waged a more value-loaded foreign policy. In 1997 the neo-conservatives' programme was launched under the title 'The Project for the New American Century', which had as its express aim 'to return to the Reagan era's military strength and moral clarity'.[22] The argument was that the USA needed to entrench its position as the world's unique superpower and be willing to use force to achieve this aim. The doctrine emphasised the importance of moral principles such as human rights and democracy. To realise their visions the neo-conservatives wanted a more ideological president than Bill Clinton, which is why they supported Bush. Boosted by the shift in opinion in US politics after 11 September 2001, they won the support of prominent conservative nationalists such as Donald Rumsfeld, Dick Cheney, and George W. Bush. Under the Bush administration neo-conservatives such as Douglas Feith, Robert Kagan, Richard Perle, Paul Wolfowitz, David Wurmser, and Elliott Abrams exercised great influence on American foreign policy. The neo-conservatives, aligned with right-wing Israeli pressure groups, questioned the stability doctrine. Since Middle East repressive regimes provide a breeding ground for terrorism, the argument went, the USA should no longer prop up these regimes; on the contrary the USA should work to eliminate them. The war against terror should be won through a war for freedom, capitalism, and democracy. In 1996 a group of neo-conservatives led by Richard Perle wrote a report to the then Israeli Prime Minister, Benjamin Netanyahu, in which they argued for a clean break in Israeli policy towards the Arab world. The report included recommendations that the Oslo Agreement about 'land for peace' should be buried, that the Israeli armed forces should intensify their incursions into Palestinian territory and into Lebanon, that pressure should be applied to Syria and Iran, and, last but not least, Saddam Husayn should be removed.[23] After 9/11 the neo-conservatives used the war on terror as a cover for achieving these aims.

In accordance with the neo-conservatives' value-loaded foreign policy, George W. Bush put democratisation of the Middle East on the political agenda. The neo-conservatives presented democratisation of the region as the solution to the problem of realism. Throughout history the problem has been to reconcile access to Middle East oil resources with support for Israel in a region where most of the oil is controlled by anti-Israeli states. For the neo-conservatives the solution was to give the region a share of the West's freedom and democracy. In this way, the argument went, the source of anti-Semitism, war and terror, would dry up. The ability to remove Saddam Husayn in Iraq and introduce a democratic regime in the country was seen as a litmus test for the new doctrine. Bush created the impression that the invasion of Iraq was 'a battle for the future of the Muslim world'. The aim of the crusade, he claimed, was to replace Saddam Husayn with a democratic regime in Baghdad, which should stand as an example to the rest of the Arab world. But the promises of democratisation from outside have proved extremely hard to fulfil.

Case study: Iraq – 'the battle for the future of the Muslim world'

> (...) [The Americans] will lead by defending liberty and justice because they are right and true and unchanging for all people everywhere. (...) America will always stand firm for the non-negotiable demands of human dignity: the rule of law; limits on the power of the state; respect for women; private property; free speech; equal justice; and religious tolerance. America will take the side of brave men and women who advocate these values around the world, including the Islamic world, because we have a greater objective than eliminating threats and containing resentment. We seek a just and peaceful world beyond the war on terror.[24]

On January 2002 in his state of the nation speech President George W. Bush emphasised the need for fundamental change in the Muslim world. In accordance with his speech the need to democratise Iraq was promoted as one of the principle aims behind the USA's occupation of the country the previous year. In hindsight, one might discuss how important this goal in fact was, but nevertheless, the American occupation authority began a process that involved the establishment of democratic institutions and elections. Soon, the USA's 'democratisation from the outside' was to face big problems. What are the lessons drawn from the American attempt to democratise Iraq?

Legacies of the 'civilised nations'

The USA's 'war for freedom' in the spring of 2003 was not the first time a Western great power took over the rule of Iraq in the name of a superior form of political organisation. As much as 80 years earlier, the United Kingdom had adopted a corresponding power position with reference to the League of Nations' principle of national sovereignty. The aim was a league of equal, self-governing national states, but to get there the West would have to take responsibility for bringing non-western states up to a level of development at which such a modern form of political organisation could work. The 'civilised nations' had, in other words, according to the League of Nations, a mission to arrange matters for a world-wide 'democracy' of independent national states. On this basis the victors of the First World War established Iraq as a mandate territory with the United Kingdom as the mandate authority.

In reality, however, the United Kingdom's interregnum in Iraq created a difficult starting point for democracy, for example, by physically controlling the territory and pursuing its colonial interests the United Kingdom deprived the national population of the possibility of 'steering their own ship' in the crucial state formation period. It meant that securing British concerns in Iraq had priority over socio-economic development and democracy promotion. It also provided ammunition for later decades' ideological currents like Arab and Kurdish Nationalism that would question the legitimacy of the state as such.

Sections of the Iraqi elite were already familiar with modern democratic principles when the state was founded as the Ottoman Empire's liberal constitution of 1876 had made its mark on the politicians that represented the provinces of Baghdad, Basra, and Mosul in the Ottoman parliaments of 1908 and 1912. These parliamentarians brought constitutional ideals with them into the new state, demanding that the United Kingdom hold democratic elections. However, the UK refused to establish a constitutional assembly before a royal house was in place that was allied to the British and in 1921, they brought the Hashemite prince Faysal to the country and proclaimed him monarch. For lack of an Iraqi national anthem, Faysal was crowned to the notes of *God Save the King*.[25]

The Iraq that the British took upon themselves to govern was a country marked by ethnic and religious diversity and deep social chasms. One stark division separated the cities from the countryside. Urban and tribal Arabs had different customs and worldview and were not used to sharing government and while the cities were regulated by a combination of Islamic and Ottoman law, the countryside remained the domain of tribal traditions.[26] The countryside itself was also very fragmented because of intra-tribal hierarchies and inter-tribal rivalries. Another line of division separated Sunni and Shiʿa Arabs. The Shiʿa had been a minority under the Sunni Ottoman Empire and lived in separate quarters and areas to strengthen security and preserve their traditions. Other religious minorities, such as the Jews, Assyrians, Armenians, and Chaldeans, were recognised as self-governed communities and also had their own urban quarters. Ethnic differences were originally less important than religion, but as events played out during the twentieth century, the existence of Persian, Turkoman, and Kurdish minorities would add to the complexity.

Notwithstanding social divisions, there were also uniting factors in the young Iraqi state. Iraq is often presented as a colonialist-fabricated entity without any roots in history, but this cliché does not support the weight of historical scrutiny. Reidar Visser has shown how proto-political conceptions of 'Iraq' existed in Ottoman times. Poets, historians, and politicians did in fact refer to 'Iraq' in the nineteenth century as a territorial entity and a cross-sectarian concept of identity. The three-way separation of Iraq in the provinces of Basra, Baghdad, and Mosul was also a recent invention (1884). Before that the Ottomans had organised the territory of present Iraq in different ways, including, in 1780–1831 and 1862–1879, as one single entity. Baghdad had always had a special status as the territory's 'proto-capital'.[27]

Great Britain fulfilled its obligations as mandate authority by granting Iraq independence in 1932. All the same it was indifferent to its role as mentor in the work of building a modern nation-state. The British made no effort to bridge the urban–tribal divide, and instead relied on separate modes of control in the two areas. As described in Chapter 2, the colonial power maintained Sunni Muslim dominance in the urban political system, and allied itself with Shi'a tribal leaders to prevent a rebellion in the Shi'a-dominated south. The Tribal Civil Dispute Regulation Act of 1919 granted the tribal leaders the authority to adjudicate in civil conflicts, including land disputes and to collect taxes on behalf of the state. These rights that in practice delegated state authority to a feudal-like power group were later integrated into the Iraqi constitution of 1925.[28] The colonial power also packed parliament with Shi'a landowners/tribal leaders that had supported them during the revolution of 1920. In other words, Great Britain chose to strengthen the patron–client system at the expense of democracy.

Furthermore, the colonial power sabotaged the central power's attempts to win control over the territory. King Faysal wanted to introduce conscription, in order to subject the tribes to the central authority in Baghdad, but the British deliberately kept the Iraqi army weak. The cities, the Sunni officer corps, and the Shi'a *'ulama* were centres of nationalist opposition while the tribal leaders were allies of the British. The central power was only able to establish its authority over the tribes after independence.[29] The United Kingdom's control over the Iraqi central power continued even after 1932. According to the British-Iraqi treaty of 1930 that regulated relations between the two countries after independence, Iraq was obliged to consult the United Kingdom in all foreign affairs and give the United Kingdom its full support in the event of war. In addition, the Royal Air Force kept its bases outside Basra and Baghdad.

Growing nationalism

Great Britain left behind an undemocratic political system in which pro-British elites dominated. At the same time and as a reaction to British rule there arose a broad Iraqi nationalist movement that aspired to a greater degree of political co-determination. The driving force in the movement was an ethnically diverse intelligentsia inspired by the Ottoman reform movement, the constitutional revolution in Iran (1905–11), and a dawning Arab nationalism. Together these impulses provided an active and liberal environment that strengthened Iraqi identity and society. The intelligentsia published newspapers and challenged authority structures in poetry, short stories, and other art forms. They invited people to debates in cafes and artists' salons and started associations across religious and class divisions. On several occasions the nationalist movement mobilised the masses in order to put pressure on the authorities.[30] The demonstrations sometimes had political consequences, for example, when the government had to resign and some twenty members of parliament withdrew in protest against the signing of a new agreement with the British, the Anglo-Iraqi Portsmouth Treaty, in 1948. In the period from 1925 to 1958, a total of sixteen parliamentary elections were held and 56 governments formed.[31]

The liberal age of Iraqi nationalism was however to cede to more militaristic nationalist expressions in the decades following the 1958 Iraqi revolution. The underlying reason for this shift, which would set back Iraqi democracy, was the growth of radical ideologies in response to increasing class inequalities and continued colonial intervention in the region. Iraq, since the late nineteenth century, was in a process of rapid integration into the capitalist world economy. As the process took place in the context of political favouring of certain allies of the British, it resulted in extreme concentration of wealth. While 80 per cent of the families of Iraq had no property, 2 480 individuals owned 55.1 per cent of all privately held agricultural land.[32] Inequalities and the poor people's suffering gave rise to a strong communist movement, but also fuelled the nationalist movement, and particularly the Pan-Arab Socialist Ba'th Party.

Strong men's rule

On 14 July 1958, inspired by Gamal 'Abd al-Nasser, a group of officers under the name 'the Free Officers' seized power from the Hashemite monarchy. The coup was led by Brigadier 'Abd al-Karim Qasim and Colonel 'Abd al-Salam 'Arif. The coup was the starting signal for a series of strong men who would subject Iraqi society to ever more repressive regimes over the next 45 years and in which the personality cult, too, grew stronger. Even if on paper Arab and Iraqi nationalists had grand visions of nation-building, the challenges of governing such a fragmented country were so great that in practice the rulers based their government on clan and network-based survival politics. The colossal oil revenues that poured into the state treasury helped to make this negative development possible. From 31 per cent of state income in 1951 oil revenues rose to 65 per cent in 1956.[33] This development peaked with the massive increase in oil prices in 1973, which in practice made the state economically independent of society.

The principle division line in 'the years of revolution' went between Iraqi nationalists and the champions of Arab unity. The former meant that Iraq, as a continuation of the Sumerian, Babylonian, and Assyrian civilisations, was a separate nation that should find expression in its own state. The Arab nationalists, however, gave top priority to the concept of Arab unity, pointing out that under the 'Abbasids, Baghdad was the centre of the entire Arab world. This basic disagreement about the framework for political community continued to create political turbulence and make democratisation difficult. A condition for establishing popular rule is a consensus about who the people are but on this issue the Iraqi political parties gradually grew further and further apart.

The Iraqi nationalist 'Abd al-Karim Qasim ruled for the first five years after Iraq became a republic. As the son of a Shi'a Kurd mother and an Arab Sunni father, he tried to create a political platform on the theme of national unity. However, his nationalist project was disliked by the Ba'thists. When Qasim refused to join Egypt and Syria in the first United Arab Republic, the Ba'th Party accused him of being an enemy of the Pan-Arab cause. In 1963 officers belonging to the Ba'th Party and several other Pan-Arab socialist parties organised a coup and executed Qasim. The leaders of the coup were General Ahmad Hassan al-Bakr and Colonel 'Abd al-Salam 'Arif. The former, who belonged to the Ba'th Party, was appointed prime minister and the latter president. Nine months later 'Arif carried out a coup, successfully eliminating Ahmad Hassan al-Bakr and other members of the Ba'th Party from the government. However, 'Arif's moment in power proved brief. In April 1966 he was killed in a helicopter accident and was immediately succeeded by his brother, General 'Abd al-Rahman 'Arif.

In the wake of the Six-Day War in 1967, however, the Ba'th Party recovered. On 17 July the following year officers belonging to the party managed to regain power. 'Abd al-Rahman Arif was deposed in a bloodless coup and Ahmad Hassan al-Bakr became the new president. Power lay in a seven-man Revolutionary Command Council, which al-Bakr in the weeks following the coup would manage to dominate. Ba'th Party communiqué no 1, issued in 1968, declared: 'We (the Ba'th Party) are against religious sectarianism (*al-ta'ifiyya*), racism, and tribalism (*al-qaba'iliyya*).'[34] The goal was national unity but the Ba'th regime's real policy was soon to deviate from this declaration. Al-Bakr had a political and military following based in the first instance on Sunnis from his hometown Tikrit. To gain full control within the power structure he purged 'disloyal elements' from military and security positions and replaced them with his townsmen and members of the al-Bu Nasir tribal confederation from the Sunni Triangle north of Baghdad. The Ba'th regime would soon be known as the 'Tikrit clan'.

Al-Bakr in particular entrusted his second cousin, Saddam Husayn, who also hailed from Tikrit and belonged to al-Bu Nasir, with the task of building up an inner circle of loyal men. Saddam Husayn gladly carried out this order and one of his first tasks was to recruit and train a lifeguard for the president. The recruits were 15–16 year-olds from Tikrit, mainly from al-Bu Nasir. Their job was to guard the president's palaces and to accompany him on his travels. The only man they were to obey was Saddam Husayn, the man to whom they owed their position, who arranged their marriages, and guaranteed their social status. After a while Saddam came to overshadow the ageing al-Bakr. In 1979 al-Bakr retired due to illness and Saddam Husayn took over as president. Al-Bakr died some time after and there were speculations as to whether Saddam had poisoned him, but this was never proved.[35]

Upon receiving power as Iraq's president, Saddam Husayn declared that a 'plot' to overthrow the regime had been uncovered and he set up a special tribunal, proceeding to execute 22 leading Ba'th party members. Among those executed were some of Saddam Husayn's most intimate associates: those surviving in the 'inner circle' were told to carry out the executions. Consequently, Saddam Husayn guaranteed that ties between himself and his most trusted men were forged in blood. He also gained the reputation as a particularly ruthless leader that would terrorise his political opponents.[36]

On the external front, the first thing the new president did was to throw Iraq into an eight-year war, from 1980 to 1988, against its neighbour, Iran. The war impoverished the Iraqi people – but consolidated Saddam's position as despot. The Ba'th regime brutally crushed all signs of opposition. At the end of the 1980s Saddam carried out military campaigns against the Kurds, who had joined the Iranians. Soon the Iraqi president led the Iraqis into a new destructive war, this time occupying Kuwait in 1990. After Western armed forces had driven Saddam's troops out of the tiny kingdom in 1991, the Kurds rose against Baghdad, and in the same year the Shi'a Islamist *intifada* broke out in southern Iraq. Both risings were short-lived. The *intifada* was suppressed by Shi'a Muslim tribal leaders in the South, and Iraqi forces rapidly took control of Kurdish towns, carrying out bombing raids and driving hundreds of thousands over the borders into Turkey and Iran. The Iraqi regime did however withdraw from North Iraq, where the Kurdish parties, Kurdistan's Democratic Party (KDP) and Kurdistan's Patriotic Front (PUK), partly in cooperation, partly in bitter strife, governed autonomously in the period 1991–2003.

Decades of survival politics, combined with war and sanctions, had dramatic consequences for the Iraqi nation. The Ba'th state's repression created an atomised society where distrust bloomed. There were no longer civil associations to facilitate social organisation across ethnic divisions. Iraq had become a vertical society, in which individuals managed as best they could by seeking safety within their own tribe, religious group, or local community. Saddam Husayn had arranged all state institutions with one aim in view, his own survival. It was on the ruins of this regime that the Bush administration planned to build a democratic Iraq, a 'democratic lighthouse' in the Middle East.

The Bush administration's mistakes

Democratisation is usually a slow process in which a mixture of pressure from below and concessions from above gradually give the people a share in political decisions. As a rule, the process takes place within the framework of well-established states that slowly change their political institutions. In contrast to this the Bush administration wanted to bring democracy to Iraq through a radical break with the old regime. With the wisdom of hindsight we can see the strategy has failed. The problem of 'the shock method' can be summed up as three fundamental mistakes.

The dissolution of the Ba'th state

The neo-conservatives intended that Saddam Husayn's Iraq had to be pulled up by the roots in order to make democratic rule possible. Through war and occupation in 2003 the USA crushed the old power apparatus and began building a new Iraq. The new country would be based on political and economic liberalism as in the 'mother country', the USA. A liberal constitution would ensure the division of power and personal liberties, and the market economy would bring development to Iraq. For the Bush administration the core of democracy was the very antithesis to the plan economics, the corporative state, and the cult of personality that characterised Saddam's Iraq. The problem of this radical break was that in order to carry out its democratisation project the USA had to build an entirely new state.

The democratisation process ran parallel to a far more fundamental battle to re-establish state control over Iraqi territory. The lawless conditions that characterised Baghdad and other big cities after the Ba'th regime's fall on 9 April 2003, gave Washington DC a foretaste of how hard it would be. The USA had overturned a powerful and threatening dictator, but could not prevent bands of thieves from plundering shops, factories, universities, public offices and buildings, including the cultural treasures in the National Library and the National Museum. Nonetheless, on 1 May 2003 Bush declared the war in Iraq ended and the 'mission accomplished'.[37]

To fill the immediate vacuum after Saddam Husayn's regime, the USA established a transitional coalition government, the Coalition Provisional Authority (CPA). The leader of the CPA was L. Paul Bremer, who reported directly to Defence Secretary Donald Rumsfeld. During his first weeks on the job Bremer decided on two breaks with the old regime that would have far-reaching consequences. First, he announced on 16 May 2003 that former leading members of the Ba'th Party were not wanted in the new state apparatus and that 'ordinary'. party members should be excluded from major public office. In this way an estimated 120,000 Iraqis – including teachers and doctors – lost their jobs.[38] Sunni Arabs who had dominated the Ba'th Party under Saddam Husayn interpreted this decision as an attack on their ethnic group. Next on 23 May Bremer threw another 430,000 civil servants out of their jobs by dissolving Iraq's armed forces. While some parts, such as Saddam Husayn's special guards, were closely linked to the former regime, others, such as the regular army, were regarded as a national institution.[39]

The army's history was far older than that of the Ba'th regime, and even if Sunni Arabs loyal to Saddam dominated the key positions in it, Kurds and Shi'as were well integrated at lower levels. In other words, it was not just the extended arm of Saddam Husayn that the CPA decided to eliminate but one of the pillars of the Iraqi state. 'The break with the old' was part of the Bush administration's concept of a new and democratic Iraq: but democracy presupposes a state. With the experiences of the country's leaders and military class made unavailable and with entire social groups excluded, the state-building project would come up against really big problems.

The legitimacy problem

In addition, the judicial basis for USA's democratisation project was highly dubious. Democracy as a form of government presupposes maintaining judicial principles, but the Bush administration chose to override international law when it attacked Iraq in 2003. Right from the beginning, the vast majority of experts on international law claimed the war was illegal. But as one of the Bush administration's key strategists put it, international law 'stood in the way of doing things right'.[40] Originally, to legitimise the attack, the USA pointed out the dangers presented by Saddam Husayn's 'weapons of mass destruction' – but thorough searches after the war failed to find any such weapons and subsequently this excuse has been revealed as a lie. The needs for a 'humanitarian intervention' and regime change therefore became the rescue buoy of the USA and the United Kingdom, but this argument was not only in conflict with international law, it was also particularly vulnerable to a backlash in the battle for the security of the people and for democracy in Iraq. With deteriorating living conditions in the first years after the fall of the Ba'th state, it became harder and harder for the USA to convince the Iraqi people that the intention really was to democratise Iraq.

The Bush administration's legitimacy problem in Iraq was aggravated by the partners it chose to cooperate with in establishing democracy. Instead of allying itself with the grass roots, the USA imported a leader class composed of exile Iraqis that had no support in local society. The very symbol of this group was Ahmad Chalabi, the leader of the exile group the Iraqi National Congress, which before the war had been one of the strongest advocates of toppling Saddam Husayn's regime. Thanks to personal contacts with influential people in the Pentagon and CPA boss Bremer, Chalabi was able to place his men in strategically important posts such as finance minister, oil minister, and trade minister in the occupation government.[41] Chalabi was also a key figure behind the exclusion of Ba'th members from leading public offices in order to make room for his own takeover of power. The Bush administration's belief in Chalabi as the leader of a democratic Iraq contrasted sharply with realities on the ground. According to opinion polls, at this time Chalabi was even less popular than Saddam Husayn.[42] The fact that the CPA had become a tool for the personal ambitions of an exiled Iraqi that had not lived in the country for 47 years (!) helped weaken the USA's credibility even more – the Bush administration had failed to build confidence with leaders and social groups that governed Iraqi opinion. For example, the CPA did not court Sunni Arab tribal chiefs in central Iraq to calm Sunni fears of marginalisation and curb resistance. Similarly, the occupation government ignored Hawza, the influential Shi'a clerics' association, until the Grand *Ayatollah* 'Ali al-Sistani criticised CPA policy in the autumn of 2003.[43] As a result, the Bush administration antagonised the Shi'a community's most influential opinion leader and ruined all chances of obstructing supporters of the radical Shi'a leader Muqtada al-Sadr.

The Bush administration also miscalculated in its belief it could 'win Iraqi hearts' by changing to a market economy. To get rid of inefficiency after decades of plan economy the CPA went in for an immediate transfer of the economy to the private sector. In just a few months the occupation government lowered tax rates from 45 per cent to 15 per cent, removed subsidies on oil and food, and announced plans for a massive privatisation.[44] But the practical significance of these measures was limited. During the previous few years Saddam Husayn's regime had in fact not levied taxes and for lack of a functioning tax authority the CPA's tax rate was just as theoretical.[45] To prevent bread riots, subsidies on food and oil were rapidly reintroduced, while the plan for the sale of state companies flopped for the lack of interested buyers. As long as the USA could not offer security and with most factories either mismanaged under the Ba'th Party's plan economy or plundered of all valuable equipment after the fall of Baghdad, investors were not exactly queuing up to take over public companies. The privatisation plan was part of the controversial Order 39 that the CPA, under free market ideologist Bremer's leadership, proclaimed on 19 September

2003. The order opened up 100 per cent foreign ownership of Iraqi firms and the unlimited and tax-free export of profits by the owners to their home countries. Furthermore, Order 39 forbade any form of favouritism of national as opposed to international companies in the country.[46] Because it broke with all earlier regimes' policies in Iraq since 1958, Order 39 was subjected to massive criticism. According to the Geneva Convention's article 64, occupation powers shall respect the laws of the country unless these constitute a security risk for the occupation power or prevent respect for the constitution. The CPA's defence was that something urgently needed doing for the Iraqi economy because the economic situation was causing turmoil in the country.[47] But Order 39 was far more than a measure to stabilise and thereby strengthen the Iraqi economy: it rode roughshod over the Iraqi tradition of protectionism and socialism while the country was occupied. As a result, Order 39 aggravated opinion in Iraq, confirming the idea that the USA had overturned Saddam Husayn in order to 'steal the country's wealth'. That the CPA awarded lucrative reconstruction contracts to companies such as Chevron, Bechtel, Halliburton, and Lockheed Martin while states that had not supported the war against Iraq were not 'invited to the party' did not make matters any better

Overall, the Bush administration did too little to reassure the Iraqis about US intentions, too little to improve the population's welfare and security, and too little to engage the population in the state and democracy-building process. Until the CPA handed over power to the interim government in the summer of 2004 the armed resistance grew in strength. The nail in the coffin of US credibility was the photographs of the mistreatment of prisoners in Abu Ghraib prison, which at the end of May, beginning of June, 2004 were published all round the world. The Bush administration's most important argument for acceptance by the population had up till then been liberation from Saddam Husayn's terror. But the pictures from Abu Ghraib showed naked Iraqi prisoners in chains, hooded, attacked by dogs, and being humiliated by American guards. With the power to influence that only photographs can have, these images tore to shreds all arguments about liberation. By a coincidence of fate these scenes of horror came from precisely the same prison where the Ba'th regime had tortured and executed its opponents. With such help from the occupation power the resistance groups had an easy job recruiting warriors against the USA. On its side the US forces were not numerous enough to defeat the opposition. Whereas in 1991 the USA had sent 550,000 soldiers to Saudi Arabia during the First Gulf War, in 2003 Defence Secretary Rumsfeld, insisting on a 'light and flexible force', sent only 160,000 men, cutting numbers to 140,000 after the invasion. Right from the start the force was too small to patrol Iraqi borders, secure the oil pipes and other installations, protect politicians and political institutions, prevent attacks on the civilian population, defeat rebel forces, and all the other tasks that the US military now had to solve. Thus gradually they lost control. When the Iraqi democracy should have been inaugurated with elections to the popular assembly and the constitutional referendum in 2005, the country was already on the verge of collapse.

Ethnic representation

After decades of divide and rule and other forms of survival politics, Iraq offered a rich potential for ethnic conflict. Through a mixture of Jacobin state control and nationalist propaganda Saddam Husayn had kept the country together. But the dissolution of the Iraqi state apparatus under the occupation power's leadership gave ethnic forces a new dynamic. The Bush administration's third mistake was therefore to think of Iraqi politics in ethnic terms.

The USA came to Iraq with a one-sided and exaggerated idea that the country was split into linguistic and religious groups.[48] On the creation of the CPA and the Iraqi Governing Council, the USA was careful to see that all groups had 'their representatives' and that the numbers reflected the demographic distribution. It was of less interest that Iraqis' identities did not just have linguistic and religious but also professional, class, ideological, and, not least, national components. What was important for getting a seat in the institutions the USA founded was linguistic and religious, so it was precisely this sort of identity the actors emphasised. The Governing Council had 25 members of which nine functioned as a rotating presidency. The representatives were elected with a view to ensure ethnic representation and distribution. The Governing Council's task was to 'prepare democracy' by starting to formulate the constitution and by appointing ministers for a transitional government until popular elections could be held. But the USA had not taken precautions against members of the council building their own power bases and adjusting the system to suit their own interests. After independence, the foremost figures on the council, 'Iyad 'Allawi, Ahmad Chalabi, Mas'ud Barzani, Jalal Talabani, Ibrahim Ja'fari, and 'Abd al-'Aziz al-Hakim, emerged as the leaders of Iraqi 'democracy'.[49]

In a system founded on ethnic rather than national representation it is not surprising that Sunni Arabs, as a minority, ended up in opposition to the proposed constitution. The opposition was based on ideological as well as political considerations. Ideologically, the many Sunni Arabs who identified with Iraqi nationalism categorically rejected the idea of constructing political institutions along ethnic lines and called for continued downplaying of ethnic identities. Politically, they had been very much marginalised through the dissolution of the armed forces and the exclusion of Ba'th Party members from the state system. In the battle for influence with their Shi'a Arab brothers the Sunnis suffered from a numerical handicap. Partly in protest, partly because the security situation did not permit it, few Sunni Arabs took part in the elections of January 2005 to the national assembly that was to be responsible for drafting the constitution. In that way they obtained even less influence on the process that should lay the foundations of Iraq's future. To reduce the damage 15 Sunni Arabs with the right to vote were allowed to join the 55 members of the big constitution committee for the negotiations. However, the Sunnis, complaining they were excluded from all the backroom negotiations between the Kurds and the Shi'as, withdrew from the process on 28 August 2005.[50] As a result the constitution that was accepted in a referendum 15 October 2005 did not unite the nation.[51] And even if the Sunni Arabs managed to get a clause accepted that the constitution should be amended in the spring of 2006, the security situation in Iraq had become so intolerable that it completely undermined democracy.

Conflict lines and unsolved issues

The Bush administration's three mis-steps have had a lingering legacy for Iraqi politics. First, the dissolution of the Ba'th state opened an agonising debate regarding the nature of the state. Politicians in the USA, both Republicans and Democrats, decided early on that the best model would be a decentralised Iraq with a weak central authority in Baghdad, but the idea of a federal Iraqi state set off a series of difficult questions. Key issues such as the degree of power sharing between the central government and the provinces, how oil revenues were to be shared, and to what extent Kirkuk should be incorporated into the Kurdish province, have remained unresolved. There are also difficulties ahead regarding the role of Islam in the state. While Islamists dominate Shi'a politics, the Kurds have a more secularist orientation.

Second, the legitimacy problem continues to haunt Iraqi politicians. In the absence of an effective state apparatus, creating confidence between the authorities and the voters seems an almost impossible task. Prime Minister Nuri al-Maliki has tried to make himself the symbol of Iraqi nationalism by defending the principle of national sovereignty and repressing challenges to the central power in Baghdad. In 2008 he led a military campaign in Basra against the followers of Muqtada al-Sadr that earned him a reputation as 'Iraq's new strongman'. However, Maliki's security apparatus could not stop bomb explosions from frequently killing Iraqi civilians, and the low-level quality of public education, healthcare, and infrastructure undermined his popularity. In July 2010, more than seven years after the invasion, even the capital Baghdad only had five hours of electricity a day.[52] In the 2010 Parliamentary election Maliki ended up second after Iyad 'Allawi with a disappointing 24,22 per cent of the votes.[53]

Third, ethnic representation has created a dominance of political leaders and parties with a sub-national focus that are unable to unite the Iraqis. Muqtada al-Sadr has tried to take the role of Iraqi nationalist, but the Sunnis do not place much trust in him since he is the leader of a Shiʻa militia. Similarly, the Islamic Supreme Council of Iraq of Ammar al-Hakim, is discredited because of its close ties to Iran. The leaders of the two biggest Kurdish parties, Jalal Talabani and Masud Barzani, insist on extensive autonomy within the framework of a loose Iraqi federation. During the civil war the above and other leaders learned to defend their interests through armed militias. Today, the existence of so many armed militias is a fundamental obstacle to democracy developing in Iraq. Successful democracy building requires that the militias be disarmed and if possible, be integrated into the regular national army so that the legitimate authorities have a monopoly of armed force. Disarmament again cannot take place without trust. If the militias do not trust the ruling authorities, it is futile to expect they will voluntarily hand over their weapons. Experiences from Hezbollah in Lebanon, who have clung to their weapons ever since the Civil War in the 1980s, illustrate just how difficult a task disarmament is.

The USA and democracy promotion after Iraq

The occupation of Iraq has proved extremely expensive, both in terms of loss of human life and purely economically,[54] and it has born few fruits, if one assumes that at the beginning the aim was to create a democratic Iraq and eliminate some of the basis for political extremism in the Middle East.

Not surprisingly, the Bush administration early on met opposition at home for its Middle East policy. In October 2004 a group of highly profiled American academics and public officials published an appeal against the occupation of Iraq. The group, which called itself the Coalition for a Realistic Foreign Policy, aimed to work against the neo-conservative idea that the USA should use its economic and military superiority to change regimes in other parts of the world.[55] Three of the coalition members, John J. Mersheimer, Christopher A. Preble, and Stephen M. Walt, pointed out that the Bush administration overlooked *nationalism*, the most important political ideology in the world. As the Soviet Union experienced in Afghanistan, Israel experienced in Lebanon, and the USA in Iraq, the road from being perceived as liberator to being perceived as invader is short, and invaders usually face nationalist risings that are hard to defeat.

The Iraqi experience even led certain neo-conservatives to do some soul searching. One of these was Francis Fukuyama. In 2006 he published the book *After the Neocons: America at the Crossroads*, in which he accused the Bush administration of having misused neo-conservative ideology to legitimise the invasion of Iraq.[56] Fukuyama argued that the administration underestimated international opposition to the invasion and the challenges of state-building in Iraq. The Pew Global Attitudes Project survey report from June 2006 showed that most nations regarded US military presence in Iraq as a bigger danger to world peace than Iran.[57] This failure would according to Fukuyama discredit the neo-conservative ideology and strengthen the position of those who argued for realism in US foreign policy.[58]

Public opinion at home also rapidly turned against the Bush administration's use of military power to democratise Iraq. In September 2005, the Program on International Policy Attitudes published the results of a national survey that showed that as many as 55 per cent of Americans were opposed to promoting democracy by force and that this method only had 35 per cent support. The poll showed that as many as 68 per cent of Americans thought that democratic government would not make the world a safer place. Almost half of those asked felt that promoting democracy ought to be a goal of American foreign policy but not the most important. In addition, the majority of those asked believed that the authorities should not promote democracy in countries where elections could bring Islamist to power.[59]

The experiences from Iraq will influence the West's approach to the issue of democratisation in the Middle East. The idea of spreading democratic government is far from dead and buried, but in the foreseeable future this will take place by using different methods from military power. Kenneth M. Pollack argues that the USA should not abandon the goal of democratisation in the Middle East simply because it was the goal of George W. Bush.[60] But democratisation should not start by forcefully removing those in power: on the contrary, the USA should start from the existing political order and involve the regimes themselves in the process. One way to do this, according to Pollack, is to offer incentives such as economic relations and aid to those who carry out liberal reform. The USA should also do more to convince the rulers that their long-time survival depends on their willingness to open up. The inability the USA has demonstrated to 'forcibly democratise' Iraq makes it highly improbable that Western states will use the same procedure on other regimes in the region.

Conclusion

The analysis shows that there are few actors that have both the will and the ability to lead a democratisation process in the Middle East. The region's people are aware of democracy and want to participate in political processes, but lack the means to put pressure on authoritarian authorities. The strongest social force is in most countries the Islamist movement. Even if the Islamists' democratic intentions have, only to a very limited extent, been put to a practical test, many have gradually come to accept democratic principles. However, the regimes exploit the West's fear of Islamism to repress these movements. Democracy's future also depends on the will of the elite to change the status quo. The rulers feel under pressure both from below and from outside and will probably continue to initiate political reforms in order to ease this pressure. But the regimes will take care not to go so far that they undermine their own power and expose themselves to real competition. The reform process the regimes have started can, however, prove hard to control: the reforms create expectations of rapid change, and if these expectations are not met, popular discontent will increase and the pressure on the regimes will grow stronger. Recent events in Iran are instructive in this respect – having been accustomed to determine the outcome of elections over 30 years in the Islamic Republic, the Iranian public reacted angrily to what they perceived as electoral fraud in June 2009. 'The Green Movement' that emerged to contest the electoral result persisted to become a broad social movement for democracy and constitutional government. This emergence of 'street pressure' constitutes a new and promising development for democratisation from below. If similar movements emerge in other countries in the region the era of authoritarian regime stability may be put to a test.

Further reading

Abdel Rahman, Maha: *Civil Society Exposed: The Politics of NGOs in Egypt.* London and New York: I.B.Tauris, 2005.

Brown, Nathan J.: *Constitutions in a Nonconstitutional World: Arab Basic Laws and the Prospects for Accountable Government.* New York: State University of New York Press, 2002.

Davis, Eric: *Memories of State: Politics, History, and Collective Identity in Modern Iraq.* Berkeley and California: University of California Press, 2005.

Diamond, Larry, Marc F. Plattner and Daniel Brumberg (eds.): *Islam and Democracy in the Middle East.* Washington: Johns Hopkins University Press, 2003.

Diamond, Larry: *Squandered Victory: The American Occupation and the Bungled Effort to Bring Democracy to Iraq.* New York: Times Books, Henry Holt & Co, 2005.

Dodge, Toby: *Inventing Iraq: The Failure of Nation Building and a History Denied.* New York: Columbia University Press, 2010.

Fattah, Moataz A.: *Democratic Values in the Muslim World.* Boulder and London: Lynne Rienner Publishers, 2006.

Gheissari, Ali and Vali Nasr: *Democracy in Iran: History and the Quest for Liberty.* Oxford and New York: Oxford University Press, 2006.

Jones, Jeremy: *Negotiating Change: The New Politics of the Middle East*. London and
    New York: I.B.Tauris, 2007.
Phillips, David L.: *Losing Iraq: Inside the Postwar Reconstruction Fiasco*. New York:
    Westview Press, 2005.
Salamé, Ghassan (ed.): *Democracy without Democrats: The Renewal of Politics in the
    Muslim World*. London: I.B.Tauris, 1994.

10 Breakdown

> Everything is breaking down: there are shortages of food, no electricity, no wages, the public services are breaking down. (...) some can live on very little, but there is a point at which things break down.[1]

Over the past few years several parts of the Middle East have been hit by economic problems, social fragmentation, and violent conflict. In September 2006, John Ging, chief of the UN aid organisation UNRWA, warned that the Gaza Strip was on the verge of breakdown. This warning came before the 2007 civil war between Hamas and Fatah and the conflict between Israel and Hamas during the winter of 2008–9, which made the situation even worse. Iraq looks equally grim: between 2006 and 2008 the Iraqi society collapsed into violence and ethnic cleansing. As the USA is pulling out its forces, the civil war nightmare still haunts the Iraqis. Yemen is also at risk of imminent political collapse, as war threatens in the north and protests turn to riots in the south, terror attacks hit the capital, and the opposition is boycotting elections. Over the past years political violence in the shape of terror and ruthless repression of the opposition has been a predominant trait in other countries in the Middle East as well. Militant Islamists have carried out violent actions throughout the region while the regimes have used such actions as a pretext for tightening their grasp of power.

In the previous chapter we saw that democratisation, at any rate in the short term, appeared challenging in the Middle East: continued stability under authoritarian regimes seemed more probable. Developments in the Palestinian areas, Iraq, Yemen, and other countries, however, give some grounds for discussing an alternative scenario, namely breakdown. We have seen how several of the regions' rulers over the last three decades have undermined national cohesion and weakened the efficiency of the state in order to hang onto power. The regimes' power strategies have had a high price.

In this chapter we shall try to answer the following question: are the Middle East states about to break down? In the second part of the chapter we shall take a closer look at Saudi Arabia: does the Sa'ud family's kingdom bear signs of weakening?

State failure

Sovereign states, which the Middle East inherited from the colonial powers, are the modern world order's 'building bricks'. As a result, in cases where the states are weakening and about to fall apart the whole order is threatened. After the Cold War the question of 'failed states' has become a central issue in international politics, both in relation to humanitarian interventions and to security. The focus on state failure has also been reflected in academia. What then is 'state failure'?

Symptoms

Robert I. Rotberg, who led the Harvard University Failed States Project from 1999 to 2003, distinguishes between weak, failed, and collapsed states. According to Rotberg, a 'weak state' is characterised by ethnic tensions that have not yet broken out into widespread violence. In some states the authorities are unable to take care of the inhabitants' legal rights, civil society is harassed, and authoritarian rulers have come to power. In other states the ruling powers lack the authority to make collective decisions or the capacity to deliver public services such as water and electricity. GDP and other critical economic indicators show a negative development, and public infrastructure is falling apart. Such signs of crisis are a rapid reduction in income and living standards, growing corruption, pressure on basic services such as health and education, increasing unemployment, and a scarcity of basic goods. A development towards a growing gap between rich and poor, in which the country's rulers grab an ever-bigger slice of the cake, is thought to be more dangerous than poverty.[2]

In a 'failed state' the above tendencies are even clearer and more serious. What is more, the state is ravaged by long-term violent conflict and the central government has lost control over parts of its territory. Often effective state control goes no further than the capital and major cities. Besides these conditions, Rotberg mentions that a failed state has inadequate institutions: as a rule only the executive is properly developed. The legislature, to the extent that it exists, does nothing more than rubber-stamp the decisions made by the executive. Democratic debate is often absent and consequently, government is frequently arbitrary. The judiciary, bureaucracy, and armed forces are reduced to instruments of power in the hands of the rulers. Lawlessness and crime characterise the towns, and weapon and drugs traffic spread in areas outside the authorities' control. In such states the inhabitants often turn to warlords, ethnic nationalists or rebel forces for protection, and one sees that ambitious leaders try to mobilise the masses by activising ethnic solidarity bonds.[3]

A 'collapsed' state is an extreme version of a failed state and is a rare phenomenon. According to Rotberg such a state is characterised by anarchy and the absence of government. In the power vacuum the rule of the strongest applies, the state being more a geographical expression than a reality.[4]

Moreover, methods have been developed to measure the degree of state failure. The most systematic method has been developed by the research institute the Fund for Peace, which yearly publishes the report the 'Failed States Index'. The extent to which a state is weakened and threatened with collapse is evaluated on the basis of twelve political, economic, military, and social indicators of instability. In 2009, a total of 177 countries were assessed. After the researchers had examined the various source materials, each individual country was allocated points from one to ten for each indicator before the countries were then ranged on the basis of the total score. In this method a high total score indicates a country in crisis while a low score shows that the country is stable[5] (see Table 12).

Symptoms in the Middle East

The 'Failed States Index' concludes that a clear majority of states with signs of failure are to be found in sub-Saharan Africa. In addition, there are such states

Table 12 Twelve indicators of the 'Failed States Index'

Social indicators

I-1	Mounting demographic pressures
I-2	Massive movement of refugees or internally displaced persons creating complex humanitarian emergencies
I-3	Legacy of vengeance-seeking group grievance or group paranoia
I-4	Chronic and sustained human flight

Economic indicators

I-5	Uneven economic development along group lines
I-6	Sharp and/or severe economic decline

Political indicators

I-7	Criminalisation and/or de-legitimisation of the state
I-8	Progressive deterioration of public services
I-9	Suspension or arbitrary application of the rule of law and widespread violation of human rights
I-10	Security apparatus operates as a 'state within a state'
I-11	Rise of factionalised elites
I-12	Intervention of other states or external political actors

in Latin America, South-east Asia – and the Middle East. According to the 'Failed States Index 2009' Iraq is the sixth most unstable country in the world. Furthermore, the report points out Yemen, Lebanon, and Iran as countries in danger of failure. Syria and Egypt also show signs of weakening. But just as interesting is the fact that many of the countries in the region score well on the ranking list. This is especially true of the monarchies on the Arabian Peninsula – including Saudi Arabia – and the countries in North Africa[6] (see Table 13).

It is on the political indicators that the Middle East states score worst. Earlier in the book we have seen that authoritarian government is the rule rather than the exception. Countries such as Algeria, Egypt, Iraq, Iran, Yemen, Libya, and Syria in particular have been noted for repressive rule.

Furthermore, the results reflect the fact that a series of countries in the Middle East have been ravaged by war and turbulence. Hundreds of thousands have been killed and millions have fled from their homes. 'The Human Security Brief 2007' concluded that the numbers killed as a result of civil war fell in all regions with the exception of the Middle East from 2002 to 2006,[7] and the main reason for this negative development was the war in Iraq.[8] In October 2009, Iraq's government claimed that more than 85,000 people had lost their lives in the country's violence from 2004 to 2008, the first official report by the government on the death toll since the USA's invasion in 2003.[9] The exact death statistics for Iraq, however, are very uncertain and disputed, and earlier assessments put the death toll significantly higher. Political violence has increased in other Middle East countries, too: in Yemen many have been killed and nearly 200,000 people forced to flee their homes since 2004, primarily because of the Salih regime's military campaigns against Shi'a rebels in the Sa'dah Province;[10] the war between Israel and Hizbollah in the summer of 2006 killed about 1,150 civilians, over 95 per cent of them Lebanese, as well as many combatants on both sides;[11] 1,400 Palestinians, more than half of them civilians, and 13 Israelis were killed in the 2009 Gaza war;[12] and over the past years many have been killed in terrorist attacks in countries such as Algeria, Egypt, Jordan, Lebanon, Morocco, Saudi Arabia, Turkey and Yemen.

Moreover, 'The Human Security Brief 2007' registered a rise in the number of human rights breaches in the Middle East, and the list of the world's worst human rights sinners was topped by Iraq.[13] Violent crimes are also an increasing problem in the region: in Iraq the collapse of Saddam Husayn's state gave criminals total freedom, and in the Palestinian areas, Lebanon, and in Yemen the weakening of the state has given crime greater opportunities. Handguns are easily available, blood feuds flourish, and the state authorities have limited capacity to keep law and order.[14]

Table 13 Middle East states' scores on the 'Failed States Index 2009'

Rank	State	I-1	I-2	I-3	I-4	I-5	I-6	I-7	I-8	I-9	I-10	I-11	I-12	Total
6	Iraq	8.7	8.9	9.7	9.1	8.6	7,6	9.0	8.4	9.3	9.7	9.6	10.0	108.6
18	Yemen	8.8	7.9	7.7	7.4	8.9	8.2	8.3	8.5	7.7	8.4	9.0	7.3	98.1
29	Lebanon	7.0	9.0	9.2	7.2	7.4	6.3	7.8	6.2	6.9	9.1	9.1	8.3	93.5
38	Iran	6.5	8.5	7.6	6.8	7.4	5.5	8.3	6.0	8.9	8.6	9.1	6.8	90.0
39	Syria	6.1	9.2	8.2	6.8	8.0	6.8	8.8	5.7	8.6	7.8	7.8	6.0	89.8
43	Egypt	7.6	6.9	8.0	6.2	7.6	7.0	8.6	6.4	8.4	6.2	8.1	8.0	89.0
58	Israel/West Bank	7.2	8.0	9.3	4.0	7.5	4.1	7.5	7.0	8.0	6.0	8.0	8.0	84.6
73	Algeria	6.7	6.7	7.7	6.2	7.3	4.6	7.7	6.7	7.6	7.0	6.7	5.7	80.6
85	Turkey	6.8	6.6	7.7	5.0	8.0	5.3	6.5	5.3	6.0	7.0	7.8	6.2	78.2
86	Jordan	6.7	7.9	6.8	5.0	7.4	6.5	6.0	5.4	6.9	6.0	6.5	6.8	77.9
89	Saudi Arabia	6.5	6.0	8.0	3.4	7.0	2.7	8.4	4.3	8.9	8.0	7.8	6.5	77.5
93	Morocco	7.0	6.7	6.8	6.2	7.8	6.5	7.4	6.5	6.7	5.1	6.2	4.2	77.1
112	Libya	5.9	4.2	5.8	4.0	7.1	5.5	7.1	4.2	8.1	5.4	7.1	5.0	69.4
121	Tunisia	5.9	3.2	5.4	5.3	7.2	4.9	6.6	6.1	7.4	6.2	6.0	3.4	67.6
125	Kuwait	5.7	4.2	5.1	4.2	6.1	3.5	6.5	3.5	6.9	5.1	7.2	5.3	63.4
133	Bahrain	5.0	3.1	6.4	3.7	5.9	3.5	6.9	3.1	5.0	4.4	6.1	5.9	59.0
138	Qatar	4.7	3.2	5.2	3.3	5.3	4.4	6.5	2.6	4.5	2.5	5.0	4.7	51.9
139	Emirates	4.6	3.4	4.7	3.3	5.7	3.2	6.7	3.6	5.8	2.3	4.0	4.5	51.8
146	Oman	4.5	1.0	3.0	1.3	2.3	4.4	6.0	4.5	6.4	5.0	6.6	2.2	47.2

The Middle East does, however, emerge better when we consider the economic and social indicators. First, the Middle East, as a whole, experienced strong economic growth in the period 2000–8, mainly as a result of higher oil prices. In 2006 the World Bank estimated the average growth to a total of 6.3 per cent, which adjusted for population increase, corresponds to 4.2 per cent growth in GDP. This was the strongest growth registered in the region in more than a decade.[15] The global downturn and financial crisis, however, have exacted a toll on growth in the Middle East. Second, income differences in the Middle Eastern countries, measured with the aid of the so-called Gini Coefficient, continue to be lower than in other major regions such as Latin America, East Asia, and the Pacific.[16]

But the figures are nowhere near as optimistic as they may appear at first sight as certainly not everyone has benefited from the least few years' economic boom. There are considerable differences from state to state. Indeed, the Middle East has more variation in per capita income than any other region, as it includes stone-rich countries such as Qatar and the Emirates and poor countries such as Yemen.[17] Most of the growth of the early 2000s was driven by the oil-rich countries of the region and according to the World Bank, 'comparing growth over the 1990s with growth over the last two years [2003 and 2004], 97 per cent of the regional growth upturn was driven by just four countries – Saudi Arabia, the Islamic Republic of Iran, Algeria, and the United Arab Emirates. In fact, nearly half of the region actually experienced growth downturns relative to the 1990s'.[18] This again means that the region's economic growth is highly vulnerable to price falls on the international market. In addition, income inequality is on the rise within the Middle Eastern states.[19]

Moreover, in many countries, the economic growth will be eaten up by rapid population growth. Despite gradual drops in fertility rate in many Middle Eastern countries since the mid-1980s, the figure is as still as high as 2.2 per cent – only Sub-Saharan Africa has a higher rate of population growth. Forecasting population is obviously difficult, but most demographers project the population to rise rapidly. UNDP expects the population to rise from 436.8 million (in 2007) to 533.8 million in 2020,[20] while others predict an even sharper rise.[21] Most countries in the region now have some kind of family planning programme, but only Iran, Turkey, Egypt, and Tunisia show clear signs of coping with the problem of ever bigger and younger populations.[22]

The population growth means that young people under the age of 24 now make up 50–60 per cent of the total population in the Middle East.[23] The young population, which will mostly live in the towns, puts strong pressure on schools, the health services, housing, and not least employment. The World Bank considers that these countries must create 4.5 million new jobs annually over the next decade, while in reality only 3 million are made each year.[24] The 'Arab Human Development Report 2002' claimed that over half of young Arabs see their future in emigration to the West. Often it is the most resourceful that leave and consequently, the region is drained of its most important resource – highly educated young people.[25] The big question, to which Graham E. Fuller calls attention is: who will be able to politically mobilise the younger generation most successfully, the state or oppositional forces? Research indicates that there is a connection between radicalism and youth. In the case of the Middle East, there is a real danger that unemployed and dissatisfied youths will turn to radical political movements.[26]

In three places, the economic signs of state failure are particularly manifest: Yemen, Iraq, and the Palestinian areas the West Bank and Gaza. Yemen ranks as number 140 of 182 countries on UNDP's 'Human Development Index' for 2009. GDP per inhabitant in the country is only 2,335 US$,[27] and 41.8 per cent of the population lives under the UN's declared poverty line.[28] The Yemenis, who live mainly in the countryside, face colossal socio-economic challenges: among which are limited access to basic social services and freshwater; import dependency on food – not least because of the cultivation of *qat*; and a birth rate as high as 6 per cent.[29] At some time between 2012 and 2018 Yemen's oil wells will dry out and at 3.02 per cent, the country has one of the highest population growth rates globally, with the population expected to rise. The future seems grim.

Iraq's economy fell abruptly from its peak in the 1980s until 2003 resulting from decades of wars and sanctions. Economic data for the years following Saddam Husayn's fall are very uncertain, but several international aid organisations have warned of the development. In July 2007 Oxfam described a humanitarian catastrophe, in which about 8 million people (around two-thirds of the population) needed emergency aid. Furthermore, it claimed that 43 per cent of all Iraqis lived under the poverty line, partly because unemployment was as high as 50 per cent. The proportion of Iraqis without access to clean water rose from 50 per cent in 2003 to 70 per cent in 2007. As many as 80 per cent of the population lacked adequate sanitary installations and diarrhoea flourished. In Baghdad most homes had electricity only two hours a day. Iraqi children were highly exposed to malnutrition and disease, and more than 800,000 children had stopped attending school and as many as 40 per cent of Iraqi teachers, engineers, and doctors had left the country since 2003.[30]

The situation is also depressing on the West Bank and in Gaza. In the years following the outbreak of the second *intifada* in 2000, living conditions for the Palestinians seriously deteriorated.[31] In June 2008 a survey carried out by The Palestinian Central Bureau of Statistics showed that as many as 45.7 per cent of all families on the West Bank and 79.4 per cent of all families on the Gaza Strip lived in poverty.[32] The survey showed that poverty in Gaza, controlled by Hamas, was on the increase, whereas it was slightly on the decline on the West Bank, controlled by the Fatah-dominated self-governing authority. Israel's blockade of Gaza has led to a dramatic rise in unemployment, scarcity of basic vital goods, and to greater poverty among Palestinians. In June 2009, the Red Cross released a report that argued that Israel's continued blockade was making it impossible for Gaza to recover from the 2009 war.[33]

Regime stability and state failure

It is easy to demonstrate symptoms of several Middle East states showing signs of weakening. But what are the reasons and effects?

Composite causes

The reasons for state failure are many and composite and will vary from country to country. The literature identifies a number of causes why states weaken and finally collapse. Paul D. Williams distinguishes between structural and contingent causes of state failure.[34] A structural explanation lays weight on the difficult inheritance of the colonial powers. In some cases the Europeans left behind 'artificial' states, where local conditions for state and nation building were poor. As a result of super power rivalry during the Cold War, the new states frequently experienced exploitation of internal strife by outside powers to further their own interests. According to Williams, many states on independence had a territory and a resource basis that made internal consolidation hard. Some states were difficult to administer because of geographical conditions and a small population, while others did not have an adequate resource basis to feed a large and growing population.

Williams identified the contingent causes of state failure as the effect of conditions such as political misgovernment, destructive activities from non-governmental actors such as warlords and criminals, unsuccessful economic policy, and undermining external intervention. Many leaders in the post-colonial world have used survival politics to hang on to power and have exploited rentier revenues to reward their own supporters and repress their opponents rather than start development projects. Hand-in-hand with poor leadership, warlords and criminals have sought profit in kindling the fires of ethnic tension, thus helping to weaken the state. The state power has problems controlling its territory and protecting its inhabitants, and its opponents can easily take to arms against the authorities. Last but not least, external intervention has contributed to state failure.

In the book *The Bottom Billion* Paul Collier tries to systematise various conditions that cause state failure. The author claims that as a rule weakened states are caught in at least one of four 'poverty traps'.[35] The first trap is conflict. According to Collier as much as 73 per cent of all countries that, at one or another point in time, have experienced state failure have gone through a civil war.[36] The second trap is to be landlocked, especially when the neighbours are poor and especially when these countries also bear symptoms of state failure. Next comes dependency on abundant natural resources. Paradoxically, overwhelming access to natural resources has a tendency to give negative effects on economic development. Only exceptionally are rich natural resources a catalyst for development as such resources hinder diversified economic growth, tend to create conflict, and not least contribute to the fourth trap, which is bad governance. By bad governance Collier refers to authoritarian rule whose prime focus is hanging on to power rather than promoting the development of the country.

The above-mentioned driving forces behind state failure strengthen each other reciprocally. In other words it is the combination of these factors that explains why certain states are weakened, fail or collapse.

The price of stability

In 'The Failed States Index' we see that three of the most colonist-crafted states rank highly: Iraq, Lebanon, and Syria, plus the country by nature poorest, Yemen. But countries that have long traditions as states and an advantageous political geography also come high on the list, respectively Egypt and Iran. This indicates that in order to explain state failure in the Middle East one should look behind the structural causes and also take into account the contingent causes. In particular, survival politics have contributed to weaken the states. A quick recall of the lessons from this book illustrates this point.

In several countries rulers lacking legitimacy have played the 'ethnic card' to protect their position in power, which involves recruiting leaders to the power apparatus on a basis of blood and friendship in order to ensure political loyalty. While this has helped ensure the regime's stability, it has also undermined national solidarity and, in certain cases prepared the ground for ethnic conflict. In countries such as Yemen, Iraq, and Syria such recruitment has led to certain clans hijacking the state system, which creates a reaction in the shape of the mobilisation of other groups. The combination of a multi-ethnic society and authoritarian rule can in this way lead to state failure in the Middle East.

Furthermore, in Chapters 3 and 4 we saw how the rulers' divide and rule tactics, corporatism, and clientelism have enfeebled society. These policies have serious consequences for the region's countries. Social scientists from John Locke and Alexis de Tocqueville to Robert D. Putnam and Sidney Verba have emphasised the importance of *trust* for a country's development. Trust, as the most important component in social capital, is a necessary condition for social integration, economic growth, and the maintenance of stable democratic government. However, the Middle East rulers have undermined confidence both between the inhabitants, and between inhabitants and state, by their policies. By keeping society divided and weak, the regimes make initiative and cooperation, vital for development, hard.

Many in the elite use their political control over the state for personal gain. King 'Abdallah of Saudi Arabia with a personal fortune of US$ 21 billion topped *Forbes Magazine*'s 2006 list of the world's richest heads of state. Next followed Abu Dhabi's *Shaykh* Khalifa in third place and Dubai's *Shaykh* Muhammad in fourth with US$ 19 and US$ 14 billion respectively. Only Sultan Hajji Hassan al-Bulkia of Brunei managed to squeeze in among the three Arab state heads at the top of the list.[37] The ruling families on the Arabian Peninsula regard their countries' oil resources as their rightful property, and consider themselves to be generous in sharing their wealth with the people. This attitude is underlined by the following commentary of Prince Bandar bin Sultan, Saudi Arabia's former ambassador to Washington:

> If you tell me that building this whole country, and spending $350 billion out of $400 billion, that we misused or got corrupted with $50 billion, I'll tell you, 'Yes'. But I'll take that any time. There are so many countries in the Third World that have oil that are still 30 years behind. But more important – who are you to tell me this? ... What I'm trying to tell you is, so what? We did not invent corruption, nor did those dissidents, who are so genius, discover it. This happened since Adam and Eve. ... I mean, this is human nature. But we are not as bad as you think. ...[38]

By liberalising the economy the rulers in the republics have also permitted their own families and their political allies to buy state companies on the cheap or get lucrative concessions and contracts. In Yemen, for example, President 'Ali 'Abdallah Salih is personally a partner in Hayl Sa'id, the country's best-known industrial and trading firm. His relatives have also gone into business: Tawfiq, the president's nephew, is the director of the Yemeni tobacco and matchstick firm; Salih's cousin, 'Abdallah al-Qadi, manages the country's pharmaceutical company; and 'Abd al-Khaliq al-Qadi, the president's son-in-law, is the boss of the Yemeni national airline. Two of the sons of deceased Grand *Shaykh* 'Abdallah al-Ahmar are making a great deal of money, too. Between them the two sons control as many as 300 businesses.[39]

In addition, authoritarian rulers' power strategies have weakened the state's official institutions. After decades of a cult of authoritarian leaders the inhabitants often equate the state and its institutions with these leaders and their clans. In some extreme cases the repressive system, the party, and the bureaucracy have all become pure instruments of power in the leaders' hands. The authorities often resort to raw power – torture, political assassination, and 'disappearances' – to terrorise oppositional elements in the population. Amnesty International, for instance, has documented how, over the last few years, the regimes in Algeria, Yemen, and Jordan have intensified the persecution of Islamists in the shadow of 'the war on terror'.[40]

The Middle East authoritarian regimes are, moreover, maintained thanks to weapons, technology, and money from external powers. The region's governments are among the world's biggest importers of arms. The trade is massive: in July 2007 Condoleezza Rice announced that the USA planned to ship arms worth US$ 63 billion to Israel, Egypt, Saudi Arabia, and the other Gulf monarchies.[41] However, other countries are also major arms suppliers to the region, including Russia, France, Germany, and the United Kingdom. For exporters, such enormous deals are valuable for keeping national jobs, and for the Middle East regimes the agreements are vital both militarily and politically. A country that exports such huge arms shipments to the Middle East will be careful of criticising its customers for breaches of human rights and authoritarian rule. The payback is considerable, however, coming in the form of rights to military bases and privileged access for Western corporations.

Failing for whom?

Morten Bøås and Kathleen M. Jennings argue that the essential question, is strictly speaking, not whether a state has failed or not but for whom and how it has failed.[42] Various actors within one and the same state may have very different interests and what is good for one group is not necessarily so for another. For example, for the ruling clans in Egypt, Yemen, and Syria, the state has not failed as long as they hang on to power and their economic privileges, and in countries such as Iraq and Lebanon the warlords and criminals have profited from the power vacuum that arose in the wake of state failure. In the Middle East states that show signs of enfeeblement, it is groups in society that fall outside the regimes' client networks that are worst hit by the symptoms of the state being in crisis.

As long as authoritarian rulers keep in with international society, they will seldom experience sanctions and isolation. Bøås and Jennings assert that the concept of state failure is used politically and mainly based on the West's security notions and interests.[43] According to the researchers, there is a tendency for states to be labelled 'failed' when they are seen as a threat to Western interests, while other states that show just as blatant signs of state failure are not labelled providing they create a favourable market for investments and international capital. In this way it is fascinating how the governments of George W. Bush and Tony Blair hesitated to talk of Iraq and Afghanistan, ranked respectively as six and seven on the 'Failed State Index', as failed states. The explanation was, of course, that the label would be a declaration of failure for both governments, which had invested considerable political prestige and financial resources in building up new governments for these two countries. Nonetheless, the Middle East regimes are allowed to continue their survival politics undisturbed as long as they sell oil and gas, purchase arms, house military bases, and are allies in 'the war on terror'.

State collapse

In spite signs of weakening, it is far from certain that states such as Egypt, Yemen, and Syria will in fact break down. Previous studies of states' breaking down show that it is almost impossible to predict when a weakened state reaches the tipping point and collapses,[44] although it is possible to imagine a number of factors that trigger such a development. With reference to the Middle East we shall concentrate on two conditions as potential triggers: external intervention and the disappearance of 'strong men'.

External intervention

In June 2006 Ralph Peters presented a map in *Armed Forces Journal*, where he sketched what he felt were the borders of a more 'logical' Middle East. Instead of following the state borders drawn up by Europeans almost a century ago, Peters drew what he called 'blood borders', which he defined as the borders between ethnic groups in conflict with each other. Peters drew several new states, including Kurdistan and Baluchistan, divided Iraq into three independent states, expanded Jordan, Yemen, and shrank Turkey, Iran, and Saudi Arabia. He made a case for this redrawing of the map as follows:

> A root cause of the broad stagnation in the Muslim world is the Saudi royal family's treatment of Mecca and Medina as their fiefdom. With Islam's holiest shrines under the police-state control of one of the world's most bigoted and oppressive regimes – a regime that commands vast, unearned oil wealth – the Saudis have been able to project their Wahhabi vision of a disciplinarian, intolerant faith far beyond their borders.

The rise of the Saudis to wealth and, consequently, influence has been the worst thing to happen to the Muslim world as a whole since the time of the Prophet, and the worst thing to happen to Arabs since the Ottoman (if not the Mongol) conquest.[45]

Peters' wild scribblings gave rise to heated debate. The map aroused anger in the Middle East in particular, where many believed his proposal reflected American neo-conservative imperialist ambitions. Neo-conservative members of the Bush administration rushed out to dismiss any idea there were plans to divide either Iraq or other countries in the region. Nevertheless, Middle East reactions are understandable in the light of the region's historical experience of external intervention.

In the Middle East there are in fact very few instances of states collapsing after 1970. The only examples are Lebanon in the middle 1970s and Iraq after 2003. External interventions were contributory causes of Lebanon's collapse and it still seems as though international and regional involvement continue to fuel the fires of Lebanon's latent ethnic tensions. Where Iraq is concerned, the country collapsed as a direct result of the USA-led military invasion. Regime changes in Syria and Iran, too, were clearly voiced aims of the Bush Administration as Washington saw new friendly regimes as necessary to secure both the survival of Israel and US oil interests in the Middle East. The lessons of Iraq, however, make Americans cautious about achieving such aims by military means. Outside powers upsetting regime stability in the Middle East is similar to opening Pandora's Box; no one knows what will pop out.

After the fall of Saddam Husayn, Washington decided to ban the Iraqi Ba'th Party, to effect a 'de-Ba'thification' of the state system. As we saw in the previous chapter, this was regarded as necessary to create a new, democratic government. Francis Fukuyama shows with examples from Congo, Sudan, Afghanistan, and Iraq that state building in collapsed states in general is an extremely difficult task.[46] Successful state building is a long-term project requiring enormous financial – and human – investment, resources decision makers in the West seldom possess. Despite the USA having long experience in state building, from the reconstruction of the South after the Civil War to Japan, and Germany after the Second World War, the country has enjoyed little success in Iraq. According to Fukuyama, an important reason for this is that the Bush Administration underestimated the challenge that lay in constructing fresh state structures. The administration had in fact planned far too inadequately what it should do after the invasion.

'Strong men' vanish

In the article 'The Day After', published in *Foreign Policy* in November/December 2003, a number of researchers speculated on what would happen if 'strong men' vanished as a result of, for example, external intervention, coups or illness. The examples came from a number of authoritarian states from Cuba's Fidel Castro to Zimbabwe's Robert Mugabe.[47] Almost all the contributors concluded that there would be a considerable risk of grave political instability and breakdown in the power vacuum that would arise in the wake of these despots. History shows that states are particularly vulnerable to breakdown when strong men vanish, for example, Yugoslavia broke down ten years after Josip Broz Tito died in 1980.

In the Middle East a wave of changes of leader started in 1999. In that year the Emir of Bahrain died and was succeeded by his son Hamad al-Khalifa. In the same year Morocco's King Hassan II was succeeded by his son Muhammad VI, while King Husayn of Jordan was followed by his son 'Abdallah II. In 2000 Hafiz al-Asad was followed by his son Bashar. In 2004 Abu Dhabi's *Shaykh* Zayid al-Nahayan died and was succeeded by his son Khalifa, while the year after, the Palestinian leader Yasir 'Arafat was followed by Mahmud Abbas. The year 2006 began with the death of the Emir of Dubai Maktum bin Rashid al-Maktum and the succession of his brother Muhammad, and Kuwait's emir Jabir al-Ahmad al-Sabah passed away and his brother Sabah took over. Most of these changes of leader took place without any immediate sign of unrest . The exception is the rise in tension between the Palestinian factions, in particular, Fatah and Hamas on the West Bank and Gaza after Yasir 'Arafat's decease. 'Arafat had an iron grip on the apparatus of power and was the personification of the Palestinian nation in its liberation struggle against Israel. He left behind a state system organised to ensure political control, for instance, he established a series of parallel security services and an almost empty treasury.

Similar problems might arise the day rulers such as Mu'ammar al-Qadhafi, Husni al-Mubarak, and 'Ali 'Abdallah Salih die. They probably wish to keep the presidency within their own families and three factors favour that a change of leadership from father to son will succeed: first, the fathers have done their very best to dispose of all potential rivals to their sons. Second, a dynastic change of leader would ensure a continuation of the privileges of those caught in the client network of the present ruler. And third, family background is generally considered very important in Middle East politics, which would make it easier for the presidents' sons to win the acceptance of the people as their new rulers. However, there is no guarantee that the opposition to the sitting regime would quietly accept that the sons inherit power from their fathers.

Case study: Saudi Arabia – family dynasty ripe for fall?

The whole system will collapse. No one can hold the balance of power. The tribal state will fall apart.[48]
Saudis are now talking almost openly about the end of the House of Sa'ud, and the inevitability – even the desirability – of a bloody revolution.[49]

Like a rotting carcass, the House of Sa'ud is beginning to decompose. (...) If nothing is done then we will have a revolution, if not in 1997, then soon after.[50]

One day, some time soon, one way or another, the House of Sa'ud is coming down.[51]

In the last part of this chapter we shall take a closer look at Saudi Arabia. The kingdom, founded in 1932, is ranked as number 89 on *The Failed States Index 2009,* and has stayed one of the most stable regimes on the Middle East despite Saudi society having undergone enormous socio-economic upheavals over the last few decades. But signs that a state is weakening are often subtle and diplomats, journalists, and researchers have repeatedly warned that the regime, *Al Sa'ud* ('the House of Sa'ud'), will soon fall. During King Fahd's reign (1982–2005) in particular the question of Saudi Arabia's stability was raised. Does the Sa'ud family's kingdom reveal signs of state failure?

Four 'pillars'

To answer the question we shall first identify and analyse the meaning of four important 'pillars' that form part of the foundations of the House of Sa'ud. These pillars are the Sa'ud family, oil income, Wahhabi Islam, and the USA.

The Sa'ud family

Saudi Arabia is often referred to as 'a family business'.[52] The country gets its name from the ruling family, al-Sa'ud and, since the middle of the eighteenth century, this family has reigned over three kingdoms on the Arabian Peninsula. The founder of the present dynasty, Ibn Sa'ud, had many wives but without breaking Islam's command never to have more than four at a time. All together the wives gave him 36 sons (and 27 daughters).[53] So far five of Ibn Sa'ud's sons have followed him on to the throne. The sons not only inherited his power but also his virility: consequently, according to *Shaykh* 'Abd al-Rahman S. al-Ruwaishid, the Al Sa'ud's unofficial genealogist, the ruling house, counting men and women of all branches, has grown to more than 4,500 members.[54]

After Ibn Sa'ud's death, Saudi Arabia became what Michael Herb calls a 'dynastic monarchy'.[55] Oil income began to pour into the treasury in earnest during the reign of King Faysal (1964–74) and this wealth gave the Sa'ud family the opportunity to dominate the local economy, distribute welfare, marginalise rival elite groups, and construct a modern state system. The result is that the ruling family that previously had ruled through alliances with elite groups in Saudi society such as religious leaders, tribal chiefs, and trading families, has become the centre of gravity in Saudi Arabia's political structure. The ruling family's many princes occupy key posts in the state system, but only a few of these have the power to influence political decisions. Today, the most powerful princes are respectively 'Abdallah (king and commander of the National

Guard), Sultan (Crown Prince and Minister of Defence), Nayif (Minister of the Interior), and Salman (Governor of Riyadh Province). It was only in 1992 that Saudi Arabia acquired a constitution, the Basic Law of Government (*an-nizam al-asasi*), which declares that the king has virtually unlimited powers.

However, the kingdom is not an absolute monarchy: the leading princes and their families live in a collective, mixing daily, and making decisions in consultation with their trusted advisors. Moreover, there are influential princes without formal positions. By reason of their age and reputation within the family they have direct access to – and can therefore influence – central decision makers. In 1992, a parliament, Majlis al-shura, and in 2000, a ruling family council were established but so far these have had little political significance.

Within the Sa'ud family, as in all families, from time to time disagreements and conflicts arise. However, they rarely get out of control as, partly, the rulers follow – at least publicly – very strict norms of behaviour, as we have seen in Chapter 7. Family members that break these norms are likely to be disciplined. The reaction is assessed according to the offense, varying from a reprimand to the withdrawal of stipends to imprisonment. In addition, the ruling family has efficient mechanisms for conflict regulation. The family council is an arena where family problems are discussed and they attempt to find solutions. When conflicts arise in the ruling family, older family members act as brokers (Arab. *wusata'*) and mediate compromises. Prince Salman is known for often playing the role of mediator.

Wahhabi Islam

Article 1 of *al-nizam al-asasi* states that the country shall be an Islamic state in which government is based on *shari'a*.[56] The state ideology builds on a more than 250-year alliance between the Sa'ud family and the Islamic revivalist Muhammad Ibn 'Abd al-Wahhab. He formulated a political doctrine inspired by Ibn Taymiyya, an Islamic cleric who lived in Baghdad from 1263 to 1326. According to Ibn Taymiyya an ideal Islamic state should be founded on two equal authorities: *umara'*, the princes, and *fuqaha'*, specialists in God's holy law. The profane should govern, but the clerics should monitor politics. Ibn Sa'ud re-established early in the twentieth century 'the alliance state', an efficient device to establish and later to consolidate the monarchy.

For Ibn Sa'ud and his successors Islam has served a number of aims. First, Al Sa'ud has used Islam, as it is interpreted by the supporters of Ibn 'Abd al-Wahhab, as an identity marker in the nation-building process. The territory Ibn Sa'ud conquered was a patchwork that consisted of a number of religious groups, tribes, and regions, each with its distinctive character and identities. To give the inhabitants a common identity Ibn Sa'ud introduced the teachings of Ibn 'Abd al-Wahhab as a state religion. Saudi Arabia's king was looked on as the leader (*imam*) of the Wahhabi community and was only subordinate to the law of God. In 1986 King Fahd (1981–2005) took the title *khadim al-haramayn al-sharifayn* ('Guardian of the Holy Places') to emphasise his leadership over the entire Muslim community by power of his rule over Mecca and Medina. Second, the Sa'ud family has used Islam to legitimise its rule. All important political decisions are justified by the country's supreme spiritual institution, the Supreme Council of Senior Scholars (*hay'at kubar al-'ulama*), issuing a religiously founded recommendation (Arab. *fatwa*). The foremost clerics, who owe their privileged position in society to the Al Sa'ud, issue *fatwas* in support of the king's policies. Third, the ruling family uses Islam as an instrument of social control. This is achieved through institutions such as the *shari'a* courts, the Committee for 'the Combating of Evil and the Promotion of Good' (*al-'amr bi-l-ma'ruf wa-l-nahy 'an al-munkar*), and 'the Moral Police' (*mutawwa'*), which enforce the Wahhabi *'ulama*'s strict interpretation of *shari'a*. Persons who have committed murder or rape or narcotics smuggling can be beheaded, thieves may have both arms and feet amputated, and those who have been guilty of immoral behaviour may be whipped or executed.

Oil

In 1938 an American oil company discovered oil under the Saudi desert sand. According to the BP Statistical Review, in 2004 Saudi Arabia controlled as much as 22.1 per cent of the world's proven oil reserves and represented 13.1 per cent of the world's total production (around 10.5 million barrels a day).[57] Nowhere on earth is oil cheaper to extract, and the profit is therefore amazing. Today oil revenue accounts for 75 per cent of the Saudi state's income and 85 per cent of its export income.[58] The princes spend a considerable part of the income on themselves, while much is spent 'buying' the loyalty of the Saudi society.

Mamoun Fandy uses a set of concentric circles to explain how the Sa'ud family distributes oil revenue.[59] The first circle includes Al Sa'ud. The princes get a yearly stipend, whose size depends on each prince's position in the state and family hierarchy, on top of which come many other privileges. In addition, many princes are involved in Saudi business. In 2003, *Forbes Magazine* named one of them, Prince al-Walid bin Talal, with a personal fortune estimated at US$ 17.7 billion, as the world's fifth richest man.[60] In the second circle you find the 'aristocratic' families that are married into the ruling family. Among the best known outside the kingdom are Al al-Shaykh, descendants of Ibn 'Abd al-Wahhab, and Al Sudayri. These families enjoy a number of privileges, for example, financial support from Al Sa'ud, and blood ties through intermarriage bind together the two innermost circles. The third circle includes Saudi trading and entrepreneurial families with limited tribal connections. Among the most important of these families are the Juffali, 'Ali Reza, Rajhi Bin Mah- fuz, al-Qusaybi, Tamimi, and Bin Ladin. The fourth circle, which is far wider, includes all Saudi citizens. They have limited political rights but enjoy a number of socio-economic goods as citizens – without paying taxes. Outside the circles are Saudi Arabia's foreign workers with neither political nor socio-economic rights. Of a total population of 23.6 million, this group number 7–8 million people, comprising more than two-thirds of the country's total labour force.[61]

The USA

A key event in modern Saudi history is the meeting between Ibn Sa'ud and President Franklin D. Roosevelt on board the warship USS Quincy on Great Bitter Lake, 14 February 1945. This meeting laid the foundations for an infor- mal alliance between Saudi Arabia and the USA that has lasted right up to today. This partnership has been advantageous for both countries. In the tur- bulent decades after the Second World War Al Sa'ud was challenged by mili- tarily stronger neighbouring states with expansionist ambitions, Gamal 'Abd al-Nasser's Egypt, *Ayatollah* Khomeini's Iran, and Saddam Husayn's Iraq. David E. Long claims that because of its historical experiences, the Saudis suffer from an 'encirclement syndrome',[62] which has led them to seek the protection of the USA. King Faysal even declared: 'the relationship with the USA is a pillar in Saudi politics'.[63] On their side, the Americans have cooperated with the Sa'ud family in order to take care of American strategic and economic interests in the Gulf. The Second World War made the importance of oil as a strategic resource clear. In 1950 the Truman Administration in Washington defined American control of Saudi Arabian oilfields, which are mainly to be found in the East- ern Province (al-Hasa), as of decisive significance in the global struggle against Communism as the panic scenario was that these fields should fall into the hands of the Soviet Union.

With the exception of the oil boycott of 1973–4, Saudi Arabia has secured stable oil supplies for the world market, thereby holding prices at an acceptable level for the Americans. In 2007 the kingdom supplied 11 per cent (1.5 million barrels a day) of the USA's total import needs for oil (13.5 million barrels a day).[64] Long-standing defence ties remain intact, and the United States has long been Saudi Arabia's leading arms supplier. From 1950 through 2006, the kingdom purchased and received from the United States weapons, military equipment, and related services worth over $62.7 billion. Saudi Arabia was the world's big- gest buyer of US weapons during a four-year span 2005–08 with $11.2 billion in deals.[65] Lastly, Saudi Arabia has supported US foreign policy. The Sa'ud family supported the Americans' global struggle against Communism during the Cold

War by, for example, financing the *mujahidun* guerrilla that fought against the Russian occupation of Afghanistan in the 1980s. Not only that but the Saʻud family paid more than half of the costs of the liberation of Kuwait in 1991, a sum estimated by Jane's International Defence Review to amount to as much as US$ 60 billion.[66]

Rotting pillars?

Each one of the four 'pillars' that are essential for maintaining the stability of the Saʻud kingdom have shown signs of rotting, something that became clear during the reign of King Fahd. But the regime's effective handling of this challenge has fully demonstrated its resources.

Brotherly strife

First, we have seen tendencies towards fragmentation within the Saʻud ruling house under Fahd's leadership. Fahd's ascension to the throne in 1982 resulted in the so-called Sudayri Seven coming to power. This branch, which today consists of the deceased Fahd's six full brothers (all sons of Hassa bint Ahmad al-Sudayri, Ibn Saʻud's favourite wife), seized control of the Ministry of Defence and Aviation and the governorate of the Riyadh Province in 1963, the Ministry of Interior in 1975, and became the single most powerful alliance within the royal family when Fahd became king. On 1 January 1996, King Fahd formally passed his authority to Crown Prince ʻAbdallah, after having been struck by an incapacitating stroke the year before. Immediately rumours began circulating about a power struggle between ʻAbdallah on the one side; and his half brother and third in line, Defence Minister Sultan, one of the Sudayri brothers, on the other. Some went as far as to indicate that fighting was about to break out between the half brothers, who command respectively the National Guard and the ordinary armed forces. These rumours, however, had no roots in reality. There was never any doubt about the order of succession: when Fahd died ʻAbdallah became king and Sultan Crown Prince.

Saudi Arabia has become a 'kingdom with several kings'. A number of dynasties are growing up within the House of Saʻud. Today there is no longer any meaning in speaking of 'the Sudayri clan' as a block within the Saʻud ruling house. Interaction within the family has shifted from brother-to-brother to father-to-son. It is possible to identify distinct power centres within Al Saʻud built up round ʻAbdallah, Sultan, Nayif, Salman, and other senior royals. These Saʻud oligarchs have their sons and advisors around them; they hold their own courts and receptions, and service their networks of loyal clients. The future fight for positions of power within the House of Saʻud – the key to colossal wealth – will take place between these family blocks.

Both 'Abdallah and Sultan are in their mid 80s. Up to now the office of king has passed horizontally through the sons of Ibn Sa'ud. If this practice should last, which is probable, there are still 15 sons who can lay claim to the throne. Among these Nayif, Salman, and Miqrin are the most likely candidates.

The Basic Law of Government from 1992 – Chapter 2, Article 5 – also makes it possible for the grandsons of Ibn Sa'ud to be kings:

> Article 5 (B) 'Power goes to the sons of King 'Abd al-'Aziz bin 'Abd al-Rahman (Ibn Sa'ud) and to their sons. To the most suitable among these the oath of allegiance shall be sworn in agreement with the principles in the Holy Qu'ran and in tradition (sunna) after the venerable Prophet.'
>
> (C) 'The king chooses his successor and releases him from his duties by royal decree.'[67]

The number of princes is rising rapidly, and there is reason to expect growing rivalry for power and resources over the next few years. The transfer of power from Ibn Sa'ud's sons to his grandsons will then be critical. Which of them emerges strongest in the struggle for the throne is an open question. The kings Sa'ud and Fahd tried to position their own sons, but were stopped by their brothers. Today none of the Sa'ud oligarchs has enough support within the ruling family to be able to give the power to one of his sons. Nonetheless, Ibn Sa'ud's sons still rule, and it may take ten to fifteen years before there is a generation shift.

Moreover, the ruling family has taken important measures towards institutionalising the succession to the throne. The Allegiance Institutional Law of 2006 prescribes the establishment of a new council, the Allegiance Institution (Arab. *hayat al-bay'a*).[68] The council, consisting of Ibn Sa'ud's 15 still-living sons and 19 of his grandsons, is intended to ensure that successions to the throne go smoothly. This new law, which does not apply to the present king and crown prince, lays down that as soon as a king is too ill to reign a medical committee shall make a report to the Allegiance Institution about the state of health of the king. If he is considered as permanently too ill to reign, the Transitory Ruling Council, composed of five members of the Allegiance Institution, will temporarily take charge of the government of the kingdom. Within a week the members of the Allegiance Institution will then choose a new king from among the sons and grandsons of Ibn Sa'ud. The new law means that the decision about who shall reign over the kingdom no longer rests in one man's hands – those of the king – but that in the future a collective of princes will decide.

Islamist opposition

Second, Fahd was challenged by Islamists opposition. One event in particular threatened Al Sa'ud's legitimacy: the Western military deployment to Saudi Arabia in connection with the Gulf War in 1990–1. Islamists criticised Fahd for not being able to guard Islam's holy land without the support of infidel soldiers. Many activist Islamic scholars have been associated with al-Sahwa al-islamiyya (the Islamic Awakening), an Islamist movement that has gradually developed since the 1960s. The most prominent members in the 1990s, a decade marked by Islamist activism in Saudi Arabia, were Salman al-'Awda and Safar al-Hawali. More marginal groups of activist preachers represented various other ideological trends. One of these was *al-wasatiyyun*, a group of modernist Islamic intellectuals, which included former *al-sahwa shaykhs* such as 'Abd al-Aziz al-Qasim, 'Abdallah al-Hamid, and Hasan al-Maliki. Another group was the *al-takfir*, militant Islamic preachers who had declared *takfir* (calling a Muslim an apostate) against the House of Sa'ud and its supporters. Among these were *shaykhs* such as Humud ibn 'Uqla al-Shu'aybi, 'Ali al-Khudayr, and Nasir al-Fahd.

A parallel development was the return of *mujahidun* from Afghanistan. In the 1980s several thousand men from Saudi Arabia and other Muslim lands went to war against the occupying Russian forces and after the Soviet withdrawal, many war veterans returned while others left for fresh conflict in areas such as Chechnya and Kosovo. It was from this environment that al-Qa'ida sprang, led by Usama bin Ladin. In 1990 this rich man's son was at odds with the Sa'ud family as King Fahd rejected his offer of a *mujahidun* army as an alternative to Western troops to protect Saudi Arabia against Saddam Husayn's war machine that had occupied Kuwait. Usama had his Saudi passport taken away and went into exile, first into Sudan, then into Taliban-controlled Afghanistan. From his hiding place in the Afghan mountains he and his followers issued *fatwas* against the Americans that 'occupied Mecca and Medina', against the Jews that 'occupied Jerusalem', and against the Sa'ud family, who were the useful idiots of 'the alliance of Zionist-Crusaders'.[69]

Saudi Arabia experienced a wave of political violence from May 2003 to December 2004. Militant Islamists carried out actions against both Western and Saudi targets, and their strategies included suicide bombings, bomb attacks, and kidnappings. This wave of violence can be seen in the context of hundreds of Saudi Afghans coming home after the fall of the Taliban regime. Specifically, the actions were a response to provocation by the Security Forces, which early in 2003, intervened to prevent militant Islamists creating disturbances in connection with the USA's invasion of Iraq.[70] The Islamists created an unstable security situation in Saudi Arabia but came nowhere near to upsetting the regime's stability. The ruling house has effectively dealt with the radicals, and by the end of 2004 most militant Islamists had been killed or arrested, including most of the group's leaders. Moreover, the Saudi authorities passed several effective 'soft' measures against the Islamists, such as offering wanted Islamists amnesty and rehabilitation. Alongside these measures the authorities have made use of the media and the influential Wahhabi establishment to condemn the militant Islamists as apostates. 'Al-Qa'ida on the Arabian Peninsula', like Juhayman al-'Utaybi's rebellious movement at the end of the 1970s, did not manage to start a broadly based rising for which there were two main reasons: to begin with, the Islamists never formulated a credible alternative to Sa'ud family rule, and, in the second place, political violence, which hurt Muslims and Arabs, had little appeal for the Saudis.

Today it is not possible to identify a political opposition that is strong enough to threaten regime stability in Saudi Arabia. Within the kingdom there are circles that want the country to go in certain directions. There is lively debate, but so far no one has formulated a credible alternative to the status quo that might win wide support. It is, by definition, hard to imagine a Saudi Arabia without the royal Sa'ud family. Liberal Saudis have spoken up for a greater degree of popular government in which the members of the Majlis al-shura would be elected. The royal house does not want such a development to come too quickly. Further, the liberal forces want more liberty for Saudi women, but the liberals are poorly organised. More Islamist-orientated circles, on the other hand, are better organised through mosques, schools, and charities. Furthermore, the local elections in spring 2005 showed that it was the Islamists that had most support among people, even in the more liberal city of Jiddah. There are still some Islamists that speak out against the regime, but most of these are isolated in exile, arrested or co-opted.

The economic challenge

Third, the economy was weakened under Fahd's reign. In accordance with Saudi Arabia's strict Islamic tradition Fahd was buried in an unmarked grave but the grave contrasts sharply with the life of luxury he led. Stories of the Sa'ud princes' extravagance are well known: the rulers enjoy generous stipends and other privileges, for instance, free telephone, electricity, water, and flights with SAUDIA. The princes show off their wealth by building opulent palaces at home and abroad and buying luxury items such as yachts and private jets. Simultaneously, many ordinary Saudis have experienced a fall in their own living standards. The last few decades' rapid migration of Saudis from the countryside, particularly in 'Asir, to the cities has contributed to slums mushrooming on the outskirts of Riyadh and Jiddah, where beggars are a common sight. According to UNDP's 'Human Development Index' for 2005, 14.9 per cent of Saudis live in poverty and around 60 per cent of Saudi Arabia's male population between 20 and 29 years of age are now without jobs.[71] Men from this segment of Saudi society are recruiting ground for militant Islamism.

The reasons why the economy was weakened in the 1980s and 1990s are twofold. On the one hand, Saudi Arabia's income fell as a result of the oil price crash in the middle of the 1980s. Prices stayed low right up to the end of the 1990s. In 1998 the price was down at 10 US$ a barrel. On the other hand, Al Sa'ud's expenses rose as the population increased so steeply. *The Economist* estimates that the population grew annually by 3.49 per cent from 1960 to 2000,[72] and as a result, the number of Saudis doubles every twenty years. Today almost half of Saudi Arabia's population is under the age of fifteen. The 'Human Development Report 2009' concludes that if this rate of growth carries on, by 2020 there may be as many as 31.6 million inhabitants in the kingdom.[73]

However, Saudi authorities have tried to counteract this negative economic development, and they have been much assisted by the gradual rise in price of oil that started in 1999. By the summer of 2008 the price peaked at a record high 147.5 US$ a barrel. In addition, Saudi private individuals have invested more at home since 11 September 2001. Ådne Cappelen and Robin Choudhury have shown that Saudi Arabia's economic prospects are positive. As long as oil prices stay over 30 US$ a barrel – which seems realistic in view of price developments in recent years – the kingdom will probably enjoy high economic growth and reduce its financial imbalance.[74] The high oil price gives Al Sa'ud resources to maintain 'the social pact', at any rate in the short term. The danger is that the influx of revenue will act as a 'cushion' taking away the focus on executing measures that will make the Saudi economy less vulnerable to the swings of oil prices in the longer term. Tim Niblock, however, shows that so far high oil prices have not stopped the promised reforms being carried out. He believes that there are three reasons for this: outside pressure for reform, both political and economic after 11 September; the growth of a Saudi commercial middle class that demands reform; and 'Abdallah's will and ability to instigate reform.[75]

11 September

Finally, the warm relations between Saudi Arabia and the USA cooled during Fahd's reign. After 11 September, Saudi Arabia's standing fell among Americans and members of the administration in Washington, DC, went so far as to suggest the Sa'ud family were involved in the terror attacks. Early in 2003, the American troops that had been stationed in the kingdom since the 1990–91 Gulf War were pulled out. One reason why the USA decided to occupy Iraq in the spring of 2003 was probably a desire to reduce dependence on Saudi Arabia. By rebuilding and further developing the oil industry in Iraq, the hawks in Washington reasoned, one would weaken the Saudi grip on the oil market.

For the Sa'ud royal house the close relationship with the USA has become a double-edged sword. On the one hand, the alliance provides protection against external enemies, but, on the other, it is a source of internal discontent. The results of an opinion poll conducted by the Arab American Institute in 2003 demonstrate Saudi scepticism towards the USA. In 2003 only 3 per cent were positive towards Americans while as many as 97 per cent were negative.[76] The consensus within the Sa'ud royal house is, however, that the kingdom cannot survive without the backing of a strong ally. Today the princes fear above all the rising Shi'a influence around the Gulf and Iran as a future nuclear power. Leading princes appear to think that Saudi Arabia must continue to rely on its relationship with the USA, because no other country can at such short notice offer corresponding economic and military support. But at the same time the Sa'ud family is trying to knit strategic bonds with other great powers, for example, China, India, Pakistan, and Russia because of discontent with the American approach to the Middle East; support of Israel, the occupation of Iraq, and the democratisation pressure. Thus it is worth noting that in January 2006 'Abdallah picked China for his first official royal trip abroad, followed by Malaysia, Pakistan, and India. The Chinese president, Hu Jintao, reciprocated the visit in April the same year. This visit resulted in 'Abdallah and Hu signing a cooperation agreement on behalf of their respective countries concerning the fields of security, defence, trade, health, and youth affairs. In addition, closer ties to Asiatic great powers will improve the Saudi negotiating position with the Americans; the USA will take care not to lose its hegemony in the Middle East. The country obtains only 16 per cent of its oil imports from the Gulf region (11 per cent from Saudi Arabia),[77] but the price of crude petroleum is decided by developments there. Difficulties in stabilising Iraq have probably strengthened the USA's need to have good relations with the Saudis, as reflected in a gradual reconciliation between Washington and Riyadh in recent years and US forces in the Gulf are still deployed so they can defend Saudi Arabia's oilfields, if supplies from the region are threatened.

The House of Sa'ud stands firm: the princes are united; no political opposition strong enough to make it fall is identifiable; oil revenues continue to fill the treasury; and relations with the USA have gradually been normalised. But in the long term there are difficult times ahead. The ruling family must handle future successions. Moreover, to avoid the weakening of legitimacy the princes must reform to create a new foundation for their rule. The Saʻud family must adjust to a new age in which globalisation brings the Saudis fresh ideas about how the state and the economy should be organised. The arenas where the people can legitimately express their opinions must be expanded. The population explosion must be halted and Saudi workers must be educated, trained, and motivated so they can replace millions of foreign workers.

Conclusion

Contrary to Saudi Arabia, a handful of states in the Middle East show grave signs of state failure. They do worst on the political indicators, particularly for authoritarian and repressive rule and violent conflict. The Middle East does better for social and economic indicators, but resource dependency and rapid population increase are factors that threaten social and political stability. The weakening of the states is to a large extent a consequence of decades of survival politics. Ruling clans have 'hijacked' the state, exploiting its resources to hang on to power, and their strategies have helped enfeeble state institutions and divide society. Through co-option, divide and rule tactics, and repression, the regimes have undermined confidence and national unity which in turn has a negative effect on the states' economic development. When, in addition, enfeebled states are exposed to intervention from outside, they are especially liable to break down. Experience from Iraq shows that once the state collapses, there is no single social structure that can fill the power vacuum. The regimes have strengthened themselves at the expense of society, the economy, and the state.

Further reading

Bronson, Rachel: *Thicker than Oil: America's Uneasy Partnership with Saudi Arabia.* Oxford and New York: Oxford University Press, 2006.

Clarke, Victoria: *Yemen: Dancing on the Heads of Snakes.* New Haven, CT: Yale University Press, 2010.

Dodge, Toby: *Iraq's Future: The Aftermath of Regime Change.* London: Routledge, 2005.

Hegghammer, Thomas: *Jihad in Saudi Arabia: Violence and Pan-Islamism since 1979.* New York: Cambridge University Press, 2010.

Hertog, Steffen: *Princes, Brokers, and Bureaucrats: Oil and the State in Saudi Arabia.* Ithaca, NY: Cornell University Press, 2010.

Hirst, David: *Beware of Small States: Lebanon, Battleground of the Middle East.* London: Faber and Faber, 2010.

Niblock, Tim and Monica Malik: *The Political Economy of Saudi Arabia.* London and New York: Routledge, 2007.

al-Rasheed, Madawi: *A History of Saudi Arabia.* Cambridge: Cambridge University Press, 2002.

Vitalis, Robert: *America's Kingdom: Mythmaking on the Saudi Oil Frontier.* Stanford C.A.: Stanford University Press, 2006.

Yamani, Mai: *Changed Identities: The Challenge of the New Generation in Saudi Arabia.* London: Royal Institute of International Affairs, 2000.

11 Conclusion

A house that is built on a solid foundation is not shaken by the wind.[1]

Regime stability can be built on both solid, or less than solid, foundations. Examples of reliable foundations are successful nation-building, social mobility, legitimacy, and efficient state institutions, while a more fragile foundation can be based on divide and rule tactics, co-optation, repression, and fear. Like most other political systems, the Middle East regimes are maintained through a combination of these factors. Their relative importance varies from country to country and from time to time. This book does not provide a basis for measuring the extent to which each factor contributes towards explaining regime stability in each state. But the book has revealed and analysed some of the most vital variables behind the stability. We shall now sum up the observations that have been made in the light of the three questions we raised by way of introduction: how have the rulers in the Middle East tightened their grip? What consequences do their power strategies have for political and socio-economic development? And what forces threaten those in power today?

A combination of historical, economic, and political conditions have pressured several regimes in the Middle East to hold on to power through destructive means. One of these conditions is the difficult heritage from the colonial powers. The European imperialists built the post First World War political order on the basis of their own strategic interests rather than the local history or the aspirations of the population with the result that, when these states won independence, they were weakly rooted in society. In addition, by their divide and rule tactics the colonial powers created tensions between groups inside these states. Relations between state and society were particularly inflamed in the so-called Fertile Crescent. As we have shown, the nation-building project was challenged from above – by identities such as Arab nationalism – and from below – by substate groups, for example, confessional communities, linguistic communities, and tribes. The plague of ethnic conflicts over recent decades cannot, however, be ascribed to the colonial heritage alone. The battle for resources so unevenly shared between social groups and external intervention have also undermined national solidarity in such countries as Iraq and Lebanon. Survival politics under rulers such as Saddam Husayn, 'Ali 'Abdallah Salih, and Hafiz al-Asad have further aggravated the ethnification of politics. By filling the state apparatus with men from their own confession, region, and tribe, the rulers have created tensions between social groups.

The reason why Middle East regimes have resorted to survival politics can be found in the development crisis and their lack of legitimacy. The deeper the legitimacy problem they have, the more the rulers resort to survival politics and the more destructive the consequences are. The rulers manage in varying degree to satisfy the people's demands and desires. Some countries have experienced strong economic growth and a considerable improvement of living standards, including states that are not rentier states, for instance, Tunisia and Turkey. Political liberalisation is making progress in countries such as Qatar and Morocco, and Islamist opposition groups have succeeded in winning elections in Iraq, Turkey, and Palestine. Private enterprise throughout the region has gained greater opportunities owing to economic liberalisation. However, the basic problem remains that political power is monopolised by a ruling elite that puts its own interests before those of the community as a whole. This development has been criticised from outside and inside. To give the impression that the critics are being accommodated the rulers have played the reform card. But reluctance to share political power has prevented them from generating profound legitimacy. On the contrary, the regimes' foremost opponents, the Islamist movements, in past decades have won more support. To ease the pressure from these movements the regimes have permitted a partial Islamisation of society by, for example, the introduction of *shari'a* in criminal and family law and stricter moral control in cultural affairs. Nonetheless, the Islamists have hardly been permitted participation in government at all.

Furthermore, the regimes' survival politics have undermined the efficiency of the state systems. Mechanisms such as clientelism, corporatism, and divide-and-rule tactics reduce the efficiency of the bureaucracy and the armed forces. The primary function of the state apparatus is in some extreme cases to uphold the privileges of the power elite and its control over the country. Considerations such as economic development or the state's capacity to wage war come second. A general feature of states in the region is that the executive completely dominates the legislature and the judiciary. In the 1960s and 1970s many saw this as a condition for creating economic growth and social progress. The principle of the division of powers was sacrificed in order to 'make up' for the arrears of the colonial era. The absence of constitutional limitations on the executive has, however, been an obstacle to these countries' development, since it permits the princes, kings, and presidents to misuse the state apparatus with impunity. The control exerted by the population on political decisions is, by and large, minimal.

There are strong forces behind the survival of the Middle East regimes. It is in the interests of a number of groups inside the states to maintain the status quo. These include not just the ruling elite but also those who have been co-opted into the regimes' huge client networks. Moreover, many support the regimes because they are scared that the disappearance of the present governments will lead to civil war, chaos, and collapse. Not least have developments in Lebanon, Algeria, and Iraq fuelled this fear. Internal opposition to the regimes has been systematically obstructed. The result is opposition movements that in most cases are too fragmented and weak to push for regime change. In other words, the regimes' survival politics have not just weakened the state but also society.

In addition, there are strong external interests connected to regime stability. Rulers that maintain stability ensure at the same time the international community's access to oil, markets, and security for Israel. The great powers have a long tradition of preserving regimes in the Middle East that serve their interests. In the wake of 9/11, the USA has given massive support to the rulers of Algeria, Egypt, Yemen, Jordan, and Saudi Arabia as part of its 'war on terror'. Countries that defy the West conversely run the risk of sanctions and military attack. In 2003. Saddam Husayn's regime was overthrown by a US-led invasion of Iraq. The rulers in Syrian and Iran have, for a long time, feared that Washington's war machine may be used to overthrow their 'defiant' regimes. Experiences in Iraq, however, show that regime change by military means can have catastrophic consequences. Rulers put in place by foreign military powers will from day one lack legitimacy in the population. An occupying power risks undermining what were unifying institutions without being able to establish state structures with new authority. The danger of collapse is therefore great when outside powers disturb stability.

Internal pressure for change will last. In all the countries of the Middle East people live who are concerned to get the best possible future for their society – and will often sacrifice a great deal to reach their goals. Many have alternative visions to today's political order and are working consciously for change. The spread of technological tools like satellite TV, mobile phones, and the internet are helping them to exchange ideas, build networks, and occasionally organise mass protests. However, as the conditions of power are in the region today, the process of change will continue at a slower tempo than the opposition wishes. The regimes have few incentives for democratisation and do their utmost to keep society weak. With the possible exception of Iran, continued regime stability seems the most likely scenario in the short term. Authoritarian rulers will pursue their survival politics at the risk of state failure.

Notes

1 Introduction

1. *BBC Monitoring Global Newsline – Middle East Political*, 31 December 2009.
2. Readers desiring a chronological presentation of the political history of each individual state in the Middle East can for example read Malcolm E. Yapp: *The Near East since the First World War: A History to 1995*. Harlow: Pearson, 2nd edition, 1996; and David E. Long and Bernard Reich (eds): *The Government and Politics of the Middle East and North Africa*. Boulder, San Francisco and Oxford: Westview Press, 4th edition, 2002.
3. For studies that emphasise the importance of internal factors see Albert Hourani: *A History of the Arab Peoples*. London: Faber & Faber, 1991; Malcolm E. Yapp: *The Making of the Modern Near East, 1792–1923*. London: Longman, 1987; M. E. Yapp: *The Near East since the First World War … op.cit.*; and William L. Cleveland: *A History of the Modern Middle East*. Boulder, CO.: Westview Press, 2000.
4. For the opposite, studies emphasising external factors, see Carl L. Brown: *International Politics in the Middle East: Old Rules, Dangerous Games*. London: I.B.Tauris, 1984; C. L. Brown (ed.): *Diplomacy in the Middle East: The International Relations of Regional and Outside Powers*. London: I.B.Tauris, 2001; and Avi Shlaim: *War and Peace in the Middle East: A Concise History, Revised and Updated*. New York: Penguin Books, 1995.
5. Alfred T. Mahan: 'The Persian Gulf and international relations', in *National Review*, 1902. The article was also published in Alfred T. Mahan: *Retrospect & Prospect: Studies in International Relations Naval and Political*. Boston: Little, Brown, & Company, 1903, pp. 209–51.
6. Leonard J. Fein: *Politics in Israel*. Boston: Little, Brown, & Company, 1967, quoted in Nils A. Butenschøn: 'Israel as a Regional Great Power: Survival and Dominance', in Iver B. Neumann (ed.): *Regional Great Powers in International Politics*. London: Macmillan, 1991, pp. 35–6.
7. See among others Nils A. Butenschøn, *op.cit.*, p. 12; Fred Halliday: *100 Myths about the Middle East*. London: al-Saqi Books, 2005, pp. 140–1.
8. Arthur Goldschmidt: *A Concise History of the Middle East*. Boulder and London: Westview Press, 3rd edition, 1988, p. 15.
9. This estimate is, however, uncertain. Egyptian Copts themselves claim to make up 10 per cent of the population, while the country's authorities assert that the group is far smaller.
10. *The Middle East and North Africa 2006*. Europa Regional Surveys of the World. London and New York: Routledge, 52nd edition, 2005, p. 167.
11. The authors' own estimate.
12. *The New International Webster's Comprehensive Dictionary of the English Language*. Trident Press International, encyclopaedic edition, 2003, p. 1061.
13. Robert M. Fishman: 'Rethinking state and regime: southern Europe's transition to democracy', in *World Politics*, vol. 42, no. 3, April, 1990, p. 428.
14. David Easton: *A Systems Analysis of Political Life*. New York: Wiley, 1965, p. 193.
15. *Ibid.*
16. The authors' own estimate.

17. UNDP, 'Arab Human Development Report 2002: Creating Opportunities for Future Generations', New York: United Nations Publications, 2003; UNDP: 'Arab Human Development Report 2003: Building a Knowledge Society', 2004; and UNDP: 'Arab Human Development Report 2004: Towards Freedom in the Arab World', 2005, http://hdr.undp.org/reports/detail_reports.cfm?view=600.

18. The Arab Fund for Economic and Social Development is a Kuwaiti-financed development fund. All members of the Arab League are associated with the fund which has a pan-Arabic profile. For the fund's home page, see http://www.arabfund.org.

19. Alfred C. Stepan and Graeme B. Robertson: 'An "Arab" more than a "Muslim" democracy gap', in *Journal of Democracy*, vol. 14, no. 3, 2003, pp. 30–44.

20. 'Times Higher Education – QS World University Rankings 2007', http://www.topuniversities.com/worlduniversityrankings/results/2007/overall_rankings/top_400_universities/.

21. Edward W. Said: *Orientalism*. London: Penguin Books, 2003.

22. Samuel P. Huntington: *The Clash of Civilizations?* New York: Council on Foreign Relations, 1993.

2   Troubled Heritage

1. David Fromkin: *A Peace to End All Peace*. London: Phoenix Press, 2000, p. 563.

2. Avi Shlaim: *War and Peace in the Middle East: A Critique of American Policy*. London: Viking, 1994.

3. See for example Barry Rubin: *The tragedy of the Middle East*. Cambridge: Cambridge University Press, 2002.

4. Ibn Khaldun: *The Muqaddimah: An Introduction to History*. Princeton, New Jersey: Princeton University Press, 1989.

5. Ilya Harik: 'The Origins of the Arab State System', in Giacomo Luciani (ed.): *The Arab State*. London: Routledge, 1990, pp. 1–28.

6. John Rudy: *Modern Algeria: The Origins and Development of a Nation*. Bloomington: Indiana University Press, 1992, p. 111.

7. Hasan Kayali: *Arabs and Young Turks: Ottomanism, Arabism, and Islamism in the Ottoman Empire, 1908–1918*. Berkeley: University of California Press, 1997.

8. William L. Cleveland: *A History of the Modern Middle East*. Boulder, San Francisco, and Oxford: Westview press, 1994, p. 238.

9. *Ibid.*, p. 241.

10. *Ibid.*, p. 249.

11. Albert Hourani: *A History of the Arab Peoples*. London: Faber & Faber, 1991, p. 372.

12. *Ibid.*, p. 370.

13. Ernest Dawn: 'The Origins of Arab Nationalism', in Rashid Khalidi (ed.): *The Origins of Arab Nationalism*. New York: Columbia University Press, 1991, pp. 3–30.

14. Jacob M. Landau: *Pan-Turkism: From Irredentism to Cooperation*. London: Hurst, 1995.

15. Erik J. Zürcher: *Turkey: A Modern History*. London and New York: I.B.Tauris, 2004, p. 129.

16. Ziya Gökalp: *The Principles of Turkism*. Leiden: E.J. Brill, 1968.

17. Meliha Benli Altunışık and Özlem Tür: *Turkey: Challenges of Continuity and Change*. London and New York: RoutledgeCurzon, 2005, p. 20.

18. Gherardo Gnoli: *The idea of Iran: An Essay on its Origins*. Roma: Instituto Italiano per il Medio ed Estremo Oriente, 1989.

19. Mostafa Vaziri: *Iran as Imagined Nation: The Construction of National Identity*. New York: Paragon House, 1993.

20. Lisa Anderson: 'Absolutism and resilience of monarchy in the Middle East', in *Political Science Quarterly*, vol. 106, no.1, 1991, pp. 3–11; and Fred Halliday: 'The Fates of Monarchy in the

Middle East', in Fred Halliday: *Nation and Religion in the Middle East*. London: al-Saqi Books, 2000, pp. 96–8.

21. Roger Owen: *State, Power and Politics in the Making of the Modern Middle East*. London and New York: Routledge, 1992, p. 14.

22. William L. Cleveland, *op.cit.*, p. 207.

23. Kamal Salibi: *The Modern History of Jordan*. London: I.B.Tauris, 1993.

3   Class

1. Mu'ammar al-Qadhafi: *The Green Book*. Tripoli, Libya: Ministry of Information, 1979, p. 47.

2. See Table 1.2 in Chapter 1.

3. *Forbes Magazine*, 2008, http://www.forbes.com/lists/2008/10/billionaires08_The-Worlds-Billionaires_Rank.html.

4. UNDP: 'Arab Human Development Report 2003', New York: United Nations Publications, 2003.

5. Pierre Bourdieu: 'The Forms of Capital', in John G. Richardson: *Handbook of Theory and Research in the Sociology of Education*. New York and London: Greenwood Press, 1986, pp. 241–58.

6. Karl Marx: *The Poverty of Philosophy*. Moscow: Progress Publishers, 1955.

7. James A. Bill: 'Class analysis and the dialectics of modernization in the Middle East', in *International Journal of Middle East Studies*, vol. 3, 1972, pp. 417–34.

8. Samira Haj: *The Making of Iraq*. New York: State University of New York Press, 1997.

9. Malcolm E. Yapp: *The Making of the Modern Near East, 1792–1923*. Longman: London, 1987.

10. Manfred Halpern: *The Politics of Social Change in Middle East and North Africa*. Princeton, New Jersey: Princeton University Press, 1963.

11. For a good description and discussion of this type of regime with Syria as an example, see Raymond Hinnebusch: *Syria: Revolution From Above*. London and New York: Routledge, 2001.

12. Nazih N. Ayubi: *Over-Stating the Arab State: Politics and Society in the Middle East*. London and New York: I.B.Tauris, 1995, p. 176.

13. Homa Katouzian: *Iranian History and Politics: The dialectic of state and society*. London and New York: Routledge Curzon, 2003.

14. Amira al-Azhary Sonbol: *The New Mamluks: Egyptian Society and Modern Feudalism*. Syracuse, NY: Syracuse University Press, 2000.

15. James A. Bill and Robert Springborg: *Politics in the Middle East*. New York: Harper Collins, 4th edition, 1994.

16. Halim Barakat: *The Arab World: Society, Culture, and State*. Berkeley, California: University of California Press, 1993, p. 20.

17. Robert Bianchi: *Unruly Corporatism: Associational Life in the Twentieth-Century Egypt*. Oxford and New York: Oxford University Press, 1989.

18. Anoushiravan Ehteshami and Emma C. Murphy: 'Transformation of the corporatist state in the Middle East', in *Third World Quarterly*, vol. 17, no. 4, 1996, pp. 753–72.

19. Nazih N. Ayubi, *op.cit.*, p. 192.

20. Alan Richards and John Waterbury: *A Political Economy of the Middle East*. Boulder, CO: Westview Press, 2nd edition, 1998, p. 314.

21. Steven Heydemann: *Authoritarianism in Syria: Institutions and Social Conflict 1946–1970*. New York: Cornell University Press, 1999; and Steven Heydemann: 'Social Pacts and the

Persistence of Authoritarianism in the Middle East', in Oliver Schlumberger: *Debating Arab Authoritarianism: Dynamics and Durability in Nondemocractic regimes*. Stanford, CA: Stanford University Press, 2007, pp. 21–38.

22. Quoted in Alan Richards and John Waterbury, *op.cit.*, p. 315.

23. *Ibid.*, p. 316.

24. Anoushiravan Ehteshami and Emma C. Murphy: 'Transformation of the corporatist state in the Middle East', *op.cit.*

25. Mu'ammar al-Qadhafi: *The Green Book: The Solution to the Problem of Democracy, the Solution to the Economic Problem, the Social Basis of the Third Universal Theory*. Ithaca, NY: Ithaca Press, 2005.

26. Emma C. Murphy: *Economic and Political Change in Tunisia*. Basingstoke and London: Macmillan Press, 1999.

27. *Ibid.*, p. 173.

28. Quoted in Emma C. Murphy, *op.cit.*, p. 174.

29. Michael Johnson: 'Political Bosses and their Gangs: *Zu'ama* and *Qabadayat* in the Sunni Muslim Quarters of Beirut', in Ernest Gellner and John Waterbury (eds): *Patrons and Clients in Mediterranean Societies*. London: Gerald Duckworth & Co, 1977, pp. 207–24.

30. Agnes Favier (ed.): *Municipalités et pouvoirs locaux au Liban*. Beirut: Cermoc, 2001.

31. May Kassem: *In the Guise of Democracy: Governance in Contemporary Egypt*. Reading: Ithaca Press, 1999.

32. Giacomo Luciani and Hazem Beblawi: *The Rentier State: Nation, State and Integration in the Arab World*. London: Croom Helm, 1987.

33. Marjane Satrapi: *Persepolis: The Story of a Childhood*. New York: Pantheon Books, 2003, p. 37.

34. Vilfredo Pareto: *The Rise and Fall of Elites*. Totowa NJ: The Bedminister Press, 1968.

35. Jean-Pierre Digard, Bernard Hourcade and Yann Richard: *L'Iran au Xx siecle*. Paris: Fayard, 1996, p. 290.

36. Azadeh Kian-Thiebaut: *Secularization of Iran: A Doomed Failure? The New Middle Class and the Making of Modern Iran*. Paris: Peeters, 1998, p. 73.

37. *Ibid.*, p. 135.

38. *Ibid.*

39. *Ibid.*, p. 137.

40. Hossein Bashiriyeh: *The State and Revolution in Iran, 1962–1982*. London: Croom Helm, 1984.

41. Ervand Abrahamian: *Iran Between Two Revolutions*. Princeton: Princeton University Press, 1982.

42. Hossein Bashiriyeh, *op.cit.*

43. Henry Coville: *L'économie de l'Iran islamique: entre l'Etat et le marché*. Teheran: Institut Français de Recherches en Iran, 1994.

44. Farhad Nomani and Sohrab Behdad: *Class and Labor in Iran: Did the Revolution Matter?* Syracuse, NY: Syracuse University Press, 2006, p. 127.

45. Bernard Hourcade: *Iran. Nouvelles idendités d'une république*. Paris: Editions Belin, 2002, p. 215.

46. Central Bank of Iran: 'Key Economic Indicators', no. 41, Second Quarter, 1384 (2005/2006).

47. Farhad Nomani and Sohrab Behdad, *op.cit.*, p. 127.

48. Bill Samii: 'Iran Report', RFE/RL, vol. 7, no. 7, 16 February, 2004.

49. Farhad Nomani and Sohrab Behdad, *op.cit.*

50. Rand Corporation: 2009 'The Rise of the Pasdaran: Assessing the Domestic Roles of Iran's Islamic Revolutionary Guard Corps', http://www.rand.org/pubs/monographs/2008/RAND_MG821.pdf.

51. Kjetil Bjorvatn and Kjetil Selvik: 'Destructive competition: factionalism and rent-seeking in Iran', in *World Development*, vol. 36, no. 11, 2008.

52. Central Bank of Iran: 'Economic Trends', no. 36, First Quarter 1383 (2004/2005).

53. Bernard Hourcade, *op.cit.*, p. 183.

54. 'Detailed Interpretation of the Sentry Committee for Presidential Candidate Mr. Mir Hossein Mousavi's vote', http://www.princeton.edu/irandataportal/other_individuals/other_individuals/Makhbalbaf_Mousavi_Electoral_Violations.pdf.

4   Ethnicity

1. Ibn Khaldun: *The Muqaddimah: An Introduction to History*. Princeton, NJ: Princeton University Press, [1377] 1989, p. 130.

2. See for example Milton J. Esman and Itamar Rabinovich: 'The Study of Ethnic Politics in the Middle East', in Milton J. Esman and Itamar Rabinovich (eds.): *Ethnicity, Pluralism, and the State in the Middle East*. Ithaca and London: Cornell University Press, 1988.

3. Fredrik Barth: 'Introduction', in Fredrik Barth (ed.): *Ethnic Groups and Boundaries*. Oslo: Universitetsforlaget, 1969.

4. Anthony D. Smith: *Theories of Nationalism*. New York: Holmes & Meier, 2nd edition, 1983.

5. Joel S. Migdal: *Strong Societies and Weak States*. Princeton, NJ: Princeton University Press, 1988.

6. *Ibid.*, pp. 206–37.

7. David McDowall: *A Modern History of the Kurds*. London: I.B.Tauris, 2000, p. 3.

8. *Ibid.*, pp. 418, 440.

9. Salem Chaker: *Berbères aujourd'hui*. Paris: L'Harmattan, 1998.

10. John Ruedy: *Modern Algeria: The Origins and Development of a Nation*. Bloomington: Indiana University Press, 1992.

11. Louay Bahry: 'The Socioeconomic Foundations of the Shiite Opposition in Bahrain', in *Mediterranean Quarterly*, Summer, 2000, p. 132.

12. 'Discrimination in Bahrain: The Unwritten Law', The Bahrain Center for Human Rights, September 2003, http://www.bahrainrights.org/node/29.

13. Louay Bahry, *op.cit.*, p. 134.

14. *Ibid.*, p. 137.

15. *Ibid.*, p. 138.

16. Anh Nga Longva: 'Reforms in Bahrain', in *Babylon*, vol. 1, no. 1, 2003, p. 53.

17. Louay Bahry, *op.cit.*, 135.

18. Mohammed Zahid Mahjoob Zweiri: 'The Victory of Al Wefaq: The Rise of Shiite Politics in Bahrain', International Relations and Security Network, 2007, http://www.isn.ethz.ch/isn/Digital-Library/Publications/Detail/?id=29901&lng=en.

19. David C. Gordon: *Lebanon: The Fragmented Nation*. London: Croom Helm, 1980, pp. 41–2.

20. Beverley Milton-Edwards: *Contemporary Politics in the Middle East*. Cambridge: Polity Press, 2000, p. 112.

21. Hassan Krayem: 'The Lebanese Civil War and the Taif Agreement', American University of Beirut, http://almashriq.hiof.no/ddc/projects/pspa/conflict-resolution.html.

22. Theodor Hanf: *Coexistence in Wartime Lebanon: Decline of a State and Rise of a Nation*. London: I.B.Tauris, 1993, p. 204.

23. Theodor Hanf: *Coexistence in Wartime Lebanon: Decline of a State and Rise of a Nation*. London: I.B.Tauris, 1993, p. 204.

24. Vali Nasr: *The Shia Revival: How Conflicts within Islam Will Shape the Future*. New York and London: W.W. Norton and Company, 2007.

25. Sabrina Mervin (ed.): *Les mondes chiites et l'Iran*. Amman, Beirut, and Damascus: IFPR, 2007.

26. Laurence Louër: *Transnational Shia Politics: Religious and Political Networks in the Gulf*. New York: Columbia University Press, 2008.

27. *The Oxford Encyclopaedia of Modern Islamic World Vol. 4, op.cit.*, p. 156. Exact figures are not available as the size of various confessions is a sensitive topic in Syria.

28. Quotation from an old Yemeni poem, found in Omar Daair: 'Authoritarian Rule in a Plural Society: The Republic of Yemen', MSc Dissertation, School of Oriental and African Studies, London, September 2001, p. 1.

29. Paul Dresch: *A History of Modern Yemen*. Cambridge and New York: Cambridge University Press, 2000, p. 1.

30. Ahmed Abdul Kareem Saif: 'A Legislature in Transition: The Parliament of the Republic of Yemen 1990–99', PhD Thesis, University of Exeter, April 2000.

31. UNDP: 'Country Profile Yemen', http://www.undp.org.ye/y-profile.php.

32. John L. Esposito (ed.): *The Oxford Encyclopaedia of the Modern Islamic World Vol. 4, op.cit.*, p. 353.

33. Fred Halliday: 'The Formation of Yemeni Nationalism: Initial Reflections', in James Jankowski and Israel Gershoni (eds.): *Rethinking Nationalism in the Arab Middle East*. New York: Columbia University Press, 1997, pp. 26–41.

34. Sheila Carapico: *Civil Society in Yemen: The Political Economy of Activism in Modern Arabia*. Cambridge, New York, Oakleigh, Madrid, and Cape Town: Cambridge University Press, 1998, p. 21.

35. Nasser Arrabyee: 'Bowing out?', in *Al-Ahram Weekly* (Cairo), 25 July 2005, http://weekly.ahram.org.eg/2005/752/re2.htm; and Sarah Phillips: 'Cracks in the Yemeni System', *Middle East Report Online*, 28 July 2005, http://www.merip.org/mero/mero072805.html.

36. Paul Dresch: 'The Tribal Factor in the Yemeni Crisis', in Jamal al-Suwaidi (ed.): *The Yemeni War of 1994: Causes and Consequences*. London: al-Saqi Books, 1995, p. 41.

37. Paul Dresch: *Tribes, Government and History in Yemen*. Oxford: Oxford University Press, 1989, p. 86.

38. Al-Ahmar Trading & Investment Co, http://www.aticoretail.com/history.htm.

39. Sheila Carapico, *op.cit.*, pp. 203–4.

40. Paul Dresch: 'Stereotypes and political styles: Islamists and tribal peoples in Yemen', in *International Journal of Middle East Studies*, vol. 27, no. 4, 1995, pp. 405–31.

41. Sheila Carapico, *op.cit.*

42. Malcolm E. Yapp: *The Near East since the First World War: A History to 1995*. Harlow: Parson Education Limited, 2nd edition, 1996, p. 366.

43. *Ibid.*, pp. 366–7.

44. Sheila Carapico, *op.cit.*, pp. 204–5.

45. Shelagh Weir: 'A Clash of fundamentalisms: Wahhabism in Yemen', in *Middle East Report*, July–September 2002; and 'Yemen's Al-Houthi rebellion: Zaidi revivalist resentments', in *Gulf States Newsletter*, vol. 33, issue 861, 28 September, 2009.

46. *Ibid.*

47. '"Scorched earth" in Yemen further raises regional temperature as US considers Iranian angle', in *Gulf States Newsletter*, vol. 33, issue 864, 9 November, 2009.

48. 'Amnesty International Report 2010: Middle East and North Africa', Amnesty International, 2010, http://thereport.amnesty.org/regions/middle-east-north-africa.

49. 'Southern Yemen's discontent comes to the boil with tribal leader's defiance', in *Gulf States Newsletter*, vol. 33, issue 852, 4 May, 2009; and 'Southern Movement under pressure', in *Gulf States Newsletter*, vol. 33, issue 859, 10 August, 2009.

50. 'How likely is Southern secession?', in *Middle East Monitor: Gulf*, August 2009.

51. 'Southern Yemen's discontent comes to the boil with tribal leader's defiance', *op.cit.*

5 Reformism

1. Michael C. Hudson: *Arab Politics: The Search for Legitimacy*. New Haven and London: Yale University Press, 1977, p. 2.

2. Max Weber: *The Theory of Social and Economic Organization*. New York: Oxford University Press, 1947, pp. 124–6.

3. Michael Hudson, *op.cit.*, p. 2.

4. Fuad Ajami: 'The end of pan-Arabism', in *Foreign Affairs*, vol. 57, no. 2, 1978, pp. 355–73.

5. Ray Bush: *Economic crisis and the politics of reform in Egypt*. Boulder, CO: Westview Press, 1999.

6. John Waterbury: *The Egypt of Nasser and Sadat: The Political Economy of Two Regimes*. Princeton, NJ: Princeton University Press, 1983.

7. Erik J. Zürcher: *Turkey: A Modern History*. London and New York: I.B.Tauris, 1998.

8. Alan Richards and John Waterbury: *A Political Economy of the Middle East*. Boulder, CO: Westview Press, 1998, p. 250.

9. Hans Hopfinger (ed.): *Economic Liberalization and Privatization in Socialist Arab Countries*. Gotha: Justus Perthes Verlag, 1996.

10. 'How the Arabs Compare. Arab Human Development Report 2002', in *The Middle East Quarterly*, vol. 9, no. 4, 2002, http://www.meforum.org/article/513.

11. Emma C. Murphy: 'Legitimacy and economic reform in the Arab world', in *The Journal of North African Studies*, vol. 3, no. 3, 1998, pp. 71–92.

12. Jason Brownlee: 'The Decline of Pluralism in Mubarak's Egypt', in Larry Diamond, Marc F. Plattner and Daniel Brumberg (eds.): *Islam and Democracy in the Middle East*. Baltimore and London: The Johns Hopkins University Press, 2003, p. 49.

13. Paul Balta: *Le grand Maghreb: Des Independences à l'an 2000*. Paris: La découverte, 1990, p. 101.

14. See for example Ghassan Salamé (ed.): *Democracy Without Democrats: The Renewal of Politics in the Muslim World*. London: I.B.Tauris, 1994; Augustus Richard Norton: *Civil Society in the Middle East*. Leiden: Brill, 1994; and Mehran Kamrava: *Democracy in the Balance: Culture and Society in the Middle East*. Chatham NJ: Chatham House, 1998.

15. Maha M. Abdelrahman: *Civil Society Exposed*. Cairo: American University of Cairo, 2004.

16. Béatrice Hibou (ed.): *Privatising the State*. London: Hurst, 2004.

17. Marsha Pripstein Posusney: 'Multiparty Elections in the Arab World: Election Rules and Opposition Reponses', in Marsha Pripstein Posusney and Michele Penner Angrist (eds.): *Authoritarianism in the Middle East: Regimes and Resistance*. Boulder, CO, and London: Lynne Rienner, 2005, pp. 91–118.

18. Ellen Lust-Okar: *Structuring Conflict in the Arab World: Incumbents, Opponents and Institutions*. Cambridge, NY: Cambridge University Press, 2005.

19. Ellen Lust-Okar: 'Opposition and Economic Crisis in Jordan and Morocco', in Marsha Pripstein Posusney and Michele Penner Angrist (eds.). *op.cit.*, pp. 143–68.

20. 'Great Man-made River Water Supply Project, Libya', http://www.water-technology.net/projects/gmr/.
21. 'Gulf Arab nations in race to build world's tallest skyscraper', in *The China Post*, 13 March, 2008.
22. 'Islam's holiest city set for 130-skyscraper redevelopment', in *The Guardian*, 29 May, 2008.
23. 'Work starts on Gulf 'Green City', in *BBC News*, 10 February 2008, http://news.bbc.co.uk/2/hi/science/nature/7237672.stm.
24. 'Nuclear Programs in the Middle East: In the Shadow of Iran', The International Institute for Strategic Studies, London, May 2008.
25. Steven Heydemann: 'Upgrading authoritarianism in the Arab world', *The Saban Center Analysis Paper*, no. 13, October 2007.
26. The Kingdom of Morocco's constitution, http://www.servat.unibe.ch/icl/mo00000_.html.
27. Max Weber: *On Charisma and Institution Building*. Chicago and London: The University of Chicago Press, 1968, p. 46.
28. *Ibid.*, p. 19.
29. Mohamed Tozy: *Monarchie et islam politique au Maroc*. Paris: Presses de Sciences Po, 1999.
30. Jawad Touhami: *Abrégé de l'histoire du Maroc*. Rabat: Les Marocains de l'émigration, 2005.
31. John Waterbury: *Commander of the Faithful: The Moroccan Political Elite – A Study in Segmented Politics*. London: Weidenfeld & Nicolson, 1970.
32. *Ibid.*
33. *Ibid.*, p. 31.
34. Abdellah Hammoudi: *Maîtres et disciples: Genèse et fondements des pouvoirs autoritaires dans les sociétés arabes. Essai d'anthropologie politique*. Paris: Maisonnevue et Larose, 2001.
35. Morocco's constitution, *op.cit.*
36. Pierre Vermeren: *Histoire du Maroc depuis l'independence*. Paris: La decouverte & Syros, 2002, p. 35.
37. See for example Clifford Geertz: *Islam observed: Religious Development in Morocco and Indonesia*. Chicago: The University of Chicago Press, 1971.
38. Zakya Daoud and Maati Monjib: *Ben Barka*. Paris: Michalon, 1996.
39. Youssef Belal: 'Le réenchantement du monde: Autorité et rationalisation en Islam marocain', Institut d'Etudes Politiques de Paris: these doctorale, 2005, p. 89.
40. *Ibid.*, p. 90.
41. Malika Zeghal: *Les islamistes marocains. Le défi à la monarchie*. Paris: La Découverte, 2005.
42. Pierre Vermeren, *op.cit.*
43. Youssef Belal, *op.cit.*, p. 332.
44. *Ibid.*
45. Pierre Vermeren: *Le Maroc en transition*. Paris: La Decouverte, 2001, p. 83.
46. *Ibid.*, p. 38.
47. *Ibid.*, p. 122. There is considerable uncertainty concerning the proportion of the population that is Berber.
48. Driss Ksikes: 'Le fantôme du père', in *Tel Quel*, no. 221, April 2006, p. 36.
49. Susan Slyomovics: 'A Truth Commission for Morocco', in *Middle East Report*, no. 218, 2001.
50. *Ibid.*
51. Royaume du Maroc: Instance Equité et Réconciliation, http://www.ier.ma/_fr_article.php?id_article=147.
52. Royaume du Maroc: Instance Equité et Réconciliation, http://www.ier.ma/_fr_article.php?id_article=1538.
53. Malika Zeghal, *op.cit.*, p. 252.

54. Saloua Zerhouni: 'Morocco: Reconciling Continuity and Change', in Volker Perthes (ed.): *Arab Elites…*, *op.cit.*, p. 66.
55. *Ibid.*, p. 67.
56. *Ibid.*
57. Interview with the research institution Bouabid, Salé, Marokko, 13 April 2006.
58. 'Le roi fustige ses ministres', *Le Journal*, April, 2004, http://www.lejournal-hebdo.com/rubrique.php3?id_rubrique=109.
59. *Ibid.*
60. Amr Hamzawy: 'The 2007 Moroccan Parliamentary Elections: Results and Implications', http://www.carnegieendowment.org/files/moroccan_parliamentary_elections_final.pdf; and Mohamed Tozy: 'Islamists, technocrats, and the palace;, in *Journal of Democracy*, vol. 19, no. 1, 2008.
61. Driss Ksikes, *op.cit.*
62. Mohamed Tozy, *op.cit.*, pp. 34–41.

6 Islamism

1. *Esteqlal, azadi, jumhuri-e eslami*, slogan for Iran's Islamic Revolution, cited in Muhammad H. Panahi: *An Introduction to the Islamic Revolution of Iran and it's [sic] Slogans*. London: al-Hoda, 2001, p. 101.
2. Albert Hourani: *Arabic Thought in the Liberal Age 1798–1939*. Cambridge, New York, Port Chester, Melbourne, and Sydney: Cambridge University Press, 1983.
3. Brynjar Lia: *The Society of the Muslim Brothers in Egypt: the Rise of an Islamic Mass Movement 1928–1942*. Reading: Ithaca Press, 1998; and Richard P. Mitchell: *The Society of the Muslim Brothers*. New York and Oxford: Oxford University Press, 1993.
4. Sayyid Qutb: *Milestones*. Karachi: International Islamic Publishers, 2nd edition, 1988.
5. Fawaz Gerges: *The Far Enemy: Why Jihad Went Global*. New York: Cambridge University Press, 2006; and Anonymous: *Through Our Enemies' Eyes*. Washington: Brassey's Inc., 2002.
6. M. Yavuz Hakan: 'Towards an Islamic liberalism?: the Nurcu movement and Fethullah Gülen', in *The Middle East Journal*, vol. 53, no. 4, 1999.
7. Thomas Pierret and Kjetil Selvik: 'Limits of "authoritarian upgrading" in Syria: private welfare, Islamic charities, and the rise of the Zayd movement', in *International Journal of Middle East Studies*, vol. 41, no. 4, 2009.
8. See Mohammed Ayoob: *The Many Faces of Political Islam: Religion and Politics in the Muslim World*. Ann Arbour, MI: University of Michigan Press, 2007.
9. We owe broad traits of this categorisation to Bjørn Olav Utvik, as presented in *The Pious Road to Development. Islamist Economics in Egypt*. London: Hurst & Co. Ltd, 2006.
10. See, for example, Bernard Lewis: *The Crisis of Islam: Holy War and Unholy Terror*. New York: The Modern Library, 2003; and Emmanuel Sivan: *Radical Islam: Medieval Theology and Modern Politics*. New Haven: Yale University Press, 1985.
11. Bruce Lawrence: *Defenders of God: The Fundamentalist Revolt against the Modern Age*. New York: Harper & Row, 1989.
12. See for instance White, Jenny B.: *Islamist Mobilization in Turkey: A Study in Vernacular Politics*. Seattle and London: University of Washington Press, 2002.
13. Nazih N. Ayubi: *Political Islam. Religion and Politics in the Arab World*. London: Routledge, 1991.
14. François Burgat: *L'islamisme au Maghreb: La Voix du Sud*. Paris: Karthala, 1988. See too the English edition: François Burgat and William Dowell: *The Islamic Movement in North Africa*. Austin, Texas: The Center for Middle Eastern Studies at the University of Texas at Austin, 1993.

15. François Burgat and William Dowell, *op.cit.*, p. 64.
16. See, for example, Alain Finkielkraut: *La défaite de la pensée: essai*. Paris: Galimard, 1989.
17. Bjørn Olav Utvik: 'The Modernizing Force of Islamism', in François Burgat and John Esposito (eds.): *Modernizing Islam: Religion and the Public Sphere in the Middle East and Europe*. London: Hurst & Co, 2003, pp. 43–67.
18. *Ibid.*, p. 43.
19. Dale F. Eickelman and James Piscatori: *Muslim Politics*. Princeton, NJ: Princeton University Press, 1996.
20. Brynjar Lia, *op.cit.*
21. Richard P. Mitchell: *The Society of the Muslim Brothers*. New York: Oxford University Press, 1993.
22. Carrie Rosefsky Wickham: *Mobilizing Islam: Religion, Activism, and Political Change in Egypt*. New York, Chichester, and West Sussex: Columbia University Press, 2002.
23. Yavuz, M. Hakan (ed.): *The Emergence of a New Turkey: Democracy and the AK Party*. Salt Lake City, UT: University of Utah Press, 2006.
24. Dale F. Eickelman and James Piscatori, *op.cit.*
25. Ali Rahnema: *An Islamic Utopian: A Political Biography of Ali Shari'ati*. London: I.B.Tauris, 1998.
26. Richard Bonney: *Jihad: From Qur'an to bin Laden*. London: Palgrave Macmillan, 2004.
27. Johannes J. B. Jansen: *The Neglected Duty*. New York: MacMillan Publishing Company, 1986.
28. Emad Eldin Shahin: *Political Ascent: Contemporary Islamic Movements in North Africa*. Boulder and Oxford: Westview Press, 1997.
29. 'Algeria puts strife tolls at 150,000', in *al-Jazeera*, 24 February 2005, http://english.aljazeera.net/NR/exeres/663E8C85–9120-4A65-BD2B-B70593A19899.htm.
30. 'Shiite politics in Iraq: the role of the Supreme Council', in *International Crisis Group*, Middle East Report N 70, 15. November 2007, http://www.crisisgroup.org/home/index.cfm?id=5158&l=1.
31. 'Islamism, violence and reform in Algeria: turning the page', in *International Crisis Group*, Middle East Report N 29, 30. July 2004, http://www.crisisgroup.org/home/index.cfm?.
32. Bjørn Olav Utvik: 'Hizb al-Wasat and the potential for change in Egyptian Islamism', in *Critique: Critical Middle Eastern Studies*, vol. 14, no. 3, 2005.
33. R. Quinn Mecham: 'From the ashes of virtue: a promise of light: the transformation of political Islam in Turkey', in *Third World Quarterly*, vol. 25, no. 2, 2004.
34. Gilles Kepel: *Jihad: The Trail of Political Islam*. London: I.B.Tauris, 2004.
35. Habib Souaidia: *La Sale Guerre: le témoignage d'un ancien officier des forces spéciales de l'armée algérienne*. Paris: La Découverte, 2001.
36. Khaled Nezzar: *L'armée algérienne face à la désinformation: le procès de Paris*. Paris: Médiane, 2005.
37. See for example Alain Finkielkraut, *op.cit.*; Slavoj Zizek: 'The antinomies of tolerant reason: a blood-dimmed tide is loosened', in *Lacan dot com*, 2006, http://www.lacan.com/zizantinomies.htm; and Hans Magnus Enzensberger: *Schreckens Männer: Versuch über den radikalen Verlierer*. Frankfurt am Main: Suhrkamp, 2006.
38. Robert Burns: 'Rumsfeld says threat to U.S. is from "a new type of fascism"', in *Northwest Florida Daily News*, 2 October 2006, http://www.nwfdailynews.com/articleArchive/aug2006/newtypefascism.php.
39. Egypt's constitution, http://www.egypt.gov.eg/english/laws/Constitution/chp_one/part_one.asp.

40. Daniel Brumberg: 'Liberalization versus Democracy: Understanding Arab Political Reform', in *Democracy and Rule of Law Paper*, no. 37, Carnegie Endowment for International Peace: Washington, DC, 2003, p. 3.
41. *Ibid.*, p. 12.
42. Daniel Brumberg: 'The Trap of Liberalized Autocracy', in Larry Diamond, Marc F. Plattner and Daniel Brumberg (eds.): *Islam and Democracy in the Middle East*. Baltimore and London: The Johns Hopkins University Press, 2003, p. 42.
43. Constitutional Proclamation, http://www.egypt.gov.eg/english/laws/Constitution/CAdocument. asp.
44. Egypt's constitution, *op.cit.*
45. Hesham al-Awadi: *In pursuit of Legitimacy. The Muslim Brothers and Mubarak, 1982–2000*. London and New York: I.B.Tauris, 2004.
46. Carrie Rosefsky Wickham: *Mobilizing Islam. Religion, Activism, and Political Change in Egypt*. New York: Columbia University Press, 2002.
47. Hesham al-Awadi, *op.cit.* p. 50.
48. *Ibid.*, p. 52.
49. *Ibid.*, p. 53.
50. *Ibid.*, p. 114.
51. *Ibid.*, p. 148.
52. Carrie Rosefsky Wickham, *op.cit.*
53. Salwa Ismail: *Rethinking Islamist Politics: Culture, the State and Islamism*. London and New York: I.B.Tauris, 2003, pp. 42–4.
54. Gilles Kepel: *The Prophet and the Pharaoh*. London: al-Saqi Books, 1985.
55. Salwa Ismail, *op.cit.*, pp. 42–4.
56. Lila Abu-Lughod: 'Islam and public culture: the politics of Egyptian television serials', in *Middle East Report*, no. 180, 1993, p. 28.
57. Salwa Ismail, *op.cit.*, p. 64.
58. *Ibid.*, p. 66.
59. Charles Onians: 'Supply and demand democracy in Egypt', in *World Policy Journal*, vol. 21, no. 2, 2004.
60. Salwa Ismail, *op. cit.*, p. 75.
61. Sabry Hafez: 'The novel, politics and Islam. Haydar Haydar's *Banquet for Seaweed*', in *New Left Review*, no. 5, 2000, p. 133.
62. *Ibid.*, p. 134.
63. *Ibid.*, p. 136.
64. Gregory Starrett: *Putting Islam to Work: Education, Politics and Religious Transformation in Egypt*. Berkeley, Los Angeles, and London: University of California Press, 1998. See too Mansoor Moaddel: 'The Saudi public speaks: religion, gender and politics', in *International Journal of Middle East Studies*, vol. 38, no. 1, 2006, which shows that Egyptians score higher than Jordanians and Saudi Arabians on almost all indicators for religiosity.
65. Michael Cook: *Commanding Right and Forbidding Wrong in Islamic Thought*. Cambridge: Cambridge University Press, 2000.
66. Joseph Schacht: *An Introduction to Islamic Law*. Oxford: Oxford University Press, 1964, p. 52.
67. Fauzi M. Najjar: 'Islamic fundamentalism and the intellectuals: the case of Nasr Hamid Abu Zayd', in *British Journal of Middle Eastern Studies*, vol. 27, no. 2, 2000, pp. 177–200.
68. Salwa Ismail, *op.cit.*, p. 65.
69. For an explanation of the theological arguments in the case, see Fauzi M. Najjar, *op.cit.*

70. Joshua A. Stacher: 'Post-Islamist rumblings in Egypt: the emergence of the Wasat Party', in *Middle East Journal*, vol. 56, no. 3, 2002, pp. 415–32.

71. Carrie Rosefsky Wickham, *op.cit.*, p. 215.

72. 'Islamism in North Africa II: Egypt's Opportunity', in *International Crisis Group*, Middle East Report no. 13, 20. April, 2004, http://www.crisisgroup.org/home/index.cfm?id=3713&l=2.

7 Monarchies

1. Quotation from a speech *Sheik* Zayid, the ruler of the Emirates from 1971 to 2004 held for his colleagues in the Supreme Federal Council. *United Arab Emirates Yearbook 2005*. London: Trident Press Ltd., 2005, p. 20.

2. The figure is based on the UNDP: 'Human Development Report 2007/2008', United Nations Publications: New York, 2008.

3. Samuel P. Huntington: *Political Order in Changing Societies*. New Haven, Conn.: Yale University Press, 1968, pp. 87–92, 126–37, 168–91, 406.

4. Manfred Halpern: *The Politics of Social Change in the Middle East and North Africa*. Princeton, NJ: Princeton University Press, 1963, pp. 41–3, 51–78.

5. 'BP Statistical Review of World Energy June 2009', http://www.bp.com.

6. Giacomo Luciani: 'Allocation versus Production States: A Theoretical Framework', in *ibid.* (ed.): *The Arab State*. Berkley: University of California Press, 1990, p. 87.

7. Adam Smith: *An Inquiry into the Wealth of Nations*. London: Penguin Press, 1956, p. 412.

8. See among others Giacomo Luciani and Hazem Beblawi: *The Rentier State*. London: Croom Helm, 1987; F. Gregory Gause III: *Oil Monarchies: Domestic and Security Challenges in the Arab Gulf States*. New York: Council of Foreign Relations, 1994; Jill Crystal: *Oil and Politics in the Gulf*. Cambridge: Cambridge University Press, 1995; and Kiren Aziz Chaudhry: *The Price of Wealth: Economies and Institutions in the Middle East*. Ithaca, NY: Cornell University Press, 1997.

9. However, in Kuwait and Saudi-Arabia – besides Iran, Jordan, Libya, Malaysia, Pakistan, and Sudan – the state collects alms (*zakat*), a tax for Islamic purposes.

10. N. Janardhan: 'Redefining the rules of engagement for expatriates in the GCC countries', paper presented at the conference *The Global Gulf*, Institute of Arab and Islamic Studies, University of Exeter, 4–6 July, 2006.

11. *Ibid.*

12. Khaldun al-Naqib, cited in Nazih N. Ayubi: *Overstating the Arab State*. London: I.B.Tauris, 1995, pp. 241–2.

13. Steffen Hertog: *Princes, Brokers, and Bureaucrats: Oil and the State in Saudi Arabia*. Ithaca, NY: Cornell University Press, 2010.

14. Jordan's constitution, see, http://www.kinghussein.gov.jo/constitution_jo.html.

15. Morocco's constitution, see, http://www.oefre.unibe.ch/law/icl/mo00000_.html.

16. 'Morocco 2005', *Freedom House*, http://www.freedomhouse.org/template.cfm?page=22&year=2005&country=6795.

17. Michael Herb: *All in the Family: Absolutism, Revolution, and Democracy in the Middle Eastern Monarchies*. Albany: State University of New York Press, 1999.

18. Michael Herb, *op.cit.*, pp. 7–10.

19. Khalid Bin Sultan and Patrick Seale: *Desert Warrior*. New York: Harper Collins, 1995, p. 48.

20. Michael Herb, *op.cit.*, pp. 150–2.

21. The Basic Law of the Sultanate of Oman, see http://www.omanet.om/english/government/basiclaw/overview.asp?cat=gov&subcat=blaw.

22. Sam Perlo-Freeman, Catalina Perdomo, Elisabeth Sköns, and Petter Stålenheim: 'Chapter 5. Military expenditure', in *SIPRI Yearbook 2009: Armaments, Disarmament and International Security 2009*, http://www.sipri.org/yearbook/2009/files/SIPRIYB0905.pdf.

23. Oman's national anthem, 'Oh Allah, protect for us His Majesty the Sultan', quoted in Anne Bouji: *This is Oman*. Muscat: al-Roya Publishing, 2003.

24. Samuel P. Huntington: *The Third Wave: Democratization in the Late Twentieth Century*. Norman, Oklahoma: University of Oklahoma Press, 1991.

25. Samuel P. Huntington: *The Soldier and the State: The Theory of Politics and Civil-Military Relations*. Cambridge, MA: Harvard University Press, 1991.

26. J.E. Peterson: *Oman's Insurgencies: The Sultanate's Struggle for Supremacy*. London, San Francisco, and Beirut: al-Saqi Books, 2007, pp. 37–8.

27. *Ibid.*, p. 38.

28. *Ibid.*, pp. 48–9.

29. *Ibid.*, pp. 54–62.

30. *Ibid.*, pp. 80–146.

31. *Ibid.*, pp. 147–52; and Francis Owtram: *A Modern History of Oman: Formation of the State Since 1920*. London and New York: I.B.Tauris, 2004, pp. 103–4.

32. J.E. Peterson: *Defending Arabia*. London, Croom Helm/New York: St. Martin's Press, 1986, p. 162.

33. Joseph A. Kechichian: 'The Throne in the Sultanate of Oman', in *ibid.* (ed.): *Middle East Monarchies: The Challenge of Modernity*. Boulder and London: Lynne Rienner Publishers, 2000, pp. 187–208.

34. The numbers are from *Jane's Sentinel – Gulf States 2001*, pp. 327–47; and Calvin Allen Jr. and W. Lynn Riggsbee: *Oman Under Qaboos: From Coup to Constitution, 1970–1996*. London and Portland, OR: Frank Class, 2000, pp. 65–95.

35. Niccolò Machiavelli: *The Prince*. Harmondsworth: The Penguin Classics, 1961.

36. Calvin Allen and W. Lynn Rigsbee, *op.cit.*, pp. 77–8.

37. *Ibid.*, p. 91.

38. See for example J.E. Peterson *op.cit.*, 1986, p. 162; and Anthony H. Cordesman: *Bahrain, Oman, Qatar, and the UAE: Challenges of Security*. Boulder, CO and Oxford: Westview Press, 1997, p. 180.

39. Francis Owtram, *op.cit.*, p. 157.

40. *Arab News*, 26 August 2002.

41. *BBC News*, 26 January 2005, http://news.bbc.co.uk/1/hi/world/middle_east/4209645.stm.

42. Anne Joyce: 'Interview with Sultan Qaboos bin Said Al Said', in *Middle East Policy*, vol. 3, April 1995, p. 1.

43. Calvin Allen Jr. and W. Lynn Riggsbee, *op.cit.*, p. 65.

44. F. Gregory Gause III, *op.cit.*, p. 124.

45. Anthony H. Cordesman, *op.cit.*, p. 171.

46. Stockholm International Peace Research Institute: *SIPRI Yearbook 2009: Armaments, Disarmament and International Security*. London and New York: Oxford University Press, revised edition, 2009.

47. See for example 'Oman – Country Profile 2008', *The Economist Intelligence Unit*, London, 2008, p. 6.

48. Calvin Allen and W. Lynn Rigsbee, *op.cit.*, p. 92.

49. *Ibid.*

50. See Calvin Allen and W. Lynn Rigsbee, *op.cit.*, p. 92; and 'Oman – Country Profile 2005', *op.cit.*, p. 10.

51. Michael Herb, *op.cit.*, pp. 34–5.

52. *Worldwide Directory of Defence Authorities 2004*.

53. Calvin Allen and W. Lynn Rigsbee, *op.cit.*, pp. 91–2.

54. Anthony H. Cordesman, *op.cit.*, pp. 273, 353.

8　Republics

1. Husni Mubarak's answer to the question of whether Egypt is a democracy. Popular joke in Cairo's coffee houses.
2. Nazih N. Ayubi, *op.cit.*, p. 204.
3. Fred Halliday: *Nation and Religion in the Middle East*. London: al-Saqi Books, 2000, pp. 101–4.
4. Hisham Sharabi: *Neopatriarchy: A Theory of Distorted Change in the Arab World*. New York: Oxford University Press, 1988, p. 4.
5. *Ibid.*, p. 7.
6. Lebanon's constitution, see http://www.servat.unibe.ch/icl/le00000_.html.
7. Ed Blanche: 'Algeria: the battle within', in *The Middle East*, May 2006, pp. 24–6; and Isabelle Werenfels: 'Algeria: System Continuity Through Elite Change', in Volker Perthes (ed.): *Arab Elites, op.cit.*, pp. 175–7.
8. Algeria's constitution, see http://www.oefre.unibe.ch/law/icl/ag00000_.html.
9. Nathan J. Brown: *Constitutions in a Nonconstitutional World: Arab Basic Laws and the Prospects for Accountable Government*. New York: State University of New York Press, 2002.
10. *Ibid.*, pp. 91–2.
11. Syria's constitution, see http://www.oefre.unibe.ch/law/icl/sy00000_.html.
12. *Ibid.*
13. 'Egypt's Emergency Laws without End', Human Rights Watch, 25 February 2005, http://hrw.org/press/2003/02/egypt022503.htm.
14. Syria's constitution, *op.cit.*
15. Yemen's constitution, see http://www.al-bab.com/yemen/gov/con94.htm.
16. *Ibid.*
17. Egypt's constitution, *op.cit.*
18. Robert Springborg: *Family Power and Politics in Egypt: Sayyed Bay Marie – His Clan, Clients, and Cohorts*. Philadelphia: University of Pennsylvania Press, 1982; and Michel Saurat: *L'Etat de Barbarie*. Paris: Editions du Seuil, 1989.
19. Steven A. Cook: *Ruling but Not Governing: The Military and Political Development in Egypt, Algeria, and Turkey*. Baltimore and London: Johns Hopkins University Press, 2007.
20. Roger Owen: *State, Power and Politics in the Making of the Modern Middle East*. London and New York: Routledge, 2nd edition, 2000, pp. 201–2.
21. Hans Günter Lobmeyer: *Opposition und Widerstand in Syrien*. Hambourg: Deutsches Orient-Institut 1995.
22. See for example 'Genocide in Iraq: the Anfal Campaign Against the Kurds', report published by The Human Rights Watch, July 1993, http://www.hrw.org/reports/1993/iraqanfal/.
23. Eberhard Kienle: *A Grand Delusion: Democracy and Economic Reform in Egypt*. London and New York: I.B.Tauris, 2001, p. 93.
24. Samir Khalil: *Republic of Fear: The Politics of Modern Iraq*. Berkley and Los Angeles: University of California Press, 1998.
25. Kevin Woods, James Lacey, and Williamson Murray: 'Saddam's delusion: The view from the inside', in *Foreign Affairs*, May/June 2006.
26. Philippe Droz-Vincent: 'Changing Role of Middle Eastern Armies', in Oliver Schlumberger (ed.): *Debating Arab Authoritarianism: Dynamics and Durability in Nondemocratic Regimes*. Stanford, California: Stanford University Press, 2007, pp. 201–3.

27. Hillel Frisch: 'Guns and butter in the Egyptian army', in *Middle East Review of International Affairs*, vol. 5, no. 2, June 2001, http://meria.idc.ac.il/journal/2001/issue2/jv5n2a1.html.

28. For a comparison of military expenses in the Middle East with other parts of the world, see 'World Development Indicators', the World Bank, 2005, http://devdata.worldbank.org/wdi2005/Section5.htm.

29. Eyal Zisser: 'The Syrian army: between the domestic and the external fronts', in *MERIA*, vol. 5, no. 1, 2001, p. 6, http://meria.idc.ac.il/journal/2001/issue1/jv5n1a1.html.

30. *Ibid.*

31. The International Institute for Strategic Studies: *The Military balance 2009*. London and New York: Routledge, 2009.

32. Stockholm International Peace Research Institute: *SIPRI Yearbook 2009, op.cit.*

33. Roger Owen, *op.cit.*, p. 157.

34. Alan George: *Syria: Neither Bread nor Freedom*. London and New York: Zed Books, 2003, p. 71.

35. Christine Moss Helms: *Iraq: Eastern Flank of the Arab World*. Washington, DC: The Brookings Institution, 1984, pp. 105–6.

36. Egypt's constitution, *op.cit.*

37. Tunisia's constitution, see http://www.oefre.unibe.ch/law/icl/ts00000_.html; and for a commentary on the constitutional amendments accepted in 2002, see for example 'Country Report: Tunisia', Commission of the European Communities, 2004, http://europa.eu.int/comm/world/enp/pdf/country/Tunisia_11_May_EN.pdf.

38. Syria's constitution, *op.cit.*

39. Nazih N. Ayubi, *op.cit.*, p. 321.

40. Nizar Qabbani, Syria, 1967, translated into English at http://oldpoetry.com/opoem/30732.

41. Charles Tilly (ed.): *The Formation of National States in Western Europe*. Princeton: Princeton University Press, 1975; and Charles Tilly: *Coercion, Capital and European States, AD 990–1990*. Oxford: Basil Blackwell, 1990.

42. Charles Tilly: *Coercion, Capital and European States, AD 990–1990, op.cit.*, pp. 99–126.

43. Georg Sørensen: 'War and state making – why doesn't it work in the Third World?', in *Security Dialogue*, vol. 32, no. 3, 2001, pp. 341–54.

44. Charles Tilly: *Coercion, Capital and European States, AD 990–1990, op.cit.*, p. 206.

45. See for example Samuel P. Huntington: *Political Order in Changing Societies, op.cit.*, 1968.

46. Niccolò Machiavelli, *op.cit.*

47. Thomas Hobbes: *Leviathan*. Oxford and New York: Oxford University Press, 1996.

48. Corey Robin: *Fear: The History of a Political Idea*. Oxford: Oxford University Press, 2004, pp. 31–50.

49. David L. Altheide: *Terrorism and the Politics of Fear*. Lanham, MD: AltaMira Press, 2005; Frank Furedi: *Politics of Fear: Beyond Left and Right*. London and New York: Continuum International Publishing Group, 2005; and Barry Glassner: *The Culture of Fear: Why Americans Are Afraid of the Wrong Things*. New York: Basic Books, 1999.

50. Steven Heydemann: *Authoritarianism in Syria: Institutions and Social Conflict 1946–1970*. Ithaca and London: Cornell University Press, 1999.

51. The Arab Socialist Ba'th Party: 'Statement of the National Leadership on the Work and Results of the 11th National Congress', quoted in Raymond Hinnebusch: *Syria: Revolution from Above*. London and New York: Routledge, 2001, p. 65.

52. Volker Perthes: 'Si Vis Stabilitatem, Para Bellum', in Steven Heydemann (ed.): *War, Institutions, and Social Change in the Middle East*. Berkeley: University of California Press, 2000.

53. Raymond Hinnebusch: *Syria: Revolution from Above*. London and New York: Routledge, 2001, pp. 76–8.
54. Volker Pertes, *op.cit.*
55. *Ibid.*
56. Eyal Zisser: 'The Syrian army: between the domestic and the external fronts', *op.cit.*, p. 6.
57. *Ibid.*
58. Raymond Hinnebusch, *op.cit.*, p. 149.
59. Volker Perthes, *op.cit.*
60. Alan George, *op.cit.*, p. 108.
61. *Ibid.*, p. 110.
62. Partick Seale: *Asad of Syria: The Struggle for the Middle East*. London: I.B.Tauris, 1988, p. 339
63. Lisa Wedeen: *Ambiguities of Domination: Politics, Rhetoric, and Symbols in Contemporary Syria*. Chicago: University of Chicago Press, 1999, p. 35.
64. *Ibid.*, pp. 20–3.
65. Raymond Hinnebusch, *op.cit.*, p. 128.
66. *Ibid.*, p. 129.
67. David W. Lesch: *The New Lion of Damascus: Bashar al-Asad and Modern Syria*. New Haven and London: Yale University Press, 2005.
68. *Ibid.*, p. 75.
69. *Ibid.*, pp. 81–2.
70. Alan George, *op.cit.*, pp. 42–5.
71. *Ibid.*, p. 52.
72. *Ibid.*, p. 53.
73. Volker Perthes: *Syria under Bashar al-Asad: Modernisation and the Politics of Change*. Adelphi Paper, Oxford and New York: Oxford University Press, 2004, p. 17.
74. *Ibid.*, p. 54.
75. *Ibid.*, p. 51.
76. Sami Moubayed: 'Syria's Ba'thists loosen the reins', in *Asia Times*, April 26, 2005, http://www.atimes.com/atimes/Middle_East/GD26Ak04.html.
77. Bashar al-Asad, 21 January 2006, quoted in Eyal Zisser: 'What does the future hold for Syria?', in *MERIA*, vol. 10, no. 2, 2006, p. 9, http://meria.idc.ac.il/journal/2006/issue2/jv10no2a6.html.
78. Bashar al-Asad, speech to the Association of Journalists' fourth conference, in *al-Thawra* (Damascus), 16 August, 2006.
79. 'Syrian workers are the victims of Lebanon-Syrian relations', in *Ya Libanon* (Beirut), 21 May 2008, http://yalibnan.com/site/archives/2008/05/syrian_workers_1.php
80. Bashar al-Asad's, 'inauguration speech', 18 July 2007, http://www.champress.net/.
81. Aurora Sottimano and Kjetil Selvik: *Changing Regime Discourse and Reform in Syria*. Boulder, CO: Lynne Rienner, 2008.
82. Rif'at Sayyid Ahmad: *Bayna al-dam wa-l nar: Suria wa-l mu'amara al-amrikiyya* [Between the Blood and the Fire: Syria and the American Conspiracy], Damascus and Cairo: Dar al-Kitab, 2007, p. 334.
83. International Crisis Group: Reshuffling the Cards?: Syria's New Hand, *Middle East Report*, no. 93, 16. December 2009.

9 Democratisation

1. UNDP: 'Arab Human Development Report 2002: Creating Opportunities for Future Generations', New York: United Nations Publications, 2003, p. 2, http://www.undp.org/rbas/ahdr/.

2. Besides UNDP both the Economist Intelligence Unit, http://www.eiu.com, and Freedom House, http://www.freedomhouse.org, have documented democracy's weak position in the Middle East.

3. See for example, Freedom House, *op.cit.*

4. Robert Dahl: *Democracy and its Critics.* New Haven, Conn.: Yale University Press, 1989.

5. Samuel P. Huntington: *The Third Wave: Democratization in the Late Twentieth Century.* Norman, Oklahoma: University of Oklahoma Press, 1991.

6. Jeremy Jones: *Negotiating Change: The New Politics of the Middle East.* London and New York: I.B.Tauris, 2007.

7. Rex Brynen, Baghat Korany, and Paul Noble (eds.): *Political Liberalization & Democratization in the Arab World.* Boulder and London: Lynne Rienner Publishers, 1995, p. 3.

8. Elie Kedourie: *Democracy and Arab Political Culture.* London: Frank Class, 1994, p. 1.

9. Marshall McLuhan: *The Global Village: Transformations in World Life and Media in the 21st Century.* Oxford: Oxford University Press, 1992.

10. *The Washington Times,* 16 June, 2009, http://www.washingtontimes.com/news/2009/jun/16/irans-twitter-revolution/.

11. Moataz A. Fattah: *Democratic Values in the Muslim World.* Boulder and London: Lynne Rienner Publishers, 2006.

12. *Ibid.,* p. 89.

13. *Ibid.,* p. 92.

14. Jean Leca: 'Democratization in the Arab World: Uncertainty, Vulnerability, and Legitimacy: A Tentative Conceptualization and Some Hypotheses', in Ghassan Salamé (ed.): *Democracy without Democrats: The Renewal of Politics in the Muslim World.* London: I.B.Tauris, 1994, pp. 48–83.

15. 'Iranian elections: Ahmadinejad's 'dirt and dust' jibe rebounds', in *The Guardian,* 18 June, 2009, http://www.guardian.co.uk/world/2009/jun/18/ahmadinejad-iran-insults-dirt-dust.

16. Two interesting contributions to this debate are Daniel Byman: 'The Implications of Leadership Change in the Arab World', in Nora Bensahel and Daniel L. Byman (eds.): *The Future Security Environment in the Middle East: Conflict, Stability, and Political Change.* RAND Corporation, 2004, pp. 163–95; and Volker Perthes (ed.): *Arab Elites, op.cit.*

17. See the interview in *Der Spiegel* (Berlin), 31 January 2005.

18. See the interviews in *Financial Times,* 11–12 September, 2004; and *International Herald Tribune,* 28 January, 2005.

19. Tim Niblock: 'Democratization: a theoretical and practical debate', in *British Journal of Middle Eastern Studies,* vol. 25, no. 2, 1998, p. 27.

20. Samuel P. Huntington: *The Third wave, op.cit.*

21. Eva Bellin: 'Coercive Institutions and Coercive Leaders', in Marsha Pripstein Posusney and Michele Penner Angrist (eds.): *Authoritarianism in the Middle East, op.cit.,* pp. 21–41.

22. For an insight into neo-conservative thinking on foreign affairs see www.newamericancentury.org.

23. 'A Clean Break: A New Strategy for Securing the Realm', Washington, DC: The Institute for Advanced Strategic and Political Studies, http://www.iasps.org/strat1.htm.

24. George Bush: 'State of the Union Speech', 29 January 2002, http://www.whitehouse.gov/news/releases/2002/01/20020129-11.html.

25. John Keay: *Sowing the Wind: The Seeds of Conflict in the Middle East.* London: John Murray, 2003.

26. Hanna Batatu: *The Old Social Classes and the Revolutionary Movements of Iraq*. Princeton, New Jersey: Princeton University Press, 1978.

27. Reidar Visser: 'Proto-political conceptions of "Iraq" in late Ottoman times', in *International Journal of Contemporary Iraqi Studies*, vol. 3, no. 2, 2009.

28. Samira Haj: *The Making of Iraq 1900–1963: Capital, Power and Ideology*. New York: State University of New York Press, 1997, pp. 29–30.

29. Charles Tripp: *A History of Iraq*. Cambridge: Cambridge University Press, 2000.

30. Eric Davis: *Memories of State: Politics, History, and Collective Identity in Modern Iraq*. Berkeley, Los Angeles and London: University of California Press, 2005.

31. Ghassan Salamé: 'Sur la causalité d'un manqué. Pourquoi le monde arabe n'est-il donc pas démocratique?', in *Revue Française de Science Politique*, vol. 41, no. 3, 1991, p. 323.

32. Hanna Batutu, *op.cit.* p. 1115.

33. Charles Tripp, *op.cit.*, p. 138.

34. Amatzia Baram: 'Neo-Ttibalism in Iraq: Saddam Hussein's tribal policies 1991–96', in *International Journal of Middle East Studies*, vol. 29, no. 1, 1997, p. 1.

35. For a more detailed account of the power structure in Saddam Husayn's Iraq, see Amatzia Baram: 'Saddam's Power Structure: The Tikritis Before, During and After the War', in Toby Dodge and Steven Simon (eds.): *Iraq at the Crossroads: State and Society in the Shadow of Regime Change*. Adelphi Paper 354. Oxford and New York: Oxford University Press, 2003, pp. 93–112.

36. Marion Farouk-Sluglett and Peter Sluglett: *Iraq Since 1958: From Revolution to Dictatorship*. London and New York: I.B.Tauris, 1990.

37. David L. Phillips: *Losing Iraq: Inside the Postwar Reconstruction Fiasco*. New York: Westview Press, 2005.

38. *Ibid.*, p. 145.

39. 'Iraq: building a new security structure', International Crisis Group. Middle East Report No 20, 23 December 2003, http://www.crisisgroup.org/home/index.cfm?l=1&id=2433.

40. Quoted in Patrick Thornberry: ' "It seemed the best thing to be up and go". On the legal case for invading Iraq', in Alex Danchev and John MacMillan (eds.): *The Iraq War and Democratic Politics*. New York: Routledge, 2005, pp. 114–33.

41. David L. Phillips, *op.cit.*, p. 147.

42. *Ibid.*, p. 164.

43. Eric Davis: 'History matters: past and prologue in building democracy in Iraq', in *Orbis*, vol. 49, no. 2, 2005, pp. 229–44.

44. 'Reconstructing Iraq', International Crisis Group, Middle East Report, no. 20, 2 September 2004, http://www.crisisgroup.org/home/index.cfm?id=2936&l=1.

45. Bathsheba Crocker: 'Reconstructing Iraq's economy', in *Washington Quarterly*, vol. 24, no. 2, pp. 73–93.

46. Antonia Juhasz: *The Bush Agenda: Invading the World, One Economy at a Time*. New York: Harper Collins, 2006.

47. Bathsheba Crocker, *op.cit.*, p. 85.

48. Ghassan Salamé: *Quand l'Amérique refait le monde*. Paris: Fayard, 2005, p. 476.

49. Jeremy Jones, *op.cit.*, p. 246.

50. 'Unmaking Iraq: A Constitutional Process Gone Awry', International Crisis Group, Middle East Briefing, no. 19, 26 September 2006, http://www.crisisgroup.org/home/index.cfm?id=3703&l=1.

51. 'Electricity shortage persists in Iraq, hobbles progress', *The New York Times*, 1 August 2010, http://seattletimes.nwsource.com/html/nationworld/2012509806_iraq02.html

52. 'Iraqi Parliamentary Election 2010', *Wikipedia*, http://en.wikipedia.org/wiki/Iraqi_parliamentary_election,_2010

53. Reidar Visser: ' COIN to Nowhere? Lessons from Iraq, Questions for Afghanistan ', in *Iraq and Gulf Analysis*, December 1, 2009. http://gulfanalysis.wordpress.com/2009/12/01/coin-to-nowhere-lessons-from-iraq-questions-for-afghanistan/

54. See for instance Joseph E. Stiglitz and Linda Bilmes: *The Three Trillion Dollar War: The True Cost of the Iraq Conflict.* New York: Norton, 2008.

55. The Committee for a Realistic Foreign Policy, http://www.realisticforeignpolicy.org/.

56. Francis Fukuyama: *After the Neocons: America at the Crossroads.* London: Profile Books, 2006.

57. 'America's Image Slips, but Allies Share U.S. Concerns over Iran, Hamas', Pew Global Attitudes Project, June 13, 2006, p. 3, http://pewglobal.org/ reports/pdf/252.pdf.

58. Francis Fukuyama: *After the Neocons: America at the Crossroads. op.cit*, p. 183.

59. 'Americans on Promoting Democracy', Chicago Council of Foreign Relations, Program on International Policy Attitudes, September 2005, pp. 1–13, http://thechicagocouncil.org/UserFiles/File/Democratization%20Report%20Sept%202005.pdf.

60. Kenneth M. Pollack: *A Path Out of the Desert: A Grand Strategy for America in the Middle East*, New York: The Random House, 2008.

10 Breakdown

1. John Ging quoted in *Agence France Presse*, 6 September 2006.

2. Robert I. Rotberg (ed.): *State Failure and State Weakness in a Time of Terror.* Washington, DC: World Peace Foundation Brookings Institution Press, 2003, pp. 4–5.

3. *Ibid.*, pp. 5–9.

4. *Ibid.*, pp. 9–10.

5. 'The Failed States Index 2009', in *Foreign Policy*, http://www.fundforpeace.org/web/index.php?option=com_content&task=view&id=391&Itemid=549.

6. *Ibid.*

7. 'Human Security Brief 2007: Dying to Lose: Explaining the Decline in Global Terrorism', Human Security Project, Simon Frasier University, Canada, http://www.humansecuritybrief.info/access.html.

8. *Ibid.*

9. *Al-Jazeera*, 14 October, 2009, http://english.aljazeera.net/news/middleeast/2009/10/2009101320124344577.html.

10. 'Amnesty International Report 2010: Middle East and North Africa', Amnesty International, 2010, http://thereport.amnesty.org/regions/middle-east-north-africa.

11. 'Why they died: civilian casualties in Lebanon during the 2006 war', Human Rights Watch, 2007, http://hrw.org/reports/2007/lebanon0907/.

12. *B'Tselem*, 9 September, 2009, http://www.btselem.org/Download/20090909_Cast_Lead_Fatalities_Eng.pdf.

13. 'Human Security Brief 2007 ...', *op.cit.*

14. See for example 'Yemen: coping with terrorism and violence in a fragile state', International Crisis Group, Middle East Report No 8, 8 January 2003, http://www.crisisgroup.org/home/index.cfm?id=1675&l=1; 'Who governs the West Bank? Palestinian administration under Israeli occupation', International Crisis Group, Middle East Report No 32, 28. September 2004, http://www.crisisgroup.org/home/index.cfm?id=3034&l=1; and 'The next Iraqi war? sectarianism and civil conflict', International Crisis Group, Middle East Report No 52, 27 February 2006.

15. 'Annual Report 2007: Middle East and North Africa', World Bank, http://web.worldbank.org/wbsite/external/extaboutus/extannrep/extannrep2k7/0,,contentMDK:21507733~menuPK:4187916~pagePK:64168445~piPK:64168309~theSitePK:4077916,00.html.

16. Klaus W. Deininger and Pedro Olinto: 'Asset Distribution, Inequality and Growth', Working Paper no. 2375, World Bank, 2002, www.worldbank.org.

17. Alan Richards and John Waterbury: *A Political Economy of the Middle East*. Boulder, CO: Westview Press, 3rd edition, 2008, p. 58.

18. 'Middle East & North Africa Region 2005: Economic Developments and Prospects: Oil Booms and Revenue Management', World Bank, 2006, p. v, http://siteresources.worldbank.org/INTMENA/Resources/MENA-EDP2005.pdf.

19. Paul Rivin: *Arab Economies in the Twenty-First Century*. Cambridge and New York: Cambridge University Press, 2009, p. 9.

20. See table 1.2.

21. For some different forecasts, see Alan Richards and John Waterbury, *op.cit.*, pp. 71–97; and Paul Rivin, *op.cit.*, pp. 7–35.

22. Alan Richards and John Waterbury, *op.cit.*, p. 71.

23. The World Bank, http://siteresources.worldbank.org/INTMENA/Resources/Environment_for_Womens_Entrepreneurship_in_MNA-3.pdf.

24. *Ibid.*

25. UNDP: 'Arab Human Development Report 2002: Creating Opportunities for Future Generations', New York: United Nations Publications, 2003.

26. Graham E. Fuller: 'The Youth Factor: The New Demographics of the Middle East and the Implications for U.S. Policy', The Saban Center for Middle East Policy at the Brookings Institution, Analysis Paper, no. 3, June 2003, p. 18, http://www.brookings.edu/~/media/Files/rc/papers/2003/06middleeast_fuller/fuller20030601.pdf.

27. See Table 1.2.

28. UNDP: 'Country Profile Yemen', http://www.undp.org.ye/y-profile.php.

29. *Ibid.*

30. 'Rising the Humanitarian Challenge in Iraq', Oxfam International, Briefing Paper 105, July 2007, http://www.oxfam.org/en/files/bp105_humanitarian_challenge_in_iraq_0707.pdf/download.

31. 'Middle East & North Africa Region 2005...', *op.cit.*, p. 15.

32. The Palestinian Central Bureau of Statistics, 2 June 2008, http://www.pcbs.gov.ps/Portals/_pcbs/PressRelease/poverty_ee.pdf.

33. *Haaretz*, 29 June 2009, http://www.haaretz.com/hasen/spages/1096443.html.

34. Paul D. Williams: 'State Failure in Africa: Causes, Consequences and Responses', in *Africa South of the Sahara 2007, 36th edition*. Europa Regional Surveys of the World/Routledge, 2007, pp. 37–42.

35. Paul Collier: *The Bottom Billion: Why the Poorest Countries Are Failing and What Can be Done About it*. New York: Oxford University Press, 2007.

36. *Ibid.*, p. 17.

37. *Forbes Magazine*, 22 May 2006, http://www.forbes.com/business/global/2006/0522/057.html.

38. Interview in *PBS's* 'Frontline Program', September 2003.

39. Paul Dresch: *A History of Modern Yemen*. Cambridge and New York: Cambridge University Press, 2000, p. 201

40. See for example http://www.amnestyusa.org/waronterror/index.do.

41. *BBC News*, 31 July 2007, http://news.bbc.co.uk/2/hi/6923430.stm.

42. Morten Bøås and Kathleen M. Jennings: 'Insecurity and development: the rhetoric of the "failed state"', in *The European Journal of Development Research*, vol. 17, no. 3, September 2005, pp. 385–95.

43. Morten Bøås and Kathleen M. Jennings: '"Failed states" and "state failure": threats or opportunities', in *Globalizations*, vol. 4, no. 4, December 2007, pp. 475–85.

44. Robert I. Rotberg (ed.): *When States Fail: Causes and Consequences*. Princeton, NJ: Princeton University Press, 2004, p. 25.

45. Ralph Peters: 'Blood borders: how a better Middle East would look', in *Armed Forces Journal*, June 2006, http://www.armedforcesjournal.com/2006/06/1833899/.

46. Francis Fukuyama: *State-Building: Governance and World Order in the 21st Century*. Ithaca: Cornell University Press, 2004; F. Fukuyama: *Nation-Building: Beyond Afghanistan and Iraq*. Washington: Johns Hopkins University Press, 2005; and F. Fukuyama: *America at the Crossroads: Democracy, Power, and the Neoconservative Legacy*. New Haven, Conn.: Yale University Press, 2006.

47. 'The day after', in *Foreign Policy*, November/December 2003, pp. 32–47.

48. Assessment sent home to the Foreign Office in London by a British diplomat in Saudi Arabia in the 1950s right after Ibn Sa'ud, the founder of the modern kingdom, died in 1953.

49. Except from a report that USA's former ambassador to Riyadh, James Akins, wrote to the White House in 1979. The note was penned in the wake of the murder of King Faysal in 1975 and the Islamic Revolution in Iran in 1978–9.

50. Said K. Aburish: *The Rise, Corruption and Coming Fall of the House of Saud*. London: Macmillan, 1995, p. 314. The book was published when Saudi Arabia was hit by internal turbulence after the Gulf War 1990–1.

51. Robert Baer: 'The fall of the House of Saud', in *Atlantic Monthly*, May 2003, http://www.theatlantic.com. The occasion for Baer's article was 11 September 2001.

52. See for example Fred Halliday: *Nation and religion in the Middle East, op.cit.*, pp. 169–76.

53. Gary Samuel Samore: 'Royal Family Politics in Saudi Arabia', unpublished PhD thesis, Harvard University, 1984, pp. 528–32.

54. Abd-al-Rahman S. al-Ruwaishid: *The Genealogical Charts of the Royal Saudi Family*. Riyadh: Al-Shibil Press, (1421) 2001, p. 19.

55. Michael Herb, *op.cit.*

56. The Basic Law of Government, see http://www.SaudiEmbassy.net.

57. 'Putting energy at the spotlight', *BP Statistical Review of World Energy*, 2005, pp. 4 and 6, http://www.bp.com/downloads.do?categoryId=9003093&contentId=7005944.

58. 'Saudi Arabia – Country Profile 2005', the Economist Intelligence Unit, London, 2005.

59. Mamoun Fandy: *Saudi Arabia and the Politics of Dissent*. London: Macmillan Press, 1999, pp. 30–1.

60. *Forbes Magazine*, 2003, http://www.forbes.com/2003/02/26/billionaireland.html.

61. See Table 7.3.

62. David E. Long: 'Kingdom of Saudi Arabia', in D.E. Long and Bernard Reich (eds.): *The Government and Politics of the Middle East and North Africa*. Boulder, San Francisco and Oxford: Westview Press, 1995, p. 84.

63. King Faysal declared this during a conversation with *Times*-correspondent Wilton Lynn in 1975.

64. 'How dependent are we on foreign oil?', Energy Information Administration (Washington), 23 April 2009, http://tonto.eia.doe.gov/energy_in_brief/foreign_oil_dependence.cfm.

65. Christopher M. Blanchard: 'Saudi Arabia: Background and U.S. Relations', Congressional Research Service, April 30, 2009, http://www.fas.org/sgp/crs/mideast/RL33533.pdf.

66. 'Shifting Sands, Changing Prospects', in *Jane's International Defence Review*, 2 November, 2000, http://www.janes.com/defence/news/jidr/jidr001102_01_n.shtml.

67. The Basic Law of Government, *op.cit.*

68. The Allegiance Institutional Law, see http://www.saudiembassy.net/2006News/Statements/TransDetail.asp?cIndex=651.

69. See for example 'Declaration of war against the Americans occupying the land of the two holy places', first published in *Al-quds al-arabi*, August 1996; and 'Jihad against Jews and Crusaders', first printed in *Al-quds al-arabi*, 1998.

70. See 'Saudi Arabia backgrounder: who are the Islamists?' ,International Crisis Group (Amman, Riyadh, and Brussels), 2004, p. 12, http://www.crisisgroup.org/home/index.cfm?id=3021&l=1.

71. UNDP: 'Human Development Report 2005', http://hdr.undp.org/statistics/data/country_fact_sheets/cty_fs_SAU.html.

72. *The Economist*, 23 March 2003.

73. See Table 1.2.

74. Ådne Cappelen and Robin Choudhury: 'Saudi-Arabia – økonomisk pusterom under politisk usikkerhet', in *Internasjonal Politikk*, vol. 63, no. 4, 2005, pp. 371–94.

75. Tim Niblock: 'The Global Economy and Economic Reform in Saudi Arabia', paper presented at the conference *The Global Gulf*, Institute of Arab and Islamic Studies, University of Exeter, 4–6 July, 2006.

76. *The Arab American Institute*, 2003, www.aaiusa.org.

77. 'How dependent are we on foreign oil?', *op.cit.*

11   Conclusion

1. *Al-bayt aladhi asasuhu qawi, la tahizzuhu.*

Index